THE COMMON LAW LIBRARY

CHITTY
ON
CONTRACTS

First Supplement
to the
Thirty-Second Edition

Up-to-date to July 31, 2016

SWEET & MAXWELL 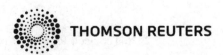 THOMSON REUTERS

Published in 2016 by
Thomson Reuters (Professional) UK Limited
trading as Sweet & Maxwell, Friars House,
160 Blackfriars Road, London, SE1 8EZ
(Registered in England & Wales, Company No 1679046.
Registered Office and address for service:
2nd floor, 1 Mark Square, Leonard Street, London EC2A 4EG)
For further information on our products and services,
visit *www.sweetandmaxwell.co.uk*

Computerset by Wright & Round Ltd, Gloucester
Printed and bound in the UK by CPI Group (UK) Ltd, Croydon, CR0 4YY

No natural forests were destroyed to make this product;
only farmed timber was used and replanted

A CIP catalogue record for this book is available from the British Library

ISBN Main Work (full set)   9780414050679

ISBN Supplement   9780414057067

HOW TO USE THIS SUPPLEMENT

This is the First Supplement to the Thirty-Second Edition of *Chitty on Contracts*, and has been compiled according to the structure of the two main work volumes.

At the beginning of each chapter of this Supplement the mini table of contents from the main volume has been included. Where a heading in this table of contents has been marked with a square pointer, this indicates that there is relevant information in the Supplement to which the reader should refer.

Within each chapter, updating information is referenced to the relevant paragraph in the main volume.

It should be noted that for this Supplement there is no material for chapters 10 and 17.

This Supplement has been prepared on the premise that, despite the referendum result in favour of "Brexit", the UK remains a member of the EU and that the status of EU law in UK law remains unchanged. See below, paras 1–013A—1–013E.

TABLE OF CONTENTS

VOLUME I

VOLUME II

TABLE OF STATUTES

Where a reference indicates significant discussion of the statute in the text, it is in **bold**. Where a reference is to a footnote, it is *italic*.

TABLE OF STATUTORY INSTRUMENTS

Where a reference indicates significant discussion of the statutory instrument in the text, it is in **bold**. Where a reference is to a footnote, it is *italic*.

TABLE OF EUROPEAN UNION LEGISLATION

Where a reference indicates significant discussion of the legislation in the text, it is in **bold**.
Where a reference is to a footnote, it is *italic*.

TABLE OF INTERNATIONAL STATUTORY MATERIAL

Where a reference indicates significant discussion of the legislation in the text, it is in **bold**. Where a reference is to a footnote, it is *italic*.

TABLE OF CASES

Where a reference indicates significant discussion of the case in the text, it is in **bold**. Where a reference is to a footnote, it is *italic*.

[xxiii]

TABLE OF CASES

TABLE OF CASES

TABLE OF CASES

TABLE OF CASES

TABLE OF EU CASES

Where a reference indicates significant discussion of the case in the text, it is in **bold**. Where a reference is to a footnote, it is italic.

[xlix]

TABLE OF EU CASES

VOLUME I

GENERAL PRINCIPLES

Part One

INTRODUCTION

CHAPTER 1

INTRODUCTORY

1. Sources Of English Contract Law

(a) *The Common Law of Contract*

The common law's dominance of the general law

1–003   [*Add to note 5, at the end: page* [5]]
See, however, Burrows, *A Restatement of the English Law of Contract* (2016), whose aim (p.x) is "to provide the best interpretation of the present English law of contract".

(d) *EU Law*

[*Insert new sub-heading before para.1–011: page* [9]]

(i) *The Current Position*

EU law governing contracts: the Union *acquis*

1–011   [*Add to note 63, line 15, after* "[1990] O.J. L158/59": *page* [9]]
(itself repealed and replaced by Directive (EU) 2015/2302 on package travel and linked travel arrangements [2015] O.J. L326/1 as from July 1, 2018 (arts 28 and 29))

[*Add to note 63, at the end: page* [9]]
; Directive 2014/17/EU on credit agreements for consumers relating to residential immovable property [2014] O.J. L2014/34 on which see Main Work, Vol.II, paras 39–003 and 39–531.

[*In note 65, line 3, delete* "Law Payment" *and substitute: page* [10]]
Late Payment

[*Add to note 66, last line, after* "[2004] O.J. L134/1.": *page* [10]]
The two 2004 directives were repealed and replaced as from April 18, 2016 by Directive 2014/24/EU on public procurement and repealing Directive

2004/18/EC [2014] O.J. L94/65 (see esp. art.91) and Directive 2014/25/EU on procurement by entities operating in the water, energy, transport and postal services sectors and repealing Directive 2004/17/EC [2014] O.J. L94/243 (see esp. art.107), which were supplemented by Directive 2014/23/EU on the award of concession contracts [2014] O.J. L94/1.

The Proposed Common European Sales Law (CESL)

[Add to note 88, at the end: page [12]]   **1–013**
This strategy has led, inter alia, to a Proposal for a Directive of the European Parliament and of the Council on certain aspects concerning contracts for the online and other distance sales of goods COM(2015) 635 final and a Proposal for a Directive of the European Parliament and of the Council on certain aspects concerning contracts for the supply of digital content COM(2015) 634.

[Add new sub-heading and new paras 1–013A—1–013E: page [13]]

(ii) "Brexit"

A note on "Brexit". After a national referendum taken on June 23, 2016 at   **1–013A**
which a majority voted in favour of the UK leaving the EU, the UK Government formed on July 16, 2016 declared its intention to end the UK's membership of the EU. At the time of writing what this may mean in terms of the future legal relationship of the UK to the EU or its individual Member States remains unclear.

The future legal relationship of the UK to the EU will clearly be determined   **1–013B**
according to whether, under the arrangement (or series of arrangements) nego- tiated by the UK and agreed by the other Member States, the UK becomes bound to retain one or more aspects or bodies of EU law (notably, as a concomitant of access to the EU internal market). If this were the case, then the legislation replacing the European Communities Act 1972 would have to provide for the continuing application of the relevant EU regulations and of relevant UK regula- tions made under the 1972 Act in order to implement other EU measures. EU law would continue to play a necessary element in UK law, and this could, depending on the EU law covered, include all or some of the measures that currently affect the law of contract. Those EU measures that are currently implemented by means of "free-standing" domestic legislation—for example, those covered by the Consumer Rights Act 2015—would remain in force unless and until the legisla- tion concerned is amended or repealed.

However, it may be that the future arrangements between the UK and the EU   **1–013C**
would not require the UK to conform to existing (and future) EU law regulating contracts. If this were the case, then the UK itself would have to choose whether it wishes to enact laws replacing EU Treaty provisions (such as those governing competition law), to give continuing effect to EU regulations affecting contracts (for example, the Denied Boarding Regulation[92a]) and to retain the UK laws (or aspects of those laws) which implement EU directives (such as the provisions on

information and cancellation rights in consumer distance and off-premises contracts[92b] or the law governing public procurement contracts.[92c] The UK would also have to determine for this purpose its general approach to the subsequent amendment or replacement of the relevant EU laws on the UK national legislation; and it would have to determine the status of existing and, possibly, future interpretation by the Court of Justice of the EU of those EU laws which underlie UK legislation, which would then be purely national law.

[92a] Regulation (EC) 261/2004 [2004] O.J. L46/1.
[92b] Consumer Contracts (Information, Cancellation and Additional Charges) Regulations 2013 (SI 2013/3134), on which see Main Work, Vol.II, paras 38–057 et seq.
[92c] On which see Main Work, Vol.I, paras 11–051—11–052.

1–013D The issue of the relationship of UK law to that of the other Member States is less obvious; but there are a number of provisions relating to contract law that require mutual recognition or co-operation between Member States. Similar points apply; the provisions may have to be kept in force or, if the UK is not required to keep them, it may still choose to negotiate a position that would enable it to do so.

1–013E All these issues remain to be determined, but at the time of writing the UK remains a Member State of the EU and will apparently remain a Member State for a period of time likely to extend to the life, certainly of this Supplement and probably of the present edition of *Chitty*. This Supplement therefore remains written on the premise that the UK is a member of the EU and that the status of EU law in UK law remains unchanged. This approach extends to examples of EU legislation which have been enacted and are expressed as requiring to be implemented by Member States within a particular timeframe. For example, in 2015 there was a new EU Package Travel Directive,[92d] which repeals the old 1990 Directive[92e] and is stated as requiring to be implemented by Member States by January 1, 2018. While this new EU legislation (and its date for implementation by Member States) is noted, these references must be read subject to the general points about the UK's future legal relations with the EU and its Member States noted above.

[92d] Directive (EU) 2015/2302 [2015] O.J. L326/1.
[92e] Directive 90/314/EEC [1990] O.J. L158/59, implemented in UK law by the Package Travel, Package Holidays and Package Tours Regulations (SI 1992/3288).

2. Definitions of Contract

Competing definitions of contract

1–014 [*In note 96, delete* "13th edn (2011), para.1–001" *and substitute: page* [13]]
14th edn (2015), para.1–001. Cf. Burrows, *A Restatement of the English Law of Contract* (2016), para.2 which defines "contract" as an agreement that is legally binding because it is supported by consideration or made by deed, certain and complete, made with the intention to create legal relations, and complies with any formal requirement needed for the agreement to be legally binding; and see the commentary at pp.44–55.

Difficulties with "contract as agreement"

[*In note 112, delete* "13th edn (2011), para.3–170" *and substitute: page* [15]]   **1–016**
14th edn (2015), para.3–170. Cf. Burrows, *A Restatement of the English Law of Contract* (2016), paras 2 and 8(1), commentary on pp.63–64, which includes agreements supported by a deed within its definition of contract, but distinguishes deeds which contain agreements and those which do not (deeds poll).

EU private international law

[*Add to note 147, line 2, after* "July 18, 2013 at para.33"*: page* [19]]   **1–021**
; *Brogsitter v Fabrication de Montres Normandes EURL* (C-548/12) March 13, 2014 at para.18; *ERGO Insurance SE v If P&C Insurance AS* (Joined Cases C-359/14 and C-475/14) January 21, 2016 at para.43; *Kolassa v Barclays Bank Plc* (C-375/13) January 28, 2015 at para.43; *Granarolo SpA v Ambrosi Emmi France SA* (C-196/15) July 14, 2016 at para.19.

[*Add to paragraph, at the end: page* [19]]
For this purpose, the Court of Justice of the EU has held that "the concept of 'contractual obligation' [under the Rome I Regulation] designates a legal obligation freely consented to by one person towards another".[152a]

[152a] *ERGO Insurance SE v If P&C Insurance AS* (Joined Cases C-359/14 and C-475/14) January 21, 2016 para.44; *Verein für Konsumenteninformation v Amazon EU Sàrl* (C-191/15) July 28, 2016 esp. at para.60 (action for cessation of use of unfair contract terms falls under Rome II as concerning a non-contractual obligation, though the assessment of the terms falls under Rome I as concerning a contractual obligation following the nature of these terms whether this arises in an action for cessation or in an individual action between a trader and a consumer); *Committeri v Club Mediterranee SA* [2016] EWHC 1510 (QB) at [45]–[48].

"Contract" in EU public procurement law

[*Add to note 163, at the end: page* [21]]   **1–024**
The conclusion of public contracts between entities in the public sector (which forms the context of this case-law) has been the subject of regulation by the Public Contracts Directive 2014: Directive 2014/24/EU on public procurement and repealing Directive 2004/18/EC [2014] O.J. L94/65 art.12 and recitals 31 and 32.

3. FUNDAMENTAL PRINCIPLES OF CONTRACT LAW

(a) *Freedom of Contract*

Freedom of contract in the modern common law

[*Add to note 179, at the end: page* [23]]   **1–027**
; *Prime Sight Ltd v Lavarello* [2013] UKPC 22, [2014] A.C. 436 at [47] (contractual recital of fact known by both parties to be untrue enforceable in

principle); *MWB Business Exchange Centres Ltd v Rock Advertising Ltd* [2016] EWCA Civ 553 at [31] and [34], following dicta in *Globe Motors Inc v TRW Lucas Varity Electric Steering Ltd* [2016] EWCA Civ 396, esp. at [100] and [119] (the general principle that parties are free to agree whatever terms they choose to undertake allows them to vary by contract an earlier contract containing an "anti-oral variation" clause); *Transocean Drilling UK Ltd v Providence Resources Plc* [2016] EWCA Civ 372 at [28] ("the principle of freedom of contract is still fundamental to [English] commercial law").

[Add to note 181, line 2, after "[1986] A.C. 80, 104–105": page [23]]
; *Marks & Spencer Plc v BNP Paribas Securities Services Trust Co (Jersey) Ltd* [2015] UKSC 72, [2015] 3 W.L.R. 1843 at [14]–[21] and [77].

[Add to note 183, at the end: page [23]]
On the views of the Supreme Court on Lord Hoffmann's approach to implied terms, see *Marks & Spencer Plc v BNP Paribas Securities Services Trust Co (Jersey) Ltd* [2015] UKSC 72, [2015] 3 W.L.R. 1843.

[Add to paragraph, at the end: page [24]]
Even where the common law recognises an exception to freedom of contract, as in the case of the law controlling penalty clauses,[185a] the courts have distinguished between the nature of this control and wider controls of contracts on the ground of fairness. According to Lord Neuberger P.S.C. and Lord Sumption J.S.C. (with whom Lord Carnwath J.S.C. agreed) in *Cavendish Square Holding BV v Makdessi, ParkingEye Ltd v Beavis*:

> "There is a fundamental difference between a jurisdiction to review the fairness of a contractual obligation and a jurisdiction to regulate the remedy for its breach. Leaving aside challenges going to the reality of consent, such as those based on fraud, duress or undue influence, the courts do not review the fairness of men's bargains either at law or in equity. The penalty rule regulates only the remedies available for breach of a party's primary obligations, not the primary obligations themselves."[185b]

In the view of the Supreme Court, the true test whether a contract term imposes a "penalty" on the party in default is whether "it imposes a detriment on the contract-breaker out of all proportion to any legitimate interest of the innocent party in the enforcement of the primary obligation".[185c] For this purpose,

> "the circumstances in which the contract was made are not entirely irrelevant. In a negotiated contract between properly advised parties of comparable bargaining power, the strong initial presumption must be that the parties themselves are the best judges of what is legitimate in a provision dealing with the consequences of breach."[185d]

And the bargaining position of the parties more generally may be relevant.[185e]

[185a] *Cavendish Square Holding BV v Makdessi, ParkingEye Ltd v Beavis* [2015] UKSC 67, [2015] 3 W.L.R. 1373 at [33] ("[t]he penalty rule is an interference with freedom of contract", per Lord Neuberger and Lord Sumption); at [257] per Lord Hodge. On this decision see below, paras 26–178 et seq.

[185b] [2015] UKSC 67, [2015] 3 W.L.R. 1373 at [13]; and see similarly at [73].

[185c] [2015] UKSC 67 at [32] per Lord Neuberger P.S.C. and Lord Sumption J.S.C. (with whom Lord Carnwath J.S.C. and Lord Clarke J.S.C. agreed. See similarly per Lord Mance J.S.C. at [152] per Lord Mance J.S.C. and [249] and [255] per Lord Hodge J.S.C.

[185d] [2015] UKSC 67 at [35] Lord Neuberger P.S.C. and Lord Sumption J.S.C. (with whom Lord Carnwath J.S.C. and Lord Clarke J.S.C. agreed. See similarly at [75]. For discussion of this point, see below, para.26–214.

[185e] [2015] UKSC 67 at [35].

Freedom of contract in EU law

[Add to paragraph, at the end: page [24]]   1–028
The principle of "party autonomy" is also important in EU private international law.[190a]

[190a] See Regulation (EC) 593/2008 on the law applicable to contractual obligations (Rome I) [2008] O.J. L177/6, art.3 and Main Work, Vol.I, paras 30–169 et seq.; Regulation (EU) 1215/2012 of 12 December 2012 on jurisdiction and the recognition and enforcement of judgments in civil and commercial matters (recast) ("the Brussels I*bis* Regulation") art.23 (on jurisdiction agreements) and recital 14, on which see Dicey, Morris and Collins, *The Conflict of Laws*, 15th edn (2014), paras 12–099 et seq.

(iii) Restricted freedom as to terms

[Add to note 227, at the end: page [28]]   1–034
A legislative regime governing a particular category of contracts may require the implication of an appropriate term by the courts: see, e.g. contracts governed by the Housing Grants, Construction and Regeneration Act 1996 and the Scheme for Construction Contracts (England and Wales) Regulations 1998 (SI 1998/649) and *Aspect Contracts (Asbestos) Ltd v Higgins Construction Plc* [2015] UKSC 38, [2015] 1 W.L.R. 2961 esp. at [23].

(b) *The Binding Force of Contract*

General significance

[Add to note 251, at the end: page [31]]   1–036
As from October 1, 2016 the provisions in the French Civil Code governing general contract law are reformed: *Ordonnance* No.2016/131 of February 10, 2016. The equivalent provision of art.1134.1 of the Civil Code as promulgated appears in art.1103 of the Civil Code as reformed; the latter's provisions on penalty clauses are contained in art.1231-5 of the Civil Code as reformed.

Limits on binding force of contracts

[In paragraph, lines 5–10, delete from "As regards . . . " up to and including note   1–038
281 and substitute: page [33]]
As regards the latter, the Supreme Court has recently clarified the limits of the law which renders a contract term unenforceable as a penalty, holding that a contract term which stipulates the payment of a sum of money on breach of contract will be classed as a penalty clause (and so unenforceable) only if it "imposes a detriment on the contract-breaker out of all proportion to any legitimate interest of the innocent party in the enforcement of the primary obligation".[280–281]

[280-281] *Cavendish Square Holding BV v Makdessi, ParkingEye Ltd v Beavis* [2015] UKSC 67, [2015] 3 W.L.R. 1373 at [32] per Lord Neuberger of Abbotsbury P.S.C. and Lord Sumption J.S.C. (with whom Lord Carnwath and Lord Clarke of Stone-cum-Ebony JJ.S.C. (at [291] agreed); and see similarly at [152] (Lord Mance J.S.C.) and [255] (Lord Hodge J.S.C., with whom Lord Toulson J.S.C. at [292] agreed on this issue). On this decision see paras 26–178 et seq.

[Add to paragraph, at the end: page [35]]
According to the Supreme Court, this provision "is deliberately framed in wide terms with very little in the way of guidance about the criteria for its application . . . It is not possible to state a precise or universal test for its application, which must depend on the court's judgment of all relevant facts", though the Supreme Court offered some general points which courts should take into account for this purpose.[293a]

[293a] *Plevin v Paragon Personal Finance Ltd* [2014] UKSC 61, [2014] 1 W.L.R. 4222 at [10] per Lord Sumption J.S.C. (with whom Baroness Hale of Richmond D.P.S.C., Lord Clarke of Stone-cum-Ebony, Lord Carnwath and Lord Hodge J.J.S.C. agreed).

(c) *A Principle of Good Faith or of Contractual Fairness?*

No general principle of good faith

1–039 *[Add to note 299, at the end: page* [35]]
Burrows, *A Restatement of the English Law of Contract* (2016) considers that it remains clear that there is no free-standing rule imposing a duty to perform in good faith in English law, though notes that English law sometimes comes to the same result by implying a term: commentary to s.5, p.50; commentary to ss.15(3)–(4), p.93; on the latter, see Main Work, Vol.I, paras 1–052—1–054A.

[Add to note 305, line 5, after "[2013] B.L.R. 265 at [105]"*: page* [36]]
; *MSC Mediterranean Shipping Co SA v Cottonex Anstalt* [2016] EWCA Civ 789 at [45].

[Add to paragraph, after note 305: page [36]]
And, very recently, Moore-Bick L.J. has observed that:

> "the better course is for the law to develop along established lines rather than to encourage judges to look for what the judge in this case called some 'general organising principle' drawn from cases of disparate kinds . . . There is . . . a real danger that if a general principle of good faith were established it would be invoked as often to undermine as to support the terms in which the parties have reached agreement."[305a]

[305a] *MSC Mediterranean Shipping Co SA v Cottonex Anstalt* [2016] EWCA Civ 789 at [45]. The judge at trial was Leggatt J., who had earlier given judgment in *Yam Seng Pte Ltd v International Trade Corp Ltd* [2013] EWHC 111 (QB), [2013] 1 Lloyd's Rep. 526, discussed in the Main Work, Vol.I, para.1–053.

1–040 *[Add to paragraph, at the end: page* [38]]
Moreover, the courts do not generally allow a party to a contract to rely on public law defences (such as one based on its legitimate expectation) against its contractual partner where the latter's claim is fundamentally for the enforcement of a commercial bargain, even if that partner was a public authority acting under

statutory powers, though it has been accepted that they could do so where "a true public law defence vitiates a contractual claim".[314a] For this purpose, in the view of Lewison L.J., it cannot "usually be an abuse of power [in a public body] to exercise contractual rights freely conferred, even if the result may appear to be a harsh one".[314b]

[314a] *Dudley Muslim Association v Dudley MBC* [2015] EWCA Civ 1123, [2016] 1 P. & C.R. 10 at [29] per Lewison L.J. (with whom Treacy and Gloster L.JJ. agreed) (local authority able to enforce covenant in lease as to re-conveyance of freehold transferred under option on the failure of a condition as to obtain timely planning permission).
[314b] *Dudley Muslim Association v Dudley MBC* [2015] EWCA Civ 1123 at [49], who noted (at [50]) that in the case before the court, private law mechanisms which preclude a person from relying on his strict legal rights such as promissory estoppel had not been pleaded.

"Good faith" and "good faith and fair dealing" in EU law

[Delete last sentence of the paragraph and note 344, "While the proposed . . . modified proposal[344]" and substitute: page [42]] **1–043**
However, the CESL Proposal was withdrawn by the Commission in 2014,[344] and the legislative proposals put forward by the EU Commission instead are of much narrower scope than the CESL and do not refer to the concept of good faith.[344a]

[344] European Commission, Annex 2 to the Commission Work Programme 2015 Com(2014) 910 final, p.12. See also the Communication from the Commission, *A Digital Single Market Strategy for Europe*, 2015 COM(2015) 192 final, pp.4–5.
[344a] Proposal for a Directive of the European Parliament and of the Council on certain aspects concerning contracts for the online and other distance sales of goods COM(2015) 635 final and Proposal for a Directive of the European Parliament and of the Council on certain aspects concerning contracts for the supply of digital content COM(2015) 634.

(i) Duties to consider other party's interest

[Add to note 350, at the end: page [43]] **1–045**
; *Alpstream AG v PK Airfinance Sarl* [2015] EWCA Civ 1318, [2016] 2 P. & C.R. 2 at [115].

(iii) Contractual interpretation

[In paragraph, after note 392, delete "Furthermore," and substitute: page [51]] **1–051**
Furthermore, while the Supreme Court in *Arnold v Britton* recently reaffirmed that the meaning of words in a contract must be seen in their "documentary, factual and commercial context", including "commercial common sense",[392a] the latter and the surrounding circumstances "should not be invoked to under-value the importance of the language of the provision which is to be construed"[392b]: "[t]he purpose of interpretation is to identify what the parties have agreed, not what the court thinks that they should have agreed".[392c] On the other hand,

[392a] [2015] UKSC 36, [2015] A.C. 1619 at [15] per Lord Neuberger of Abbotsbury P.S.C. (with whom Lord Sumption and Lord Hughes JJ.S.C. agreed); Lord Hodge J.S.C. in a separate judgment also agreed with Lord Neuberger, at [66]).
[392b] [2015] UKSC 36 at [15].

392c [2015] UKSC 36 at [20] per Lord Neuberger of Abbotsbury P.S.C.; *Globe Motors Inc v TRW Lucas Varity Electric Steering Ltd* [2016] EWCA Civ 396 at [62].

(iv) Implied terms

1-052   [*Add to paragraph, at the end: page* [53]]
Moreover, even in those types of contract which involve "a high degree of communication, co-operation and predictable performance based on mutual trust and confidence and expectations of loyalty", in which the courts may be willing to imply a duty of good faith, this will depend on the terms of the particular contract405a: "an implication of a duty of good faith will only be possible where the language of the contract, viewed against its context, permits it".405b

405a *Globe Motors Inc v TRW Lucas Varity Electric Steering Ltd* [2016] EWCA Civ 396 at [67].
405b *Globe Motors Inc v TRW Lucas Varity Electric Steering Ltd* [2016] EWCA Civ 396 at [68] per Beatson L.J.

A general implied term to perform in good faith?

1-053   [*In note 406, lines 2–3, delete* "See also *MSC Mediterranean* . . . [97] (Leggatt J.)": *page* [53]]

[*Add to note 413, at the end: page* [54]]
; *Acer Investment Management Ltd v Mansion Group Ltd* [2014] EWHC 3011 (QB) at [101]–[109]; *Globe Motors Inc v TRW Lucas Varity Electric Steering Ltd* [2016] EWCA Civ 396 at [67]; *Monde Petroleum SA v WesternZagros Ltd* [2016] EWHC 1472 (Comm) at [249]–[259]; *Apollo Window Blinds Ltd v McNeil* [2016] EWHC 2307 (QB) (no implied term in contract of franchise requiring one party (the franchisor) to inform the other (the franchisee) of its contractual rights). See also *MSC Mediterranean Shipping Co SA v Cottonex Anstalt* [2016] EWCA Civ 789 at [45] (disapproving of the establishment of a general principle of good faith, contrary to the suggestion by Leggatt J. at trial).

[*Add to note 415, at the end: page* [54]]
cf. *Hockin v Royal Bank of Scotland* [2016] EWHC 925 (Ch) at [44]–[47] (no strike out of claim for breach of implied term as to the exercise of a right/ discretion under a contract in the absence of factual matrix to be established at trial).

[*Add to paragraph, at the end: page* [54]]
Moreover, the approach of the Supreme Court to the implication of terms in *Marks & Spencer Plc v BNP Paribas Securities Services Trust Co (Jersey) Ltd*415a may lead to a greater reluctance in the courts to imply terms requiring good faith in at least some commercial contracts: as Lord Neuberger of Abbotsbury P.S.C. there observed, "a term should not be implied into a detailed commercial contract merely because it appears fair".415b

415a [2015] UKSC 72, [2015] 3 W.L.R. 1843.
415b [2015] UKSC 72 at [21] and see for an example of this approach being adopted in the context of good faith: *Hockin v Royal Bank of Scotland* [2016] EWHC 925 (Ch) at [46] (high threshold for

the implication of a term in a standard commercial contract). On the decision of the SC in *Marks & Spencers Plc* generally, see below, para.14–007.

Implied restrictions on broad contractual powers

[*Add to note 432, line 16, after* "at [110]–[112]"*: page* [56]]   **1–054**
; *Monde Petroleum SA v WesternZagros Ltd* [2016] EWHC 1472 (Comm) at [261]–[275]. In *British Telecommunications Plc v Telefónica O2 UK Ltd* [2014] UKSC 42, [2014] 4 All E.R. 907 at [37] Lord Sumption J.S.C. observed that, although the matter remains a matter of construction, it is "well established that in the absence of very clear language to the contrary, a contractual discretion must be exercised in good faith and not arbitrarily or capriciously".

[*Add to note 437, at the end: page* [57]]
; applied in *Monde Petroleum SA v WesternZagros Ltd* [2016] EWHC 1472 (Comm) at [261]–[275] (contractual right to terminate a contract not a discretion and may be exercised irrespective of the party's reasons for doing so); *Monk v Largo Foods Ltd* [2016] EWHC 1837 (Comm) at [52]–[60].

[*Add to note 437h, at the end: page* [58]]   **1–054A**
Cf. *Patural v DB Services (UK) Ltd* [2015] EWHC 3659 (QB) at [61].

(v) Reasonableness and legitimate interest in relation to remedies for breach

[*In note 441, lines 1–4, delete* "This law . . . [2015] 1 Lloyd's Rep. 359 at [97]" *and*   **1–055**
substitute: page [59]]
While this law was seen by Leggatt J. in *MSC Mediterranean Shipping Co SA v Cottonex Anstalt* [2015] EWHC 283 (Comm), [2015] 1 Lloyd's Rep. 359 at [97] as reflecting an "increasing recognition in the common law world of the need for good faith in contractual dealings" as it implies "some constraint on the decision-maker's freedom to act purely in its own self-interest", on appeal the CA (which did not see the *White & Carter* principle as applicable on the facts) did not encourage judges to recognise a "general organising principle" drawn from cases of disparate kinds in this way: [2016] EWCA Civ 789 at [43] and [45] respectively.

[*Add to paragraph, after note 441: page* [59]]
And the Supreme Court has held that a contract term stipulating payment of a sum of money on breach of contract will be a penalty clause at common law (and so unenforceable) only if the term does not serve a legitimate interest and if in the circumstances its amount is extravagant, exorbitant or unconscionable.[441a]

[441a] *Cavendish Square Holding BV v Makdessi, ParkingEye Ltd v Beavis* [2015] UKSC 67, [2015] 3 W.L.R. 1373 at [32] and [152] and see, below, paras 26–178 et seq.

[*In paragraph, line 9, delete* "And" *and substitute: page* [59]]
Finally,

4. The Human Rights Act 1998 and Contracts

(a) *Contracts made before October 2, 2000*

(ii) *Contracts made by "Public Authorities"*

Effect of any unlawful performance by a public authority

1–063 *[In note 489, update reference to Treitel on The Law of Contract to: page* [65]]
14th edn (2015)

(b) *Contracts made on or after October 2, 2000*

(i) *The Construction and Review of Legislation Governing Contracts*

Sections 3 and 4 of the 1998 Act: primary or secondary legislation governing the contract and Convention rights

1–066 *[Add to note 500, at the end: page* [66]]
This approach was applied in *Winstanley v Sleeman* [2013] EWHC 4792 (QB) at [58]–[59] (rule against scrutiny of academic judgments in claims for breach of contract does not bar access to the courts).

(ii) *Contracts made by "Public Authorities"*

"Hybrid bodies" and "functions of a public nature"

1–074 *[Add to note 557, at the end: page* [73]]
The approach taken by the HL was applied in *TH v Chapter of Worcester Cathedral* [2016] EWHC 1117 (Admin) (decision by the Chapter of a cathedral affecting the claimant's ability to perform his hobby of bell-ringing was held not to be an act of a "hybrid" public authority within s.6(3) of the Human Rights Act 1998).

(iii) *The Duty of Courts as "Public Authorities" in Relation to Contracts*

New implied terms

1–088 *[In paragraph, line 5, delete* "even under a" *and substitute: page* [85]]
under the established

[Add to note 641, at the end: page [85]]
; *Marks & Spencer Plc v BNP Paribas Securities Services Trust Co (Jersey) Ltd* [2015] UKSC 72, [2015] 3 W.L.R. 1843 at [14]–[21] and [77].

[In paragraph, line 8, delete "And since" *and substitute: page* [85]]
And under

[In paragraph, line 9, delete "of asking" *and substitute: page* [85]]
which asks

[Add to note 643, line 2, before "and see below"*: page* [85]]
. In *Marks & Spencer Plc v BNP Paribas Securities Services Trust Co (Jersey) Ltd* [2015] UKSC 72, [2015] 3 W.L.R. 1843 a majority of the SC considered that Lord Hoffmann's guidance on implied terms in the *Belize* case should not be seen as "authoritative guidance on the law of implied terms": [2015] 3 W.L.R. 1843 at [31];

5. CLASSIFICATION OF CONTRACTS

(a) *Classification of Contracts According to their Subject Matter*

General

[Add to note 688, at the end: page [90]]   **1–096**
(as promulgated); art.1101 C.civ. (as inserted by *Ordonnance* No.2016/131 of February 10, 2016).

(c) *Classification of Contracts According to their Form or Means of Formation*

Express and implied contracts

[Add to note 731, line 2, after "per Mance L.J."*: page* [95]]   **1–104**
; *Heis v MF (Global) Services Ltd* [2016] EWCA Civ 569 at [36]–[47]

6. CONTRACTS CONTAINED IN DEEDS

(a) *General*

General abolition of the requirement of sealing

[Add to note 769, at the end: page [99]]   **1–114**
The recognition of "electronic seals" by Regulation (EU) 910/2014 of 23 July 2014 on electronic identification and trust services for electronic transactions in the internal market and repealing Directive 1999/93/EC [2014] O.J. L257/73 (the "eIDAS Regulation"), see esp. arts 2(25), 35–40, does not affect the law described in the text of the Main Work, as art.2(3) provides that the Regulation does not affect national or Union law related to the conclusion and validity of contracts or other legal or procedural obligations relating to form: see further below, para.5–008.

Electronic documents and deeds

1–116   [*Add new note 780a at the end of the title of this paragraph: page* [101]]

[780a] "Electronic documents and deeds" for the purposes of the Land Registration Act 2002 (which are the subject of the present paragraph) are to be distinguished from "electronic seals" recognised by Regulation (EU) 910/2014 of 23 July 2014 on electronic identification and trust services for electronic transactions in the internal market and repealing Directive 1999/93/EC [2014] O.J. L257/73 (the "eIDAS Regulation"), see below, para.5–008.

[*Delete text of note 783 and substitute: page* [101]]

The relevant dispositions are specified by the Land Registration Act 2002 s.91(2).

[*Add to note 785, at the end: page* [101]]

See further Law Commission, *Updating the Land Registration Act 2002, A Consultation Paper* (Consultation Paper No.227, 2016), Part 8, which notes (at para.20.6) that the electronic system provided for by Pt 8 of the 2002 Act which would have implemented the model which it had earlier recommended has not been developed, and instead makes recommendations for a "new vision for electronic conveyancing" (at para.20.11).

(b) *Intention, Form and Delivery*

(i) *Deeds executed on or after July 31, 1989 and before or on September 14, 2005*

Deeds executed by an individual

1–118   [*Add to note 791, at the end: page* [102]]

The question whether the requirement of signature may be satisfied other than by a party writing his or her name or mark with his or her own hand remains unclear. There is authority for the purposes of s.2 of the 1989 Act that requires such writing (*Firstpost Homes Ltd v Johnson* [1995] 1 W.L.R. 1567, on which see Main Work, Vol.I, para.5–037), but a more liberal position has been taken for the purposes of the (less demanding) formalities of s.4 of the Statute of Frauds: *J Pereira Fernandes SA v Mehta* [2006] EWHC 813 (Ch), [2006] 2 All E.R. 881 at [31]; *Golden Ocean Group Ltd v Salgaocar Mining Industries Pvt Ltd* [2012] EWCA Civ 265, [2012] 1 Lloyd's Rep. 542 at [32] (on which see Main Work, Vol.II, para.45–057). In *Ramsay v Love* [2015] EWHC 65 (Ch) at [7], Morgan J. observed (in the context of s.1(3) of the 1989 Act, obiter) that the position in *Firstpost Homes Ltd v Johnson* (which requires signature by an executing party with a pen in his own hand) was not designed to distinguish between signing in such a way and by use of a signature writing machine. For further discussion of the significance of "signature" see *Emmet & Farrand on Title* (looseleaf and electronic version updated to June 2016) paras 2–041—2–041.06. For the possibility that an "electronic signature" may satisfy this requirement by way of s.7 of the Electronic Communications Act 2000 see below, para.5–008.

[14]

(iii) *Common Aspects*

Estoppel preventing reliance on formal invalidity

[*Add to note 859, at the end: page* [110]]   **1–132**
; *Bank of Scotland Plc v Waugh* [2014] EWHC 2117 (Ch), [2015] 1 P. & C.R.
DG3 at [68]–[79].

Delivery of deed as an escrow

[*In note 863, update reference to Treitel on The Law of Contract to: page* [110]]   **1–133**
14th edn (2015), para.3–173

(c) *Consideration*

No consideration required

[*Add to paragraph, at the end: page* [112]]   **1–136**
Where a promise or agreement unsupported by consideration is enforceable by
reason of its being contained in a deed, it may be avoided on the ground of
special equitable rules of mistake which are distinct from the rules of mistake
applicable to contracts.[881a]

[881a] *Pitt v Holt* [2013] UKSC 26, [2013] 2 A.C. 108 esp. at [115]; applied in *Van der Merwe v
Goldman* [2016] EWHC 790 (Ch), [2016] 4 W.L.R. 71 at [26]–[32]. On the common law rules
applicable to mistakes in contracts, see Main Work, Vol.I, Chs 3 and 6.

(d) *Other Aspects*

Non est factum

[*Delete title of paragraph and substitute: page* [114]]   **1–139**

Non est factum and mistake

[*Add to paragraph, at the end: page* [114]]
This position is to be contrasted with mistakes made in making gifts or other
voluntary dispositions (including those made by deed), where equitable rules
apply which differ from the common law rules applicable to mistake in contracts
(whether or not contained in deeds).[899a]

[899a] *Pitt v Holt* [2013] UKSC 26, [2013] 2 A.C. 108 esp. at [115]; applied in *Van der Merwe v
Goldman* [2016] EWHC 790 (Ch), [2016] 4 W.L.R. 71 at [26]–[32]. On the common law rules
applicable to mistakes in contracts, see Main Work, Vol.I, Chs 3 and 6.

Variation or discharge

[*Add to note 918, at the end: page* [116]]   **1–143**
The parties to a contract contained in a deed (as in the case of a simple contract)
may vary or discharge that contract by simple contract despite its containing an

"anti-oral variation clause" by which, for example, any variation may be effected only by deed or only in signed writing: *MWB Business Exchange Centres Ltd v Rock Advertising Ltd* [2016] EWCA Civ 553 at [19]–[34], following dicta in *Globe Motors Inc v TRW Lucas Varity Electric Steering Ltd* [2016] EWCA Civ 396 esp. at [100] and [119], and reviewing earlier conflicting authorities.

7. The Relationship between Contract and Tort

(b) Differences of Substance between Contract and Tort

General

1–148 [*In note 963 update reference to Treitel on The Law of Contract: page* [120]] 14th edn (2015), para.20–021

(c) Concurrence of Actions in Contract and Tort

(i) Pre-contractual Liability

Damages for misrepresentation

1–161 [*In note 1036, update reference to Treitel on The Law of Contract to: page* [129]] 14th edn (2015), paras 9–050—9–058

(ii) Torts Committed in the Course of Performance of a Contract

Effect of broad liability in tort

1–172 [*Add new note 1112a after* "paid for or not" *in line 8: page* [139]]
[1112a] See, e.g. *Burgess v Lejonvarn* [2016] EWHC 40 (TCC), [2016] T.C.L.R. 3 esp. at [185]–[186] (claimants' friend providing project management services in a professional context to them not under a contract (for lack of agreement as to terms, intention to create legal relations and consideration) held to duty of care in tort based on an assumption of responsibility).

Contractual exclusions of liability in tort

1–181 [*In paragraph, line 7, delete* "contra proferentum" *and substitute: page* [145]] *contra proferentem*

Remoteness of damage

1–195 [*Add to note 1262, line 1, after* "cf. at 413": *page* [158]]
; *Wellesley Partners LLP v Withers LLP* [2015] EWCA Civ 1146, [2016] 2 W.L.R. 1351 at [74] and [146]

[In note 1274, delete from "See also . . . " in line 4 to the end: page [160]]

[Add new paragraph 1–195A: page [160]]
However, in *Wellesley Partners LLP v Withers LLP*[1276a] the Court of Appeal **1–195A**
expressed the opposite view as to the proper approach to remoteness of damage
in cases of concurrence of liability in contract and tort from the one which that
court (differently constituted[1276b]) had expressed in *Yapp v Foreign and Commonwealth Office*,[1276c] which was not discussed in *Wellesley Partners LLP*. In
Wellesley Partners LLP, the claimants were a partnership of executive recruitment consultants which had instructed the defendant firm of solicitors to draft
amendments to their partnership agreement so as to allow a third party investor
to gain an interest in the partnership. The amendments which were drafted (and
agreed) allowed the investor to withdraw half its funds *within* a period of 41
months from its formation, rather than (as instructed by the partnership) only
outside such a period: this failure was held to constitute negligence in the
solicitors.[1276d] One issue before the Court of Appeal was whether the claimants
could recover a percentage of the profits which might have been made if the
investment had remained in place until the end of 41 months, in particular in
relation to a recruitment handling contract or contracts with a major bank. In this
respect, it held that where a claimant is able to sue either for breach of contract
or for pure economic loss in the tort of negligence based on an assumption of
responsibility which is assumed under a contract, the contract law test for
remoteness of damage applies even if the claim is brought in tort: "[i]t would be
anomalous . . . if the party pursuing the remedy in tort in these circumstances
were able to assert that the other party has assumed a responsibility for a wider
range of damage than he would be taken to have assumed under the contract".[1276e] In so holding, the Court of Appeal related the remoteness of damage
rule for breach of contract (as reformulated by Lord Hoffmann in *The Achilleas*
in terms of assumption of responsibility[1276f]) to the basis of liability in tort in the
context (assumption of responsibility as explained by *Henderson v Merrett
Syndicates Ltd*[1276g]). The Court of Appeal therefore disagreed with the judge at
trial on the remoteness test applicable, though it held that the application of the
contract test rather than the tort test did not make any difference on the facts as
the damage claimed by the partnership was of a kind for which the solicitors had
assumed responsibility under their contract and was in the reasonable contempla-
tion of the parties as not unlikely to result from a breach.[1276h] The Court of
Appeal in *Wellesley Partners LLP* therefore took a different view on the question
as to the proper test of remoteness applicable to a claim in the tort of negligence
concurrent with a claim for breach of contract from the one which it had taken
in *Yapp*.[1276i] In neither case were these views necessary for the courts' decisions
on the facts before them, as in both cases they held that the two tests of
remoteness (in tort and in contract) would have led to the same result.[1276j]
Moreover, the two approaches to the proper test of remoteness, while apparently
opposing, may be reconciled by reference to their contexts. In *Yapp,* the claim
was for damages by an employee against his employer for psychiatric injury
suffered as a result of withdrawing him from his post without informing him of
the case against him for doing so (which was held to have been unfair)[1276k] and
the Court of Appeal held (summarising the authorities in that context) that in
such a claim "for breach of the common law duty of care" it is immaterial that
the duty arises in contract as well as tort.[1276l] In such a context, therefore, the

defendant's liability in the tort in respect of psychiatric injury (which did not rest on any assumption of responsibility) could be seen as primary as compared with its contractual liability arising from breach of the term implied in law on the employer to take reasonable care of the employee's health and safety.[1276m] By contrast, in *Wellesley Partners LLP* the defendant's liability in contract was for breach of an express term of the contract (that is, to follow their client's instructions as to the terms of the amendment agreement) whereas its liability in tort was for pure economic loss based on an assumption of responsibility where the assumption stemmed from the contract itself: indeed, the judges in the Court of Appeal restricted their decision on the test of remoteness to the situation where the tort was based on such a contractual assumption of responsibility.[1276n] A distinction between claims for psychiatric injury (and, it is submitted, other harms, such as personal injury and damage to property) where liability in tort in the defendant does not rest on an assumption of responsibility (*Yapp*) and claims for pure economic loss where it does (*Wellesley Partners LLP*) would echo the approach of Lord Denning M.R. in his minority reasoning in *H Parsons (Livestock) Ltd v Uttley Ingham & Co Ltd* (who distinguished between concurrent claims for physical damage and pure economic loss[1276o]) with the difference that under *Wellesley Partners LLP* the contract test of remoteness would apply to a claim for pure economic loss in tort only where it is based (as would normally be the case) on an assumption of responsibility. More generally, while the Court of Appeal in *Wellesley Partners LLP* acknowledged that the House of Lords in *Henderson v Merrett Syndicates Ltd* treated liability in the tort of negligence that is based on a "broad principle" of assumption of responsibility in *Hedley Byrne* as independent from any liability in contract,[1276p] its own decision treats the liability of the defendant solicitors in tort for negligence as dependent on their liability for breach of the contract of retainer.[1276q] However, a better approach would be to hold that the contract test should apply whenever one party has had the opportunity to alert the other to the type of loss of which he is at risk, and that such an opportunity should be assumed (or perhaps presumed) where the parties are in a contractual relationship.[1276r]

[1276a] [2015] EWCA Civ 1146, [2016] 2 W.L.R. 1351.

[1276b] The Court of Appeal in *Yapp* consisted of Underhill, Davis and Patten L.JJ; the Court of Appeal in *Wellesley Partners LLP* consisted of Longmore and Floyd L.JJ. and Roth J.

[1276c] [2014] EWCA Civ 1512, [2015] I.R.L.R. 112 (discussed in Main Work, Vol.I, para.1–195).

[1276d] [2015] EWCA Civ 1146 at [41], [54] and [58]–[59] (decision at trial not appealed on this point).

[1276e] [2015] EWCA Civ 1146 at [68] per Floyd L.J. and see also at [75], explicitly approving the position proposed by *McGregor on Damages* at n.1265, para.22–009 that was rejected by the CA in *Yapp* [2014] EWCA Civ 1512, [2015] I.R.L.R. 112 at [119] n.8 and at [80]. See similarly, at [151] (approving the view of Burrows in Burrows and Peel (eds), *Commercial Remedies* (2003) 27 at 35), [157] and [163] (Roth J.); [183]–[186] (Longmore L.J.).

[1276f] *Transfield Shipping Inc v Mercator Shipping Inc (The Achilleas)* [2009] 1 A.C. 61. In this respect, the CA in *Wellesley Partners LLP* adopted a similar approach to Akenhead J. in *How Engineering Services Ltd v Southern Insulation (Medway) Ltd* [2010] EWHC 1878 (TCC), [2010] B.L.R. 537 (noted in the Main Work, Vol.I, para.1–195), though the earlier decision was not discussed by the CA.

[1276g] [1995] 2 A.C. 145. See [2015] EWCA Civ 1146 at [69], [74], [80]–[83] (Floyd L.J.) and [155] (Roth J.). In this respect, the CA in *Wellesley Partners LLP* adopted a similar approach to Akenhead J. in *How Engineering Services Ltd v Southern Insulation (Medway) Ltd* [2010] EWHC 1878 (TCC), [2010] B.L.R. 537 (noted in the Main Work, Vol.I, para.1–195), though the earlier decision was not discussed.

1276h [2015] EWCA Civ 1146 at [81]–[89] (Floyd L.J.); [179] (Roth L.J.) and [188] (Longmore L.J.).

1276i [2014] EWCA Civ 1512 and see Main Work, Vol.I, para.1–195.

1276j In *Yapp* the CA held that the claimant's depressive illness was not reasonably foreseeable under the *tort* test (seen as more favourable to the claimant), and therefore was also too remote in his claim for breach of contract: [2014] EWCA Civ 1512 at [121]–[124], [133]. In *Wellesley Partners LLP* the partnerships losses were held not too remote under the contract test thereby leading to the CA affirming the result at trial which had held them not too remote under the tort test: [2015] EWCA Civ 1146 at [81] (Floyd L.J.); [179] (Roth L.J.) and [188] (Longmore L.J.).

1276k [2014] EWCA Civ 1512 at [60] and [67].

1276l [2014] EWCA Civ 1512 at [119].

1276m [2014] EWCA Civ 1512 at [42]–[43]. The CA also referred to breach of the implied term of mutual trust and confidence, but this was not seen as paralleled with any breach of duty at common law.

1276n [2015] EWCA Civ 1146 at [80] and [151].

1276o [1978] Q.B. 791 at 802–804 noted in Main Work, Vol.I, para.1–195 n.1265.

1276p [2015] EWCA Civ 1146 at [68].

1276q Cf. the discussion in the Main Work, Vol.I, paras 1–188—1–190 on the question whether one party to a contract can be held to have "assumed responsibility" to the other contracting party under the *Hedley Byrne* principle even where the contract contained no express or implied term as to the claimed subject-matter of such an assumption of responsibility. See also Main Work, Vol.I, paras 1–169—1–172 on assumption of responsibility under *Hedley Byrne* more generally.

1276r Peel (ed.), *Treitel on The Law of Contract*, 14th edn (2015) para.20–112 and see similarly *McGregor on Damages* 19th edn (2014) para.22–009.

The conflict of laws: jurisdiction

[*Add to paragraph, at the end: page* [164]]   **1–199**
In a series of recent cases, the Court of Justice of the EU has confirmed its approach to the relationship of the contract and tort provisions in the Brussels Regulation taken in *Kalfelis v Schröder* in relation to the Brussels Convention[1301a] and has therefore made clear that the question whether a particular claim falls within "matters relating to contract" or "matters relating to tort, delict or quasi-delict" must be judged by reference to autonomous EU law understandings of these concepts; and that for this purpose the latter concept "covers all actions which seek to establish the liability of the defendant and do not concern 'matters relating to a contract' within the meaning of Article 5(1)(a)" of the Brussels Regulation.[1301b] As a result, where a national court finds that a claim is a "matter relating to a contract", a national court does not enjoy jurisdiction on the basis that the claim could be viewed as relating to tort as a matter of national law.[1301c]

1301a C-189/87 [1988] E.C.R. 5565 at para.17, discussed in this paragraph of the Main Work.

1301b *Brogsitter v Fabrication de Montres Normandes EURL* (C-548/12) March 13, 2014 at para.20; *ERGO Insurance SE v If P&C Insurance AS* (Joined Cases C-359/14 and C-475/14) January 21, 2016 paras 43–45; *Kolassa v Barclays Bank Plc* (C-375/13) January 28, 2015 at para.44; *Granarolo SpA v Ambrosi Emmi France SA* (C-196/15) July 14, 2016 at para.20.

1301c *Granarolo SpA v Ambrosi Emmi France SA* (C-196/15) July 14, 2016 at para.28.

Conflict of laws: applicable law

[*Add to note 1306, at the beginning: page* [164]]   **1–200**
ERGO Insurance SE v If P&C Insurance AS (Joined Cases C-359/14 and C-475/14) January 21, 2016 paras 43–45; *Verein für Konsumenteninformation v*

Amazon EU Sàrl (C-191/15) July 28, 2016 paras 36–53 and 58. See also *Committeri v Club Mediterranee SA* [2016] EWHC 1510 (QB) at [49]–[53].

(d) *The Influence of Contract on Tort beyond Privity*

Subsequent cases

1–215   [*Add to note 1398, at the end: page* [176]]
; *Summit Advances Ltd v Bush* [2015] EWHC 665 (QB), [2015] P.N.L.R. 18.

Part Two

FORMATION OF CONTRACT

CHAPTER 2

THE AGREEMENT

1. PRELIMINARY

The objective test

[Add to note 9, at the end: page [192]]   2–002
; *Newbury v Sun Microsystems Ltd* [2013] EWHC 2180 (QB) where Lewis J.
held that it is neither legitimate nor helpful to take into account subsequent
communications to determine whether documents gave rise to a binding agreement.

2. The Offer

Inactivity as an offer

2–006   [*In note 35, delete* "Contrast, Trunk Flooring . . . This was not a case of inactivity."
in line 6 to the end and substitute: page [196]]
In *Trunk Flooring Ltd v HSBC Asset Finance (UK) Ltd, Costi Righi SpA* [2015]
NICA 68, the Court of Appeal held that the parties had not abandoned the
contract, as there was no evidence by way of conduct or correspondence, or of
inactivity, to support such a finding; both parties were incontrovertibly actively
engaged in the arbitration process until an impasse was created by the costs issue;
and the respondent who contributed to the situation whereby the costs of the
reference were increased, could not benefit from this action. Although the
reference to arbitration had been terminated this was distinct from the underlying
arbitration agreement.

3. The Acceptance

(a) *Definition*

Acceptance by conduct

2–029   [*Add to note 154, at the end: page* [210]]
(decision to grant summary judgment overturned on appeal on other grounds,
[2015] EWCA Civ 715).

[*Add to paragraph, after note 161: page* [211]]
Nor is a managing director's proposal of an employment contract accepted by the
company paying him at the stated rate, if there is doubt over whether the
company accepted the other terms.[161a]

[161a] *Arley Homes North West Ltd v Cosgrave* Unreported April 14, 2016 EAT.

(d) *Prescribed Mode of Acceptance*

Other equally efficacious mode

2–065   [*Add to note 335, at the end, page* [232]]
; *A Ltd v B Ltd* [2015] EWHC 137 (Comm).

Method of acceptance waived

2–066   [*Add new note 335a, after* "no doubt be bound by," *in line 2: page* [232]]
[335a] *A Ltd v B Ltd* [2015] EWHC 137 (Comm).

Terms of offer drawn up by offeree

[*Add to paragraph, at the end: page* [233]]   **2–067**
In another case,[339a] the Court of Appeal, approving this and the previous paragraphs of the 32nd edition of the Main Work, set out the rules in play here[339b] and found a concluded contract despite the contract document remaining unsigned by the offeree as required by the contract, because[339c]: the contract was on the offeree's standard form and the signature requirement was for its benefit; the requirement was waived by the offeree performing the contract as contemplated; there was no prejudice to the offeror, who had benefitted from and had actively facilitated the offeree's performance; subsequent conduct on both sides confirmed the existence of the contract; and finding a contract "accords with what would be the reasonable expectations of Lord Steyn's honest, sensible business people". Nevertheless, the Court acknowledged that the offeree's failure to sign "was at the expense of certainty as to the precise date the contract was formed", although this was not significant on the facts.[339d]

[339a] *Reveille Independent LLC v Anotech International (UK) Ltd* [2016] EWCA Civ 443.
[339b] [2016] EWCA Civ 443 at [40]–[41].
[339c] [2016] EWCA Civ 443 at [53].
[339d] [2016] EWCA Civ 443 at [53].

5. Special Cases

Difficulty of offer and acceptance analysis in certain cases

[*Add to note 573, line 4, after* "[1999] S.T.C. 821": *page* [264]]   **2–118**
; *Assuranceforeningen Gard Gjensidig v International Oil Pollution Compensation Fund* [2014] EWHC 3369 (Comm); *Price v Euro Car Parks Ltd* [2015] EWHC 3253 (QB); and *Burgess v Lejonvarn* [2016] EWHC 40 (TCC); [2016] T.C.L.R. 3.

6. Incomplete Agreement

Agreement complete despite lack of detail

[*Add to note 592, at the end: page* [266]]   **2–120**
In *Hughes v Pendragon Sabre Ltd (t/a Porche Centre Bolton)* [2016] EWCA Civ 18 the Court of Appeal held that a customer had entered into a binding contract with a car dealership to buy a limited edition Porsche, even though the contract did not stipulate the price, specification or delivery date of the vehicle. These could be resolved by reference to the Sale of Goods Act 1979.

Duty to negotiate outstanding details?

[*Add to paragraph, at the end: page* [290]]   **2–146**
Similarly, a dispute resolution clause in an existing and enforceable contract which requires the parties to seek to resolve a dispute by friendly discussions in

good faith and within a limited period of time before the dispute may be referred to arbitration is enforceable. It is not incomplete; not uncertain (it has an identifiable standard, namely, fair, honest and genuine discussions aimed at resolving a dispute, the difficulty of proving a breach in some cases does not mean that the clause lacks certainty); and not inconsistent with the position of a negotiating party since the parties voluntarily accepted a restriction upon their freedom not to negotiate. Moreover, it is in the public interest, since courts should enforce freely agreed obligations and because it may avoid expensive and time-consuming arbitration.[783a]

[783a] *Emirates Trading Agency v Prime Mineral Exports Private Ltd* [2014] EWHC 2104 (Comm), [2015] 1 W.L.R. 1145 at [63]–[64].

9. CONTRACTUAL INTENTION

Burden of proof: agreements inferred from conduct

2–169   [*Add to paragraph, at the end: page* [305]]
Likewise, in *Re MF Global UK Ltd (In Special Administration)*[879a] the court implied a contract between two companies in administration, pursuant to which one company paid the expenses of staff seconded to a second company within the same group. The established relationship between the companies was only explicable in the particular circumstances on the basis that it had a contractual foundation. In contrast, the burden of proof was not discharged in *Assuranceforeningen Gard Gjensidig v International Oil Pollution Compensation Fund*[879b] where, following a serious oil spill from an insured ship, the insurer asserted a contract with an international fund, set up to compensate for damage caused by oil pollution, to indemnify the insurer in respect of aspects of its liability. On the facts, it was impossible to construe the international fund's communications as making the offer alleged expressly or impliedly, let alone clearly and unequivocally.[879c]

[879a] [2016] EWCA Civ 569.
[879b] [2014] EWHC 3369 (Comm).
[879c] [2014] EWHC 3369 at [102], [110], [114] and [123].

Intention judged objectively

2–170   [*Add to paragraph, line 10, after* "her pupil masters."*: page* [306]]
In *New Media Holding Co LLC v Kuznetsov*[884a] the court found an intention to create legal relations in respect of a "Term Sheet" signed by both parties. On the one hand: the language of the document was brief and did not mention consideration; the document was prepared in a casual and informal way; further formalities were required; and the rights transferred were not capable of immediate enforcement. On the other hand: the parties were experienced and sophisticated businessmen; the document contained clear express terms; the language was consistent with a legally binding agreement; and the "Term Sheet" was consistent with an intention that this be part of a package agreement (with other terms, including the consideration, to be dealt with elsewhere) and with the

[24]

parties' pre-existing relationship, which itself raised a strong presumption that the parties intended to be legally bound. Where there has been substantial performance, courts are especially reluctant to reach the unrealistic conclusion that the parties lacked intention to be legally bound.[884b]

[884a] [2016] EWHC 360 (QB).
[884b] *Purton (t/a Richwood Interiors) v Kilker Projects Ltd* [2015] EWHC 2624 (TCC) at [7].

[*Add to note 885, at the end: page* [306]]
In contrast, no intention to be bound was concluded in *Price v Euro Car Parks Ltd* [2015] EWHC 3253 (QB) where the claimant put a business proposal and sent an "In Principle Heads of Agreement" that neither signed, to the defendant. The defendant never accepted any offer made by the claimant; it merely allowed the claimant to go ahead (at his own risk) to research his business proposal. Moreover, the "In Principle Heads of Agreement" was too indefinite. Nor was there intention to be bound in *Burgess v Lejonvarn* [2016] EWHC 40 (TCC), [2016] T.C.L.R. 3, where an architect, for no fee, had found a contractor to landscape her friends' garden with a view to her providing subsequent design input for consideration. There was no contract to project manage the landscaping because the written discussions were simply too inchoate, there was no intention to be legally bound and there had been no consideration.

CHAPTER 3

MISTAKES AS TO THE TERMS OR AS TO IDENTITY

1. INTRODUCTION TO MISTAKE

Types of mistake

3–001   [*In note 6, update reference to Anson's Law of Contract, 29th edn to: page* [340]]
30th edn (2015), Ch.8

Mistakes as to terms and mistakes as to facts

3–002   [*In note 12, update reference to Anson's Law of Contract to: page* [340]]
30th edn (2015), p.300

Mistakes that are not legally relevant

3–008   [*In note 26, delete* "29th edition by Beatson, Burrows and Cartwright (eds) (2010)" *and substitute: page* [342]]
30th edition by Beatson, Burrows and Cartwright (eds) (2015)

[*In note 26, delete* "pp.277–278" *and substitute: page* [342]]
p.300

2. MISTAKES AS TO TERMS OR IDENTITY

(a) *Underlying Principles*

Older "subjective" notions

[In note 63, update reference to Anson's Law of Contract to: page [347]]
30th edn (2015), p.270

3–017

(c) *Unilateral Mistake as to Terms*

(ii) *Effect on Contract*

Effect of mistake as to terms: mistaken party's intention known to other

[In note 125, update reference to Anson to: page [355]]
Beatson, Burrows and Cartwright (eds), *Anson's Law of Contract*, 30th edn
(2015), p.278

3–029

[In note 125, update reference to Treitel on The Law of Contract to: page [355]]
14th edn (2015), para.8–053

(d) *Mistaken Identity*

Offer to B cannot be accepted by C

[In note 148, update reference to Anson to: page [359]]
Beatson, Burrows and Cartwright (eds), *Anson's Law of Contract*, 30th edn
(2015), p.290

3–038

Identity and attributes

[In note 194, update reference to Treitel on The Law of Contract to: page [365]]
14th edn (2015), para.8–037

3–045

4. RECTIFICATION OF WRITTEN AGREEMENTS

(b) *Common Mistake*

Issue may be solved by construction

[Add to note 247, at the end: page [372]]
Compare *LSREF III Wight Ltd v Millvalley Ltd* [2016] EWHC 466 (Comm) ("no
ambiguity, no syntactical difficulty in construing the language used and the

3–060

reference to the 1992 form of ISDA Agreement cannot be said to be such a commercial nonsense as to make it absurd for the parties to refer to it": at [62]).

Parol evidence

3–061   [*Add to note 257, at the end: page* [374]]
See also *Procter and Gamble Co v Svenska Cellulosa Aktiebolaget SCA* [2012] EWHC 498 (Ch) at [104]–[106]; *DS-Rendite-Fonds Nr.106 VLCC Titan Glory GmbH & Co Tankschiff KG v Titan Maritime SA* [2013] EWHC 3492 (Comm) at [48]; *LSREF III Wight Ltd v Millvalley Ltd* [2016] EWHC 466 (Comm) at [121]–[123].

Outward expression of accord

3–064   [*Add to note 274, at the end: page* [376]]
In *Prowting 1968 Trustee One Ltd v Amos-Yeo* [2015] EWHC 2480 (Ch), [2015] B.T.C. 33 rectification was ordered when an agreement did not reflect the parties' intention to transfer enough shares to entitle the claimants to tax relief, although the parties had left the number to be determined by a trustee, who had miscalculated the number (see at [37]–[38]).

(c) *Unilateral Mistake*

Inequity

3–072   [*Add to paragraph, at the end: page* [383]]
A party with little experience or few bargaining resources who has noticed a possible mistake made by a much stronger party may be entitled to assume that the stronger party "knew what it was doing".[332a] This may be explained in terms of whether the weaker party was acting unconscionably[332b]; but it can equally be seen as a question of whether the weaker party had the requisite degree of knowledge—a party who did not actually know a mistake had been made but who shut his eyes to the obvious or failed to make enquiries is treated as "knowing of it" only if he acted dishonestly.[332c]

[332a] See *George Wimpey UK Ltd v VI Construction Ltd* [2005] EWCA Civ 77, [2005] B.L.R. 135 at [65]–[67] (Sedley L.J.).
[332b] *NHS Commissioning Board v Silovsky* [2015] EWHC 3141 (Comm) at [42]–[43].
[332c] As by the majority in *George Wimpey UK Ltd v VI Construction Ltd* [2005] EWCA Civ 77, [2005] B.L.R. 135, see at [47] and [79]; see Main Work, Vol.I, para.3–070.

(d) *The Extended Notion of Common Mistake*

Criticism of the *Chartbrook* decision

3–081   [*Add to note 367, at the end: page* [388]]
In *NHS Commissioning Board v Silovsky* [2015] EWHC 3141 (Comm), Leggatt J. respectfully agreed with Lord Neuberger MR but held that he was bound to

apply Lord Hoffmann's "strong" objective approach: at [31]. See also *Magellan Spirit ApS v Vitol SA (The Magellan Spirit)* [2016] EWHC 454 (Comm) at [42].

(e) *General Principles*

A discretionary remedy

[*Add to note 422, at the end: page* [395]]   **3–093**
See also *Equity Syndicate Management Ltd v Glaxosmithkline Plc* [2015] EWHC 2163 (Comm), [2016] Lloyd's Rep. I.R. 155 at [46]–[47] (on the facts it would have been inequitable to withhold the remedy).

CHAPTER 4

CONSIDERATION

3. ADEQUACY OF CONSIDERATION

Courts generally will not judge adequacy

4–014   [*Add to note 81, at the end: page* [409]]
For the possible legal status, after the completion of "Brexit", of UK legislation which has been passed to implement EU legal requirements, see above, paras 1–013A—1–013E.

8. Existing Duties as Consideration

(b) *Duty Imposed by Contract with Promisor*

Factual benefit to promisor

[Add to note 369, line 5, after "[1998] 2 Lloyd's Rep. 428 at 435": page [445]]   **4–069**
; *Stevensdrake Ltd v Hunt* [2016] EWHC 1111 (Ch) at [61]; *MWB Business Exchange Centres Ltd v Rock Advertising Ltd* [2016] EWCA Civ 553, discussed below, para.4–119A.

[Add to note 377, at the end: page [446]]   **4–070**
A passage in the judgment of Arden L.J. in *MWB Business Exchange Centres Ltd v Rock Advertising Ltd* [2016] EWCA Civ 553 at [79] could be said to support the view that the decision in *Stilk v Myrick* (1809) 2 Camp. 317, Main Work, para.4–067, might now go the other way on the ground that the master of the ship had obtained a "practical benefit" which would constitute consideration within the reasoning of the *Williams* case [1991] 1 Q.B. 1, see Main Work, Vol.I, para.4–069; but there is no reference to *Stilk v Myrick* (above) in the *MWB* case, above.

[Add a new note 378a at the end of the paragraph: page [447]]
378a The above sentence in the Main Work is cited with apparent approval by Arden L.J. in *MWB Business Exchange Centres Ltd v Rock Advertising Ltd* [2016] EWCA Civ 553 at [80]. The question whether in that case the requirement of consideration was satisfied is discussed below, para. 4–119A.

9. Discharge and Variation of Contractual Duties

(b) *Variation*

(iii) *Equitable Mitigations*

The promise or representation must be "clear" or "unequivocal"

[Add to note 473, at the end: page [461]]   **4–091**
The requirement that, for the purpose of an estoppel by representation, the representation must be "clear or unequivocal" or "precise and unambiguous" is stated by Carr J. in *Spliethoff's Bevrachtingskantoor BV v Bank of China* [2015] EWHC 999 (Comm), [2015] 2 Lloyd's Rep. 123 at [156] citing, with apparent approval, para.3–090 of the 31st edition of the Main Work, replaced by para.4–091 of the 32nd (present) edition.

[Add to note 475 at the end: page [461]]
; *MWB Business Exchange Centres Ltd v Rock Advertising Ltd* [2016] EWCA Civ 553 at [51], [52] and *passim;* as the promise in this case was supported by consideration (see below, para.4–119A) it was not strictly necessary to decide the estoppel issue: see at [50].

Whether "detriment" required

4–095   [*Add to note 513, at the end: page* [465]]
; *MWB Business Exchange Centres Ltd v Rock Advertising Ltd* [2016] EWCA
Civ 553 at [54]; for this case (so far as it relates to estoppel) see also above,
para.4–091 n.475.

Effect of the doctrine generally suspensive

4–097   [*Add to note 526, line 13, after* "no promissory estoppel had arisen": *page* [467]]
; *MWB Business Exchange Centres Ltd v Rock Advertising Ltd* [2016] EWCA
Civ 553 at [56] ("may only be suspensive"). No promissory estoppel would have
arisen in this case as reasonable notice had been given to terminate the "variation
agreement" (described below, see para.4–119A); for this point see at [63], [67]
and [92].

[*Add to note 526, at the end: page* [467]]
Notice is not required to bring an end to the suspension where, on the true
construction of the representation, the circumstances in which it was intended to
apply had come to an end: see *Dunbar Assets plc v Butler* [2015] EWHC 2546
(Ch) at [50]; or where notice of termination was not necessary "to allow a
reasonable period for the party to whom notice is given to make alternative
arrangements" (*ibid.*, at [51]).

Analogy with waiver

4–105   [*Add to note 595, line 13, after* "and promissory estoppel");": *page* [477]]
MWB Business Exchange Centres Ltd v Rock Advertising Ltd [2016] EWCA Civ
553 at [64], describing "waiver" in the context of para.4–015 of the Main Work,
Vol.I, as "akin to promissory estoppel";

Distinguished from estoppel by convention

4–108   [*Add to note 620, penultimate line, after* "without further reference to estoppel.":
page [481]]
F G Wilson (Engineering) Ltd v John Holt & Co (Liverpool) Ltd [2013] EWCA
Civ 1232, [2014] 1 W.L.R. 2365 is doubted in *PST Energy 7 Shipping LLC v O
W Bunker Malta Ltd (The Res Cogitans)* [2016] UKSC 23, [2016] 2 W.L.R.
1193, but not on the estoppel point for which it is cited in this footnote in the
Main Work.

[*Add to note 620, at the end: page* [481]]
The requirements of estoppel by convention are summarised in *Spliethoff's
Bevrachtingskantoor BV v Bank of China* [2015] EWHC 999 (Comm), [2015] 2
Lloyd's Rep. 123 at [159], citing "paras. 3–107 [of the 31st edition of the Main
Work] and following" with apparent approval; the corresponding paragraphs in
the present, 32nd edition are paras 4–108 et seq. Carr J. would have held those
requirements to have been satisfied but it was "strictly unnecessary" (at [154])
to decide the point since his "primary conclusion" (at [170]) was that the facts

which the claimant sought to estop the defendant from denying had been established by the evidence (see at [147]–[154]).

[*Add to note 622, at the end: page* [482]]
For discussions of estoppel by convention, see also *Mitchell v Watkinson* [2014] EWCA Civ 1472, [2015] L. & T.R. 22 at [51], where para.3–107 of the 31st edition of the Main Work (para.4–108 of the present, 32nd edition) is cited with apparent approval; in that case the defence of estoppel by convention failed for want of a common assumption (at [60]—but the appeal was dismissed on other grounds: at [95]); *Edray Ltd v Canning* [2015] EWHC 2744 (Ch), where the two requirements of estoppel by convention stated at notes 620 and 621 of the Main Work (that there must be a common assumption and that it must be unjust to allow the party alleged to be estopped to resile from that assumption (at [38]) were held to have been satisfied (at [48]); and *Roundlistic Ltd v Jones* [2016] UKUT 325 where the requirements of estoppel are stated at [47] and [48] and no such estoppel was held to arise as the parties had not made any "common assumption" (at [50] and [56]).

Assumption of law

[*Add to note 645, at the end: page* [485]]   **4–111**
and [2015] EWCA Civ 751, [2016] 2 All E.R. (Comm) 333 at [43].

Whether estoppel by convention creates new rights

[*Add to note 676, at the end: page* [488]]   **4–114**
In this case the Court of Appeal allowed the appeal: see [2015] EWCA Civ 751, [2016] 2 All E.R. (Comm) 333 at [59]. The Court held that the judge below had been wrong to conclude that the contract contained the term giving effect to the allegedly shared assumption (at [50]); and that he had also been wrong in holding that, if there was no "relevant contractual term," then the lender in that case was "estopped on the basis of some sort of contractual estoppel, estoppel by convention or estoppel by representation" from denying that the borrower was protected as if there had been some such term (at [56]); but the Court further held that the lender's representations gave rise to liability under the Misrepresentation Act 1967 and as "contractual warranties" (at [57]), presumably collateral to the main contract.

[*Add to note 682, at the end: page* [489]]
See also *Rivertrade Ltd v EMG Finance Ltd* [2015] EWCA Civ 1295, where estoppel by convention did not "create an enforceable right" but was relied upon "to bind the parties to [the] agreement to an interpretation that would not otherwise be correct" (at [50]).

[*Add to paragraph, after note 683: page* [489]]
In *Rivertrade Ltd v EMG Finance Ltd*[683a] Kitchin L.J., with whose judgment Moore-Bick and Ryder L.JJ. agreed, said that the case was not one "in which an estoppel [was] relied upon to create an enforceable right where none previously existed. It is instead one of those cases in which the estoppel is relied upon to

bind the parties to an agreement to an interpretation which it would not otherwise bear"[683b]; and that, where this was the position, an estoppel by convention could "enlarge the effect of an agreement."[683c] The view that estoppel by convention can have such an effect can, where the common assumption on which the estoppel is based increases the obligation of the party alleged to be estopped, give rise to the same difficulty as that discussed in the context of promissory estoppel in Main Work, Vol.I, para.4–100: it could, for example, if applied in circumstances resembling those of *Stilk v Myrick*[683d] have the effect of allowing the claim that was there dismissed. It is respectfully submitted that the *Rivertrade* case[683e] should not be regarded as concluding the point. In that case, counsel for the defendant conceded the point; and although the Court approved of this concession,[683f] it also seemed to attach importance to the fact that the estoppel in that case did *not* "create an enforceable right where none previously existed."[683g] The tension between these two positions should, it is respectfully submitted, not be regarded as having been finally resolved in the *Rivertrade* case; in particular the question whether there are limits to the extent to which estoppel by convention can "enlarge the effect of an agreement" remains an open one. The answer to this question requires fuller argument[683h] than it received in the *Rivertrade* case.

[683a] [2015] EWCA Civ 1295.
[683b] At [50].
[683c] At [48].
[683d] (1809) 2 Camp. 317, 6 Esp. 129, Main Work, Vol.I, para.4–067.
[683e] Above, at note 683a.
[683f] [2016] EWCA Civ 1295 at [48].
[683g] At [50], quoted above at note 683b.
[683h] The concession referred to at note 683f had the effect that the point was not fully argued.

"Contractual estoppel"

4–116   *[Add to note 693, at the end: page* [491]]
The Court of Appeal allowed the appeal in the *NRAM* case: see [2015] EWCA Civ 751, [2016] 2 All E.R. (Comm) 333 at [59]. The judgment of the Court of Appeal contains two references to "estoppel by convention and/or contractual estoppel" (at [52] and [56]). Neither of these passages refers to any requirement that the statement or common assumption must relate to a "past" state of affairs to be capable of giving rise (in cases of alleged "contractual estoppel") to a cause of action.

10. Part Payment of a Debt

(a) *General Rule*

Effects of the rule

[Add new paragraph 4–119A: page [494]]
4–119A   The discussion in para.4–119 of the likely relationship between, on the one hand, the general rule stated in *Pinnel's*[714a] case and in *Foakes v Beer*,[714b] and, on the

other, the more recently developed view stated in *Williams v Roffey Brothers & Nicholls (Contractors) Ltd*[714c] now calls for further discussion in the light of the decision of the Court of Appeal in *MWB Business Exchange Centres Ltd v Rock Advertising Ltd*[714d] ("the *MWB* case"). In that case, office premises managed by the claimants were occupied by the defendants under a licence agreement between themselves and the claimants. The defendants having fallen into arrears with payments due from them to the claimants, the parties agreed on February 27, 2012 to vary their original licence agreement by "re-scheduling" the payments due from the defendants to the claimants (so as in effect to give the defendants extra time to pay). One of the re-scheduled payments (of £3,500) was made on that day, but on March 30, 2012 the claimants exercised their right under the original contract to lock the defendants out of the premises.[714e] On March 30, 2012 the claimants gave notice terminating the (original) agreement[714f]; they then sued for arrears of licence fees and damages. The defendants relied on the variation agreement (re-scheduling their payments); and one of the issues before the Court of Appeal was whether the claimants' promise to (in effect) give the defendants extra time to pay was supported by consideration. In answering this question in the affirmative,[714g] the Court applied the reasoning of the *Williams* case[714h]: that is, it held that the requirement of consideration was satisfied because the variation agreement had conferred "practical benefits"[714i] on the claimants. *Foakes v Beer*[714j] and *Re Selectmove*[714k] were distinguished on the ground that they applied only where the sole benefit accruing to the creditor from the performance of the variation agreement took the form of receiving part payment of a debt already legally due to him, instead of insisting on payment of the whole.[714l] Indeed, this view is supported, as Arden L.J. points out in the *MWB* case, by the well known statement in *Pinnel's* case that the rule there laid down, and approved in *Foakes v Beer*, is subject to the "rider" that "the gift of a horse, hawk or robe etc. shall be good satisfaction . . . ".[714m] It is sometimes assumed that the provision of such benefits satisfies the requirement of consideration because the debtor was not bound by the original contract to provide them[714n]; but the ensuing discussion will show that the requirement of consideration may (though it will not necessarily) be satisfied where the debtor's performance which confers the "practical benefit" on the creditor was already due from the debtor to the creditor under the original contract between these parties before that contract was varied by agreement between them; indeed that was the position in the *Williams* case[714o] itself. It is convenient here to begin the discussion of the consideration issue in the *MWB* case by reference to the way in which Arden L.J. there discusses this question. Her starting point is to refer to the way in which the judge in the Court below had dealt with the point: he had found that the "variation agreement conferred on [the claimant] the practical benefit of continuing occupation by" the defendant and thus (in Arden L.J.'s own words) that "of avoiding a void", the noun "void" being here used "in the sense in which it is used in property management to refer to unoccupied and therefore unproductive property, which may cause loss in the form of loss of rent *and in other ways.*"[714p] Substantially the same point is made by Kitchin L.J.,[714q] who in addition agreed with Arden L.J. on this issue[714r]; while McCombe L.J. agreed with both of the other judgments.[714s] Both these judgments also identify a second "practical benefit" obtained by the claimants. This was the benefit which they obtained by reason of the facts that, in performance of the variation agreement they had received a payment of £3,500 and that they would, under that agreement, be "likely to recover more than [they] would by enforcing the terms of the original agreement."[714t] This second "practical benefit" seems closely to resemble the benefit described by Lord Blackburn in *Foakes v Beer*,[714u] but reluctantly there regarded by him as *not* amounting to consideration, a point on which that case was followed in *Re Selectmove*.[714v] It is therefore hard to accept that the second "practical benefit" identified in the *MWB* case would, on its own, have satisfied the requirement of consideration. That benefit differs, or may differ, from the benefit that a debtor may provide by way of a horse, a hawk or a robe[714w] in that those benefits are assumed to be of a kind that the debtor is *not* obliged under the original contract to provide;[714x] and it is not clear from the report of the Court of Appeal's decision in the *MWB* case whether the original contract in that case imposed any obligation on the defendants to continue to occupy the premises for the term of the licence.[714y] The *Anangel Atlas* case[714z] supports the view that a benefit may satisfy the requirement of consideration even though it takes the form of an act which the debtor *was* bound under the contract to do, in that case taking delivery of the contractual subject-matter. This benefited the creditor in that the debtor's refusal to take delivery might have prejudiced the creditor's relations with other actual or potential customers; and from a commercial point of view this resembled the benefit that the claimants in the *MWB* case obtained from "avoiding a void."[714aa] The only situation in which a "practical benefit" conferred by the debtor on the creditor will *not* satisfy the requirement of consideration because the debtor was already bound by the contract to confer that benefit on the creditor is that in which the benefit consists of part payment (or the promise of part payment) of a debt already due. In the *MWB* case, this was said to be the only situation squarely covered by *Foakes v Beer* and *Re Selectmove*.[714ab] Where the benefit is of a different kind, the *MWB* case recognises that it can constitute consideration for the creditor's promise and it can do so whether or not the debtor was already bound by the original contract to confer that benefit on the creditor. The remaining puzzle arising from this part of the reasoning of the *MWB* case is that the defendants' continuing in occupation was regarded as a benefit to the claimants in spite of the fact that, by locking the defendants out of the premises, the claimants had shown that they did not themselves so regard it.[714ac]

[714a] (1602) 5 Co. Rep. 117a; Main Work, Vol.I, para.4–117.
[714b] (1884) 9 App. Cas. 605; Main Work, Vol.I, para.4–117.
[714c] [1991] 1 Q.B. 1; Main Work, Vol.I, paras 4–069, 4–070.
[714d] [2016] EWCA Civ 553.
[714e] At [4].
[714f] *ibid.*
[714g] [2016] EWCA Civ 553 at [49], [66], [67], [87].
[714h] Above, at note 714c.
[714i] [2016] EWCA Civ 553 at [42].
[714j] (1884) 9 App. Cas. 605; Main Work para.4–117.
[714k] [1995] 1 W.L.R. 474; Main Work para.4–119 n.713.
[714l] See [2016] EWCA Civ 553 at [39], [85]–[87].
[714m] At [85].
[714n] *e.g.* at [41] ("some other act that he was not bound by the contract to perform"); *cf.* at [84], explaining *Re Selectmove* (above, n.714k) on the ground that there was no "extra" benefit to the promisor.
[714o] [1991] 1 Q.B. 1, Main Work paras 4–069, 4–070.
[714p] [2016] EWCA Civ 553 at [72], italics supplied; *e.g.*, perhaps by reducing the rental value of other units in the same building.

[714q] At [48] ("would retain [the defendant] as licensee").

[714r] At [49].

[714s] At [67].

[714t] At [48].

[714u] (1884) 9 App. Cas. 605 at 622, quoted in the *MWB* case [2016] EWCA Civ 553 at [39].

[714v] [1995] 1 W.L.R. 474, Main Work, para.4–119 n.713.

[714w] See above, at note 714m.

[714x] See above at note 714n.

[714y] *Cf.* , for example, *Co-operative Insurance Society Ltd v Argyll Stores (Holdings) Ltd*, Main Work, Vol.I, para.27–031, for a clause of this kind. No issue of consideration arose in this case.

[714z] [1990] 2 Lloyd's Rep. 526, 544, discussed in the Main Work, Vol.I, para.4–125.

[714aa] [2016] EWCA Civ 553 at [72].

[714ab] See [2016] EWCA Civ 553 at [48], [49], [67] and [82]–[87].

[714ac] Perhaps the resolution of the above reasoning may be sought by reasoning similar to that of para.4–024 of the Main Work.

(c) *Limitations in Equity*

Equitable forbearance

[*Add new note 759a, after* "had come to an end." *in line 18: page* [500]]   4–130

[759a] For similar reasoning, see *Dunbar Assets plc v Butler* [2015] EWHC 2546 (Ch) where the issue was not one of part payment of a debt, but was one of the postponement of a liability. In that case A had lent money to two companies, in the management of which a "prominent part" (at [2]) was played by B for whom and whose family most of the shares in the companies were held in trust and who, without charging any fees, managed development properties owned by the companies (at [11]). B had guaranteed debts of the companies, and in an action to enforce these guarantees, B relied on the defence of promissory estoppel; such an estoppel was alleged to have arisen from a representation or promise by A that any such enforcement would be "postponed indefinitely" for so long as B continued with his (unpaid) work for the companies (at [18]). B's defence of promissory estoppel was rejected on the ground that A's statement was intended to affect the rights of the parties "only for the intended duration of the arrangement" (at [49]), *i.e.* for so long as B continued to provide the (unpaid) management work "with the concurrence of" A (*ibid.*). It no longer applied after A had made it clear that B's work was no longer required; and, once B had ceased to do the work, his reliance on A's representation, and hence the suspension of B's liability, had come to an end (at [50]).

Suspensive nature of the doctrine

[*Add to note 775, at the end: page* [501]]   4–131

In *Stevensdrake Ltd v Hunt* [2016] EWHC 1111 (Ch), at [65], it was held that, where the creditor's "agreement permanently to forego rights" was "clear and unequivocal", and the other requirements of promissory estoppel were satisfied it would be wrong to treat the agreement as "merely suspensory", with the result that "the doctrine of promissory estoppel [was] engaged" and made it "inequitable" for the creditor to pursue its claim against the debtor. In treating the issue of the extinctive (as opposed to the "suspensory") effect of the doctrine as a matter of construction, this conclusion, though it may in the circumstance have been desirable as a matter of policy, is not easy to reconcile with earlier authorities (for example *Foakes v Beer* (1884) 9 App. Cas. 605, Main Work, Vol.I, para.4–117) cited in the *Stevensdrake* case (above) at [42].

11. PROPRIETARY ESTOPPEL

(a) *Nature of the Doctrine*

Scope of proprietary estoppel

4–140   [*Add new note 825a, after* "can be divided broadly" *in line 3: page* [507]]
[825a] A proprietary estoppel does not "have to fit neatly" into the "pigeon holes" of the "pure acquiescence" or "assurance" (or "encouragement") categories discussed in para.4–140 of Vol.I of the Main Work: *Hoyl Group Ltd v Cromer Town Council* [2015] EWCA Civ 782, [2015] H.L.R. 43 at [72]. In this case a finding that the claimant company was entitled to a right of way on the basis of proprietary estoppel, partly by reason of the defendant's encouragement and partly by its acquiescence in allowing use of the right of way for three years, was accordingly upheld by the Court of Appeal: see at [71]–[78]. It was further held that a party (A) could be found to have encouraged the other's (B) belief in the existence of the right claimed even though A was not aware of that belief: it sufficed for A's conduct to be consistent only with B's having the right in question (at [73]).

(b) *Bases of Liability*

Expenditure on another's land in reliance on a promise

4–141   [*Add to note 836, line 2, after* "[1994] E.G.C.S. 134;"*: page* [509]]
cf. Arif v Anwar [2015] EWHC 124 (Fam), [2016] 1 F.L.R. 359, where the person claiming to be entitled to the benefit of the proprietary estoppel had allowed money to which he was entitled to be used in improving the property; and this fact was held to be sufficient detrimental reliance (at [68]) to give rise to the proprietary estoppel (at [69]); for this requirement, see Main Work, Vol.I, para.4–158);

Proprietary estoppel and constructive trust

4–142   [*Add to the paragraph, after note 849: page* [510]]
It is also possible, in cases of the first kind described in para.4–142 of the Main Work[849a] for relief to be given on the ground of proprietary estoppel[849b] even though the facts do *not,* give rise for want of a sufficiently "clear agreement" give rise to any constructive trust.[849c]

[849a] At note 847.
[849b] *Arif v Anwar* [2015] EWHC 124 (Fam) at [69].
[849c] At [47], [68].

(c) *Conditions giving rise to Liability*

Main elements of proprietary estoppel

4–146   [*Add to note 880, line 2, after* "[2012] 2 All E.R. 754 at [114];"*: page* [514]]
Burton v Liden [2016] EWCA Civ 275 at [16];

[Add to note 880, line 6, after "or overlap with each other;"*: page* [514]]
see also *Davies v Davies* [2016] EWCA Civ 463, restating the main elements of proprietary estoppel and repeating the point that they could not be divided into "watertight compartments" (at [38]);

[Add to note 880, at the end: page [514]]
For a case in which a daughter's claim against her mother's estate, based on proprietary estoppel, was rejected because none of the three requirements stated in para.4–146 of Vol.I of the Main Work had been satisfied, see *Wright v Waters* [2014] EWHC 3614, [2015] W.T.L.R. 353. See also *MWB Business Exchange Centres Ltd v Rock Advertising Ltd* [2016] EWCA Civ 553, where the "three main elements" of proprietary estoppel are stated at [65] but it was held that no such estoppel arose because (1) the right claimed by the person relying on the estoppel was not "a proprietary right" and (2) that person had not "suffered any detriment."

Kinds of promises capable of giving rise to proprietary estoppel

[Add to paragraph, at the end: page [516]]   **4–147**
Where the property in question was held in trust by two trustees, it was held that the promise of only one of the trustees, who had no authority to bind the other, did not give rise to a proprietary estoppel on which the promisee sought to rely by way of defence to a claim for possession of the property, that claim having been made by both trustees.[897a]

[897a] *Preedy v Dunne* [2015] EWHC 2713 (Ch), [2015] W.T.L.R. 1795.

"Clear enough" in context

[Add to note 918, at the end: page [518]]   **4–150**
See also *Burton v Liden* [2016] EWCA Civ 275 at [24], where the context in which the representation was made was said to be "hugely important" and Lord Walker's test of reasonable clarity in that context (stated in *Thorner v Major* [2009] UKHL 18, [2009] 1 W.L.R. 776 at [56], quoted in para.4–150 of Vol.I of the Main Work) was held to have been satisfied.

(d) *Effects of the Doctrine*

Remedy: principled discretion

[Add to note 1094, line 4, after "reliance: above, para.4–158;"*: page* [538]]   **4–173**
For the importance of "proportionality" in assessing the amount of monetary relief available to the promisee, see also *Davies v Davies* [2016] EWCA Civ 463 at [38], quoting from the Court below. On appeal, it was no longer disputed that compensation in money was in this case the appropriate form of relief.

CHAPTER 5

FORM

1. IN GENERAL

Duties of information as requirements of form

5–003   [*Add to note 18, at the end: page* [565]]
The 1990 directive is repealed by Directive (EU) 2015/2302 on package travel and linked travel arrangements [2015] O.J. L326/1, art.4 of which sets a general principle of full harmonisation and must be implemented by January 1, 2018.

Electronic signatures

5–008   [*Delete text of paragraph including footnotes and substitute: pages* [568]–[569]]
In 1999, the EU legislator enacted the Electronic Signatures Directive,[51] whose purposes were to facilitate the use of "electronic signatures" and to contribute to their legal recognition, and to establish a legal framework for electronic signatures and certain certification-services: it expressly did not cover aspects relating to the conclusion or validity of contracts or other legal obligations where there are requirements as regards form required by national or Community law, nor the rules and limits governing the use of documents.[52] An "electronic signature" was defined by the Directive as "data in electronic form which are attached to or logically associated with other electronic data and which serve as a method of authentication".[52a] The United Kingdom implemented the Electronic

Signatures Directive 1999 by two instruments. First, s.7 of the Electronic Communications Act 2000 provided for the admissibility in evidence of electronic signatures and certification by any person of such a signature "in relation to any question as to the authenticity of the communication or data or as to the integrity of the communication or data, and followed for this purpose the definition of "electronic signature" in the Directive.[52b] On its terms, this provision is broad enough to include evidence for the purposes of formal requirements of a contract (such as s.2 of the Law of Property (Miscellaneous Provisions) Act 1989[52c]), but, if it were so interpreted, it would go beyond the scope of the requirements of the 1999 Directive. Secondly, the Electronic Signatures Regulations 2002 provided for the supervision and liability of "certification-service-providers" (i.e. persons who issue certificates or provide other services related to electronic signatures) and for consequential matters relating to data protection.[52d] However, the Electronic Signatures Directive 1999 was repealed and replaced by the EU Electronic Identification and Electronic Trust Services Regulation 2014 (the "eIDAS Regulation", applicable in general from July 1, 2016),[52e] which lays down the conditions under which Member States mutually recognise "electronic identification means of natural persons and legal persons falling under a notified electronic identification scheme of another Member State", and "rules for trust services, in particular for electronic transactions"; and which establishes "a legal framework for electronic signatures, electronic seals, electronic time stamps, electronic documents, electronic registered delivery services and certificate services for website authentication".[52f] Following the pattern of the 1999 Directive, the eIDAS Regulation provides expressly that it "does not affect national or Union law related to the conclusion and validity of contracts or other legal or procedural obligations relating to form".[52g] Instead, its main purpose is to ensure that businesses and individuals can use their own national electronic identification schemes (eIDs) to access public services in other EU countries where electronic identification schemes are available; it also aims to create a European internal market for electronic trust services—electronic signatures, electronic seals, time stamps etc.—by ensuring that they will work across borders and have the same legal status as traditional paper-based processes.[52h] By way of implementation of some aspects of the eIDAS Regulation, the UK revoked and replaced the Electronic Signature Regulations 2002 by the Electronic Identification and Trust Services for Electronic Transactions Regulations 2016, which came into force on July 22, 2016.[52i] The 2016 Regulations also amended s.7 of the Electronic Communications Act 2000 so as to follow the simplified definition of "electronic signature" in the eIDAS Regulation as:

"so much of anything in electronic form as–
   (a) is incorporated into or otherwise logically associated with any electronic communication or electronic data; and
   (b) purports to be used by the individual creating it to sign."[52j]

The main import of s.7 remains the same, viz. to make general provision for the recognition of electronic signatures as evidence in legal proceedings.[52k] The 2016 Regulations also make new provision for electronic seals and related certificates, electronic time stamps and related certificates, electronic documents and related certificates and electronic registered delivery service and related certificates.[521] However, the eIDAS Regulation itself (as earlier noted[52m]) does not affect the law governing the definitions of signature for the purposes of formal requirements of English contract law[52n]; nor does its provision for "electronic seals" affect the common law or statutory requirements for the execution of a deed.[52o] It is submitted that the uncertainty as to the impact of s.7 of the Electronic Communications Act 2000 in relation to these same formalities remains after its amendment by the 2016 Regulations.[52p]

[51] Directive 1999/93 on a Community framework for electronic signatures [2000] O.J. L13/12.

[52] Directive 1999/93 art.1.

[52a] Directive 1999/93 art.2(1).

[52b] Electronic Communications Act 2000 s.7(2) (as enacted).

[52c] On which see Main Work, Vol.I, paras 5–010 et seq.

[52d] SI 2002/318.

[52e] Regulation (EU) 910/2014 of 23 July 2014 on electronic identification and trust services for electronic transactions in the internal market and repealing Directive 1999/93/EC [2014] O.J. L 257/73 art.52(2) (with the exceptions there noted).

[52f] Regulation (EU) 910/2014 art.1.

[52g] Regulation (EU) 910/2014 art.2(3) and recital 21.

[52h] See EU Commission, *https://ec.europa.eu/digital-single-market/en/trust-services-and-eid*.

[52i] SI 2016/696.

[52j] SI 2016/696 reg.5, Sch.3 para.1(2). The definition of certification of such an electronic signature was amended to similar effect: SI 2016/696 reg.5, Sch.3 para.1(3).

[52k] Electronic Communications Act 2000 s.7(1).

[52l] Electronic Communications Act 2000 ss.7A–7D (as inserted by SI 2016/696 reg.5, Sch.3 para.1(4)).

[52m] Regulation (EU) 910/2014 art.2(3). Later general statements, such as the statement in art.25(2) that "[a] qualified electronic signature shall have the equivalent legal effect of a handwritten signature" must be read subject to the general definition of the scope of the Regulation in art.2(3).

[52n] "Signature" is relevant to the formal requirements imposed, inter alia, by the Law of Property (Miscellaneous Provisions) Act 1989 s.1 in relation to deeds (on which see Main Work, Vol.I, para.1–118); by s.2 of the same Act in relation to contracts for the sale or other disposition of an interest in land (on which see Main Work, Vol.I, paras 5–010 et seq. and esp. para.5–037); and by the Statute of Frauds s.4 in relation to contracts of guarantee (on which see Main Work, Vol.II, paras 45–042 et seq. and esp. para.45–057). The position as regards the so-called rule in *L'Estrange v F Graucob Ltd* [1934] 2 K.B. 394 which governs the incorporation of written terms by signature (on which see Main Work, Vol.I, para.13–002) is more arguable as it is not clear that the incorporation of contract terms relates to the "conclusion and validity of contracts or other legal or procedural obligations relating to form" within the exclusion from the scope of the eIDAS Regulation reg.2(3).

[52o] See Main Work, Vol.I, paras 1–113 et seq.

[52p] For further discussion of "signature" and electronic communications see *Emmet & Farrand on Title* (updated to June 2016), paras 2–041—2–041.06.

Electronic documents and deeds

5–009   [*Add to paragraph, at the end: page* [569]]

However, the system of electronic conveyancing which these legislation provisions envisaged has not been brought into being and the Law Commission has consulted on a different scheme.[54a]

[54a] See further Law Commission, *Updating the Land Registration Act 2002, A Consultation Paper* (Consultation Paper No.227, 2016) Ch.20.

2. Contracts for the Sale or Other Disposition of an Interest in Land

(a) *Contracts within s.2 of the Law of Property (Miscellaneous Provisions) Act 1989*

"Sale or other disposition of an interest in land"

[*Add new note 70a at the end of paragraph: page* [571]]   **5–014**
70a Thus, e.g. a contract which would create an option the exercise of which would release a charge on land falls within s.2: *Tuscula (110) Ltd v Y2K Co Ltd* [2016] EWHC 1124 (Ch) at [205]–[213] (though it was held that no such contract had been concluded).

"Contracts for the disposition of an interest" and "contracts of disposition"

[*Add to note 87, at the end: page* [573]]   **5–017**
See further *Keay v Morris Homes (West Midlands) Ltd* [2012] EWCA Civ 900, [2012] 1 W.L.R. 2855 at [8]; *Rollerteam Ltd v Riley* [2015] EWHC 1545 (Ch) at [45].

(b) *Formal Requirements*

"All the terms which the parties have expressly agreed in one document": generally

[*In note 184, line 5, delete* "and [91(f)]" *and substitute: page* [584]]   **5–033**
and [91] (one of joined cases reversed on other grounds sub nom. *Marlbray Ltd v Laditi* [2016] EWCA Civ 476)

"Exchange of contracts"

[*Add to note 203, at the end: page* [587]]   **5–035**
While the judgment in *Rabiu v Marlbray Ltd* was the subject of considerable criticism (and was reversed in part) by the CA sub nom. *Marlbray Ltd v Laditi* [2016] EWCA Civ 476 (on which see below, para.5–038), the point in the text of the Main Work was not subject to appeal.

[*Add to note 204, at the end: page* [587]]
While the judgment in *Rabiu v Marlbray Ltd* was the subject of considerable criticism (and was reversed in part) by the CA sub nom. *Marlbray Ltd v Laditi* [2016] EWCA Civ 476 (on which see below, para.5–038), the point in the text of the Main Work was not subject to appeal.

Meaning of "signature"

[*Add to note 211, at the end: page* [588]]   **5–037**
For criticism of this view of "signature" for the purposes of s.2 of the 1989 Act see *Emmet & Farrand on Title* (updated to June 2016), paras 2–041—2–041.06.

Nevertheless, *Emmet & Farrand on Title* concludes that "conveyancers should be as cautious as practicable and prefer in practice 'wet ink' signatures for contracts for the sale of land": *Emmet & Farrand on Title* at para.2.041.05, not following the view expressed by the Law Society in its practice note, *Execution of documents at virtual means* (February 16, 2010) (available at *http://www.law society.org.uk*). In *Ramsay v Love* [2015] EWHC 65 (Ch) at [7], Morgan J. observed (obiter and in the context of s.1(3) of the 1989 Act rather than s.2 of the same Act) that the statements in *Firstpost Homes Ltd v Johnson* which require signature by an executing party to be made with a pen in his own hand were not designed to distinguish between signing in such a way and by the use of a signature writing machine.

Signature by agent

5–038   [*In note 216, delete from "Rabiu v Marlbray Ltd" in line 9 to the end and substitute: page* [589]]
Simpole v Chee [2013] EWHC 4444 (Ch) at [8]–[10]. Where A signs a document setting out a contract of sale with B in respect of obligations expressed as joint and several, not only on his own behalf but also on behalf of C in respect of her joint and several obligations but without her authority, in principle the contract is valid between A and B as long as it is, on an objective interpretation, not conditional on C's having authorised him to sign on her behalf, as the joint and several provision of the contract make it clear that A and C do not constitute a "composite" purchaser: *Marlbray Ltd v Laditi* (on appeal from sub nom. *Rabiu v Marlbray Ltd*) [2016] EWCA Civ 476 at [56] and [68]. If in these circumstances the document signed by A and B contains all the terms of the several contract, then it satisfies the requirements of s.2 of the 1989 Act, it being irrelevant that A did not sign identifying the precise capacity in which he did so, i.e. as principal obligor under his several contract: [2016] EWCA Civ 476 at [71]. A is therefore bound under his contract with B, even though C is not.

[*Add to note 217, line 4, after* "Companies Act 1985": *page* [589]]
(now s.51 of the Companies Act 2006)

[*Add to note 217, at the end: page* [589]]
; *Royal Mail Estates Ltd v Maple Teesdale (a firm)* [2015] EWHC 1890 (Ch), [2016] 1 W.L.R. 942.

(c) *The Effect of Failure to Comply with the Formal Requirements*

Promissory estoppel ("forbearance in equity")

5–042   [*Add to paragraph, at the end: page* [594]]
Moreover, as Lewison L.J. has observed, "it would be surprising if one could do by promissory estoppel what one could not do by informal contract"[259a] and, moreover, in the case of promissory estoppel, "there is no question of a constructive trust of land arising" so as to fall within the exception to the formality requirements provided by the 1989 Act s.2(5).[259b]

259a *Dudley Muslim Association v Dudley MBC* [2015] EWCA Civ 1123, [2016] 1 P. & C.R. 10 at
[33].
259b [2015] EWCA Civ 1123 at [33].

Cobbe v Yeoman's Row Management Ltd

[*Add to note 284, line 1, after* "[2008] UKHL 55 at [29]"*: page* [597]]   **5–046**
; *Dudley Muslim Association v Dudley MBC* [2015] EWCA Civ 1123, [2016] 1
P. & C.R. 10 at [33] (doubting the law as expressed in *Yaxley v Gotts* [2000] Ch.
162 noted in the Main Work, Vol.I, para.5–045) by reference to Lord Scott of
Foscote's view).

Herbert v Doyle

[*Add to note 288, at the end: page* [598]]   **5–048**
; *Ghazaani v Rowshan* [2015] EWHC 1922 (Ch) at [192] and [197] (allowing the
possibility of proprietary estoppel/constructive trust in the "exceptional circumstances" of the case); *Muhammad v ARY Properties Ltd* [2016] EWHC 1698
(Ch) at [32]–[50].

Restitution: recovery of money paid by purchaser on a failure of consideration

[*Add to note 307, at the end: page* [600]]   **5–051**
Sharma v Simposh was applied by the CA in *Marlbray Ltd v Laditi* (on appeal
from sub nom. *Rabiu v Marlbray Ltd*) [2016] EWCA Civ 476 at [81]–[93], [96],
esp. at [92] where it was held that a deposit paid by a joint and several purchaser
off-plan of a long lease of a flat in a large block should not be returned on the
basis of a failure of consideration, even if the contract was void under s.2 of the
1989 Act (which it was held not to be), as the purchaser had the benefit of the
specific unit chosen being taken off the market; the flat had been secured at a
specific price; the developer had (apparently) completed the works with the
deposit as collateral; and the purchaser had become entitled to 10 free days at a
London hotel. For this purpose, it made no difference that the deposit was held
by a third-party stakeholder: [2016] EWCA Civ 476 at [99].

COMMON MISTAKE

1. INTRODUCTION TO MISTAKE

Types of mistake

6–001   [*In note 7, update reference to Anson's Law of Contract, 29th edn to: page* [606]]
30th edn (2015), Ch.8.

Mistakes as to facts and mistakes as to terms

6–002   [*In note 12, update reference to Anson's Law of Contract to: page* [606]]
30th edn (2015), p.300

Mistakes that are not legally relevant

6–005   [*In note 23, delete* "29th edition by Beatson, Burrows and Cartwright (eds) (2010)" *and substitute: page* [607]]
30th edition by Beatson, Burrows and Cartwright (eds) (2015)

[*In note 23, delete* "pp.277–278" *and substitute: page* [607]]
p.300

[*Add to note 25, at the end: page* [608]]
Whether a transaction is subject to the narrower rules that apply to contracts or the wider grounds that apply to voluntary settlements depend on whether there was consideration for the transfer: *Van der Merwe v Goldman* [2016] EWHC 790 (Ch), [2016] 4 W.L.R. 71.

3. DIFFERENT APPROACHES BEFORE *BELL v LEVER BROS*

Kennedy's case

[*In note 92, update references to Treitel on The Law of Contract to: page* [616]]   **6–020**
14th edn (2015)
[*The paragraph numbers remain unchanged.*]

4. MISTAKE AT COMMON LAW

(b) *The Modern Doctrine*

(ii) *Conditions for Common Mistake to Render Contract Void*

Non-existence of the state of affairs must not be attributable to the fault of either party

[*In note 165, update reference to Treitel on The Law of Contract to: page* [626]]   **6–038**
14th edn (2015), para.8–005

Section 6 cases

[*In note 181, update reference to Treitel on The Law of Contract to: page* [628]]   **6–045**
14th edn (2015), para.8–010

[*In note 182, update reference to Atiyah's Sale of Goods to: page* [629]]
Twigg-Flessner, Canavan and MacQueen (eds), *Atiyah and Adams' Sale of Goods*, 13th edn (2016), p.80

[*In note 182, update reference to Treitel on The Law of Contract to: page* [629]]
14th edn (2015), para.8–010

What mistakes may frustrate contractual venture?

[*In note 206, update reference to Treitel on The Law of Contract to: page* [632]]   **6–051**
14th edn (2015), para.8–019

[*In note 207, update reference to Treitel on The Law of Contract to: page* [632]]
14th edn (2015), para.8–020

7. MISTAKE AND CONSTRUCTION

Contract void as a matter of construction where no common mistake

6–063   [*In note 287, update reference to Treitel on The Law of Contract to: page* [640]]
14th edn (2015), para.2–066

CHAPTER 7

MISREPRESENTATION

2. WHAT CONSTITUTES EFFECTIVE MISREPRESENTATION

(a) *False Statement of Fact*

Statements of fact

[Add to note 25, at the end: page [646]]   **7–006**
It has been said that whether the representee was entitled to rely on the representation is partly a question of reasonableness: *Monde Petroleum SA v WesternZagros Ltd* [2016] EWHC 1472 (Comm) at [219].

Statement of opinion may carry implication that grounds for belief

7–009   [*In note 34, delete last sentence, "While a party . . . " and substitute: page* [648]]
A party who merely gives a contractual warranty does not necessarily represent
that the fact warranted is true (see *Sycamore Bidco Ltd v Breslin* [2012] EWHC
3443 (Ch) at [203]–[209] and *Idemitsu Kosan Co Ltd v Sumitomo Corp* [2016]
EWHC 1909 (Comm), declining to follow the unreported decision in *Invertec
Ltd v De Mol Holding BV* [2009] EWHC 2471 (Ch)). Merely offering for
signature a document containing the warranty is not a representation of the truth
of the facts warranted: [2016] EWHC 1909 (Comm) at [28]–[30]. If there was a
previous representation, followed by a warranty, the fact of the warranty does
tend to imply that the party giving the warranty has reasonable grounds for
believing the facts warranted: *Avrora Fine Arts Investment Ltd v Christie,
Manson & Woods Ltd* [2012] EWHC 2198 (Ch) at [133].

Representation ceases to be true

7–021   [*Add to note 112, line 8, after "111 L.Q.R. 385": page* [658]]
; *Abu Dhabi Investment Company v H Clarkson and Co Ltd* [2007] EWHC 1267
(Comm) at [232] (rev'd on other grounds [2008] EWCA Civ 699).

[*Add new paragraph 7–021A: page* [658]]
7–021A   **Withdrawals and corrections.** A misrepresentation will cease to have effect
if it is withdrawn or corrected before the contract is made, as then it will not have
induced the contract.[113a] The burden of establishing a correction or withdrawal
rests on the person making the correction and the correction must be sufficiently
clear in all the circumstances of the case.[113b]

[113a] *Cramaso LLP v Viscount Reidhaven's Trustees* [2014] UKSC 9, [2014] 2 W.L.R. 317 at [20].
On inducement see Main Work, Vol.I, paras 7–035 et seq.
[113b] *Mortgage Express v Countrywide Surveyors Ltd* [2016] EWHC 224 (Ch) at [194], referring to
Arnison v Smith (1889) 41 Ch. D. 348, 370, 373 and *Abu Dhabi Investment Company v H Clarkson
and Co Ltd* [2007] EWHC 1267 (Comm).

(c) *Other Requirements*

The representee or person intended to act on the representation

7–031   [*In note 160, update reference to Gower & Davies, Principles of Modern Company
Law to: page* [664]]
10th edn, 2016, para.25–32.

Inducement

7–035   [*In note 186, delete from the second sentence "In Hayward v Zurich . . . " to the end
and substitute: page* [667]]
In *Hayward v Zurich Insurance Co Plc* [2016] UKSC 48 the Supreme Court,
reversing the decision of the Court of Appeal ([2015] EWCA Civ 327) held that
a settlement of an insurance claim could be avoided by the insurer when it

discovered that the amount of loss had been exaggerated fraudulently, even though at the time the insurer had doubts over the extent of the claim. It was sufficient that the false claim influenced the insurer in the sum offered in settlement. It is not necessary that the insurer believed that the claim made was true.

[Add to note 187, at the end: page [667]]
If it would have been unreasonable of the representee to rely upon the representation, that may go to show that the representee did not in fact rely on it: *Monde Petroleum SA v WesternZagros Ltd* [2016] EWHC 1472 (Comm) at [219].

Material misrepresentation and a presumption of inducement

[Add to note 214, at the end: page [670]]   **7–040**
Hayward v Zurich Insurance Co Plc [2016] UKSC 48 at [34], quoting this paragraph, and [37].

Materiality

[*In note 216, update reference to Treitel on The Law of Contract to: page* [670]]   **7–041**
14th edn (2015), para.9–020

Unforeseeable reliance

[*In note 224, update reference to Treitel on The Law of Contract to: page* [672]]   **7–042**
14th edn (2015), para.9–020

Representee could have discovered truth: rescission

[*In note 230, update reference to Treitel on The Law of Contract to: page* [673]]   **7–043**
14th edn (2015), para.9–028

3. DAMAGES FOR MISREPRESENTATION

(a) *Fraudulent Misrepresentation*

Definition of fraud

[Add a new note 255a, at end of paragraph: page [676]]   **7–048**
255a "I can conceive of many cases where the fact that an alleged belief was destitute of all reasonable foundation would suffice of itself to convince the Court that it was not really entertained, and that the representation was a fraudulent one.": Lord Herschell (1889) 14 App. Cas. 337, 375, cited in *Mortgage Express v Countrywide Surveyors Ltd* [2016] EWHC 224 (Ch) at [164].

Principal and agent

[Add to note 265, at the end: page [677]]   **7–053**
This sentence was quoted with approval in *Greenridge Luton One Ltd v Kempton Investments Ltd* [2016] EWHC 91 (Ch) at [77].

[51]

Measure of damages for fraudulent misrepresentation

7–055   [*Add to note 274, at the end: page* [679]]
; *Wemyss v Karim* [2016] EWCA Civ 27 at [23].

Property worth less than paid for it

7–060   [*Add to note 286, at the end: page* [681]]
; *Wemyss v Karim* [2016] EWCA Civ 27 at [24]–[25].

[*Insert new paragraph 7–060A: page* [681]]
7–060A   **Difference in value at time of acquisition.** As Lord Browne-Wilkinson states in his propositions (3) and (4),[286a] the general rule is that the claimant is entitled to the difference between what he paid and the value of the property he received at the date he acquired it. The court will not reduce the damages to reflect that fact that, as it turned out, various risks that, at that date, reduced the value of the property, did not in fact materialise.[286b] The claimant will normally recover the difference between the price paid and the value of the property bought, and also any consequential loss.[286c]

[286a] See Main Work, Vol.I, para.7–057.
[286b] *OMV Petrom SA v Glencore International AG* [2016] EWCA Civ 778 ("The purpose of the flexibility of approach about the valuation date to which Lord Browne-Wilkinson referred was to ensure that the person duped should not suffer an injustice by failing to recover full compensation in the type of circumstances to which he referred. There is no need to adopt such an approach in order to relieve the fraudster from the general rule as to damages, especially if to do so means that the person defrauded ends up paying more than the cargo was worth at the time that he bought it." (at [39]).
[286c] [2016] EWCA Civ 778 at [66].

(b) *Negligent Misrepresentation*

Misrepresentation Act s.2(1)

7–075   [*Add new note 334a after title to paragraph: page* [688]]
[334a] Note that under s.2(4) of the Misrepresentation Act 1967 (added by Consumer Protection (Amendment) Regulations 2014 (SI 2014/870) reg.5), a consumer who has a right to redress under Pt 4A of the Consumer Protection from Unfair Trading Regulations 2008 (on which see Main Work, Vol.I, para.7–002 and Vol.II, paras 38–145 et seq.) in respect of the conduct constituting misrepresentation no longer has a right to damages under s.2 of the Act: see Main Work, Vol.II, para. 38–188.

Application of rules on damages for fraud

7–078   [*In note 366, update reference to Treitel on The Law of Contract to: page* [691]]
14th edn (2015), para.9–072

Relationship between manufacturer and purchaser of goods

7–094   [*In paragraph, line 31, delete* "when it comes into force the Consumer Rights Act 2015" *and substitute: page* [700]]
(for contracts made on or after October 1, 2015) the Consumer Rights Act 2015

Other legislative provisions creating liability for negligent misrepresentations: financial services

[*In note 449, delete the last sentence, "For the possibility" and substitute: page* [701]]

7–098

For the possibility of a restitution order on the basis that the conduct may constitute market abuse within the Market Abuse Regulation (Regulation (EU) 596/2014) see Gower & Davies, *Principles of Modern Company Law*, 10th edn (2016), paras 30–51 and 30–55 and cf. *Securities and Investments Board Ltd v Pantell SA (No.2)* [1993] Ch. 256, decided under Financial Services Act 1986.

[*In note 450, update reference to Gower & Davies, Principles of Modern Company Law to: page* [701]]

10th edn (2016), paras 25–10 et seq.

[*In note 453, update reference to Gower & Davies, Principles of Modern Company Law: page* [702]]

10th edn (2016), paras 25–36—25–39

(c) *Innocent Misrepresentation*

No damages for innocent misrepresentation

[*Add to note 471, at the end: page* [703]]

7–102

If the statement amounts to a contractual term, the promisee need not show reliance: *Wemyss v Karim* [2016] EWCA Civ 27 at [26], citing Slade L.J. in *Harlingdon and Leinster Enterprises Ltd v Christopher Hull Fine Art Ltd* [1991] 1 Q.B. 564, 584. The measure of damages will also differ: see above, para. 7–055.

Misrepresentation Act section 2(2)

[*Add new note 479a, after title to paragraph: page* [704]]

7–104

479a Note that under s.2(4) of the Misrepresentation Act 1967 (added by Consumer Protection (Amendment) Regulations 2014 (SI 2014/870) reg.5), a consumer who has a right to redress under Pt 4A of the Consumer Protection from Unfair Trading Regulations 2008 (on which see Main Work, Vol.I, para.7–002 and Vol.II, paras 38–145 et seq.) in respect of the conduct constituting mis-representation no longer has a right to damages under s.2 of the Act: see Main Work, Vol.II, para. 38–188.

4. RESCISSION FOR MISREPRESENTATION

(a) *General*

Misrepresentation Act section 1(a)

[*Add to note 518, line 11, after* "and representations': at [202].".: *page* [710]]

7–113

See also *Idemitsu Kosan Co Ltd v Sumitomo Corp* [2016] EWHC 1909 (Comm) (above, para.7–009).

Misrepresentation as defence to proceedings

7–117   [*In note 526, update reference to Treitel on the Law of Contract to: page* [712]]
14th edn (2015), para.9–088

Court order not required

7–119   [*Add to note 535, at the end: page* [713]]
See also Turner (2016) 132 L.Q.R. 388.

5. EXCLUSION OF LIABILITY FOR MISREPRESENTATION

Misrepresentation Act s.3

7–146   [*Delete text of note 643 and substitute: page* [728]]
With the coming into force of the Consumer Rights Act 2015 (for contracts made
on or after October 1, 2015), s.3 of the Misrepresentation Act 1967 is amended
so as to no longer apply to "a term in a consumer contract within the meaning
of Pt 2 of the Consumer Rights Act 2015": see next paragraph.

Consumer cases

7–147   [*Delete first three sentences of paragraph and substitute: pages* [728]–[729]]
With the coming into force of the Consumer Rights Act 2015 (for contracts made
on or after October 1, 2015), s.3 of the Misrepresentation Act 1967 is amended
so as to no longer apply to "a term in a consumer contract within the meaning
of Pt 2 of the Consumer Rights Act 2015".[646] These terms are controlled under
the 2015 Act by the general test of unfairness provided by s.62.[647] This has the
effect of making the application of the legislation (the Misrepresentation Act
1967 s.3 on the one hand, the Consumer Rights Act on the other) turn on the
distinction between a person who contracts as a "consumer" with a "trader"
within the meanings of the Act and otherwise.

[646] Consumer Rights Act 2015 s.75; Sch.4 para.1. On the effect of the Act on the law on unfair
terms, see Main Work, Vol.II, paras 38–196 and 38–334 et seq. It should be noted that (with
exceptions that are not relevant here) s.62 applies to any term of a consumer contract, not just terms
that were not individually negotiated, as was the case under the Unfair Terms in Consumer Contracts
Regulations 1999 (on which see Main Work, Vol.II, paras 38–201 et seq.).
[647] On which see Main Work, Vol.II, paras 38–359 et seq.

Section 3 and no reliance clauses

7–150   [*Add to note 666, at the end: page* [731]]
But in *Thornbridge Ltd v Barclays Bank Plc* [2015] EWHC 3430 (QB) at
[97]–[121] H.H. Judge Moulder, sitting as a judge of the High Court, said "the
test is not whether the clause attempts to rewrite history or parts company with
reality. The first step is to determine as a matter of construction whether the terms
define the basis upon which the parties were transacting business or whether they

were clauses inserted as a means of evading liability" (at [105]); and in *Sears v Minco Plc* [2016] EWHC 433 (Ch) at [74]–[84] H.H. Judge Hodge, sitting as a judge of the High Court, said "I respectfully agree with Judge Moulder's analysis and conclusions [in *Thornbridge*]" (at [80]).

[*Add to note 667, at the end: page* [731]]
Similarly, a clause has been held to prevent a duty of care arising in tort rather than excluding liability, so the clause did not fall within s.2(2) of the Unfair Contract Terms Act 1977: *Crestsign Ltd v National Westminster Bank Plc* [2014] EWHC 3043 (Ch).

[*Add to paragraph, after note 667: page* [731]]
Or, even if it had relied on a statement made by the other party, it was not "entitled to do so" as the statement was not put forward as one of fact.[667a]

[667a] cf. Main Work, Vol.I, para.7–006.

Unfair Contract Terms Act 1977 s.3(2)(b)(ii)

[*Amend the title of this paragraph and the reference in line 5 to: pages* [731]–[732]]   **7–151**
Unfair Contract Terms Act 1977 s.3(2)(b)(i)

Clauses covering breach

[*In note 680, update reference to* Treitel on The Law of Contract *to: page* [733]]   **7–153**
14th edn (2015), para.9–130

[*In note 681, update reference to* Treitel on The Law of Contract *to: page* [733]]
14th edn (2015), para.9–131

6. CONTRACTS WHERE A DUTY OF DISCLOSURE

(b) *Contracts to take Shares in Companies*

Companies

[*In note 766, update reference to* Gower & Davies, Principles of Modern Company Law *to: page* [742]]   **7–169**
10th edn (2016), paras 25–8 to 25–43

[*In note 769, update reference to* Gower & Davies, Principles of Modern Company Law *to: page* [742]]
10th edn (2016), para.25–39

CHAPTER 8

DURESS AND UNDUE INFLUENCE

2. DURESS

(f) *Threats of Actions not in Themselves Wrongful*

Threat to commit otherwise lawful act

8–047 *[Add to note 198, line 1, after "[1994] 4 All E.R. 715": page [775]]*
; *Marsden v Barclays Bank Plc* [2016] EWHC 1601 (QB)

[Add to note 200, at the beginning: page [776]]
Marsden v Barclays Bank Plc [2016] EWHC 1601 (QB) at [35].

(h) *General Effects of Duress*

[*Add new paragraph 8–054A: page* [780]]

Right to rescind cannot be excluded. The right to rescind an agreement   **8–054A**
reached under duress cannot be excluded by the terms of the agreement.[237a]

[237a] *Borrelli v Ting* [2010] UKPC 21, [2010] Bus. L.R. 1718 at [40]. Compare the right to rescind
for fraud, Main Work, Vol.I, para.7–143.

3. UNDUE INFLUENCE

(a) *Introduction*

When the stronger party's conscience is engaged

[*Add to paragraph, at the end: page* [786]]   **8–059**
It is submitted, however, that in the light of the decision of the House of Lords
in *Royal Bank of Scotland v Etridge (No.2)*[284a] that there are not two classes of
undue influence, actual and presumed, but merely two methods of proving undue
influence (by direct proof or by use of a presumption that arises when there is a
relationship of trust and confidence between the parties[284b] and a transaction
between them that "requires explanation"[284c]) to insist that undue influence is
limited to cases of wicked exploitation would involve at least a substantial
re-working of the authorities.[284d]

[284a] [2001] UKHL 44, [2002] 2 A.C. 773. See Main Work, Vol.I, para.8–061.
[284b] See Main Work, Vol.I, paras 8–073 et seq.
[284c] See Main Work, Vol.I, paras 8–065 and 8–090 et seq.
[284d] See Beale in Dyson, Goudkamp and Wilmot-Smith (eds), *Defences in Contract* (forthcoming),
Ch.5, where it is argued that while the primary purpose of the doctrine may be to prevent "tyranny,
trickery and fraud", those are not requirements. First, exploitation may be passive. Secondly, the
defendant's behaviour need not be dishonest: it can consist of a failure to ensure that the claimant was
properly informed, was thinking through the consequences and was acting free of the defendant's
influence. Thirdly, the transaction need not always be apparently to the claimant's disadvantage at the
time.

(f) *Undue Influence by a Third Party*

Constructive notice: *Barclays Bank v O'Brien*

[*Add to note 544, line 2, after* "rev. October 2014": *page* [817]]   **8–112**
and September 2015

[*Add to note 544, at the end: page* [817]]
On July 21, 2016, the Lending Standards Board published a new Standards of
Lending Practice, which come into force on October 1, 2016. The Standards of
Lending Practice will replace the Lending Code. The Standards of Lending
Practice apply to personal customers and cover loans, credit cards and current
account overdrafts. The new Standards represent a move away from the Lending

Code, which was focused more on compliance with provisions than customer outcomes. It is anticipated that new standards for business lending, which will include small and medium-sized businesses (SMEs), will be published in 2017. In the interim the existing protections of the Lending Code will continue to apply to micro-enterprises (Standards of Lending Practice, p.3). The issue of guarantees provided by individuals is dealt with in a separate document issued by the Lending Standards Board, *The Standards of Lending Practice for personal customers: Account maintenance and servicing* (September 2016), Pt 8.

Transaction not on its face to the advantage of the surety

8–117   *[In note 567, delete last sentence* "A change in ... " *and substitute: page* [819]]
Nor is a bank excused from making enquiry when the wife is the husband's partner in the business, especially if there is a change in the nature or scale of the lending: *O'Neill v Ulster Bank Ltd* [2015] NICA 64 at [17].

4. Unconscionable Bargains and Inequality of Bargaining Power

Unconscionable bargains with poor and ignorant persons

8–132   *[In note 609, update reference to Treitel on The Law of Contract to: page* [826]]
14th edn (2015), para.10–044

An oppressive bargain

8–134   *[Add to note 628, at the end: page* [828]]
It is arguable that if the effect of a clause in the contract is that the bargain is worth a great deal less to the claimant than he thought, this may make the bargain oppressive: see Beale in Dyson, Goudkamp and Wilmot-Smith (eds), *Defences in Contract* (forthcoming), Ch.5.

The complainant's circumstances

8–135   *[Add to note 635, at the end: page* [829]]
It is arguable that relief may be given when the claimant's "bargaining weakness" took the form of not knowing of a clause in the contract he was signing, or not appreciating its possible effect: relief can then be given if the result is that the deal is worth a great deal less to the claimant than he thought, and if the other party deliberately took advantage of the claimant's ignorance or lack of understanding. This form of bargaining weakness seems to fall within Fullagar J.'s words in *Blomley v Ryan* (1956) 99 C.L.R. 362, 405, quoted in the text of the paragraph, which included "lack of assistance or explanation where assistance or explanation is necessary": see Beale in Dyson, Goudkamp and Wilmot-Smith (eds), *Defences in Contract* (forthcoming), Ch.5.

Part Three

CAPACITY OF PARTIES

CHAPTER 9

PERSONAL INCAPACITY

2. MINORS

(b) *Contracts Binding on a Minor*

(i) *Liability for Necessaries*

Executory contracts for necessary goods

[*In note 58, update reference to Treitel on The Law of Contract to: page* [844]] **9–014**
14th edn (2015), para.12–008

Goods necessary when delivered, but not when sold, and vice versa

9–015 [*In note 65, update reference to Treitel on The Law of Contract to: page* [845]]
14th edn (2015), para.12–008

(ii) *Apprenticeship, Employment and Other Beneficial Contracts*

Statutory "apprenticeship agreements"

9–029 [*Delete text and footnotes from start of paragraph to* " . . . rule of law".[135]" *in line 6 and substitute: page* [850]]
The Apprenticeships, Skills, Children and Learning Act 2009 recognised a new form of apprenticeship founded on an "apprenticeship agreement", and set out rules governing, inter alia, its form and certification.[134] In 2015, the 2009 Act was amended so as to distinguish between "approved English apprenticeships"[135] and "Welsh apprenticeships".[135a] Under the 2009 Act as so amended, both "approved English apprenticeships" and "Welsh apprenticeships" are to be treated as "contracts of service" and are not to be treated as "contracts of apprenticeship" for "the purposes of any enactment or rule of law".[135b]

[134] Apprenticeships, Skills, Children and Learning Act 2009 Pt 1 (as enacted). The provisions on the "prescribed form" were contained in s.32(2)(b) and this form was later designated as being either "a written statement of particulars of employment" given to the employee/apprentice or "a document in writing in the form of a letter of engagement" as foreseen by the Employment Rights Act 1996: the Apprenticeships (Form of Apprenticeship Agreement) Regulations 2012 (SI 2012/844) reg.2, referring to the Employment Rights Act 1996 ss.2 and 7A respectively (with the exceptions specified by the Regulations). In 2015, s.32 was amended so as to apply only to "Welsh apprenticeships", as explained in the following text and notes.
[135] Apprenticeships, Skills, Children and Learning Act 2009, esp. Ch.A1 as inserted by the Deregulation Act 2015 Sch.1 para.1 (in force May 26, 2015).
[135a] Apprenticeships, Skills, Children and Learning Act 2009 ss.2, 7–12, 18–22, 28–36 (as amended).
[135b] Apprenticeships, Skills, Children and Learning Act 2009 s.A5 (approved English apprenticeships) and s.35 (Welsh apprenticeships).

(c) *Contracts Binding on a Minor Unless Repudiated*

Contracts for an interest of a permanent nature

9–037 [*In note 176, update reference to Treitel on The Law of Contract to: page* [855]]
14th edn (2015), paras 12–025—12–026

Partnerships

9–046 [*In note 213, update reference to Treitel on The Law of Contract to: page* [859]]
14th edn (2015), para.12–020 n.89

(f) *Liability of Minor in Tort and Contract*

Torts independent of the contract

9–054 [*In note 263, update reference to Treitel on The Law of Contract to: page* [863]]
14th edn (2015), para.12–031

(g) *Liability of Minor to Make Restitution*

Restoration of gains

[*In note 286, update reference to Anson's Law of Contract to: page* [866]]   **9–058**
30th edn (2016) pp.263–264

[*In note 286, update reference to Treitel on The Law of Contract to: page* [866]]
14th edn (2015) para.12 046

"Property"

[*In note 298, update reference to Treitel on The Law of Contract to: page* [867]]   **9–062**
14th edn (2015) para.12–041

3. PERSONS LACKING MENTAL CAPACITY

(a) *The Rule in* Imperial Loan Co Ltd v Stone

(ii) *Constructive Knowledge of a Party's Mental Incapacity*

Summary

[*Add new note 424a, at end of paragraph: page* [883]]   **9–088**
[424a] See similarly Peel (ed.), *Treitel on The Law of Contract*, 14th edn (2015) para.12–055 n.179;
Beatson, Burrows and Cartwright, *Anson's Law of Contract*, 30th edn (2016), p.267 at n.194 (stating
the rule as being that the other party needs to have been aware of the incapacity, though noting
Baroness Hale J.S.C.'s view that constructive knowledge is sufficient).

(iii) *The Nature of Mental Capacity and Establishing Incapacity*

Nature of understanding required

[*Add to note 428, line 1, after* "Mr Martin Nourse QC"*: page* [883]]   **9–089**
; *A County Council v MS* (2014) 17 C.C.L. Rep. 229, [2014] W.T.L.R. 931 at
[64]–[72].

Relationship of common law and statutory tests of mental capacity

[*Add to note 446, at the end: page* [885]]   **9–092**
cf. *A County Council v MS* (2014) 17 C.C.L. Rep. 229, [2014] W.T.L.R. 931 at
[64]–[72] (capacity to make gift for purposes of Mental Capacity Act 2005).

(b) *Liability for Necessaries*

Liability for necessaries: the new law

9-096   [*Add to note 468, at the end: page* [888]]
; permission to appeal on the application of s.7 of the 2005 Act was refused and
the provider of the services' appeal regarding the existence of the local authority's duty under the 1948 Act was rejected: [2014] EWCA Civ 1350, [2014]
P.T.S.R. 1507 (note).

[*Add to paragraph, line 27, after* "were provided by": *page* [888]]
the service provider under an arrangement with

(d) *Property and Affairs Under the Control of the Court*

9-099   Position under Mental Capacity Act 2005

[*In note 487, update reference to Treitel on The Law of Contract to: page* [890]]
14th edn (2015) paras 12-056—12-057

CHAPTER 11

THE CROWN, PUBLIC AUTHORITIES AND THE EUROPEAN UNION

3. PUBLIC AUTHORITIES

(a) *The Scope of Statutory Powers*

(i) *Express Powers*

[*Insert new paragraph 11–023A: page* [963]]

Procedural irregularity. An authority's failure to follow its own procedures **11–023A** for entering a contract does not render the agreement ultra vires. As the Privy Council put it in *Central Tenders Board v White*, "There is a difference between a case of procedural irregularity in the formation of a contract of a kind which a public body has power to enter, and a case of a public body purporting to

[63]

conclude a contract of a kind which it has no power to make".[157a] In that case the authority had accepted a tender for a building project despite the tenderer failing to comply with the authority's instructions that all tenderers must state, on their form of tender, what the duration of the works would be. The authority was found not to have departed from its own procedures (since the procedures permitted non-conforming tenders to be considered), but the court went on to express the view that, assuming there had been a procedural irregularity on the facts, it would not have made the ensuing contract void. The court explained that any attempt to nullify a contract entered into following a procedural irregularity would have to be assessed in the light of "the seriousness of the breach and the degree of any injustice and public inconvenience which may be caused by invalidating the act", as well as "any alternative remedies available to a person legitimately aggrieved by the conduct of the public body".[157b] The court observed that it would be "a serious denial of [a party's] rights" to invalidate a contract because of a procedural defect in the contractual process,[157c] and indicated that "it would be wrong for a court to [quash an administrative decision] in such a way as to nullify a contract made between a public body pursuant to a legal power and a person acting in good faith, except possibly on terms which adequately protect that person's interest".[157d] Where a tenderer had been unfairly disadvantaged by the authority's failure to follow its own procedures, the Privy Council envisaged that recourse could be had to an implied tender process contract, of the kind recognised in *Blackpool and Fylde Aero Club Ltd v Blackpool Borough Council*.[157e]

[157a] [2015] UKPC 39, [2015] B.L.R. 727 at [19]. Cf. the public procurement regulatory regime, outlined at para.11–051, below.
[157b] [2015] UKPC 39, [2015] B.L.R. 727 at [22].
[157c] [2015] UKPC 39, [2015] B.L.R. 727 at [25].
[157d] [2015] UKPC 39, [2015] B.L.R. 727 at [26].
[157e] [1990] 1 W.L.R. 1195. See Main Work, Vol.I, paras 11–042 et seq.

4. TENDER PROCESS CONTRACTS

(a) *Conditions for the Implication of a Tender Process Contract*

Factual conditions

11–044   [*Add to note 307, at the end: page* [979]]
; *Central Tenders Board v White* [2015] UKPC 39, [2015] B.L.R. 727 at [28].

6. PUBLIC PROCUREMENT

(a) *European Union Legislation*

11–051   [*Delete the text of note 352 and substitute: page* [984]]
Public Contracts Regulations 2015 (SI 2015/102) and Utilities Contracts Regulations 2016 (SI 2016/274).

Remedies for failure to follow the contract award procedure commenced after December 20, 2009

[In paragraph, line 12, delete "Treasury" *and substitute: page* [984]]   **11–052**
Minister for the Cabinet Office

[Delete text of note 355 and substitute: page [984]]
Public Contracts Regulations 2015 (SI 2015/102) reg.98(2)(c) and Utilities Contracts Regulations 2016 (SI 2016/274) reg.113(2)(c).

[Delete text of note 356 and substitute: page [984]]
Public Contracts Regulations 2015 (SI 2015/102) reg.99 and Utilities Contracts Regulations 2016 (SI 2016/274) reg.114.

[Delete text of note 357 and substitute: page [984]]
Public Contracts Regulations 2015 (SI 2015/102) reg.98(2)(a) and Utilities Contracts Regulations 2016 (SI 2016/274) reg.113(2)(a).

[Delete text of note 358 and substitute: page [984]]
Public Contracts Regulations 2015 (SI 2015/102) reg.100 and Utilities Contracts Regulations 2016 (SI 2016/274) reg.115.

[Delete text of note 359 and substitute: page [984]]
Public Contracts Regulations 2015 (SI 2015/102) regs 98(2)(b) and 102; Utilities Contracts Regulations 2016 (SI 2016/274) regs 113(2)(b) and 117.

[Delete text of note 360 and substitute: page [984]]
Public Contracts Regulations 2015 (SI 2015/102) reg.101 and Utilities Contracts Regulations 2016 (SI 2016/274) reg.116.

[Delete text of note 361 and substitute: page [984]]
Public Contracts Regulations 2015 (SI 2015/102) reg.102(7) and Utilities Contracts Regulations 2016 (SI 2016/274) reg.117(7).

[Delete text of note 362 and substitute: page [984]]
Public Contracts Regulations 2015 (SI 2015/102) reg.102(3) and Utilities Contracts Regulations 2016 (SI 2016/274) reg.117(3).

[Delete text of note 363 and substitute: page [985]]
Public Contracts Regulations 2015 (SI 2015/102) reg.101(4) and Utilities Contracts Regulations 2016 (SI 2016/274) reg.116(4).

CHAPTER 12

POLITICAL IMMUNITY AND INCAPACITY

1. FOREIGN STATES, SOVEREIGNS, AMBASSADORS AND INTERNATIONAL ORGANISATIONS

Foreign states and sovereigns: the common law rule

12–001   [*Add to note 1, at the end: page* [987]]
The immunity is not available to a State before its own Courts: *Iraqi Civilians v Ministry of Defence (No.2)* [2016] UKSC 25, [2016] 1 W.L.R. 2001 at [11].

Sovereign immunity and human rights

12–003   [*Add to note 18, at the end: page* [989]]
See also *Ogelegbanwei v President of the Federal Republic of Nigeria* [2016] EWHC 8 (QB) at [21]–[26]; *Al Attiya v Al Thani* [2016] EWHC 212 (QB) at [82].

State Immunity Act 1978

12–004   [*Add to note 21, at the end: page* [990]]
See also *LR Avionics Technologies Ltd v Federal Republic of Nigeria* [2016] EWHC 1761 (Comm), [2016] 4 W.L.R. 120.

[*Add to note 24, line 2, after* "[1997] 4 All E.R. 108": *page* [990]]
; *Al Attiya v Al Thani* [2016] EWHC 212 (QB) (former prime minister of Qatar)

[*Add to note 25, line 9, after* "[2011] EWCA Civ 616": *page* [991]]
; *Pearl Petroleum Co Ltd v Kurdistan Regional Government of Iraq* [2015] EWHC 3361 (Comm), [2016] 4 W.L.R. 2.

[*Add to note 27, penultimate line, after* "[2015] EWCA Civ 835 at [39]–[48]": *page* **12–005**
[992]]
; *Gold Reserve Inc v Bolivarian Republic of Venezuela* [2016] EWHC 153
(Comm), [2016] 1 W.L.R. 2829; *LR Avionics Technologies Ltd v Federal Republic of Nigeria* [2016] EWHC 1761 (Comm), [2016] 4 W.L.R. 120

[*Add to paragraph, after note 29: page* [992]]
If a State grants a lease of its premises to a privately owned company to which
the State outsources consular activities such as the handling of passport and visa
applications, the property is not being used for commercial purposes within the
meaning of s.13(4) of the 1978 Act.[29a]

[29a] *LR Avionics Technologies Ltd v Federal Republic of Nigeria* [2016] EWHC 1761 (Comm),
[2016] 4 W.L.R. 120.

[*Add to note 40, at the end: page* [993]]
; *Gold Reserve Inc v Bolivarian Republic of Venezuela* [2016] EWHC 153
(Comm), [2016] 1 W.L.R. 2829; *LR Avionics Technologies Ltd v Federal Republic of Nigeria* [2016] EWHC 1761 (Comm), [2016] 4 W.L.R. 120.

[*Add to note 42, at the end: page* [994]] **12–006**
; *Gold Reserve Inc v Bolivarian Republic of Venezuela* [2016] EWHC 153
(Comm), [2016] 1 W.L.R. 2829.

[*Update note 45: page* [994]]
Khurts Bat v Investigating Judge of the German Federal Court [2011] EWHC
2029 (Admin) is reported at [2013] Q.B. 349

Acts of sovereign states

[*Add to paragraph, after note 50: page* [994]] **12–007**
The principle of non-justiciability under the "act of state" doctrine may also
extend to the acts of a foreign sovereign state performed on territory other than
its own territory.[50a]

[50a] *Belhaj v Straw* [2014] EWCA Civ 1394, [2015] 2 W.L.R. 1105 at [127]–[133]; *High Commissioner for Pakistan in the United Kingdom v Prince Mukkaram Jah* [2016] EWHC 1465 (Ch) at
[84]–[87]. cf. *Yukos Capital Sarl v OJSC Rosneft Oil Co (No.2)* [2012] EWCA Civ 855, [2013] 3
W.L.R. 1329 at [66].

[*Add to paragraph, at the end: page* [996]]
Unlike sovereign immunity, the principle of non-justiciability under the "act of
state" doctrine is not capable of being waived, because it is a matter going to the
substantive jurisdiction of the Court.[54a]

[54a] *R. v Bow Street Metropolitan Stipendiary Magistrate Ex p. Pinochet Ugarte (No.3)* [2000] 1
A.C. 61, 90; *High Commissioner for Pakistan in the United Kingdom v Prince Mukkaram Jah* [2016]
EWHC 1465 (Ch) at [89]–[90].

Foreign heads of state, ambassadors and their staffs

[*Update note 56: page* [996]] **12–008**
Harb v Aziz [2015] EWCA Civ 481 is reported at [2016] Ch. 308

[*Add to note 56, at the end: page* [996]]
See also *Al Attiya v Al Thani* [2016] EWHC 212 (QB) (civil claim against former prime minister of Qatar).

Categories of persons entitled to diplomatic immunity

12–010   [*Delete the second sentence of note 60 and substitute: page* [996]]
As a matter of customary international law and the common law, a receiving State is obliged to secure, for the duration of a special or ad hoc mission, personal inviolability and immunity from criminal jurisdiction for the members of the mission accepted as such by the receiving State: see *Khurts Bat v Investigating Judge of the German Federal Court* [2011] EWHC 2029 (Admin), [2013] Q.B. 349; *R. (on the application of the Freedom and Justice Party) v Secretary of State for Foreign and Commonwealth Affairs* [2016] EWHC 2010 (Admin) at [116]–[120].

Diplomatic agents

12–011   [*Add to paragraph, at the end: page* [997]]
The Diplomatic Privileges Act 1964 applies only to permanent diplomatic missions; the status of special or ad hoc missions is a matter for the common law.[65a]

[65a] *R. (on the application of the Freedom and Justice Party) v Secretary of State for Foreign and Commonwealth Affairs* [2016] EWHC 2010 (Admin).

Period of immunity

12–014   [*Add to note 72, at the end: page* [998]]
See also *Al Attiya v Al Thani* [2016] EWHC 212 (QB) at [48], [81].

Certificate of entitlement

12–015   [*Add to note 79, at the end: page* [998]]
Al Attiya v Al Thani [2016] EWHC 212 (QB) at [37], [59], [83]; *R. (on the application of the Freedom and Justice Party) v Secretary of State for Foreign and Commonwealth Affairs* [2016] EWHC 2010 (Admin) at [174].

Waiver of immunity: common law

12–020   [*Add to note 112, at the end: page* [1002]]
By contrast, the principle of non-justiciability under the "act of state" doctrine is not capable of being waived by a State, because it is a matter going to the Court's substantive jurisdiction, whereas sovereign immunity is no more than a procedural bar to the Court's jurisdiction: *R. v Bow Street Metropolitan Stipendiary Magistrate Ex p. Pinochet Ugarte (No.3)* [2000] 1 A.C. 61, 90; *High Commissioner for Pakistan in the United Kingdom v Prince Mukkaram Jah* [2016] EWHC 1465 (Ch), at [89]–[90].

Submission to jurisdiction

[*Add to note 121, penultimate line, after* "[2015] EWHC 55 (Ch) at [72]–[76]":   **12–021**
page [1002]]
; *Gold Reserve Inc v Bolivarian Republic of Venezuela* [2016] EWHC 153
(Comm), [2016] 1 W.L.R. 2829; *LR Avionics Technologies Ltd v Federal Republic of Nigeria* [2016] EWHC 1761 (Comm), [2016] 4 W.L.R. 120 at
[20]–[23].

Part Four

THE TERMS OF CONTRACT

EXPRESS TERMS

1. Proof of Terms

(b) *Standard Form Contracts*

Meaning of notice

13–013   *[Add to note 61, at the end: page* [1020]*]*
However, the court may be slower to incorporate a term into a contract where that term is to be found in a contract between two other parties or between one of the contracting parties and a third party: *Barrier Ltd v Redhall Marine Ltd* [2016] EWHC 381 (QB); *Habas Sinai Ve Tibbi Gazlar Isthisal Endustri AS v Sometal SAL* [2010] EWHC 29 (Comm), [2010] 1 Lloyd's Rep. 661; *TTMI SARL v Statoil ASA* [2011] EWHC 1150 (Comm), [2011] 2 Lloyd's Rep 220.

2. Classification of Terms

(a) *Conditions*

Conditions and other contract terms

[Add to note 107, at the end: page [1027]]   **13–026**
Where the contract uses the term "condition" once and provides that "It is a
condition of the agreement . . . " that should generally suffice to constitute the
term as a condition: *Personal Touch Financial Services Ltd v Simplysure Ltd*
[2016] EWCA Civ 461 at [28].

(c) *Intermediate Terms*

Force majeure clauses

[Add new note 195a, after "right to rely on the clause." *in line 8: page* [1036]]   **13–039**
195a However, the analogy with an intermediate term may not be exact, given that it has been held
that there is no rule of law according to which the consequence of a breach of a procedural
requirement specified in the contract is the loss of the right to claim relief on the ground of force
majeure. The inability of a party to invoke the force majeure clause in the contract arises as a
consequence of the construction of the contract and would appear not to follow from the application
of a rule of law: *Scottish Power UK Plc v BP Exploration Operating Co Ltd* [2015] EWHC 2658
(Comm), [2016] 1 All E.R. (Comm) 536 at [234].

Conclusion

[Add to note 202, line 3, after "[1987] Q.B. 527": *page* [1036]]   **13–040**
; *Personal Touch Financial Services Ltd v Simplysure Ltd* [2016] EWCA Civ 461
at [28]–[31]

3. Construction of Terms

[In note 207, update reference to Lewison, The Interpretation of Contracts to: page
[1037]]
6th edn (2015)

(a) *General Principles of Construction*

"Intention of the parties"

[Add to note 220, last line, after "[2015] EWHC 110 (Comm) at [24]": *page*   **13–044**
[1039]]
; *Arnold v Britton* [2015] UKSC 36, [2015] A.C. 1619 at [77]; *Europa Plus SCA
SIF v Anthracite Investments (Ireland) Plc* [2016] EWHC 437 (Comm) at
[29].

"Striking a balance"

13–046 [*Add new note 222a, after* "uncertainty or tension in the case-law" *in line 4: page* [1040]]

[222a] In a number of cases there is agreement on the principles to be applied to the facts of the case (see, for example, *BSI Enterprises Ltd v Blue Mountain Music Ltd* [2015] EWCA Civ 1151 at [38]; *Canary Wharf Finance II Plc v Deutsche Trustee Co Ltd* [2016] EWHC 100 (Comm) at [16] and *Videocon Global Ltd v Goldman Sachs International* [2016] EWCA Civ 130 at [50]), and the disagreement relates to the application of these principles to the facts of the case and the weight to be attached to the various principles.

[*Add to note 224, at the end: page* [1040]]
The need to strike a balance between the indications given by the language and the implications of rival constructions was explicitly acknowledged by Christopher Clarke L.J. in *Wood v Sureterm Direct Ltd* [2015] EWCA Civ 839 at [30]. The current approach of the courts appears to give more weight to the natural and ordinary meaning of the words, at least in the case where the parties are commercially experienced and have access to skilled legal advice: *Canary Wharf Finance II Plc v Deutsche Trustee Co Ltd* [2016] EWHC 100 (Comm) at [17] and *Vitol E & P Ltd v Africa Oil and Gas Corp* [2016] EWHC 1677 (Comm).

(b) *Ordinary Meaning to be Adopted*

Meaning of words

13–051 [*Add to note 246, at the end: page* [1043]]
; *Persimmon Homes Ltd v Ove Arup & Partners Ltd* [2015] EWHC 3573 (TCC), [2016] B.L.R. 112 at [21].

Absurdity, inconsistency, etc.

13–056 [*Add to note 266, at the end: page* [1047]]
; *LSREF III Wight Ltd v Millvalley Ltd* [2016] EWHC 466 (Comm); *Bouygues (UK) Ltd v Febrey Structures Ltd* [2016] EWHC 1333 (TCC).

Badly drafted contracts

13–058 [*Add to note 272, at the end: page* [1048]]
But the mere fact that the contract does not achieve what one party subsequently states was its object does not necessarily result in the conclusion that the contract was badly drafted: *Fairway Lakes Ltd v Revenue & Customs Commissioners* [2015] UKFTT 605 (TC).

(c) *Whole Contract to be Considered*

Control by recitals

13–068 [*Add to note 314, at the end: page* [1053]]
; *Mr H TV Ltd v ITV2 Ltd* [2015] EWHC 2840 (Comm) at [38].

Several instruments

[*Add to note 321, at the end: page* [1054]]   **13–069**
; and *BNY Mellon Corporate Trustee Services Ltd v LBG Capital No.1 Plc* [2016]
UKSC 29 at [30], although it was acknowledged that in the case of a contract or
trust deed which governs the terms upon which a negotiable instrument is held
"very considerable circumspection" is appropriate before the contents of such
other documents are taken into account.

(d) Making sense of the agreement

Meaning of agreement

[*Add to note 334a, at the end: page* [1056]]   **13–074**
The importance of giving appropriate weight to the language of the contract,
especially where the parties have access to skilled legal advice, has been recognised in more recent case law: see, for example, *Canary Wharf Finance II Plc v
Deutsche Trustee Co Ltd* [2016] EWHC 100 (Comm) at [17] and *Vitol E & P Ltd
v Africa Oil and Gas Corp* [2016] EWHC 1677 (Comm).

Modifying

[*Add to note 349, at the end: page* [1058]]   **13–077**
; *Bouygues (UK) Ltd v Febrey Structures Ltd* [2016] EWHC 1333 (TCC); *LSREF
III Wight Ltd v Millvalley Ltd* [2016] EWHC 466 (Comm); *Hayfin Opal Luxco 3
SARL v Windermere VII CMBS Plc* [2016] EWHC 782 (Ch).

Inconsistent or repugnant terms

[*Add to paragraph, line 7, after* "construction of documents": *page* [1059]]   **13–080**
When considering how to interpret a contract in the case of alleged inconsistency,
the courts distinguish between a case where the contract makes provision for the
possibility of inconsistency and the case where there is no such provision. In the
latter case the contract documents should as far as possible be read as com-
plementing each other and therefore as expressing the parties' intentions in a
consistent and coherent manner.[363a] However, matters are otherwise in the case
where there is a term in the contract dealing with the possibility of inconsistency.[363b] In such a case court should approach the interpretation of the
contract without any pre-conceived assumptions and should neither strive to
avoid nor to find an inconsistency but rather should approach the documents in
a "cool and objective spirit to see whether there is inconsistency or not".[363c]

[363a] *RWE Npower Renewables Ltd v JN Bentley Ltd* [2014] EWCA Civ 150.
[363b] *Pagnan SpA v Tradax Ocean Transportation SA* [1987] 2 Lloyd's Rep. 342; *Alexander (as
representative of the "Property 118 Action Group") v West Bromwich Mortgage Co Ltd* [2016]
EWCA Civ 496.
[363c] *Pagnan SpA v Tradax Ocean Transportation SA* [1987] 2 Lloyd's Rep. 342, 350; *Alexander (as
representative of the "Property 118 Action Group") v West Bromwich Mortgage Co Ltd* [2016]
EWCA Civ 496.

[Add to note 364, at the end: page [1059]]
; *Alexander (as representative of the "Property 118 Action Group") v West Bromwich Mortgage Co Ltd* [2016] EWCA Civ 496.

[Add to note 365, at the end: page [1059]]
; *Mercuria Energy Trading Pte Ltd v Citibank NA* [2015] EWHC 1481 (Comm), [2015] 1 C.L.C. 999 at [76].

[In note 368, delete "Alexander v West Bromwich Mortgage Co Ltd [2015] EWHC 135 (Comm), [2015] 2 All E.R. (Comm) 224" *and substitute: page* [1060]]
; *Alexander (as representative of the "Property 118 Action Group") v West Bromwich Mortgage Co Ltd* [2016] EWCA Civ 496.

Unforeseen events: change of circumstances

13–081   *[Add to note 371, at the end: page* [1060]]
There are, however, no special rules of interpretation applicable to long term or relational contracts other than the need to recognise that terms in such contracts must often be phrased in broad, flexible terms to enable parties to adjust their bargain to meet changing circumstances and the courts should therefore not be too astute to declare such terms to be unenforceable on the ground of uncertainty or vagueness: *Globe Motors Inc v TRW Lucas Varity Electric Steering Ltd* [2016] EWCA Civ 396 at [64]–[68].

Party cannot rely on his own breach

13–085   *[Add to note 389, at the end: page* [1063]]
; *Eurobank Ergasias SA v Kalliroi Navigation Co Ltd* [2015] EWHC 2377 (Comm).

(e) *Construction against Grantor*

Construction against grantor

13–086   *[Add to note 395, at the end: page* [1064]]
; *Hut Group Ltd v Nobahar-Cookson* [2016] EWCA Civ 128 (although note the difference of view between Briggs L.J. (who at [12]–[21] invoked the *contra proferentem* rule) and Hallett L.J. and Moylan J. who did not (see paras [40] and [41]).

[Add to note 396, at the end: page [1064]]
; *Transocean Drilling UK Ltd v Providence Resources Plc* [2016] EWCA Civ 372 at [20].

13–088   *[Add to note 408, at the end: page* [1065]]
There is a possibility that the rule in its application to exclusion clauses might now develop separately from the *contra proferentem* rule. Instead of searching for the *proferens* to whom the rule may be applicable, the courts may regard the

rule as a general rule of construction applicable to exclusion clauses according to which ambiguity in an exclusion clause may have to be resolved by a narrow construction because an exclusion clause cuts down or detracts from the ambit of some important obligation in a contract, or a remedy conferred by the general law: *Hut Group Ltd v Nobahar-Cookson* [2016] EWCA Civ 128 at [18].

[*Add to note 409, at the end: page* [1065]]
But note that in *Bloomberg LP v Sandberg (A Firm)* [2015] EWHC 2858 (TCC), [2016] B.L.R. 72 at [24] Fraser J. held that the rule was of "no assistance" because he could not identify the *proferens*.

4. ADMISSIBILITY OF EXTRINSIC EVIDENCE

(a) *The Parol Evidence Rule*

Law Commission Report

[*In note 462, update reference to Treitel on The Law of Contract to: page* [1072]]   **13–102**
14th edn (2015), para 6–014

(d) *Evidence to Interpret or Explain the Written Agreement*

Evidence of surrounding circumstances

[*Add to note 564, penultimate line, after* "(2007) 111 Const. L.R. 48 at [150]":   **13–122**
page [1085]]
; *Globe Motors Inc v TRW Lucas Varity Electric Steering Ltd* [2016] EWCA Civ 396 at [61].

[*Add to note 571, line 4, after* "[2007] 1 All E.R. (Comm) 421 at [63]": *page* [1085]]
; *Scottish Power UK Plc v BP Exploration Operating Co Ltd* [2015] EWHC 2658 (Comm), [2016] 1 All E.R. (Comm) 536 at [21].

Subsequent acts

[*Add to note 613, at the end: page* [1090]]   **13–129**
; *Reveille Independent LLC v Anotech International (UK) Ltd* [2016] EWCA Civ 443 at [41].

CHAPTER 14

IMPLIED TERMS

Implication of terms

14–002   *[In paragraph, delete from after note 2 to the end and substitute: pages*
[1095]–[1096]]

However, in *Att-Gen of Belize v Belize Telecom Ltd*[3] Lord Hoffmann challenged
the validity of this difference in treatment on the ground that in both cases the
court is seeking to establish what the contract would reasonably have been
understood to mean having regard to the commercial purpose of the contract as
a whole and the relevant available background of the transaction.[4] The extent to
which the process of implication can be assimilated with the principles applicable
to the interpretation of the express terms of a contract has since been the subject
of much judicial comment[5] and academic controversy.[6] More recently the
Supreme Court has sought to distance itself from the approach of Lord Hoffmann, with a majority describing his analysis in *Belize* as "a characteristically
inspired discussion rather than authoritative guidance on the law of implied
terms".[7] However, it does not follow from this that there is no relationship at all
between the principles that govern the implication of terms and those which
apply to the construction of express terms. While the process of interpretation
precedes implication and thus may be described as "the precursor of implication",[7a] the two processes, while "logically distinct" have nevertheless been held
to be "closely related" in that "both involve taking into account the words used
in the contract, the surrounding circumstances known or available to the parties
at the time of the contract, commercial common sense and the reasonable reader
or reasonable parties".[7b]

---

[3] [2009] UKPC 10, [2009] 1 W.L.R. 1988 at [17]–[27]. For an earlier statement of Lord Hoffmann's views, expressed extra-judicially, see Lord Hoffmann (1997) 56 S.A.L.J. 656 and (1995) 29
Law Teacher 127.

[4] *Att-Gen of Belize v Belize Telecom Ltd* [2009] UKPC 10, [2009] 1 W.L.R. 1988 at [19]–[21].

[5] While the courts regularly applied *Belize* and recognised it for a period of time as the leading
modern authority on the implication of terms into a contract, cases can be found in which the courts
expressed some uncertainty about the precise scope of the decision and its relationship with earlier
case-law: see, for example, *Stena Line Ltd v Merchant Navy Ratings Pension Fund Trustees Ltd*
[2011] EWCA Civ 543, [2011] Pens. L.R. 22 at [44]; *Spencer v Secretary of State for Defence* [2012]
EWHC 120 (Ch), [2012] 2 All E.R. (Comm) 480 at [52] and *Wuhan Ocean Economic and Technical
Co-operation Co Ltd v Schiffahrts-Gesellschaft "Hansa Murcia" mbH & Co KG* [2012] EWHC 3104
(Comm), [2013] 1 All E.R. (Comm) 1277 at [15]. The reaction to *Belize* in the Commonwealth has
been more mixed. Thus the courts in Singapore have declined to follow *Belize* (see *Foo Jong Peng
v Phua Kiah Mai* [2012] SGCA 55, [2012] 4 S.L.R. 1267 and *Sembcorp Marine Ltd v PPL Holdings*

Pte Ltd [2013] SGCA 43, [2013] 4 S.L.R. 193) but it has been followed by the courts in New Zealand (*Dysart Timbers Ltd v Nielsen* [2009] NZSC 43, [2009] 3 N.Z.L.R. 160).

[6] See, for example, McLauchlan [2014] L.M.C.L.Q. 203; Courtney and Carter (2014) 31 J.C.L. 151; Hooley [2014] C.L.J. 315; McCaughran [2011] C.L.J. 607; Davies [2010] L.M.C.L.Q. 140; Macdonald (2009) 26 J.C.L. 97; Kramer [2004] C.L.J. 384; McMeel, *The Construction of Contracts*, 2nd edn (2011), Ch.11.

[7] *Marks & Spencer Plc v BNP Paribas Securities Services Trust Co (Jersey) Ltd* [2015] UKSC 72, [2016] A.C. 742 at [31] per Lord Neuberger. Not all members of the Supreme Court are, however, of the same view. Thus in *Marks & Spencer* Lord Carnwath (at [74]) saw no sufficient reason to question the "continuing authority" of the judgment of Lord Hoffmann in *Belize* and the judgment of Lord Clarke (at [76]) is more equivocal, as is the judgment of Lord Mance in *Trump International Golf Club Scotland Ltd v Scottish Ministers* [2015] UKSC 74, [2016] 1 W.L.R. 85 at [42]–[44]. However, the judgment of Lord Neuberger represents the majority view, so that the authority of Lord Hoffmann's judgment has now been considerably diminished.

[7a] *Trump International Golf Club Scotland Ltd v Scottish Ministers* [2015] UKSC 74, [2016] 1 W.L.R. 85 at [35] per Lord Hodge.

[7b] *Europa Plus SCA SIF v Anthracite Investments (Ireland) Plc* [2016] EWHC 437 (Comm), [34] per Popplewell J. The relationship between the two may be particularly close in the case where it is alleged that something has been omitted from the contract. As was noted by Snowden J. in *Hayfin Opal Luxco 3 SARL v Windermere VII CMBS Plc* [2016] EWHC 782 (Ch) at [68], the gap in such a case can be filled either by a process of corrective interpretation or by the implication of an appropriate term in the contract. But in either case it is important to note that the test applied by the court is a strict one, so that a court will not lightly correct the contract by supplying the alleged missing term, whether by corrective interpretation or by implication.

Att-Gen of Belize v Belize Telecom Ltd

[*Delete text of paragraph from after note 23 to the end: page* [1095]]   **14–006**

[*Delete text of paragraph 14–007 and substitute: page* [1098]]   **14–007**

Marks and Spencer v BNP Paribas. Initially, Lord Hoffmann's judgment received the endorsement of both the Court of Appeal[24] and it was applied or referred to in a number of cases at first instance.[25] As a result, the traditional "tests" for the implication of terms into a contract were treated as guidelines to be applied by the courts when seeking to answer the single question: Is this what the instrument, read as a whole against the relevant background, would reasonably be understood to mean? However, in *Marks & Spencer Plc v BNP Paribas Securities Services Trust Co (Jersey) Ltd*[26] the Supreme Court re-established the traditional principles applicable to the implication of terms and "qualified"[27] the judgment of Lord Hoffmann in *Belize*. In doing so the Supreme Court emphasised that Lord Hoffmann had not diluted the requirements which must be satisfied before a term will be implied into a contract.[28] The test which must be applied by the courts when seeking to imply a term into a contract as a matter of fact is whether the term satisfies the test of "business necessity".[29] It is not enough to show that the term is a reasonable one for it to be implied into the contract.[30] Reasonableness may be a necessary requirement before a term will be implied but it is not sufficient. Thus a term should not be implied into a detailed commercial contract merely because it appears fair or because the parties might have agreed to it had it been suggested to them.[31] The test remains one of necessity, albeit not "absolute necessity" but whether, without the term, the contract would lack commercial or practical coherence or whether it is necessary to imply the term "in order to make the contract work".[32] In short, in order to imply a term into an ordinary business contract, the term must be necessary to give business efficacy to the contract; it must be so obvious that it goes without saying; it must be capable of clear expression; and it must not contradict any express term of the contract.[32a]

[24] *Mediterranean Salvage & Towage Ltd v Seamar Trading & Commerce Inc (The Reborn)* [2009] EWCA Civ 531, [2009] 2 Lloyd's Rep. 639 at [8]–[14]; *Chantry Estates (South East) Ltd v Anderson* [2010] EWCA Civ 316, 130 Con. L.R. 11; *KG Bominflot Bunkergesellschaft für Mineralöle mbh v Petroplus Marketing AG* [2010] EWCA Civ 1145, [2011] 1 Lloyd's Rep. 442 at [44]; *Beazer Homes Ltd v Durham CC* [2010] EWCA Civ 1175 at [36]; *Crema v Cenkos Securities Plc* [2010] EWCA Civ 1444, [2011] 1 W.L.R. 2066 at [36]; *Garratt v Mirror Group Newspapers Ltd* [2011] EWCA Civ 425, [2011] I.R.L.R. 591 at [46]; *Stena Line Ltd v Merchant Navy Ratings Pension Fund Trustees Ltd* [2011] EWCA Civ 543, [2011] Pens. L.R. 22 at [36]; *BDW Trading Ltd v JM Rowe (Investments) Ltd* [2011] EWCA Civ 548, [2011] 20 E.G. 113 (C.S.) at [34]; *Consolidated Finance Ltd v McCluskey* [2012] EWCA Civ 1325, [2012] C.T.L.C. 133; *Procter and Gamble Co v Svenska Cellulosa Aktiebolaget SCA* [2012] EWCA Civ 1413; *Rathbone Brothers Plc v Novae Corporate Underwriting Ltd* [2014] EWCA Civ 1464 at [84].

[25] *Durham Tees Valley Airport Ltd v BMI Baby Ltd* [2009] EWHC 852 (Ch), [2009] 2 Lloyd's Rep. 246 at [89]; *Inta Navigatiori v Ranch Investments Ltd* [2009] EWHC 1216 (Comm), [2010] 1 Lloyd's Rep. 74 at [42]; *AET Inc Ltd v Arcaola Petroleum Ltd* [2009] EWHC 2337 (Comm), [2010] 1 Lloyd's Rep. 593 at [4]; *ENE 1 Kos Ltd v Petroleo Brasileiro SA* [2009] EWHC 1843 (Comm), [2010] 1 Lloyd's Rep. 87 at [42]; *Fortis Bank SA/NV v Indian Overseas Bank* [2010] EWHC 84 (Comm), [2010] 2 Lloyd's Rep. 641 at [60]; *Redmayne Bentley Stockbrokers v Isaacs* [2010] EWHC 1504 (Comm) at [84]; *Cassa di Risparmio della Repubblica di San Marino SpA v Barclays Bank Ltd* [2011] EWHC 484 (Comm), [2011] I.C.L.C. 701 at [541]; *F & C Alternative Investments (Holdings) Ltd v Barthelemy* [2011] EWHC 1731 (Ch) at [271]; *Leander Construction Ltd v Mulalley & Co Ltd* [2011] EWHC 3449 (TCC) at [41]; *Spencer v Secretary of State for Defence* [2012] EWHC 120 (Ch); *SNCB Holding v UBS AG* [2012] EWHC 2044 (Comm); [2012] All E.R. (D) 259 (Jul); *Graiseley Properties Ltd v Barclays Bank Plc* [2012] EWHC 3093 (Comm) at [28]; *Wuhan Ocean Economic & Technical Co-operation Co Ltd v Schiffahrts-Gesellschaft "Hansa Murcia" mbH & Co KG* [2012] EWHC 3104 (Comm), [2013] 1 All E.R. (Comm) 1277 at [15]; *Greatship (India) Ltd v Oceanografia SA de CV* [2012] EWHC 3468 (Comm), [2013] 1 All E.R. (Comm) 1244 at [41]; *Yam Seng Pte Ltd v International Trade Corp Ltd* [2013] EWHC 111 (QB), [2013] 1 All E.R. (Comm) 1321 at [132]; *TSG Building Services Plc v South Anglia Housing Ltd* [2013] EWHC 1151 (TCC), [2013] B.L.R. 484 at [44]; *Lombard North Central Plc v Nugent* [2013] EWHC 1588 (QB); *Marex Financial Ltd v Creative Finance Ltd* [2013] EWHC 2155 (Comm), [2014] 1 All E.R. (Comm) 122 at [72]; *Straw v Jennings* [2013] EWHC 3290 (Ch) at [99]; *Carewatch Care Services Ltd v Focus Care Services Ltd* [2014] EWHC 2313 (Ch) at [104]; *Rosserlane Consultants Ltd v Credit Suisse International* [2015] EWHC 384 (Ch).

[26] [2015] UKSC 72, [2016] A.C. 742.

[27] *Walter Lilly & Co Ltd v Clin* [2016] EWHC 357 (TCC), [2016] B.L.R. 247 at [39] and *Manor Asset Ltd v Demolition Services Ltd* [2016] EWHC 222 (TCC) at [45].

[28] *Marks & Spencer Plc v BNP Paribas Securities Services Trust Co (Jersey) Ltd* [2015] UKSC 72, [2016] A.C. 742 at [24], [66] and [77].

[29] [2015] UKSC 72 at [17].

[30] [2015] UKSC 72 at [23]. See also *Rosenblatt (A Firm) v Man Oil Group SA* [2016] EWHC 1382 (QB) at [59].

[31] [2015] UKSC 72 at [21].

[32] [2015] UKSC 72 at [21] and [77].

[32a] *Hallman Holding Ltd v Webster* [2016] UKPC 3 at [14]. See also *Europa Plus SCA SIF v Anthracite Investments (Ireland) Plc* [2016] EWHC 437 (Comm) at [33].

Implied restriction on contractual discretion

14–029   [*Add to note 178, at the end: page* [1117]]

; *Hockin v Royal Bank of Scotland* [2016] EWHC 925 (Ch) at [37]; *Monde Petroleum SA v WesternZagros Ltd* [2016] EWHC 1472 (Comm) at [242]–[276].

Implied term as to trust and confidence

[*Add to note 184, line 3, after* "[2015] EWHC 1322 (Ch)": *page* [1117]]   **14–030**
; *Mr H TV Ltd v ITV2 Ltd* [2015] EWHC 2840 (Comm) at [43]–[51].

Implied term as to good faith

[*Add to note 188, line 4, after* "[2013] B.L.R. 484": *page* [1118]]   **14–031**
; *Globe Motors Inc v TRW Lucas Varity Electric Steering Ltd* [2016] EWCA Civ
396 at [68].

[*Add to note 190, at the end: page* [1118]]
See also *Monde Petroleum SA v WesternZagros Ltd* [2016] EWHC 1472 (Comm)
at [242]–[276].

[*Add to note 191, at the end: page* [1118]]
; *Apollo Window Blinds Ltd v McNeil* [2016] EWHC 2307 (QB); *T and L Sugars
Ltd v Tate and Lyle Industries Ltd* [2015] EWHC 2696 (Comm) at [152] ("while
it would be right to imply a term that the Defendant would act in good faith and
honestly in carrying out the process envisaged in clauses 3.7.1 and 3.7.3, there is
no proper basis for the implication of the very much more onerous term for which
the Claimant argues").

CHAPTER 15

EXEMPTION CLAUSES

1. IN GENERAL

Generally

15–001   [*Add new note 3a, after* "expected to insure." *in line 16: page* [1128]]

³ᵃ See, e.g. *Nobahar-Cookson v Hut Group Ltd* [2016] EWCA Civ 128, noted below, para.15–012.

Types of exemption clause

15–003   [*Add to paragraph, line 11, after* "rescind the agreement.": *page* [1129]]
Similarly, an exemption clause can subject a party's liability for breach of contract to an onerous condition, such as a number of days within which the injured party must serve notice of the breach or bring proceedings.¹²ᵃ

[12a] e.g. *Nobahar-Cookson v Hut Group Ltd* [2016] EWCA Civ 128 (contractual time-bar an exclusion clause for the purposes of the principle of strict construction) and see the definition of the "exclusion or restriction" of liability in the Unfair Contract Terms Act 1977 s.13 and Main Work, Vol.I, para.15–069.

[Add to note 17, line 3, after "[1981] C.L.J. 108": page [1129]]
; White [2016] J.B.L. 373

Exemption clauses distinguished from other similar clauses

[Add to paragraph, after note 18: page [1129]] **15–004**
Whereas an agreed damages clause entitles the injured party to recover the sum stipulated without proof of loss, an injured party subject to a limitation clause must prove its actual loss sustained and can recover this loss up to the limitation stipulated[18a]; and an agreed damages clause (unlike a limitation clause) is for the benefit of both the injured party and the party in breach.[18b] The form of the clause is not decisive of the difference between the two: rather "it is the fact that the clause is expressed as one agreeing a figure [as a pre-estimate of damage], and not as imposing a limit".[18c]

[18a] *Suisse Atlantique Société d'Armement SA v NV Rotterdamsche Kolen Centrale* [1967] 1 A.C. 361 at 395 and 420 (demurrage clause in charterparty). As is explained below, paras 26–178 et seq., the Supreme Court has recently reframed the common law governing penalty clauses so as to reduce the significance of the distinction between "liquidated damages clauses" and penalty clauses, but this does not affect the distinction drawn in the text between agreed damages clauses and limitation clauses.
[18b] [1967] 1 A.C. 361 at 420–421.
[18c] [1967] 1 A.C. 361 at 436 per Lord Wilberforce.

Legislative control of exemption clauses

[In paragraph, lines 33–35, delete from "As the relevant parts ... " to " ... this **15–005**
chapter will" and substitute: page [1131]]
The relevant provisions in Pts 1 and 2 of the 2015 Act affecting exemption clauses (and the resultant amendments of the 1977 Act[32a]) were brought into force so as to apply to contracts made on or after October 1, 2015, with the exception that Pt 1's provisions governing "services contracts" apply to "consumer transport services" (as specially defined) only if made on or after October 1, 2016.[32b] This chapter will therefore

[32a] These are contained in the 2015 Act s.75, Sch.4 paras 2–27; the Consumer Rights Act 2015 (Commencement No.3, Transitional Provisions, Savings and Consequential Amendments) Order 2015 (SI 2015/1630) art.3(c).
[32b] The Consumer Rights Act 2015 (Commencement No.3, Transitional Provisions, Savings and Consequential Amendments) Order 2015 (SI 2015/1630) arts 3–4 and 6(2) as amended by the Consumer Rights Act 2015 (Commencement No.3, Transitional Provisions, Savings and Consequential Amendments) (Amendment) Order 2016 (SI 2016/484) art.2. SI 2015/1630 art.6(4) provides that the Unfair Terms in Consumer Contracts Regulations 1999 continue to have effect in relation to any contract or notice relating to any contract entered into before October 1, 2015 despite their revocation by the 2015 Act Sch.4 para.34.

2. Principles of Construction

General principles

15–007   [*In note 35, lines 3–4, delete* "; *Kudos Catering (UK) Ltd* ... 1192 (QB);":: *page* [1131]]

[*Add to note 37, at the end: page* [1132]]
; *Persimmon Homes Ltd v Ove Arup & Partners Ltd* [2015] EWHC 3573 (TCC), [2016] B.L.R. 112 at [25]–[28].

[*Add to note 41, at the end: page* [1132]]
cf. the restrictive interpretation of the decision on the construction of a clause disapplying a statutory limitation of liability in *Clarke v Earl of Dunraven and Mount-Earl, The Satanita* [1897] A.C. 59 by the PC in *Bahamas Oil Refining Co International Ltd v Owners of the Cape Bari Tankschiffahrts GmbH & Co KG* [2016] UKPC 20 at [49], in part on the basis that the earlier case was decided "at a time when the relevant principles of construction were much less developed than they are today".

[*In note 42, lines 3–4, delete* "*Transocean Drilling UK Ltd* ... para.7–017" *and substitute: page* [1133]]
Nobahar-Cookson v Hut Group Ltd [2016] EWCA Civ 128, esp. at [12]–[22] but cf. *Transocean Drilling UK Ltd v Providence Resources Plc* [2016] EWCA Civ 372 at [14] and [19] ("artificial approaches to construction" should not be applied to a contract by which the parties entered "mutual undertakings to accept the risk of consequential loss flowing from each other's breaches of contract"). And see Peel (ed.), *Treitel on The Law of Contract*, 14th edn (2015) para. 7–016.

Clear and unambiguous expression

15–008   [*Add to note 43, line 16, after* "(ordinary rules of construction apply)": *page* [1133]]
; *Persimmon Homes Ltd v Ove Arup & Partners Ltd* [2015] EWHC 3573 (TCC), [2016] B.L.R. 112 at [33] (commercial and contractual context *may* make it improbable that one party would have assumed responsibility for the negligence of another, so that clear words are needed); and cf. *Bahamas Oil Refining Co International Ltd v Owners of the Cape Bari Tankschiffahrts GmbH & Co KG* [2016] UKPC 20 at [31]–[40] (exclusion of limitation of liability arising by statute and international convention).

[*Add to note 43, line 19, after* "payment obligation)": *page* [1133]]
(though the CA was overruled on other grounds in *PST Energy 7 Shipping LLC v OW Bunker Malta Ltd* [2016] UKSC 23, [2016] 2 W.L.R. 1193 at [58]).

[*In note 50, lines 3–4, delete* "*Kudos Catering (UK) Ltd* ... 1192 (QB)" *and substitute: page* [1134]]
Nobahar-Cookson v Hut Group Ltd [2016] EWCA Civ 128 at [19]; *Transocean Drilling UK Ltd v Providence Resources Plc* [2016] EWCA Civ 372 at [28] and [35]

[In note 51, lines 2–3, delete "; Transocean Drilling UK Ltd ... [2015] B.L.R. 190 at [39]": page [1134]]

Clause must extend to event

[Add to note 56, at the end: page [1135]]   **15–009**
However, some of these earlier cases may be decided differently today given that the courts are now more willing to recognise that words take their meaning from their context and that the same word or phrase may mean different things in different documents: *Transocean Drilling UK Ltd v Providence Resources Plc* [2016] EWCA Civ 372 at [15].

Inconsistency with main purpose of contract

[In note 62, lines 6–7, delete "; Transocean Drilling UK Ltd ... [2015] B.L.R. 190 **15–010**
at [167]": page [1135]]

[Add to paragraph, at the end: page [1137]]
And it has been said recently that the principle in *Tor Line A/B v Alltrans Group of Canada Ltd*[72a] "should be seen as one of last resort" and that there is authority that "it applies only in cases where the effect of the clause is to relieve one party from all liability for breach of any of the obligations which he has purported to undertake" as "[o]nly in such a case could it be said that the contract amounted to nothing more than a mere declaration of intent".[72b]

[72a] [1984] 1 W.L.R. 48.
[72b] *Transocean Drilling UK Ltd v Providence Resources Plc* [2016] EWCA Civ 372 at [27] per Moore-Bick L.J. (with whom McFarlane and Briggs L.JJ. agreed) referring to *Great North Eastern Railway Ltd v Avon Insurance Plc* [2001] EWCA Civ 780, [2001] 1 Lloyd's Rep. I.R. 793 (the relevant passages are at [31]).

Construction *contra proferentem*

[Add to note 83, line 2, after "[1992] 2 Lloyd's Rep. 127, 134": page [1138]]   **15–012**
; *Nobahar-Cookson v Hut Group Ltd* [2016] EWCA Civ 128, esp. at [14] and [16] (distinguishing "the *contra proferentem* rule in its classic form", which is "a rule designed to resolve ambiguities against the party who prepared the document", and the principle that, if necessary to resolve ambiguity, [exclusion clauses] should be narrowly construed"); *Transocean Drilling UK Ltd v Providence Resources Plc* [2016] EWCA Civ 372 at [20] (*contra proferentem* has no role to play where the meaning of the words is clear or where a clause favours both parties equally).

[Add to paragraph, after note 85: page [1138]]
For example, in *Nobahar-Cookson v Hut Group Ltd* a clause in a commercial contract provided that the sellers of a company would not be liable for any claim unless the buyer served notice of it within 20 business days "after becoming aware of the matter".[85a] The Court of Appeal held that "there remains a principle that an ambiguity" in the meaning of such a clause (which was rightly to be treated as an exclusion clause) "may have to be resolved by a preference for the

narrower construction, if linguistic, contextual and purposive analysis do not disclose an answer to the question with sufficient clarity".[85b] The Court recognised that the phrase "after becoming aware of the matter" could have three possible meanings, but held that, given that the commercial purpose of the term was to prevent the buyer from keeping claims of which it was aware "up its sleeve", and assisted by the principle which it had stated, the phrase should be interpreted as referring to an awareness of a claim and not merely an awareness of facts which could give rise to a claim.[85c] However, the Court of Appeal considered that:

> "This approach to exclusion clauses is not now regarded as a presumption, still less as a special rule justifying the giving of a strained meaning to a provision merely because it is an exclusion clause. Commercial parties are entitled to allocate between them the risks of something going wrong in their contractual relationship in any way they choose. Nor is it to be mechanistically applied wherever an ambiguity is identified in an exclusion clause. The court must still use all its tools of linguistic, purposive and common-sense analysis to discern what the clause really means."[85d]

Rather, the principle is "essentially one of common sense; parties do not normally give up valuable rights without making it clear that they intend to do so".[85e] It will be seen, therefore, that this aspect of the construction *contra proferentem* is clearly related to the approach of the courts which requires clear and unambiguous language effectively to exclude liability for breach.[85f]

[85a] [2016] EWCA Civ 128 at [5].
[85b] [2016] EWCA Civ 128 at [21] per Briggs L.J.
[85c] [2016] EWCA Civ 128 at [36] (with whom Hallett L.J. and Moylan J. agreed, though placing greater emphasis on the commercial sense of the resulting decision: [2016] EWCA Civ 128 at [40] and [41]).
[85d] *Nobahar-Cookson v Hut Group Ltd* [2016] EWCA Civ 128 at [19] per Briggs L.J.
[85e] *Seadrill Management Services Ltd v OAO Gazprom* [2010] EWCA Civ 691, [2011] 1 All E.R. (Comm) 1077 at per Moore-Bick L.J. quoted by Briggs L.J. in *Nobahar-Cookson v Hut Group Ltd* [2016] EWCA Civ 128 at [19].
[85f] On which see Main Work, Vol.I, para.15–008.

Liability for negligence

15–013   *[In note 91, lines 5–6, delete* "; *Transocean Drilling UK Ltd* ... [2015] B.L.R. 190 at [40]–[54]": *page* [1139]]

Words wide enough to cover negligence

15–014   *[Add to note 105, at the end: page* [1141]]
; *Persimmon Homes Ltd v Ove Arup & Partners Ltd* [2015] EWHC 3573 (TCC), [2016] B.L.R. 112 at [42]–[44] and [50].

Indemnity clauses

15–018   *[Add to note 134, line 7, after* "[2014] 1 W.L.R. 3517 at [94]": *page* [1144]]
; *Capita (Banstead 2011) Ltd v RFIB Group Ltd* [2015] EWCA Civ 1310, [2016] 2 W.L.R. 1429 at [10].

[Add to paragraph, after note 136: page [1144]]
In the case of dishonest wrongdoing, "general words will not serve", as "the language used must be such as will alert a commercial party to the extraordinary bargain he is invited to make".[136a]

[136a] *HIH Casualty & General Insurance Ltd v Chase Manhattan Bank* [2003] UKHL 6, [2003] 2 Lloyd's Rep. 61 per Lord Bingham of Cornhill (exemption clause); *Capita (Banstead 2011) Ltd v RFIB Group Ltd* [2015] EWCA Civ 1310, [2016] 2 W.L.R. 1429 at [10] (indemnity clause).

[Add to note 137, line 15, after "[2014] 1 W.L.R. 3517 at [96]"*: page* [1145]]
; *Capita (Banstead 2011) Ltd v RFIB Group Ltd* [2015] EWCA Civ 1310, [2016] 2 W.L.R. 1429.

4. APPLICATION OF PRINCIPLES OF CONSTRUCTION TO PARTICULAR CONTRACTS

Sale of goods: terms as to quality, etc.

[Delete text of note 200 and substitute: page [1153]]   **15–030**
The relevant provisions of the 2015 Act were brought into force so as to apply to consumer contracts made on or after October 1, 2015: see above, para.15–005 and also below, para.38–335.

Hire purchase

[Add to paragraph, line 1, after "October 1, 2015 (when the"*: page* [1154]]   **15–031**
relevant provisions of

Carriage of goods: deviation

[Add to note 213, at the end: page [1155]]   **15–032**
However, the provisions in the 2015 Act relating to the exclusion or restriction of liability in "services contracts" do not apply to certain "consumer transport services" (certain rail passenger services, carriage by air, and sea and inland waterway transport, all as specially defined by the 2015 Order art.2) until October 1, 2016: 2015 Order arts 4 and 6(2) as amended by the Consumer Rights Act 2015 (Commencement No.3, Transitional Provisions, Savings and Consequential Amendments) (Amendment) Order 2016 (SI 2016/484) art.2. See further below, para.38–403.

Bailment: acts inconsistent with bailment

[Add to note 236, at the end: page [1158]]   **15–037**
On the qualifications on the general temporal application of the relevant provisions of the 2015 Act, see above, para.15–005.

5. Exemption Clauses and Third Parties

Effect of the 1999 Act: burden

15–044   [*Add to paragraph, line 23, before* "liability for negligence": *page* [1161]]
business

[*Add to note 265, at the end: page* [1162]]
On the qualifications on the date of the coming into force of the relevant
provisions of the 2015 Act in the case of "consumer transport services" see
above, para.15–005.

6. Legislative Control of Exemption Clauses

(a) *Unfair Contract Terms Act 1977*

(i) *Overview*

Consumer Rights Act 2015

15–064   [*Delete text of note 351 and substitute: page* [1175]]
The relevant provisions of Pts 1 and 2 of the 2015 Act came into force (with
certain qualifications in relation to "consumer transport services") on October 1,
2015, on which see above, para.15–005 and below, para.38–335.

[*In paragraph, line 16, delete* "will be two principal legislative" *and substitute:
page* [1175]]
are two principle legislative

(ii) *The Pattern of Control: Key Definitions*

Varieties of exemption clause

15–070   [*Add to note 378, line 4, after* "[1981] C.L.J. 108": *page* [1177]]
; White (2016) J.B.L. 373

[*Add to note 386, last line, after* "see above, para.7–149": *page* [1178]]
; *Crestsign Ltd v National Westminster Bank Plc* [2014] EWHC 3043 (Ch) at
[112]–[119] (permission to appeal on other grounds: [2015] EWCA Civ 986);
Thornbridge Ltd v Barclays Bank Plc [2015] EWHC 3430 (QB) at [97]–[111]
(appeal pending) (on "basis clauses" stipulating that defendants were not providing advice in relation to interest rate "swap agreements")

The new law: "dealing as consumer" deleted from the 1977 Act

15–079   [*Add to note 410, at the end: page* [1181]]
On the qualifications on the date of the coming into force of the relevant
provisions of the 2015 Act in the case of "consumer transport services" see
above, para.15–005.

(iii) *The Controls Provided by the 1977 Act*

Negligence liability: the new law

[*Add to note 430, at the end: page* [1183]]
On the qualifications on the date of the coming into force of the relevant
provisions of the 2015 Act in the case of "consumer transport services" see
above, para.15–005.

15–083

Liability arising in contract: the old law

[*Add new note 435a, after* "reference or by course of dealing." *in line 12: page*
[1183]]
435a This sentence was quoted without disapproval by Phillips J. in *African Export-Import Bank v
Shebah Exploration and Production Co Ltd* [2016] EWHC 311 (Comm) at [20], though the learned
judge observed (at [27]) that where legally-represented commercial parties have used a "neutral"
industry model form as the basis for a complex and detailed financial contract, executed after
negotiation and revision, cogent evidence would be required to raise even an arguable case that the
resulting contract is made on the written standard terms of one of those parties.

15–084

[*Add to note 436, last line, after* "[2015] EWHC 1280 (QB) at [91]–[95]"*: page*
[1184]]
; *Commercial Management (Investments) Ltd v Mitchell Design & Construct Ltd*
[2016] EWHC 76 (TCC) at [61]–[73] (A's standard terms incorporated only to
the extent to which B's terms did not prevail over them, term held still one of A's
"written standard terms of business")

Liability arising in contract: the new law

[*Add to note 455, at the end: page* [1186]]
On the qualifications on the date of the coming into force of the relevant
provisions of the 2015 Act in the case of "consumer transport services" see
above, para.15–005.

15–087

Indemnity clauses: the new law

[*Add to note 465, at the end: page* [1187]]
On the qualifications on the date of the coming into force of the relevant
provisions of the 2015 Act in the case of "consumer transport services" see
above, para.15–005.

15–090

(iv) *Test of Reasonableness*

Guidelines

[*Add to note 508, at the end: page* [1192]]
cf. *Thornbridge Ltd v Barclays Bank Plc* [2015] EWHC 3430 (QB) at [116]
(appeal pending) (equal bargaining power evidenced by party threatening to go
elsewhere).

15–097

[*Add to note 511, at the end: page* [1193]]
; *Commercial Management (Investments) Ltd v Mitchell Design & Construct Ltd* [2016] EWHC 76 (TCC) at [86]–[88].

(v) *Exclusions from the Scope of the 1977 Act or Some of its Provisions*

Specific exceptions

15–116   [*Add to note 584, after* "The Act": *page* [1203]]
generally

Schedule 1

15–118   [*Add to paragraph, line 5, before* "the Consumer Rights Act": *page* [1204]]
the relevant provisions of

[*Add to note 594, at the end: page* [1204]]
The general date of the coming into force of the 2015 Act on October 1, 2015 has an exception as regards "consumer transport services" (as specially defined) in relation to which the relevant provisions of the 2015 Act come into force only for contracts made on or after October 1, 2016: the Consumer Rights Act 2015 (Commencement No.3, Transitional Provisions, Savings and Consequential Amendments) Order 2015 (SI 2015/1630) art.4 and 6(2) as amended by the Consumer Rights Act 2015 (Commencement No.3, Transitional Provisions, Savings and Consequential Amendments) (Amendment) Order 2016 (SI 2016/484) art.2. This applies to the amendments to Sch.1 of the 1977 Act: SI 2015/1630 art.4(c) referring, inter alia, to the 2015 Act Sch.4 paras 26 and 27.

15–119   [*Add to note 600, at the end: page* [1205]]
For the special position of "consumer transport services" see above, para.15–118 n.594.

[*Add to paragraph, line 13, before* "coming into force of": *page* [1205]]
the relevant provisions of

International supply contracts

15–122   [*Add to note 607, at the end: page* [1205]]
As regards "consumer transport services" the deletion of the reference to s.4 of the 1977 Act applies only to contracts made or on after October 1, 2016: SI 2015/1630 arts 4(c) and 6(2) (as amended by the Consumer Rights Act 2015 (Commencement No.3, Transitional Provisions, Savings and Consequential Amendments) (Amendment) Order 2016 (SI 2016/484) art.2) referring to the 2015 Act Sch.4 para.23.

Contractual provisions authorised or required by statute or international agreement

15–123   [*In note 614, delete second sentence and substitute: page* [1206]]
This amendment generally comes into force as regards contracts made on or after October 1, 2015, but this finds an exception as regards "consumer transport

[88]

services" where the relevant date is October 1, 2016: SI 2015/1630 arts 3(g), 4(c) and 6(2) (as amended by SI 2016/484 art.2) referring to the 2015 Act Sch.4 para.25.

Choice of English law clauses

[*Add to paragraph, line 10, before* "the Consumer Rights Act": *page* [1207]] **15–125**
the relevant provisions of

[*Add new note 622a, after* "came into force" *in line 11: page* [1207]]
622a The changes noted in the text apply to "consumer transport services" where made on or after October 1, 2016: SI 2015/1630 arts 4(c) and 6(2) (as amended by SI 2016/484 art.2) referring to the 2015 Act Sch.4 para.24.

(b) *Misrepresentation Act 1967*

Liability for misrepresentation: the old law

[*Add to paragraph, line 2, before* "the Consumer Rights Act": *page* [1209]] **15–130**
relevant provisions of

[*Delete text of note 639 and substitute: page* [1209]]
See below, para.15–131, n.642.

Liability for misrepresentation: the new law

[*In paragraph, line 2, delete* "the Consumer Rights Act 2015," *and substitute: page* **15–131**
[1209]]
of the relevant provisions of the Consumer Rights Act 2015 on October 1, 2015,

[*Delete text of note 642 and substitute: page* [1209]]
Consumer Rights Act 2015 (Commencement No.3, Transitional Provisions, Savings and Consequential Amendments) Order 2015 (SI 2015/1630) arts 3I and 6(1) and (4); the relevant provisions of the 2015 Act are ss.61–76 and Sch.4 para.1. For contracts made before October 1, 2015 see Main Work, Vol.II, para.38–334.

(c) *Other Legislation*

Consumer protection legislation on unfair contract terms

[*Add to paragraph, line 2, before* "Consumer Rights Act": *page* [1212]] **15–142**
relevant provisions of the

[*Add to note 675, at the beginning: page* [1212]]
Consumer Rights Act 2015 (Commencement No.3, Transitional Provisions, Savings and Consequential Amendments) Order 2015 (SI 2015/1630) arts 3(c), (g) and 6(4).

Mandatory character of much consumer protection legislation

15–143 *[Add to note 682, line 5, before* "See further Vol.II, para.38–134"*: page* [1213]]
The 1990 Directive is repealed and replaced by Directive (EU) 2015/2302 on package travel and linked travel arrangements [2015] O.J. L326/1, art.23 of which provides for the "imperative nature" of its provisions.

7. COMMON LAW QUALIFICATIONS

Acknowledgements

15–147 *[Add to note 703, at the end: page* [1216]]
; *Crestsign Ltd v National Westminster Bank Plc* [2014] EWHC 3043 (Ch) at [112]–[119] (permission to appeal on other grounds: [2015] EWCA Civ 986); *Thornbridge Ltd v Barclays Bank Plc* [2015] EWHC 3430 (QB), at [97]–[111] (appeal pending) (on "basis clauses" stipulating that defendants were not providing advice in relation to interest rate "swap agreements").

8. FORCE MAJEURE CLAUSES

Burden of proof

15–155 *[Add to note 739, line 12, after* "[2013] EWCA Civ 1628 at [22]"*: page* [1220]]
(the application of the "prohibition clause" was not in issue before the SC [2015] UKSC 43, [2015] Bus. L.R. 987).

"Prevented" clauses

15–156 *[Add to note 748, penultimate line, after* "connection must be shown"*: page* [1222]]
(the application of the "prohibition clause" was not in issue before the SC [2015] UKSC 43, [2015] Bus. L.R. 987).

15–157 *[Add to note 754, at the end: page* [1223]]
(the application of the "prohibition clause" was not in issue before the SC [2015] UKSC 43, [2015] Bus. L.R. 987).

"Force majeure"

15–162 *[Add to note 777, at the end: page* [1225]]
The French Civil Code as promulgated did not define *cause étrangère* or force majeure but its provisions on general contract law were revised (with effect from October 1, 2016) and the new art.1218 al.1 (as enacted by *Ordonnance* No.2016-131 of February 10, 2016) provides that: "[i]n contractual matters, there is force majeure where an event beyond the control of the debtor, which could not

reasonably have been foreseen at the time of the conclusion of the contract and whose effects could not be avoided by appropriate measures, prevents performance of his obligation by the debtor" (trans. Cartwright, Fauvarque-Cosson and Whittaker).

[Add to note 803, line 7, after "[2002] C.L.Y. 4043 (Cty Ct)"*: page* [1228]]   **15–164**
The 1990 Directive is repealed and replaced by Directive (EU) 2015/2302 on package travel and linked travel arrangements [2015] O.J. L326/1, which does not use the expression "force majeure" but instead refers to "unavoidable and extraordinary circumstances", which art.3(12) defines as "a situation beyond the control of the party who invokes such a situation and the consequences of which could not have been avoided even if all reasonable measures had been taken". In addition, art.14(3)(b) of the 2015 Directive provides that the organiser does not have to pay the traveller compensation in respect of "non-conformity" of the package where he proves, inter alia, that this is "attributable to a third party unconnected with the provision of the travel services included in the package travel contract and is unforeseeable or unavoidable".

Part Five

ILLEGALITY AND PUBLIC POLICY

CHAPTER 16

ILLEGALITY AND PUBLIC POLICY

1. Introduction

Underlying principle

[Add to paragraph, after note 2: page [1236]]   **16–001**
As a result of the recent decision of the Supreme Court in *Patel v Mirza*[2a] this is
now the question that the court poses in addressing the question of the effect of
illegality in contractual claims.

[2a] [2016] UKSC 42, [2016] 1 W.L.R. 399.

[In paragraph, lines 20–22, delete "As will be seen . . . parties to illegal
contracts.[4]"*: page* [1236]]

A problematic topic

[In paragraph, line 11, delete "*Jetivia SA v Bilta (UK) Ltd*" *and substitute: page*   **16–002**
[1236]]
Jetivia SA v Bilta (UK) Ltd (reported sub nom. *Bilta (UK) Ltd v Nazir (No.2)*)

[Add to paragraph, line 14, after "as appropriately possible . . . ""*: page* [1237]]
This the Supreme Court did in *Patel v Mirza*.[11a]

[11a] [2016] UKSC 42, [2016] 1 W.L.R. 399.

2. The Position At Common Law

(a) *Generally*

Scope of public policy

[Add to note 35, at the end: page [1240]]   **16–006**
: *Hounga v Allen* [2014] UKSC 47, [2014] 1 W.L.R. 2889.

(b) *Contracts involving the commission of a legal wrong*

(i) *Introduction*

Nature of the public policy when contracts involve commission of a legal wrong

[Add to note 44, at the end: page [1241]]   **16–009**
See also *Patel v Mirza* [2016] UKSC 42.

[Add to note 46, at the end: page [1241]]
; and *Patel v Mirza* [2016] UKSC 42.

How illegality may affect a contract

16–011 [*In paragraph, lines 29–32, delete* "The defence of illegality . . . to any particular dispute".⁵²" *and substitute: page* [1242]]
However many of these criticisms are no longer valid in the light of the Supreme Court decision in *Patel v Mirza*.[52]

[52] [2016] UKSC 42, [2016] 1 W.L.R. 399; see below, para.16–014B.

A more flexible approach adopted by the Court of Appeal

16–012 [*Delete the existing title to the paragraph and add to the beginning of paragraph: page* [1242]]
Developments before *Patel v Mirza.* In the light of the judgment in *Patel v Mirza*[53a] the text in paras 16–612—16–614 is mainly of historical interest.

[53a] [2016] UKSC 42, [2016] 1 W.L.R. 399.

Disagreement in the Supreme Court

16–014 [*In paragraph, lines 19–20, delete* "In the latest illegality case . . . v Nazir (No.2)" *and substitute: page* [1246]]
In *Jetivia SA v Bilta (UK) Ltd* (reported sub nom. *Bilta (UK) Ltd v Nazir (No.2)*)

[*In paragraph, line 30, delete* "is a pressing need" *and substitute: page* [1246]]
was a pressing need

[*In paragraph, sentence after note 89, delete* "*Jetivia*" *and substitute: page* [1246]]
Bilta (UK) Ltd

[*Add to note 91, at the end: page* [1247]]
In *Top Brands Ltd v Sharma* [2015] EWCA Civ 1140 the Court of Appeal pointed out the different approaches and considered "that the proper approach to the defence of illegality needs to be addressed by the Supreme Court (conceivably with a panel of nine Justices) as soon as appropriately possible . . . " at [38], a view identical to that of Lord Neuberger in *Bilta (UK) Ltd* [2015] UKSC 23, [2016] A.C. 1 at [15], see Main Work, Vol.I, para.16–002.

[*In paragraph, before note 93, delete* "*Jetivia*" *and substitute: page* [1247]]
Bilta (UK) Ltd

[*Delete sentence of sub-paragraph beginning* "Therefore for the time being . . . " *and substitute: page* [1247]]
Therefore after the *Bilta (UK) Ltd* case it had to be assumed that the flexible approach advocated by the Law Commission and adopted by the Court of Appeal[92] did not represent the law, though the issue remained open for review by the Supreme Court.

[92] See above, para.16–012.

[*Add to note 94, at the end, page* [1247]]
, [2016] Q.B. 23, [2015] 4 All E.R. 495

[Add new paragraphs 16–014A—16–014L: page [1247]]

A new approach. In *Patel v Mirza*[101a] the Supreme Court fundamentally   **16–014A**
recast the doctrine of illegality in contract. The law remains that the court will not
order performance or grant damages for breach of a contract if the claim should
not be enforced because of illegality, but the question is to be decided on a
"factors-based approach". However, the court will normally order restitution of
any money or property transferred under it.[101b] The result is that much of the
previous law on judicial remedies with respect to illegal contracts is mainly of
historical interest.[101c]

[101a] [2016] UKSC 42, [2016] 1 W.L.R. 399.
[101b] See paras 16–014B et seq.
[101c] This is particularly so of law set out in Main Work, Vol.I, paras 16–008—16–014.

Patel v Mirza. In *Patel v Mirza*[101d] P transferred £620,000 to M for the   **16–014B**
purchase of shares in a listed company on the basis of information from contacts
in the listed company. The information from the company contacts was an
anticipated government announcement which would affect the price of the
shares. The agreement between P and M constituted the criminal offence of
insider trading under s.52 of the Criminal Justice Act 1993. The government
announcement did not materialise and P brought an action against M to recover
the £620,000 he had transferred to M. The claim was put on various grounds, one
of which was unjust enrichment; as the money had been transferred for a
consideration that failed, P claimed to be entitled to recover it. In order to show
such failure P had to disclose the illegality involving the insider trading. The
Supreme Court held that the doctrine of illegality (ex turpi causa) applied to
unjust enrichment actions[101e] but on the facts P was entitled to rescind the
contract and recover his money. Both the first instance judge and the Court of
Appeal[101f] considered that the claim for unjust enrichment was precluded by the
decision in *Tinsley v Milligan*[101g] as the claimant had to rely on his illegality.
However, the Court of Appeal, disagreeing with the court at first instance, held
that the claimant could rely on the *locus poenitentiae* principle.[101h] In *Patel v
Mirza*[101i] the Supreme Court considered that the reasoning in *Tinsley* "should no
longer be followed"[101j] but the result was considered correct as it would "have
been disproportionate to have prevented her from enforcing her equitable interest
in the property and conversely to have left Miss Tinsley unjustly enriched."[101k]

[101d] [2016] UKSC 42, [2016] 1 W.L.R. 399 (a panel of nine Justices).
[101e] *Patel v Mirza* [2016] UKSC 42 at [2]: "Illegality has the potential to provide a defence to civil
claims of all sorts, whether relating to contract, property, tort, or unjust enrichment, and in a wide
variety of circumstances".
[101f] [2015] Ch. 271. Gloster L.J. held that the claimant could recover as he did not have to rely on
the illegal contract to recover his money.
[101g] [1994] 1 A.C. 340. The Supreme Court in *Patel* considered this judgment to be wrong: see
below, para.16–198.
[101h] See below, paras 16–205—16–207.
[101i] [2016] UKSC 42.
[101j] [2016] UKSC 42 at [110].
[101k] [2016] UKSC 42 at [112].

16–014C   **A "factors-based" approach.** Lord Toulson gave the majority judgment of the court in *Patel v Mirza*,[1011] which upheld the Court of Appeal's judgment in favour of recovery by the claimant but on a different basis than that of the court. The action in *Patel v Mirza* was not an action to enforce an illegal contract but to obtain restitution and recover money transferred under an illegal contract.[101m] However, the Court laid down a fundamentally different approach to the effect of illegality with respect to contract, tort, restitutionary and property claims. The issue before the court was "whether the policy underlying the rule which made the contract . . . illegal would be stultified"[101n] if the claim (on the facts, a claim for unjustified enrichment) were to succeed. In answering the question of whether allowing recovery for a claim tainted with illegality would be harmful to the integrity of the legal system, the court could not do so without[101o]

> "a) considering the underlying purpose of the prohibition that has been transgressed, b) considering conversely other relevant public policies which may be rendered ineffective or less effective by denial of the claim, and c) keeping in mind the possibility of overkill unless the law is applied with a due sense of proportionality."

Thus the law in illegality in contract is no longer a prescriptive, mechanical rule but rather involves a determination of whether the policy underlying a particular rule would be advanced or frustrated by the application of the rule. The court granted restitutionary recovery to prevent the unjust enrichment of the defendant.

[1011] [2016] UKSC 42 (the minority judgments also favoured recovery).
[101m] On the remedy of restitution see para.16–194.
[101n] [2016] UKSC 42 at [115].
[101o] [2016] UKSC 42 at [101].

16–014D   **Rule-based approach vs range of factors approach.** In *Patel v Mirza*[101p] Lord Toulson set out two alternative approaches in analysing the law of illegality in contract developed by Professor Burrows—the "rule-based approach" and the "range of factors approach".[101q]

[101p] [2016] UKSC 42.
[101q] Burrows, *Restatement of the English Law of Contract* (OUP, 2016) at pp.221–223.

16–014E   **Rule-based approach.** A possible example of a rule-based approach given by Burrows would be a single master rule involving reliance:

> "If the formation, purpose or performance of a contract involves conduct that is illegal (such as a crime) or contrary to public policy (such as a restraint of trade), a party cannot enforce the contract if he has to rely on that conduct to establish its claim."[101r]

Burrows then sets out a more extended analysis of the rule-based approach which goes beyond the reliance rule. This approach involved two core rules: Rule 1 refers to "illegality in formation", that is, the contract is illegal as made, and Rule 2 referring to "illegality in performance".[101s] Burrows considers that the rule-based approach is fatally flawed because it will simply be too complex, it fails to distinguish between serious and trivial illegalities, in practice it does not give rise to greater certainty, and it is well nigh impossible to formulate comprehensive rules with appropriate exceptions to cover all eventualities.[101t] The law of illegality needs to have a greater degree of flexibility than that allowed by a rule-based approach.

[101r] Burrows, *Restatement of the English Law of Contract* (2016) at p.224.
[101s] Burrows, *Restatement of the English Law of Contract* (2016) at p.225.
[101t] [2016] UKSC 42 at [87]–[92] where Lord Toulson sets out the criticisms of Burrows, *Restatement of the English Law of Contract* (2016) at pp.224–229.

Range of factors approach. A possible formulation of range of factors **16–014F**
approach is set out by Burrows as follows[101u]:

"If the formation, purpose or performance of a contract involves conduct that is illegal (such as a crime) or contrary to public policy (such as a restraint of trade), the contract is unenforceable by one or either party if to deny enforcement would be an appropriate response to that conduct, taking into account where relevant–
(a) how seriously illegal or contrary to public policy the conduct was;
(b) whether the party seeking enforcement knew of, or intended, the conduct;
(c) how central to the contract or its performance the conduct was;
(d) how serious a sanction the denial of enforcement is for the party seeking enforcement;
(e) whether denying enforcement will further the purpose of the rule which the conduct has infringed;
(f) whether denying enforcement will act as a deterrent to conduct that is illegal or contrary to public policy;
(g) whether denying enforcement will ensure that the party seeking enforcement does not profit from the conduct;
(h) whether denying enforcement will avoid inconsistency in the law thereby maintaining the integrity of the legal system."[101v]

Lord Toulson found the Burrows list "helpful" but that he "would not attempt to lay down a prescriptive or definitive list because of the infinite variety of cases".[101w]

[101u] Burrows, *Restatement of the English Law of Contract* (2016) at pp.229–230 cited in *Patel v Mirza* [2016] UKSC 42 at [93].
[101v] Burrows notes that the final factor could be given a wider or narrower interpretation depending on the meaning attached to inconsistency: Burrows, *Restatement of the English Law of Contract* (2016) at p.230.
[101w] [2016] UKSC 42 at [107]. Lord Neuberger also considered that it was not "helpful to list all the potentially relevant factors": [2016] UKSC 42 at [173].

Lord Neuberger's view. Lord Neuberger saw the issue in *Patel v Mirza*[101x] as **16–014G**
involving:

"a claim for the return of money paid by the claimant to the defendant pursuant to a contract to carry out an illegal activity, and the illegal activity is not in the event proceeded with owing to matters beyond the control of either party."

He considered that in such a case "the general rule should ... be that the claimant is entitled to the return of the money which he has paid".[101y] He referred to this as "the Rule".[101z] The Rule should apply in appropriate cases "even where the contemplated illegal activity has been performed in part or in whole".[101aa] The Rule required a determination of what constitutes an illegal contract. Lord Neuberger considered that this would involve "a contract where the illegality would result in the court (if it could otherwise do so) not being able to award specific performance of the contract or damages for its breach",[101ab] this would obviously apply to a contract whose whole purpose or essential ingredient was the commission of a crime.[101ac] The application of the Rule was subject to possible exceptions, two of which were identified by Lord Neuberger. The first was where the criminal legislation was designed to protect one of the parties to the contract.[101ad] The second was where the defendant was "unaware of the facts which gave rise to the illegality"[101ae] particularly where "he had received money and had altered his position so that it might be oppressive to expect him to repay it".[101af] This second exception, ignorance of the facts and alteration of position, adds considerable flexibility to the illegality principle. Lord Neuberger also addressed the criticism that the Rule would come close to enforcing the contract. He conceded that this was indeed the case and that "application of the Rule would sometimes involve the court making an order whose effect in practice is similar to performance of the illegal contract".[101ag] An example, not given by Lord Neuberger, would be an illegal lending contract where the borrower had to repay the money. He considered that there was nothing to this point that the Rule could produce an outcome equivalent to performance; if a "particular outcome is correct, then the mere fact that the same outcome could have been arrived at on a wrong basis does not make it a wrong outcome".[101ah] This view was questioned by Lord Sumption. As Lord Sumption pointed out "an order for restitution would be functionally indistinguishable from an order for enforcement, as in the case of an illegal loan or a foreign exchange contract".[101ai] Citing *Boissevain v Weil*[101aj] for the principle that "if the law will not enforce an agreement it will not give the same financial relief under a different label",[101ak] he was "inclined to think that the principle is sound"[101al] but preferred not to express a concluded view.

[101x] [2016] UKSC 42 at [145].
[101y] [2016] UKSC 42 at [146].
[101z] [2016] UKSC 42 at [146].
[101aa] [2016] UKSC 42 at [167].
[101ab] [2016] UKSC 42 at [159].
[101ac] [2016] UKSC 42 at [159].
[101ad] [2016] UKSC 42 at [162].
[101ae] [2016] UKSC 42 at [162].
[101af] [2016] UKSC 42 at [162].
[101ag] [2016] UKSC 42 at [171].
[101ah] [2016] UKSC 42 at [171].
[101ai] [2016] UKSC 42 at [255].
[101aj] [1950] A.C. 327.
[101ak] [2016] UKSC 42 at [255].
[101al] [2016] UKSC 42 at [255].

16–014H   In relation to contract claims generally, Lord Neuberger favoured the approach of Lord Toulson,[101am] and although his "analysis might be slightly different" there was no difference in practice.[101an] He preferred this to the "multi-factorial" approach of Burrows as the approach of Lord Toulson was a "structured approach" and not "akin in practice to a discretion . . . ".[101ao]

[101am] [2016] UKSC 42 at [174]–[175], referring to Lord Toulson's judgment at [101].
[101an] [2016] UKSC 42 at [186]. Lord Clarke considered that Lord Neuberger "expressed some support for the approach of Lord Toulson" but he was not persuaded by his reasoning that it was appropriate: [2016] UKSC 42 at [223].
[101ao] [2016] UKSC 42 at [175].

16–014I   **The minority approach: Lord Mance.** Lord Mance, agreeing with Lord Sumption,[101ap] considered that the right of a party to recover property or money transferred under an illegal transaction was a consequence of the exercise of the right of rescission and this "right should be restored to its former significance and generalised".[101aq] The principle of rescission should not be restricted, "the logic of the principle is that the illegal transaction should be disregarded, and the parties restored to the position in which they would have been, had they never entered into it".[101ar] There should be no objection to permitting rescission after part performance "by making, where possible appropriate adjustments for benefits received . . . ".[101as] He specifically dissented from the decision of Lord Neuberger on certain points.[101at] He could not see how "an imbalance or lack of parity of delict between the parties could act as a necessary or even probable bar to rescission".[101au] More generally, Lord Mance considered that Lord Toulson and the majority had attempted to rewrite the law of illegality on the basis of the reasoning of the Canadian Supreme Court in *Hall v Hebert*[101av] which is set out in Lord Toulson's judgment.[101aw] Lord Mance was critical of such an approach as it would "introduce not only a new era but entirely novel dimensions into an issue of illegality".[101ax] Under such an approach the[101ay]:

> "Courts would be required to make a value judgment, by reference to a widely spread, mélange of ingredients, about the overall 'merits' or strengths, in a highly unspecific non-legal sense, of the prospective claims of the public interest and of each of the parties."

[101ap] [2016] UKSC 42 at [245]–[252].
[101aq] [2016] UKSC 42 at [197].
[101ar] [2016] UKSC 42 at [197]. In his opinion this principle had considerable lineage citing Mellish L.J. in *Taylor v Bowers* [1876] 1 Q.B.D. 291 at 300.
[101as] [2016] UKSC 42 at [198].
[101at] Set out at [2016] UKSC 42 at [162] and dealt with above, para.16–014E.
[101au] [2016] UKSC 42 at [198].
[101av] [1993] 2 S.C.R. 159.
[101aw] Lord Toulson also referred to the Burrows range of factors approach: [2016] UKSC 42 at [93].
[101ax] [2016] UKSC 42 at [206].
[101ay] [2016] UKSC 42 at [206].

The minority: Lord Sumption. Lord Sumption considered that as regards the enforcement of a claim founded on an illegal act the underlying principle is that for reasons of consistency the court will not give effect, at the suit of a person who committed the illegal act (or someone claiming through him), to a right derived from that act. By "consistency", citing extensively from the judgment of McLachlin J. in *Hall v Hebert*,[101az] he meant that the law should not "allow a person to profit from illegal or wrongful conduct or would permit an evasion or rebate of a penalty prescribed by the criminal laws".[101ba] The law "cannot give with one hand what it takes away with the other".[101bb]   **16–014J**

[101az] [1993] 2 S.C.R. 159 at 169 (now Chief Justice McLachlin). Also analysed by Lord Toulson at [2016] UKSC 42 at [55]–[61].
[101ba] [2016] UKSC 42 at [230] citing the judgment of McLachlin J. in *Hall v Hebert* [1993] 2 S.C.R. 159 at 169.
[101bb] *Hounga v Allen* [2014] UKSC 47, [2014] 1 W.L.R. 2889 at [55] (a dissenting judgment but not on this point) cited in *Patel v Mirza* [2016] UKSC 42 at [232].

Lord Sumption considered that the test for determining the effect of illegality was whether a party was relying on the illegality, the "reliance test".[101bc] The   **16–014K** reliance test was the "narrowest test of connection" between the illegality and the contract, all alternative tests would widen the application of the defence of illegality and render its application more uncertain.[101bd] The strength of the test was that (a) it gave "effect to the basic principle that a person may not derive a legal right from his own illegal act",[101be] (b) it established a direct causal link between the illegality and the claim and distinguished between collateral or background facts,[101bf] and (c) it ensured that the illegality principle would not be applied more widely than was needed to prevent legal rights from being derived from illegal acts.[101bg] In opting for the reliance test, Lord Sumption rejected the test that the facts relied on should be "inextricably linked" with the illegal act on the grounds that it is "far from clear what the test means".[101bh]

[101bc] *Patel v Mirza* [2016] UKSC 42 at [239].
[101bd] [2016] UKSC 42 at [239].
[101be] [2016] UKSC 42 at [239].
[101bf] [2016] UKSC 42 at [239].
[101bg] [2016] UKSC 42 at [239].
[101bh] [2016] UKSC 42 at [240].

16–014L   Lord Sumption also dealt with the "range of factors" approach[101bi] put forward by Burrows[101bj] which he considered was derived from the Law Commission Consultative Report[101bk] on illegality.[101bl] As regards the range of factors identified by the Law Commission and Professor Burrows the important issue for Lord Sumption was whether these factors are to be regarded[101bm]:

> "(i) as part of the policy rationale of a legal rule and the various exceptions to that rule, or (ii) as matters to be taken into account by a judge deciding in each case whether to apply the legal rule at all."

Lord Sumption considered that the former approach represents the law. The latter would require the courts to "weigh or balance, the adverse consequences of respectively granting or refusing relief on a case by case basis"[101bn] an approach that had been rejected in *Tinsley v Milligan*.[101bo] He considered that as the principle of illegality was based on public policy, the "operation of the principle cannot depend on the evaluation of the equities as between the parties or the proportionality of its impact upon the claimant".[101bp] The range of factors approach would largely devalue the principle of consistency because it resulted in the court making an evaluative judgment as to the weights to be attributed to the various factors.[101bq] He considered that factor (g) of the Burrows schema ("whether denying enforcement will ensure that the party seeking enforcement does not profit from his conduct") was "fundamental to the principle of consistency, and not just a factor to be weighed against others".[101br]

Lord Sumption also strongly objected to factor (a) ("how seriously illegal or contrary to public policy the conduct was") as it was "difficult to reconcile with any kind of principle the notion that there may be degrees of illegality as Professor Burrows' factor (a) seems to envisage".[101bs] Such a rule would depend "on the court's view of how illegal the illegality was or how much it matters"[101bt] and there would be "no principle whatever to guide the evaluation other than the judge's gut instinct".[101bu] The adoption of the range of factors approach would discard "any requirement for an analytical connection between the illegality and the claim"[101bv] by making it one factor in a broad evaluation of the case without offering "guidance as to what sort of connection might be relevant".[101bw]

Lord Sumption dissented from the conclusion of Lord Toulson[101bx] that the illegality principle should depend on the "policy factors involved and . . . and the circumstances of the illegal conduct".[101by] Lord Sumption considered that this was:

> " . . . far too vague and potentially far too wide to serve as the basis on which a person may be denied his legal rights. . . . it converts a legal principle into an exercise of judicial discretion, in the process exhibiting all the vices of 'complexity, uncertainty, arbitrariness and lack of transparency'."[101bz]

He considered that the remedy of restitution would not give effect to the illegal act but "return the parties to the status quo ante where they should always have been . . . This was Gloster LJ's main reason for upholding Mr Patel's right to recover the money".[101ca]

Lord Clarke gave a brief judgment agreeing with Lord Sumption's reasons[101cb] for rejecting the "range of factors" approach.[101cc]

[101bi] [2016] UKSC 42 at [259].
[101bj] Burrows, *Restatement of the Law of Contract* (2016) at pp.229–231.
[101bk] *The Illegality Defence* (LCCP 189, 2009).
[101bl] [2016] UKSC 42 at [259].
[101bm] [2016] UKSC 42 at [261].
[101bn] [2016] UKSC 42 at [261].
[101bo] [1994] 1 A.C. 340.
[101bp] [2016] UKSC 42 at [262(i)].
[101bq] [2016] UKSC 42 at [262(ii)].
[101br] [2016] UKSC 42 at [262(ii)] Lord Sumption mistakenly refers to this as factor (f).
[101bs] [2016] UKSC 42 at [262(iii)].
[101bt] [2016] UKSC 42 at [262(iii)].
[101bu] [2016] UKSC 42 at [262(iii)].
[101bv] [2016] UKSC 42 at [262(iii)].
[101bw] [2016] UKSC 42 at [262(iii)].
[101bx] [2016] UKSC 42 at [265].
[101by] Lord Toulson at [2016] UKSC 42 at [109].
[101bz] [2016] UKSC 42 at [265].
[101ca] [2016] UKSC 42 at [268]. Lord Sumption considered that a possible objection to this is that the court should not sully itself by being involved with the illegality as not being a "reputable foundation for the law of illegality": [2016] UKSC 42 at [268].
[101cb] These are set out in para.16–014K.
[101cc] [2016] UKSC 42 at [216]. See also [223] where he disagrees with Lord Neuberger in so far as the latter supports the opinion of Lord Toulson. The criticisms of the "range of factors approach" are set out above, para.16–014L.

Illegality as to formation

[Add to paragraph, at the beginning: page [1248]] **16–016**
The following paragraphs[106a] reflect "a rules based approach" to illegality as this was the basis on which the cases were decided. However, *Patel v Mirza*[106b] has adopted "a range of factors approach",[106c] although even if this had been applicable it is questionable whether the cases would have been differently decided.

[106a] Main Work, Vol.I, paras 16–016—16–027.

106b [2016] UKSC 42, [2016] 1 W.L.R. 399.
106c See above, para.16–014F.

(ii) Acts or Objects Which are Illegal by Common Law or by Statute

Other civil wrongs

16–027   [Add to paragraph, at the end: page [1257]]
Patel v Mirza[181a] does not discuss the law on when a court will find that a civil wrong would render a contract illegal. However, the range of factors approach could well produce a result similar to that in Les Laboratoires Servier v Apotex Inc.[181b]

181a [2016] UKSC 42.
181b [2012] EWCA Civ 593.

(c) Objects Injurious to Good Government

(i) Domestic Affairs

Procurement of honours

16–030   [Add to paragraph, after note 189: page [1258]]
In Parkinson v College of Ambulance Ltd[189a] the plaintiff had brought an unsuccessful action to recover money from a charity to which he had made a donation on the undertaking by the charity to secure a knighthood for the plaintiff. As Lord Toulson pointed out, where the bribe had been made to a public body such as a political party or the holder of a public office, it might be regarded "as more repugnant to the public interest that the recipient should keep it than that it should be returned".[189b] In Patel v Mirza[189c] Lord Neuberger stated that he considered that Parkinson v College of Ambulance Ltd[189d] had been "wrongly decided".

189a [1925] 2 K.B. 1.
189b [2016] UKSC 42 at [118]. See also [2016] UKSC 42 at [228].
189c [2016] UKSC 42 at [150].
189d [1925] 2 K.B. 1.

(ii) Foreign Affairs

Contract forbidden at place of performance

16–041   [Add to note 244, at the end: page [1264]]
In Eurobank Ergasias SA v Kalliroi Navigation Co Ltd [2015] EWHC 2377 (Comm) at [36] the court considered "that Ralli remains good law" despite the Convention on the Law Applicable to Contractual Obligations (Rome Convention): see Main Work, Vol.I, paras 30–017 et seq.

(f) *Contracts in Restraint of Trade*

(i) *Scope of Doctrine*

Competition Law

[Delete the last two sentences of the paragraph, after note 518 and substitute: pages **16–086**
[1291]–[1292]]
This matter is now dealt with by art.101 of the Treaty on the Functioning of the
European Union.

Injunctions

[Add to paragraph, at the end: page [1306]] **16–112**
An injunction may also be refused if there has been unreasonable delay in
seeking an order.[637a]

> [637a] *Legends Live Ltd v Harrison* [2016] EWHC 1938 (QB).

(ii) *Employer and Employee*

Employee's activities after determination of employment

[Add to paragraph, line 3, after note 646: page [1307]] **16–114**
An employer is entitled to protect the "general goodwill of the business including
potential clients",[646a] as the prospect of obtaining new clients from recommendations is an intrinsic part of a business.[646b]

> [646a] *One Step (Support) Ltd v Morris-Garner* [2016] EWCA Civ 180, [2016] I.R.L.R. 435 at
> [32].
> [646b] *Allied Dunbar (Frank Weisinger) Ltd v Weisinger* [1988] I.R.L.R. 60 at [26].

(iii) *Vendor and Purchaser of Business*

Vendor and purchaser

[Add to note 778, at the end: page [1320]] **16–126**
A failure by a solicitor to advise the purchaser of a business that the agreement
did not contain a restraint against competition has been held to constitute
negligence: see *Luffeorm Ltd v Kitsons LLP* [2015] P.N.L.R. 30 QB.

4. Enforcement of Collateral and Proprietary Rights

(a) *The Maxim Ex Turpi Causa Non Oritur Actio and Related Rules*

Ex turpi causa non oritur actio

[Add to paragraph, line 42, after " . . . which vary in different circumstances".": **16–174**
page [1346]]
The "range of factors" principle applied in *Patel v Mirza*[960a] endorses this
approach.[960b]

960a [2016] UKSC 42, [2016] 1 W.L.R. 399.
960b See above, para.16–014B.

Attribution and the law of illegality

16–175   *[In paragraph, lines 6–7, delete "Bilta (UK) Ltd v Nazir (No.2)" and substitute: page* [1346]]
Jetivia SA v Bilta (UK) Ltd (reported sub nom. *Bilta (UK) Ltd v Nazir (No.2)*)

[In paragraph, line 9, delete "Jetivia SA" and substitute: page [1346]]
Bilta (UK) Ltd

The *Stone & Rolls case*

16–179   *[In paragraph, line 11, delete "Jetivia SA" and substitute: page* [1348]]
Bilta (UK) Ltd

16–180   *[In paragraph, line 2, delete "Jetivia SA" and substitute: page* [1349]]
Bilta (UK) Ltd

[Add to paragraph, at the end: page [1349]]
The principles of attribution are not affected by the judgment in *Patel v Mirza*1001a as there will still need to be a determination of whether the wrongful act should be attributed to the company.

1001a [2016] UKSC 42. See above, paras 16–014A et seq.

(c) *Recovery of Money Paid or Transferred under Illegal Contracts*

Non-recovery of consideration

16–194   *[Delete paragraph and substitute: page* [1361]]
   Restitution of benefits under an illegal contract. The decision in *Patel v Mirza*1098 has changed the law governing the restitution of benefits conferred under a contract that is unenforceable because of illegality in a fundamental way. It would normally permit the recovery of any money or property transferred under the contract. As Lord Toulson stated1099:

> "a person who satisfied the ordinary requirements of a claim in unjust enrichment will not prima facie be debarred from recovering money paid or property transferred by reason of the fact that the consideration which has failed was an unlawful consideration".

Lord Toulson, speaking for the majority, was here applying the factors-based approach1100; but the minority also considered that restitution should be available, as explained earlier.1101

1098 [2016] UKSC 42. See above, paras 16–014B—16–014C.
1099 [2016] UKSC 42 at [116].

1100 See above, para.16–014F.
1101 See above, paras 16–014G—16–014L.

[Insert new paragraph 16–194A: page [1361]]
Quantum meruit. It seems that the restitutionary remedies available may   **16–194A**
include a quantum meruit for services rendered under the unenforceable contract.
In *Patel v Mirza*[1102] Lord Toulson pointed out that the courts in *Hounga v
Allen*[1102a] did not consider whether the claimant was "entitled to be paid for the
services she rendered on a quantum meruit". Such a claim would be independent
of the illegality and a strong argument can be made that it should be available.
Lord Sumption, citing *Hounga v Allen*[1102b] was of the opinion that "a claim for
a quantum meruit for services performed" may well have been successful.[1102c]

1102 [2016] UKSC 42 at [74].
1102a [2014] UKSC 47, [2014] 1 W.L.R. 2889. Lord Neuberger considered that there was real room
for debate that the principle was applicable: [2016] UKSC 42 at [180].
1102b [2014] UKSC 47, [2014] 1 W.L.R. 2889 at [243]. See para.16–013 for analysis of *Hounga v
Allen*.
1102c [2016] UKSC 42 at [243].

Determination of limited interests created by illegal transactions

[Add to note 1124, at the end: page [1364]]   **16–198**
See also *Davies v O'Kelly* [2015] 1 W.L.R. 2725 at [20].

[Add to paragraph, at the end: page [1365]]
In *Patel v Mirza*[1132a] Lord Neuberger considered that "it would have been
disproportionate to have refused to enforce Miss Milligan's equitable interest in
the relevant property on grounds of the illegal activity". Lord Toulson agreed, he
considered that it "would have been disproportionate to have prevented her from
enforcing her equitable interest in the property and conversely to have left Miss
Tinsley unjustly enriched".[1132b] Also, as Lord Mance pointed out as the court in
Tinsley v Milligan was reversing rather than enforcing the illegal transaction it
could therefore "take into account both the objective fact of joint contributions
and the parties' actual and by itself, legal purpose of joint ownership".[1132c]

1132a [2016] UKSC 42 at [181].
1132b [2016] UKSC 42 at [112]. See also Lord Neuberger [2016] UKSC 42 at [164], decision in
"*Tinsley,* is generally thought to be unsatisfactory", Lord Neuberger endorsed the judgment of Lord
Toulson: [2016] UKSC 42 at [181].
1132c [2016] UKSC 42 at [201].

Locus poenitentiae: presumption of advancement

[Add to note 1135, line 1, after "[2002] B.P.I.R. 1057.".: *page* [1365]]   **16–199**

"It is . . . now accepted on all sides that, if *Collier v Collier* [2002] BPIR 1057 came
before the courts today it would be decided differently": *Patel v Mirza* [2016] UKSC
42 at [221], per Lord Clarke. This was not accepted by Lord Sumption who
considered that if "*Collier v Collier* were to come before the courts today, the result
should be the same . . . ": *Patel v Mirza* [2016] UKSC 42 at [238].

Class-protecting statutes

16–202   *[In paragraph, line 1, delete* "The action for money had and received will" *and substitute: page* [1366]]
Quite apart from the decision in *Patel v Mirza*,[1142a] which opens the way in most cases for the recovery of benefits conferred under a contract that is unenforceable because of illegality,[1142b] the action for money had and received would

[1142a] [2016] UKSC 42, [2016] 1 W.L.R. 399.
[1142b] See above, para.16–194.

Oppression and fraud

16–203   *[In paragraph, line 1, delete* "A person can" *and substitute: page* [1367]]
Even before the decision in *Patel v Mirza*[1148a] a person could

[1148a] [2016] UKSC 42, [2016] 1 W.L.R. 399; see above, para.16–194.

Mistake

16–204   *[In paragraph, line 1, delete* "There is" *and substitute: page* [1368]]
Although in the light of *Patel v Mirza*[1156a] it may seldom be necessary to rely on it, there is

[1156a] [2016] UKSC 42, [2016] 1 W.L.R. 399; see above, para.16–194.

Locus poenitentiae: general

16–205—   *[Delete paragraphs 16–205—16–207 and substitute: pages* [1368]–[1371]]
16–207

16–205–   *Locus poenitentiae.* The *locus poenitentiae* principle enabled a party to resile
207   from an executory contract and recover anything paid or transferred under the contract.[1158] Lord Toulson stated in *Patel v Mirza*[1159] that it was "not necessary to discuss the question of *locus poenitentiae*" as the court was permitting the claimant to recover his consideration. He added that the principle had "only acquired importance because of the strictness of the basic rule" on the effect of illegality on the enforcement of contracts, and the fact that the courts had adopted the "wrong approach" to the effect of illegality on contracts.[1160] Lord Mance was unable to accept this as the "concept behind *locus poenitentiae* is restitutionary".[1161] Lord Sumption considered that the "notion of penitence" or "the voluntary character of the plaintiff's withdrawal" were irrelevant when dealing with the consequences of an unenforceable illegal contract as the right of restitution follows from the "legal ineffectiveness of the contract".[1162] Although the minority did not set out a definitive view on the principle of *locus poenitentiae* it is clear that money or property transferred under an illegal contract is recoverable provided such recovery is not against public policy.[1163–1178]

[1158] *Bone v Ekless* (1860) 29 L.J. Ex. 438, 440; *Palaniappa Chettiar v Arunasalam Chettiar* [1962] A.C. 294, 302–303. The right to resile was subject to a number of qualifications which need not be addressed.
[1159] [2016] UKSC 42 at [116]. See also Lord Neuberger at [193].

¹¹⁶⁰ [2016] UKSC 42 at [116].

¹¹⁶¹ [2016] UKSC 42 at [202]. He considered that "it would be desirable to avoid the moral undertones of the Latin brocard" and simply recognise the claimant's restitutionary right: [2016] UKSC 42 at [202].

¹¹⁶² [2016] UKSC 42 at [252].

^{1163–1178} See [2016] UKSC 42 at [110] where Lord Toulson considered it appropriate to refuse assistance where this would "assist the claimant in a drug trafficking operation".

6. Pleading and Practice

Pleading of illegality

[Add to note 1248, at the end: page [1379]]   **16–222**
; *AB (by his litigation friend CD) v Royal Devon & Exeter NHS Foundation Trust* [2016] EWHC 1024 (QB) at [81].

Part Six

JOINT OBLIGATIONS, THIRD PARTIES AND ASSIGNMENT

CHAPTER 18

THIRD PARTIES

2. THE COMMON LAW DOCTRINE

(a) *Parties to the Agreement*

Who are the parties?

18–004 [*Add to note 21, line 7, after* "[2015] 1 Lloyd's Rep. 216 at [68], [73]–[76];": *page* [1400]]
Navig8 Inc v South Vigour Shipping Co [2015] EWHC 32 (Comm), [2015] 1 Lloyd's Rep. 436 at [94] per Teare J. (" ... identification of the parties to a contract is a question of fact" the answer to which is generally governed by an objective test, the subjective intentions of one party are relevant only "where such intentions are communicated to the other" (*ibid.*));

Collateral contracts

18–005 [*Add new note 25a, after* "paint would last for seven years." *in line 10: page* [1401]]

[25a] Contrast *Royal Bank of Scotland Plc v McCarthy* [2015] EWHC 3626 (QB), where the argument that there was a collateral contract between one of the parties to the main contract and a

person who was not a party to the main contract was rejected for want of the requisite "assurance" (at [158]) from the former to the latter person.

Consideration in collateral contracts

[Add to note 62, at the end: page [1404]]   **18–010**
For another case (again not involving any third party) in which the claimant provided consideration for the defendant's promise giving rise to a collateral contract by entering into the main contract, see *Hughes v Pendragon Sabre Ltd* [2016] EWCA Civ 18, [2016] 1 Lloyd's Rep. 311 at [32], [35]. For this case, see also this Supplement paras 2–120, 44–020.

3. Scope

(a) *Liability in Negligence to Third parties*

Tort and contract damages contrasted

[Add to note 225, at the end: page [1427]]   **18–038**
The Scottish Law Commission's proposals for the reform and clarification of this branch of Scots law are contained in the Commission's *Review of Contract Law: Report on Third Party Rights*, Scot Law Com No.245 (2016), which contains, in its Ch.2, a summary of the present law on the subject. The Draft Contract (Third Party Rights) (Scotland) Bill appended to this Report differs significantly from the English Contracts (Rights of Third Parties) Act 1999 (discussed in Main Work, Vol.I, paras 18–090 et seq.).

4. Contracts for the Benefit of Third Parties

(a) *Effects of a Contract for the Benefit of a Third Party*

(i) *Promisee's Remedies*

Damages in respect of third party's loss: exceptions in general

[Add to note 339, line 3, after "[1987] 1 Lloyd's Rep. 465;": page [1441]]   **18–054**
the reasoning of *Obestain Inc v National Mineral Development Corp Ltd (The Sanix Ace)* [1987] 1 Lloyd's Rep. 465 was followed in *Titan Europe 2006-3 Plc v Colliers International UK Plc* [2015] EWCA Civ 1083, [2016] 1 All E.R. (Comm) 999 at [30] to enable an owner of property to recover damages in tort in respect of negligent valuation of property (in this case, choses in action) by virtue of his ownership of that property, even though that owner was not a party to the contract with the valuer.

[Add to note 339, line 10, after "[1977] C.L.J. 24.": page [1441]]
Albacruz (Cargo Owners) v Albazero (Owners) (The Albazero) [1977] A.C. 774
was distinguished in *Titan Europe 2006-3 Plc v Colliers International UK Plc*
[2015] EWCA Civ 1083 at [32] on the ground that the loss in the latter case had
been suffered by an owner in respect of property which he had retained while the
claimant in the former case had, at the relevant time, parted with the property in
question.

The "narrower ground": loss suffered by third party as transferee of the affected property

18-057   *[Add to note 356, at the end: page [1443]]*
For the distinction between *Albacruz (Cargo Owners) v Albazero (Owners) (The
Albazero)* [1977] A.C. 774 and *Titan Europe 2006-3 Plc v Colliers International
UK Plc* [2015] EWCA Civ 1083, [2016] 1 All E.R. (Comm) 999 at [32] see
above, para.18–054.

Third party having independent contractual rights against promisor

18-060   *[Add to note 379, at the end: page [1446]]*
For the distinction between *Albacruz (Cargo Owners) v Albazero (Owners) (The
Albazero)* and *Titan Europe 2006-3 Plc v Colliers International UK Plc* [2015]
EWCA Civ 1083, [2016] 1 All E.R. (Comm) 999 at [32], see above, para.18–054
note 339.

(b) *Exceptions to the Doctrine*

(ii) *Contracts (Rights of Third Parties) Act 1999*

Term purporting to confer a benefit on third party

18-093   *[Add new note 564a, after "to confer a benefit on him"" in line 3: page [1468]]*
[564a] A term may purport to confer a benefit on C even though it is also for the benefit of B. This
was held to be the position in *Cavanagh v Secretary of State for Work and Pensions* [2016] EWHC
1136 (QB), where a contract of employment contained a term by which the employer promised the
employee to make specified deductions from the employee's pay and to pay these deductions to the
employee's trade union. It was held that this term was enforceable against the employer by the union:
the term purported to confer a benefit on the union even though it could also be said to benefit the
employee.

[Add to note 565, at the beginning: page [1468]]
See *Royal Bank of Scotland Plc v McCarthy* [2015] EWHC 3626 (QB), where an
alternative ground for the decision (i.e., alternative to that stated in note 569
below) was that the fact that the third party had other remedies than enforcement
of the term in the contract between A and B indicated that A and B did not intend
the term in the contract between them to be enforceable by C (at [143]), so that
C's claim under the Contracts (Rights of Third Parties) Act failed by virtue of s.
1(2) of that Act.

[Add to note 569, at the end: page [1468]]
See also *Royal Bank of Scotland Plc v McCarthy* [2015] EWHC 3626 (QB),
where the mere fact that a benefit to the third party was an "incidental effect" (at
[137]) of the performance of the contract was held not to satisfy the requirement
set out in s.1(1)(b) of the 1999 Act. The question whether the contract purported
to confer a benefit on the third party was one of the "construction" of the contract
(at [123], [129]), and this requirement had not been satisfied. In support of this
conclusion, the Court who relied on the *Dolphin Maritime* case [2009] EWHC
716 (Comm), [2009] 2 Lloyd's Rep. 123, cited in Main Work, Vol.I, para.18–093
note 568.

Third party to be "expressly" identified

[Add to note 607, at the end: page [1473]]   **18–097**
Lord Hoffmann's description in *Attorney General of Belize v Belize Telecom Ltd*
[2009] UKPC 10, [2009] 1 W.L.R. 1988 of the process of implication as one of
"the construction of the instrument as a whole" was extensively discussed by the
Supreme Court in *Marks & Spencer Plc v BNP Paribas Security Services Trust
Co (Jersey) Ltd* [2015] UKSC 72, [2016] A.C. 742. Lord Neuberger (with whose
judgment Lord Sumption and Lord Hodge agreed) there said (at [26]) that Lord
Hoffmann's observation (quoted above) "could obscure the fact that construing
the words used and implying additional words are different processes governed
by different rules" and (at [31]) that they (i.e. those observations) should
"henceforth be treated as a characteristically inspired discussion rather than
authoritative guidance on the law of implied terms." For the same view, see also
Globe Motors Inc v TRW Varity Electric Steering Ltd [2016] EWCA Civ 396 at
[58], following the *Marks & Spencer* case. The majority view in the *Marks &
Spencer* case was not there shared by Lord Carnwath (see at 1347); while Lord
Clarke said that both processes (i.e. construction and implication) could "properly be said" to be "part of the construction of the contract in a broad sense." The
judgments in the *Marks & Spencer* case on the present point are more fully
discussed above, para.14–007. Even before that case the scope of Lord Hoffmann's views in the *Belize* case had been narrowed by judicial statements to the
effect that those views applied only to the implication of terms in fact, and not
to the implication of terms in law: see *Société Générale, London Branch v Geys*
[2012] UKSC 63, [2013] 1 A.C. 523 at [55] per Baroness Hale and *Yam Seng Ltd
v International Trade Corp Ltd* [2013] EWHC 111 (QB), [2013] 1 Lloyd's Rep.
526 at [131], [132], per Leggatt J.; for the difference between these two types of
implied terms, see Main Work, Vol.I, para.14–004.

The second group of exceptions

[Add to note 684, at the end: page [1484]]   **18–118**
In *Cavanagh v Secretary of State for Work and Pensions* [2016] EWHC 1136
(QB), see above, para.18–093 note 564a, enforcement of the term by the union
was held not to amount to enforcement of it "against the employee" within s.6(3)
of the Contracts (Rights of Third Parties) Act 1999 (see at [75]).

(iii) *Other Statutory Exceptions*

Third parties' rights against insurers

18–136   [*In note 766, delete the words from* "will be made" *in line 15 to the end and substitute: page* [1495]]
have been made by the Third Parties (Rights against Insurers) Regulations 2016 (SI 2016/570) which came into force immediately after the coming into force of the 2010 Act and of Insurance Act 2015 s.20 and Sch.2. Section 19 of the Insurance Act 2015 (which replaces s.19 of the Third Parties (Rights against Insurers) Act 2010) came into force on April 12, 2015: see s.23(3)(a) of the 2015 Act. The rest of the 2010 Act is brought into force by the Third Parties (Rights against Insurers) Act 2010 (Commencement) Order 2016 (SI 2016/550) with effect from August 1, 2016.

The Motor Insurers' Bureau

18–137   [*Add to note 771, line 6, after* "March 21, 1997"*: page* [1496]]
; Uninsured Drivers Agreement 2015 (in force August 1, 2015).

5. ENFORCEMENT AGAINST THIRD PARTIES

Third party's knowledge: the time factor

18–151   [*Add to note 845, at the end: page* [1505]]
For the defence of "justification" to the tort of inducing a breach of contract, see also *Royal Bank of Scotland Plc v McCarthy* [2015] EWHC 3626 (QB) at [107], [114], [115]. The tort claim was also rejected on the ground that there had been no "inducement" of any breach (at [105]).

ASSIGNMENT

1. ASSIGNMENT

Assignment of choses in action: at common law

19–001

[In note 1 update the reference to Tolhurst, The Assignment of Contractual Rights to: page [1509]]
2nd edn (2016).

(c) *Principles Applicable to Statutory and Equitable Assignments*

(i) *What rights are Assignable*

Rights declared to be incapable of assignment

19–044

[Add to note 159, at the end: page [1529]]
The validity of "no-assignment" clauses has been thought to be inconvenient in
the context of "factoring", where a company buys up multiple debts the precise
terms of which cannot be realistically checked. For this reason, s.1 of the Small
Business, Employment and Enterprise Act 2015 authorises regulations invalidating some "no assignment" clauses. So s.1(1) authorises provisions for the

purpose of securing that any "non-assignment of receivables term" of a relevant contract has no effect, or has no effect in relation to persons of a prescribed description, or has effect in relation to persons of a prescribed description only for such purposes as may be prescribed. By s.1(2), a "non-assignment of receivables term" of a contract is a term which prohibits or imposes a condition, or other restriction, on the assignment by a party to the contract of the right to be paid any amount under the contract or any other contract between the parties. By s.1(3), a contract is a relevant contract if it is a contract for goods, services or tangible assets which is not an excluded financial services contract and at least one of the parties has entered into it in connection with the carrying on of a business. The Secretary of State has not yet made any regulations under this power.

(iv) Assignments "subject to equities"

Assignments "subject to equities"

19–071   [Add to note 258, at the end: page [1542]]
In *Bibby Factors Northwest Ltd v HFD Ltd* [2015] EWCA Civ 1908, [2016] 1 Lloyd's Rep 517, there was a helpful application and clarification of the passage from Templeman J.'s judgment, cited in this paragraph, in *Business Computers Ltd v Anglo-African Leasing Ltd* [1977] 1 W.L.R. 578, 585. The assignor supplied goods to customers. The customers were contractually entitled to a rebate on the money owing under those contracts. The question was whether the rebate applied—that is, whether the customers were entitled to set-off the rebate—as against the assignee (who had bought the debts as a factor). The rebate arose in respect of debts owing both before and after notice of the assignment. It was held that the customers (i.e. the debtors) could set-off the rebate against the claims brought by the assignees. It did not matter whether the debts to which the rebate related were before or after the notice of assignment. This was because the rebate fell to be set-off applying the rules of equitable set-off. By those rules, there is an equitable set-off if the monetary cross-claim is so closely connected to the claim that it would be manifestly unjust to enforce payment without taking into account the cross-claim (see *Geldof Metaalcon-structie NV v Simon Carves Ltd* [2010] EWCA Civ 667, [2011] 1 Lloyd's Rep. 517). The passage from Templeman J.'s judgment in the *Business Computers* case was therefore setting out alternatives. Where equitable set-off applies, it does not matter whether the debt to which the set-off relates accrues before or after the notice of assignment because the principle being applied is that the assignment is subject to equities and the assignee cannot be in a better position than the assignor. This is distinct from the principle that the debtor cannot "take away" the rights of the assignee (referred to in the text of this paragraph), to which the timing of the accrual of the debt is relevant.

CHAPTER 20

DEATH AND BANKRUPTCY

2. BANKRUPTCY

(f) *Contracts Made After Adjudication*

After-acquired property

[Add to paragraph, after note 263: page [1579]]   **20–054**
The fact that the property does not automatically vest in the trustee allows the trustee to assess whether such vesting would be in the interests of the estate and avoids the cost of having to disclaim onerous property.[263a]

[263a] *Viscount St Davids v Lewis* [2015] EWHC 2826 (Ch) at [26].

Part Seven

PERFORMANCE AND DISCHARGE

Chapter 21

PERFORMANCE

1. In General

When notice to perform is required

21–009   [*Add to note 39, at the beginning: page* [1590]]
Edwards v Kumarasamy [2016] UKSC 40, [2016] 3 W.L.R. 310 at [29]–[38];

[*Add to note 40, at the beginning: page* [1590]]
In most of these cases the obligation of the tenant to give notice operates as an implied term of the contract, so that the implication is based on the normal principles applicable to the implication of terms, namely necessity or obviousness: *Edwards v Kumarasamy* [2016] UKSC 40, [2016] 3 W.L.R. 310 at [30], [47], [57] and [63]. See also

[*Add to paragraph, at the end: page* [1590]]
The obligation on the tenant to give notice does not normally apply to premises which are not in the possession of the tenant.[47a] However, exceptionally, the law may imply an obligation on the part of the tenant to give notice where the property is neither in the possession of the landlord nor the tenant and the tenant, but not the landlord, is in a position to know of the disrepair.[47b]

[47a] *Edwards v Kumarasamy* [2016] UKSC 40, [2016] 3 W.L.R. 310 at [42].
[47b] *Edwards v Kumarasamy* [2016] UKSC 40, [2016] 3 W.L.R. 310 at [48]–[59]. However, as a general rule, the obligation to give notice is unlikely to apply to the common parts of a block of flats let by the landlord because the landlord would ordinarily be in possession of the common parts.

2. Time of Performance

[In note 57, update reference to Treitel on The Law of Contract, to: page [1591]]
14th edn (2015), paras 18–096—18–107

3. Partial Performance of an Entire Obligation

[In note 177, update reference to Treitel on The Law of Contract to: page [1605]]
14th edn (2015), paras 17–031—17–048

Substantial performance

[In note 201, update reference to Treitel on The Law of Contract, to: page [1608]]   **21–033**
14th edn (2015), para.17–040

4. Payment

(a) *In General*

Place of payment

[Add to note 325, at the end: page [1620]]   **21–056**
The presumption that the debtor must seek out the creditor at his place of
business and pay him there is of long standing but it is readily displaced
implicitly and not just expressly; in considering whether the presumption has
been displaced the court can take account of modern ways of making commercial
payment based on its daily experience: *Canyon Offshore Ltd v GDF Suez E&P
Nederland BV* [2014] EWHC 3810 (Comm), [2015] Bus. L.R. 578 at [38].

(b) *Appropriation of Payments*

Rights to appropriate payments

[Add to note 355, at the end: page [1623]]   **21–061**
; *Lomas v Burlington Loan Management Ltd* [2015] EWHC 2269 (Ch), [2016]
B.C.C. 239 at [40].

Appropriation as between principal and interest

[Add to note 383, at the end: page [1626]]   **21–069**
; *Lomas v Burlington Loan Management Ltd* [2015] EWHC 2269 (Ch), [2016]
B.C.C. 239 at [41]; *CBRE Loan Servicing Ltd v Gemini (Eclipse 2006-3) Plc*
[2015] EWHC 2769 (Ch) at [48]. The presumption is based on what is normally

the commercially sensible course that a creditor would take, but it will be displaced if unusually the circumstances indicate otherwise: see *Smith v Law Guarantee & Trust Society Ltd* [1904] 2 Ch. 569.

5. TENDER

Actual production of the money

21–090   [*Add to note 483, at the end: page* [1637]]
; *Novoship (UK) Ltd v Mikhaylyuk* [2015] EWHC 992 (Comm) at [10]; *Marksans Pharma Ltd v Peter Beck & Partner VVW GmbH* [2015] EWHC 1608 (Comm).

CHAPTER 22

DISCHARGE BY AGREEMENT

2. RELEASE

Construction of release

[*Add to note 18, penultimate line, after* "[2015] EWHC 992 (Comm) at [14]": *page* **22–005**
[1643]]
; *Marsden v Barclays Bank Plc* [2016] EWHC 1601 (QB) at [46] (where one of
the issues before the court was whether the settlement agreement applied to a
claim in deceit and it was held that the "reference to 'all causes of action which
arise directly or indirectly . . . ' was wide enough, and was clearly intended, to
encompass an existing threat of misrepresentation claims, including those in
deceit").

[*Add to note 23, at the end: page* [1643]]
(affirmed by the Court of Appeal: *Leslie v News Group Newspapers Ltd* [2016]
EWCA Civ 79).

[*Add to note 25, at the end: page* [1644]]
(affirmed by the Court of Appeal: *Leslie v News Group Newspapers Ltd* [2016]
EWCA Civ 79).

[*Add to note 26, at the end: page* [1644]]
(affirmed by the Court of Appeal: *Leslie v News Group Newspapers Ltd* [2016]
EWCA Civ 79).

3. ACCORD AND SATISFACTION

Payment in different form, at earlier time, in different place

22–017   *[Add to paragraph, at the end: page* [1648]]
More generally, a court is likely to find the existence of consideration where the creditor receives a practical benefit over and above that derived merely from accommodating the debtor.[70a]

> [70a] *MWB Business Exchange Centres Ltd v Rock Advertising Ltd* [2016] EWCA Civ 553 (where the practical benefit obtained by the creditor landlord as a result of the re-scheduling of the tenant's payment obligations under the licence was that the tenant would continue to occupy the property and it would not be left standing empty for some time at further loss to the tenant). On this case see further above, para.4–119A. See also *Stevensdrake Ltd v Hunt* [2016] EWHC 1111 (Ch).

4. RESCISSION

Rescission by agreement

22–025   *[Add to paragraph, after note 94: page* [1650]]
It must also be distinguished from a contractual right to rescind the contract under which the party exercising the right to rescind is entitled to forfeit and keep any deposit and accrued interest, resell the property and any chattels included in the contract and claim damages.[94a]

> [94a] *Hardy v Griffiths* [2014] EWHC 3947 (Ch), [2015] 2 W.L.R. 1239 at [115].

6. WAIVER

Contracting out of waiver

22–045   *[Delete text of the paragraph and substitute: pages* [1661]–[1662]]
It is not uncommon for contracting parties to seek by a term of their contract to exclude or restrict the operation of the doctrine of waiver. Thus a contract term may provide that in no event shall any delay, neglect or forbearance in enforcing any term of the contract be or be deemed a waiver of that term. Another frequently encountered term is one which provides that the contract can only be altered if the parties go through a prescribed formality (such as a written amendment, signed by both parties). Contracting parties are free to stipulate that a particular act, such as payment of a rental instalment under an equipment lease, should not be taken to waive a right to terminate for an earlier breach.[193] But the effect of such a term is not necessarily to deprive a waiver of effect. Nor does a contract term which requires that any amendment be made in writing and signed by both parties necessarily have the effect of depriving an oral variation of the contract of validity. Such terms do not deprive the parties of their freedom to

vary, waive or otherwise depart from the terms of their original contract.[194] Freedom of contract, or party autonomy, does not only apply at the time of entry into the contract: it also applies to the variation and the unmaking or discharge of the contract.[195] The effect of a term which purports to restrict the ability of the parties to amend their contract or to deprive an apparent waiver of effect may be to cause the court to question whether the parties have in fact agreed to amend their contract or waive their rights when they have not gone through the pre-scribed formality,[196] but it does not formally alter the burden of proof, nor is it the case that the courts will require "strong evidence" before giving effect to an amendment or a variation which does not comply with the agreed formality.[196a] If the court is satisfied on the balance of probabilities that the contracting parties have agreed an oral variation of their contract or that one party has orally agreed to waive its rights under the contract, then the court should give effect to the variation or the waiver notwithstanding the existence of a term in the original contract which purports to deprive the amendment or waiver of validity.[196b]

[193] *State Securities Plc v Initial Industry Ltd* [2004] EWHC 3482 (Ch), [2004] All E.R. (D) 317.

[194] *Globe Motors Inc v TRW Lucas Varity Electric Steering Ltd* [2016] EWCA Civ 396; *MWB Business Exchange Centres Ltd v Rock Advertising Ltd* [2016] EWCA Civ 553. The consideration of the issue in *Globe Motors* is obiter because the case was decided on another ground, whereas in *MWB Business Exchange Centres* it was part of the *ratio* of the case. The point was previously the subject of apparently conflicting decisions of the Court of Appeal (contrast *United Bank Ltd v Asif* Unre-ported, February 11, 2000, in which it was held that the contract could only be altered by going through the prescribed formality, and *World Online Telecom Ltd v I-Way Ltd* [2002] EWCA Civ 413 where the Court of Appeal refused summarily to give effect to a term which provided that "no addition, amendment or modification of this Agreement shall be effective unless it is in writing and signed by or on behalf of both parties"). The relationship between these apparently conflicting decisions and their precedent value is considered by Beatson L.J. in *Globe Motors* at [110]–[114] and was followed by Kitchin L.J. in *MWB Business Exchange Centres Ltd* at [26].

[195] *Globe Motors Inc v TRW Lucas Varity Electric Steering Ltd* [2016] EWCA Civ 396 at [100] and [119] and *MWB Business Exchange Centres Ltd v Rock Advertising Ltd* [2016] EWCA Civ 553 at [34].

[196] *Globe Motors Inc v TRW Lucas Varity Electric Steering Ltd* [2016] EWCA Civ 396 at [120].

[196a] *MWB Business Exchange Centres Ltd v Rock Advertising Ltd* [2016] EWCA Civ 553 at [28] (Kitchin L.J.), following the judgment of Beatson L.J. in *Globe Motors Inc v TRW Lucas Varity Electric Steering Ltd* [2016] EWCA Civ 396 at [120] and declining to follow *Spring Finance Ltd v HS Real Co LLC* [2011] EWHC 57 (Comm) at [57] and *World Online Telecom Ltd v I-Way Ltd* [2002] EWCA Civ 413 at [33], which had adopted the "strong evidence" requirement.

[196b] *MWB Business Exchange Centres Ltd v Rock Advertising Ltd* [2016] EWCA Civ 553 at [28], following in this respect the judgment of Gloster L.J. in *Energy Venture Partners Ltd v Malabu Oil & Gas Ltd* [2013] EWHC 2118 (Comm) at [273] and Beatson L.J. in *Globe Motors Inc v TRW Lucas Varity Electric Steering Ltd* [2016] EWCA Civ 396 at [120].

Waiver of breach

[*In note 202, update reference to Treitel on The Law of Contract: page* [1663]]   **22–047**
14th edn (2015), para.18–082

[*In note 204, update reference to Treitel: page* [1663]]
Treitel on The Law of Contract, paras 18–079—18–088

7. Provision for Discharge in the Contract Itself

Relationship with right to terminate at common law

22–049   [*In note 217, line 20, after* "[2010] B.L.R. 267 at [1366]", *delete* "and": *page* [1665]]

[*Add to note 217, line 21, after* "[2014] EWHC 661 (Comm) at [49]–[54]": *page* [1665]]
; *Vinergy International (PVT) Ltd v Richmond Mercantile Ltd FZC* [2016] EWHC 525 (Comm).

CHAPTER 23

DISCHARGE BY FRUSTRATION

2. THE TEST FOR FRUSTRATION

[*In note 24, update reference to Treitel on The Law of Contract to: page* [1674]]
14th edn (2015), paras 19–114—19–123

[*In note 24, update reference to Anson's Law of Contract to: page* [1674]]
30th edn (2016), pp.509–514

Practical differences between the tests

[*In note 76, update reference to Treitel on The Law of Contract to: page* [1682]]   **23–018**
14th edn (2015), paras 19–114—19–123

3. ILLUSTRATIONS OF THE DOCTRINE

(b) *Common types of Frustrating Events*

(ii) *Cancellation of an Expected Event*

Herne Bay Steamboat Co v Hutton

23–034   [*In note 144, update reference to Treitel on The Law of Contract to: page* [1690]]
14th edn (2015), paras 19–041—19–043

(c) *Application of the Doctrine to Common Types of Contracts*

(ii) *Charterparties*

[*In note 190, update reference to Scrutton on Charterparties and Bills of Lading to: page* [1695]]
23rd edn (2015), Art.21

Examples not amounting to frustration

23–045   [*In note 206, update reference to Scrutton on Charterparties and Bills of Lading to: page* [1698]]
23rd edn (2015) at Arts 122–135

4. THE LIMITS OF FRUSTRATION

Significance of a foreseen event

23–059   [*In note 278, update reference to Treitel on The Law of Contract to: page* [1708]]
14th edn (2015), paras 19–076—19–081

[*In note 279, update reference to Treitel on The Law of Contract to: page* [1708]]
14th edn (2015), paras 19–076—19–081

[*In note 285, update reference to Treitel on The Law of Contract to: page* [1708]]
14th edn (2015), para.19–076

The Super Servant Two

23–063   [*In note 302, update reference to Treitel on The Law of Contract to: page* [1711]]
14th edn (2015), paras 19–086—19–088

Partial excuse at common law

[In note 328, update reference Treitel on The Law of Contract to: page [1714]]
14th edn (2015), paras 17–059 and 19–049—19–050

23–068

Limits of partial excuse

[In note 333, update reference Treitel on The Law of Contract to: page [1715]]
14th edn (2015), para.19–088

23–069

5. The Legal Consequences of Frustration

Breaches before discharge

[In note 364, update reference to Treitel on The Law of Contract to: page [1720]]
14th edn (2015), para.19–105

23–079

Burden of proof

[In note 383, update reference to Treitel on The Law of Contract to: page [1722]]
14th edn (2015), paras 19–098

23–082

Destruction of the end product

[In note 393, update reference to Treitel on The Law of Contract to: page [1724]]
14th edn (2015), para.19–103

23–086

Contracts excluded from the Act

[In note 415, update reference to Treitel on The Law of Contract to: page [1728]]
14th edn (2015), paras 19–111—19–113

23–096

CHAPTER 24

DISCHARGE BY BREACH

1. IN GENERAL

A middle ground

24–002   [*In note 15, update reference to Treitel on The Law of Contract to: page* [1734]] 14th edn (2015), paras 18–001—18–027

Affirmation irrevocable

24–004   [*In note 30, update reference to Treitel on The Law of Contract to: page* [1736]] 14th edn (2015), para.17–091

[*Add to note 33, at the end: page* [1736]]
In the context of an ongoing relationship such as a contract of employment it was held in *Vairea v Reed Business Information Ltd* UKEAT/0177/15/BA at [81] that an "entirely innocuous" act cannot "revive" a previous fundamental breach so that it is necessary, in order to be entitled to terminate the contract on the ground of the other party's breach, to establish that there has been a new breach entitling the innocent party to make a second election. Where there has been a series of breaches, followed by an affirmation of what would otherwise have been the "last straw" entitling the innocent party to terminate the contract, the scale does not remain loaded and ready to be tipped by adding another "straw". Rather, the scale has been emptied by the affirmation and the new "straw" lands in an empty scale (*Vairea* at [84]).

Effect of affirmation

24–010   [*In note 73, update reference to Treitel on The Law of Contract to: page* [1742]] 14th edn (2015), paras 21–011—21–015

[Add to note 74, at the end: page [1742]]
However, the Court of Appeal in *MSC Mediterranean Shipping Co SA v Cottonex Anstalt* [2016] EWCA Civ 789 at [45] did not find it necessary to invoke a duty of good faith in order to decide the outcome of the case and expressed its concern about the dangers which may follow were a general principle of good faith to be established and invoked in a case such as the present. In any event, the Court of Appeal concluded that Lord Reid's legitimate interest test was not applicable in a case where the commercial purpose of the adventure had been frustrated such that further performance had become impossible (at [42]–[43] and [61]).

[Add to paragraph, at the end: page [1743]]
Finally, it would appear that the innocent party cannot continue to hold the contract open in a case where the contractual purpose of the adventure has been frustrated such that further performance of the contract is either impossible or would be something radically different from what had been agreed by the parties at the time of entry into the contract.[79a]

[79a] *MSC Mediterranean Shipping Co SA v Cottonex Anstalt* [2016] EWCA Civ 789 at [41]–[44] and [61]–[64].

Acceptance of repudiation

[Add new note 102a, after "will be sufficiently unequivocal for this purpose" *six lines from the end: page* [1747]]   **24–013**
[102a] However, where the innocent party does nothing, in circumstances where it is not failing to perform a particular contractual obligation, a court is likely to conclude its inactivity is at best equivocal and so does not amount to an acceptance of the repudiation: *Alan Ramsay Sales & Marketing Ltd v Typhoo Tea Ltd* [2016] EWHC 486 (Comm), [2016] E.C.C. 12 at [79].

No reason or bad reason given

[Add to note 108, at the end: page [1748]]   **24–014**
In *C&S Associates UK Ltd v Enterprise Insurance Co Plc* [2015] EWHC 3757 (Comm) at [93] Males J. held that this exception applies only to anticipatory breaches or, to the extent that this is different, to situations where if the point had been taken steps could have been taken to avoid the party being in breach altogether, either by giving it an opportunity to perform its obligation in time or by enabling it to perform in some other valid way.

Both parties in breach

[In note 119, update reference to Treitel on The Law of Contract to: page [1749]]   **24–016**
14th edn (2015), para.18–094

2. RENUNCIATION

Reconciliation of the case-law

[Add to note 145, at the end: page [1753]]   **24–020**
and for a case in which it was not satisfied see *Mr H TV Ltd v ITV2 Ltd* [2015] EWHC 2840 (Comm) at [269]–[275].

3. Impossibility Created by One Party

Anticipatory breach

24–031   [*In note 187, update reference to Treitel on The Law of Contract to: page* [1759]]
14th edn (2015), para.17–077

[*In note 188, update reference to Treitel to: page* [1759]]
Treitel on The Law of Contract, paras 17–087—17–088

No anticipation of express right to terminate

24–032   [*In note 189, update reference to Treitel to: page* [1760]]
Treitel on The Law of Contract, para.17–084

4. Failure of Performance

"Frustration by breach" and frustration

24–048   [*Add to note 262, at the end: page* [1769]]
; *MSC Mediterranean Shipping Co SA v Cottonex Anstalt* [2016] EWCA Civ 789
at [25].

5. Consequences of Discharge

Obligations which survive discharge

24–050   [*Add to note 280, at the end: page* [1771]]
; *Involnert Management Inc v Aprilgrange Ltd* [2015] EWHC 2225 (Comm),
[2016] 1 All ER (Comm) 913 at [171]–[178].

Rights acquired before discharge

24–053   [*In note 297, line 2, delete* ". Contrast *Lowe v Hope* [1970] Ch. 94" *and substitute:*
page [1773]]
; *Hardy v Griffiths* [2014] EWHC 3947 (Ch), [2015] 2 W.L.R. 1239. Contrast
Lowe v Hope [1970] Ch. 94, although the latter decision has been regarded as
incorrectly decided since the decision of the Court of Appeal in *Damon Compa-
nia Naviera SA v Hapag-Lloyd International SA*: see *Hardy v Griffiths* [2014]
EWHC 3947 (Ch) at [102] and [108].

[*Add to note 298, at the end: page* [1773]]
; *Hardy v Griffiths* [2014] EWHC 3947 (Ch), [2015] 2 W.L.R. 1239.

[*Add to note 299, line 7, after* "[2014] 1 All E.R. (Comm) 593;"*: page* [1773]]
Hardy v Griffiths [2014] EWHC 3947 (Ch), [2015] 2 W.L.R. 1239.

OTHER MODES OF DISCHARGE

1. MERGER

Issues not raised previously

[*Add to note 64, at the end: page* [1784]]   **25–013**
See also *Dickinson v UK Acorn Finance Ltd* [2015] EWCA Civ 1194 at [20]
("the principles of abuse of process . . . are quite different from the somewhat
technical doctrines of cause of action estoppel and issue estoppel").

Part Eight

REMEDIES FOR BREACH OF CONTRACT

CHAPTER 26

DAMAGES

1. THE NATURE OF DAMAGES FOR BREACH OF CONTRACT

(a) *General*

Introduction

[*Add new note 7a, after* "terminated for breach" *in line 14: page* [1799]]   **26–001**
[7a] Thus a football club that has terminated a contract for improvements to its pitch before paying the price cannot recover the full price of employing a third party to carry out the work instead: *Gartell & Son v Yeovil Town Football & Athletic Club Ltd* [2016] EWCA Civ 62.

[*Add to paragraph, after note 8: page* [1799]]
Where the claimant is to be compensated for loss of an income stream, a capital sum will be awarded with an appropriate discount for accelerated receipt.[8a]

[8a] *Zodiac Maritime Agencies Ltd v Fortescue Metals Group Ltd (The Kildare)* [2010] EWHC 903 (Comm), [2011] 2 Lloyd's Rep. 360 at [73]; *Mitsui Osk Lines Ltd v Salgaocar Mining Industries Private Ltd* [2015] EWHC 565 (Comm), [2015] 2 Lloyd's Rep. 518 at [56]–[58].

[*Add new paragraph 26–006A: page* [1801]]
Abatement of price. The victim of a breach of contract who has not yet paid   **26–006A**
the other party may be entitled to rely on the fact that what he has received is

worth less than it would have been, had the contract been performed, as a ground for abatement of the price. In *Multiplex Constructions (UK) Ltd v Cleveland Bridge UK Ltd*[43a] Jackson J. reviewed a number of authorities[43b] and said[43c]:

> "Although there is not a complete harmony of approach to be discerned from this line of cases, I derive seven legal principles from the authorities cited:
>
> (i) In a contract for the provision of labour and materials, where performance has been defective, the employer is entitled at common law to maintain a defence of abatement.
>
> (ii) The measure of abatement is the amount by which the product of the contractor's endeavours has been diminished in value as a result of that defective performance.
>
> (iii) The method of assessing diminution in value will depend upon the facts and circumstances of each case.
>
> (iv) In some cases, diminution in value may be determined by comparing the current market value of that which has been constructed with the market value which it ought to have had. In other cases, diminution in value may be determined by reference to the cost of remedial works. In the latter situation, however, the cost of remedial works does not become the measure of abatement. It is merely a factor which may be used either in isolation or in conjunction with other factors for determining diminution in value.
>
> (v) The measure of abatement can never exceed the sum which would otherwise be due to the contractor as payment.
>
> (vi) Abatement is not available as a defence to a claim for payment in respect of professional services.
>
> (vii) Claims for delay, disruption or damage caused to anything other than that which the contractor has constructed cannot feature in a defence of abatement."

The fact that the innocent party has paid the price in full does not prevent a later claim for damages[43d]; nor does an abatement of the price to reflect the diminution in value of the performance preclude a later claim for other kinds of loss.[43e] Similarly, s.53 of the Sale of Goods Act 1979 provides that

> "(1) Where there is a breach of warranty by the seller, or where the buyer elects (or is compelled) to treat any breach of a condition on the part of the seller as a breach of warranty, the buyer is not by reason only of such breach of warranty entitled to reject the goods; but he may—
>
> (a) set up against the seller the breach of warranty in diminution or extinction of the price
>
> . . .
>
> (4) The fact that the buyer has set up the breach of warranty in diminution or extinction of the price does not prevent him from maintaining an action for the same breach of warranty if he has suffered further damage."[43f]

Under the Consumer Rights Act 2015 a consumer who has received goods, digital content or services that do not conform to the contract may have the right to a "price reduction".[43g] There are, however, certain cases in which there is no right to abatement of the price, in addition to contracts for professional services (as noted by Jackson J.). Claims in respect of cargo cannot be deducted from freight,[43h] and an employer has no right to make deductions from an employee's salary on account of bad work unless there is provision to that effect in the contract.[43i]

[43a] [2006] EWHC 1341 (TCC).

43b *Mondel v Steel* [1841] 8 M. & W. 858; *Davis v Hedges* [1871] L.R. 6 Q.B. 687; *H. Dakin & Co v Lee* [1916] 1 K.B. 566; *Gilbert-Ash (Northern) Ltd v Modern Engineering (Bristol) Ltd* [1974] A.C. 689; *Hutchinson v Harris* [1978] 10 B.L.R. 19; *Acsim (Southern) v Danish Contracting and Development Co* [1989] 47 B.L.R. 55; *Duquemin Ltd v Raymond Slater* [1993] 65 B.L.R. 124; *Foster Wheeler Wood Group Engineering v Chevron UK Ltd* Unreported February 29, 1996; *Mellowes Archital Ltd v Bell Projects Ltd* [1997] 87 B.L.R. 26.

43c [2006] EWHC 1341 (TCC) at [652].

43d *Davis v Hedges* [1871] L.R. 6 QB 687.

43e *Mondel v Steel* [1841] 8 M. & W. 858.

43f See Main Work, Vol.II, para.44–411.

43g See Consumer Rights Act 2015 ss.19(4)(b) and 24 (goods), ss.42(2)(b) and 44 (digital content) and ss.54(3)(b) and 56 (services); Main Work, Vol.II, para.38–483.

43h *Aries Tanker Corp v Total Transport Ltd (The Aries)* [1977] 1 W.L.R. 185 HL.

43i *Sagar v H Ridehalgh & Son Ltd* [1931] 1 Ch. 310 CA.

(g) *Difficulty in the Assessment of Damages*

Difficulty of assessment

[*Add new note 85a, line 7, after* "deprive the claimant of a remedy."*: page* [1806]]   **26–015**
85a The preceding sentences were quoted with apparent approval in *Wemyss v Karim* [2016] EWCA Civ 27 at [43].

[*Add to note 87, line 2, after* "Toulson L.J."*: page* [1807]]
See also *Wellesley Partners LLP v Withers LLP* [2015] EWCA Civ 1146 at [95]–[96].

[*Add to note 87, at the end: page* [1807]]
The principle applies where the defendant has suppressed or failed to produce evidence to which it has access, not when the evidence is simply incomplete or involves a measure of conjecture, see *Porton Capital Technology Funds v 3M UK Holdings Ltd* [2011] EWHC 2895 (Comm) at [244]; *University of Wales v London College of Business Ltd* [2016] EWHC 888 (QB) at [10].

[*Add to paragraph, at the end: page* [1807]]
When the profit-earning capacity of a business sold was less than had been warranted by the seller and there was no evidence of either the business's actual value or the value it would have had if the warranty had been met, damages were assessed by working out the ratio between the price the buyer was willing to pay and the warranted earning capacity, and then applying that to the shortfall in earning capacity.89a

89a *Wemyss v Karim* [2016] EWCA Civ 27 at [49].

3. MEASURES OF COMPENSATION

(c) *Claimant's Original Purpose Fulfilled Despite Breach*

Sale of goods cases

[*Add new note 210a, after* "purpose without any loss." *in line 5: page* [1824]]   **26–040**
210a This situation must be distinguished from the case in which the claimant has been able to mitigate its loss by subsequent action that reduced or eliminated it: see Main Work, Vol.I, para.26–095. Most of the cases cited in that paragraph concern the recovery of loss beyond the value

of the promised performance itself, but it is thought that mitigation may also reduce the claim below the difference in value between the promised performance and the performance in fact rendered. For example, if the buyer has the goods repaired so that they conform to the contract for less than the difference in value, the buyer will recover only the cost of repair not the difference in value between the goods as they should have been and as they were delivered.

Shortcomings in contracts for services

26–041   [Add to note 219, at the end: page [1826]]
But see above, para.26–040, n.210a.

[Add new paragraph 26–041A: page [1826]]

26–041A   **Landlord's failure to maintain or repair.** A slightly different approach has been taken by the Court of Appeal in a case in which a landlord had failed to repair premises that had been flooded.[219a] The Court held that the loss consists in the impairment to the rights of amenity afforded to the lessee by the lease; discomfort, inconvenience and distress (and even the deterioration of the health of a loved one) are only symptoms. Therefore the lessee may claim for loss of amenity even though for reasons unconnected with the disrepair itself he may have chosen not to make full use, or even any use, of them during part or all of the relevant period. But the non-use of the premises may be seen as a form of mitigation of loss, and non-use of the premises for other reasons may also be taken into account, so that the lessee will not necessarily recover the full market rental for the period of disrepair. If the lessee has to rent other premises, then the cost of doing so may be the best measure of his loss and may be recoverable even if it exceeds the market rental value of the original property[219b]; conversely,

" . . . the court is entitled and, I would say, obliged to temper the rigour of those rules which seek to implement the compensatory principle which lies at the heart of the law of damages, where particular circumstances make it just to do so".[219c]

The cases on goods and services cited in the previous paragraphs[219d] were not cited. It is not obvious why a buyer of goods or services should recover the difference between the value of the goods or services that should have been provided and the value of what was provided, but a lessee who has been deprived of the use of the property because of a failure to repair will not recover the full market rental irrespective of whether he would have used the property.

[219a] *Moorjani v Durban Estates Ltd* [2015] EWCA Civ 1252, [2016] H.L.R. 6.

[219b] [2015] EWCA Civ 1252 at [35]–[39] (Briggs L.J., with whom the other members of the court agreed).

[219c] [2015] EWCA Civ 1252 at [40]. Briggs L.J. relied in particular on *Earle v Charalambous* [2006] EWCA Civ 1090, [2007] H.L.R. 8, in which the lessee had gone to live with his parents and the Court of Appeal limited his damages to 50 per cent of the notional market rent for the period: see [2015] EWCA Civ 1252 at [37].

[219d] See Main Work, Vol.I, paras 26–040—26–041.

The "performance interest"

26–042   [Add new note 219e, after "benefit a third person" in line 7: page [1826]]

[219e] Thus a party who has been deprived by the defendant's breach of the chance to earn freight suffers a substantial loss even if the first party would have directed the money to be paid to a

third party who was not the first party's agent nor bound to account for it: *Glory Wealth Shipping Pte Ltd v Flame SA* [2016] EWHC 293 (Comm), [2016] 1 Lloyd's Rep. 571.

4. Measures that are not Strictly Compensatory

(c) *Depriving the Defendant of Part of his Profit*

Hypothetical bargain damages on the *Wrotham Park* basis

[Add to note 276, at the end: page [1832]]   **26–051**
See also *One Step (Support) Ltd v Morris-Garner* [2016] EWCA Civ 180 at [81].

Breach of contract cases

[Add to paragraph, after note 290: page [1833]]   **26–053**
In cases of a breach of non-competition clauses in a sale of a business, a fourth factor is whether it is doubtful that interim relief could be obtained.[290a]

[290a] Longmore L.J. in *One Step (Support) Ltd v Morris-Garner* [2016] EWCA Civ 180 at [151] (defendant's furtive conduct deprived claimant of opportunity to obtain interim relief).

[In note 291, update reference to One Step (Support) Ltd v Morris-Garner to: page [1834]]
[2016] EWCA Civ 180 at [126] and [149].

[In paragraph, after note 294, delete "However, it" *and substitute; page* [1834]]
However, in *One Step (Support) Ltd v Morris-Garner* the Court of Appeal declined to follow this dictum and held that *Wrotham Park* damages may be awarded when it will be very difficult to prove the loss that has been caused by the breach; the question is whether an award would be a just response.[294a] It

[294a] [2016] EWCA Civ 180 at [122] and [145]–[146].

[Add to paragraph, after note 295: page [1834]]
; or possibly if the real loss would be suffered by a third party.[295a]

[295a] cf. *ParkingEye Ltd v Beavis* [2015] UKSC 67, [2015] 3 W.L.R. 1373, below, paras 26–195 et seq.

5. Causation and Contributory Negligence

(a) *Causation*

Duty to prevent third party's act

[In note 342, update reference to Treitel on The Law of Contract to: page [1840]]   **26–062**
14th edn (2015), para.20–097

[*In note 344, update reference to Treitel on The Law of Contract to: page* [1840]]
14th edn (2015), para.20–097

The claimant's lost opportunities: hypothetical consequences

26–069   [*Add new note 364a, after* "deficient in some other way." *in line 7: page* [1843]]
    [364a] Where the defendant's negligence has allegedly led to the claimant losing an opportunity to pursue a claim in litigation or in commercial negotiation, the defendant may bear an evidential burden to prove that there is no causal link between the negligence and the loss: see *Mount v Barker Austin* [1998] P.N.L.R. 493, 510, applied in *Harding Homes (East Street) Ltd v Bircham Dyson Bell* [2015] EWHC 3329 (Ch) at [34]. Where there are multiple contingencies that are not independent, the court should make an overall assessment rather than simply multiplying the percentage chances of each one: *Tom Hoskins Plc v EMW Law* [2010] EWHC 479 (Ch), [2010] E.C.C. 20 at [133]–[134]; *Harding Homes (East Street) Ltd v Bircham Dyson Bell* [2015] EWHC 3329 (Ch) at [42].

A hypothetical action of a third party

26–071   [*Add to note 369, line 5, after* "out of court settlement)": *page* [1844]]
    ; *Wellesley Partners LLP v Withers LLP* [2015] EWCA Civ 1146 (distinguishing, at [96]–[98], the different exercise of assessing or quantifying the loss once the loss of chance has been established; on assessment, see Main Work, Vol.I, para.26–015); *Commodities Research Unit International (Holdings) Ltd v King and Wood Mallesons LLP* [2016] EWHC 727 (QB).

Contingency has occurred at time of trial

26–074   [*Add to note 378, line 8, after* "at [35]–[38]": *page* [1845]]
    (but for a contrary suggestion, see *OMV Petrom SA v Glencore International AG* [2016] EWCA Civ 778 at [56])

6. MITIGATION OF DAMAGE

(a) *The Principles of Mitigation*

"Reasonable steps"

26–082   [*Add to note 411, at the end: page* [1851]]
    Nonetheless it requires an objective analysis that may involve more than just fact-finding, so an appellate court may interfere if the trier of fact has clearly gone wrong: *LSREF III Wight Ltd v Gateley LLP* [2016] EWCA Civ 359, [2016] P.N.L.R. 21 at [39].

    [*Add to note 412, at the end: page* [1851]]
    The claimant may have to take an obvious step even if it is not part of its ordinary business: *LSREF III Wight Ltd v Gateley LLP* [2016] EWCA Civ 359, [2016] P.N.L.R. 21 (lender on security of lease should have pursued lessor's offer to remove clause providing for forfeiture on lessee-borrower's insolvency).

(c) *Timing of Mitigation and the Assessment of Damages*

The time for mitigating action

[*In note 445, update reference to Treitel to: page* [1855]]   **26–087**
Peel (ed.), *Treitel on The Law of Contract*, 14th edn (2015), para.20–072

(e) *Savings to be Taken into Account*

Loss which is avoided cannot be recovered

[*In note 493, delete last sentence and substitute: page* [1861]]   **26–095**
The authorities were analysed and helpfully summarised by Popplewell J. in
Fulton Shipping Inc of Panama v Globalia Business Travel SAU [2014] EWHC
1547 (Comm), but the Court of Appeal ([2015] EWCA Civ 1299) did not accept
his summary in full: see below, para.26–099.

Benefits independent of mitigation

[*Add to paragraph, at the end: page* [1864]]   **26–099**
In the *Fulton Shipping* case the owners of a vessel that the time-charterer had, in
breach of contract, re-delivered early could find no alternative employment for
her and sold her for some US $23m, whereas by the end of the charter (after the
financial crisis of 2007–08) she would have been worth only US $7m. The
arbitrator had held that the price obtained on resale should be taken into account.
Popplewell J. held that the owner's decision to sell the vessel was independent
of the breach and should not be taken into account. The Court of Appeal,
however, allowed the charterer's appeal. Longmore L.J. said:

> " . . . if a claimant adopts by way of mitigation a measure which arises out of the
> consequences of the breach and is in the ordinary course of business and such
> measure benefits the claimant, that benefit is normally to be brought into account in
> assessing the claimant's loss unless the measure is wholly independent of the
> relationship of the claimant and the defendant. That should be a principle sufficient
> to guide the decision of the fact-finder in any particular case."[512a]

Where there is an available market, the innocent party is expected to make use
of it, and any further profit as well as any further losses will normally be
irrelevant.[512b] Conversely, where there is no market but the claimant is able to
make spot contracts that reduce the loss, these should be taken into account; and
where there are no such opportunities and the owner decides to sell the vessel, the
resale price should equally be taken into account.[512c] Longmore L.J. accepted
Popplewell J's principle (8),[512d] but principle (6) was criticised as over-elaborate;
the arbitrator had correctly asked himself whether the breach was the effective
cause of the benefit.[512e] The fact that the owner's might have sold the vessel

during the charter period, irrespective of the breach, which seemed to have influenced the judge's decision,[512f] was "something of a side-issue": the central question was whether the breach caused the sale.[512g] Fairness and justice (principle (11)) are relevant but "hardly a principle of law which must be followed in all cases".[512h] The Court re-emphasised the fundamental principle that a claimant who sustains loss is, so far as money can do it, to be placed in the same situation as if the contract had been performed.[512i]

[512a] at [23]. For the application of a similar principle in a case of a solicitor's negligence in failing to discover a restriction on use of property the client was buying, where subsequently the client was able to get the restriction lifted at minimal cost, see *Bacciottini v Gotelee & Goldsmith* [2016] EWCA Civ 170, [2016] 4 W.L.R. 98.

[512b] at [24] and [49].

[512c] at [30] and [50].

[512d] at [37].

[512e] at [38] and see Christopher Clarke L.J. at [46]–[48].

[512f] See at [32].

[512g] at [35].

[512h] at [39].

[512i] at [39], referring to *Robinson v Harman* (1848) 1 Exch. 850, 855 see Main Work, Vol.I, para.26–001. Longmore L.J. answered the question whether benefits resulting from the resale should be taken into account as: "Yes, provided the acquisition of the benefit arose out of the consequences of the breach in the ordinary course of business and by way of mitigation of the claimant's loss" (at [43]). This should not be taken to mean that the resale cannot be taken into account unless it was required by way of mitigation; that would be inconsistent with *British Westinghouse* decision, [1912] A.C. 673, 689, see Main Work, Vol.I, para.26–095; and *Bacciottini v Gotelee & Goldsmith* [2016] EWCA Civ 170, [2016] 4 W.L.R. 98 at 60.

(g) *Choosing between Remedies*

"Legitimate interest" in performing

26–106   *[Add to note 545, at the end: page* [1868]*]*
Strictly speaking the point did not arise in *MSC Mediterranean Shipping Co SA v Cottonex Anstalt* [2016] EWCA Civ 789 (see below, n.547), but the Court of Appeal clearly accepted the "legitimate interest" qualification as part of the law.

[Add to paragraph, line 12, after "accepted this qualification,": page [1868]*]*
it has been referred to by the Supreme Court with apparent approval,[545a]

[545a] *Cavendish Square Holding BV v Makdessi* and *ParkingEye Ltd v Beavis* [2015] UKSC 67, [2015] 3 W.L.R. 1373 at [29].

[Add to note 547, at the end: page [1869]*]*
The Court of Appeal in that case ([2016] EWCA Civ 789) held that the issue did not arise because it was impossible to continue to perform the contract, as the contractual adventure had been frustrated (at [41]) but agreed that had it been open to the carrier to affirm the contract, the carrier would have had no legitimate interest in continuing to insist on performance by the shipper (at [43]).

7. Remoteness of Damage and Assumption of Responsibility

(b) *Remoteness*

The type or kind of loss

[Add to note 582, line 4, after "[1996] 4 All E.R. 119, 126": page [1874]]   **26–116**
; *Transfield Shipping Inc v Mercator Shipping Inc (The Achilleas)* [2008] UKHL
48, [2009] 1 A.C. 61 at [21]; *Wellesley Partners LLP v Withers LLP* [2015]
EWCA Civ 1146 at [74].

The degree of probability

[In note 608, delete from "The difference between the rules" *in line 1 to the end:*   **26–118**
page [1877]]

[Add new paragraph 26–118A: page [1877]]
Concurrent liability. The difference between the remoteness rule in contract   **26–118A**
and the remoteness rule in tort has given rise to difficulty in cases of concurrent
liability.

> "Damage may be of a kind which is reasonably foreseeable (and therefore recover-
> able in tort) yet highly unusual or unlikely (and therefore irrecoverable in con-
> tract).[608a]

In *Parsons (Livestock) Ltd v Uttley, Ingham & Co Ltd*[608b] Lord Denning M.R.
said that in the test for remoteness of damage in contract there is a distinction
between loss of profit (or only economic loss) cases, and physical damage (or
expense) cases[608c]; but this distinction was not accepted by the other members of
the Court of Appeal,[608d] and seemed to lack supporting authority. However, no
clear answer emerged from the other judgments. Academic writers suggested that
where a claimant was in previous communication with the defendant, the contract rule should apply.[608e] The question has recently been subject to apparently
conflicting decisions of the Court of Appeal.[608f] In *Yapp v Foreign and Commonwealth Office*,[608g] an employment case, Underhill L.J., with whom the other
members of the court agreed, held that whether psychiatric injury was too remote
a consequence of a breach of the employer's duty of care was to be determined
by the test applicable in tort.[608h] But in *Wellesley Partners LLP v Withers LLP*[608i]
(in which *Yapp's* case was not cited) the Court accepted the academic arguments
and held that in cases of concurrent liability the contract rule should apply.[608j]
The members of the Court saw this as consistent with the decisions of the House
of Lords in the *SAAMCo* case[608k] and *The Achilleas*[608l] that the extent of liability
should be determined by the scope of the defendant's duty and what responsibility the defendant could reasonably be taken to have assumed.[608m] It may be
necessary[608n] to distinguish the *Wellesley* case and the *Yapp* case on the ground
that *Yapp's* case was concerned with a breach of the common law duty of care[608o]
leading to psychiatric injury, whereas the *Wellesley* case involved economic loss,
which requires an assumption of responsibility[608p]; indeed Floyd L.J's view was
that "the test for recoverability of damage for economic loss should be the same,

and should be the contractual one",[608q] while Roth J. referred to tort cases in which liability was based on a voluntary assumption of responsibility and Longmore L.J. to the liability of solicitors for failing to carry out their instructions—both thus seeming to refer also to economic losses for which the defendant had assumed responsibility.

[608a] Floyd L.J. in *Wellesley Partners LLP v Withers LLP* [2015] EWCA Civ 1146 at [86].
[608b] [1978] Q.B. 791.
[608c] See at 804–805 (Orr L.J.) and at 805–806 (Scarman L.J.).
[608d] See at 804–805 (Orr L.J.) and at 805–806 (Scarman L.J.).
[608e] See A Burrows, "Limitations on Compensation" in Burrows and Peel, *Commercial Remedies* (2003), pp.27, 35; *McGregor on Damages*, 19th edn (2014), para.22–009; Peel (ed.), *Treitel on The Law of Contract*, 14th edn (2015), para.20–112.
[608f] See also above, para.1–195A.
[608g] [2014] EWCA Civ 1512.
[608h] See [2014] EWCA Civ 1512 at [119]. Underhill L.J.'s propositions are summarised in Main Work, Vol.I, para.26–147.
[608i] [2015] EWCA Civ 1146, [2016] 2 W.L.R. 1351.
[608j] See [2015] EWCA Civ 1146 at [80], [157] and [186].
[608k] *South Australia Asset Management Corp v York Montague Ltd* [1997] A.C. 191 (see Main Work, Vol.I, para.26–168).
[608l] *Transfield Shipping Inc v Mercator Shipping Inc (The Achilleas)* [2008] UKHL 48, [2009] 1 A.C. 61. See Main Work, Vol.I, paras 26–126 et seq.
[608m] See [2015] EWCA Civ 1146 at [74], [152]–[157] and [182]–[187]
[608n] While in *Yapp's* case the claim for psychiatric injury failed even on the wider tort test and in *Wellesley* the claim for loss of profit succeeded even on the narrower contract test, in each case the applicable test was discussed at length and the discussion cannot be treated as obiter.
[608o] Underhill L.J. specifically noted that he was not following the approach taken by the academics, remarking that "as regards the common law duty of care owed to employees the position seems to be the opposite" see note 8 to [119] of the judgment.
[608p] See above, para.1–195A.
[608q] [2015] EWCA Civ 1146 at [80].

Loss of a kind that is "not unusual"

26–121   [*In note 617, update reference to Treitel on The Law of Contract to: page* [1878]]
14th edn (2015), para.20–106

(c) *Assumption of Responsibility*

Assumption of responsibility

26–126   [*In note 635, update reference to Treitel on The Law of Contract 13th edn (2011) to: page* [1881]]
14th edn (2015), paras 20–098 and 20–106

The Achilleas

26–128   [*Add new note 666a, at the end of paragraph: page* [1885]]
[666a] An award of damages for loss beyond the end date of the broken charter was upheld in *Louis Dreyfus Commodities Suisse SA v MT Maritime Management BV (The MTM Hong Kong)* [2015] EWHC 2505 (Comm). It appears that no argument on assumption of responsibility had been put to the arbitrators: at [72].

8. Particular Restrictions on Recovery of Damages

(a) *Non-pecuniary Losses*

Inconvenience and discomfort

[*Add to paragraph, at the end: page* [1894]]   **26–142**
; and the Court of Appeal has held that distress and inconvenience caused by
disrepair are not freestanding heads of claim, but are symptomatic of interference
with the lessee's enjoyment of the premises.[730a] It follows that care should be
taken to ensure that any award for distress and inconvenience does not overlap
with an award of loss of the market rental value of the property.[730b]

[730a] *Earle v Charalambous* [2006] EWCA Civ 1090, [2007] H.L.R. 8 at [32], applied in *Moorjani
v Durban Estates Ltd* [2015] EWCA Civ 1252, [2016] H.L.R. 6 at [31].
[730b] See *Wallace v Manchester City Council* (1998) 30 H.L.R. 1111, 1121. On recovery of the
market rental value see above, para.26–041A.

Employment cases

[*Add new note 748a, after* "must have been foreseeable)." *in line 12: page* [1896]]   **26–147**
[748a] But contrast above, para.26–118A.

Loss of reputation

[*Add to note 757, at the end: page* [1897]]   **26–148**
On when a specific award of stigma damages may be necessary, see *Abbey
National Plc v Chagger* [2009] EWCA Civ 1202, [2010] I.C.R. 397 at
[97]–[99].

9. Illustrations of the Assessment of Damages

(b) *Sale of Goods*

Delay in delivery

[*In note 800, update reference to Treitel on The Law of Contract to: page* [1902]]   **26–158**
14th edn (2015), para.20–049

Delivery of defective goods

[*In note 809, update reference to Treitel on The Law of Contract to: page* [1903]]   **26–159**
14th edn (2015), para.20–051

[*Add to note 809, at the end: page* [1903]]
In *OMV Petrom SA v Glencore International AG* [2016] EWCA Civ 778
Christopher Clarke L.J. seemed to think that the *Bence Graphics* case could not
stand with *Slater v Hoyle Smith Ltd*, but left the matter open (at [45]–[46]).

(d) *Contracts Concerning Land*

Valuer-surveyor's report to a lender

26–168   [*Add to note 852, at the end: page* [1908]]
Although the lender may suffer a form of loss when it makes the loan, it will
normally be appropriate to calculate the lender's loss at the date of trial when the
amount of loss may have crystallised: *Nykredit* case [1997] 1 W.L.R. 1627, 1633;
LSREF III Wight Ltd v Gateley LLP [2016] EWCA Civ 359, [2016] P.N.L.R. 21
at [33].

10. LIQUIDATED DAMAGES, DEPOSITS AND FORFEITURE OF SUMS PAID

26–178 to   [*Delete paragraphs 26–178 to 26–216 and substitute: pages* [1912]–[1941]]
26–216

(a) *Liquidated Damages or Penalty*

26–178   **Introduction.** Where the parties to a contract agree that, in the event of a
breach, the contract-breaker shall pay to the other a specified sum of money, the
sum fixed may be classified by the courts either as a penalty (which is irrecoverable) or as liquidated damages (which are recoverable).[891] The law on this
topic has been fundamentally re-written by the decision of the Supreme Court in
the cases (heard together) of *Cavendish Square Holding BV v Makdessi* and
ParkingEye Ltd v Beavis.[892] A clause is enforceable if it meets the traditional test
that it does not extravagantly exceed a genuine attempt to estimate in advance the
loss which the claimant would be likely to suffer from a breach of the obligation
in question,[893] but the true test is whether the party to whom the sum is payable
had a legitimate interest in ensuring performance by the other party and the sum
payable in the event of breach is not extravagant or unconscionable in comparison to that interest. This supersedes a number of decisions suggesting that a
clause which provides for an additional payment to be made by a party who is in
breach of the contract may also be enforceable, even if it was not strictly
speaking a pre-estimate of the likely loss, if it was "commercially justifiable,
provided always that its dominant purpose was not to deter the other party from
breach".[894]

[891] A valid agreed damages clause is probably not subject to the Unfair Contract Terms Act 1977
(see Main Work, Vol.I, paras 15–062 et seq.), even if it is set at a figure below the likely loss, see
below, para.26–180. cf. however, the Unfair Terms in Consumer Contracts Regulations 1999 and
Consumer Rights Act 2015 (below, para.26–180).
[892] [2015] UKSC 67, [2015] 3 W.L.R. 1373, noted by Conte (2016) 132 L.Q.R. 382 and Morgan
[2016] C.L.J. 11. In what follows the decisions will frequently be referred to as "*Cavendish Square*"
and "*ParkingEye*".
[893] See the test laid down by Lord Dunedin in *Dunlop Pneumatic Tyre Co Ltd v New Garage &
Motor Co Ltd* [1915] A.C. 79, below, para.26–182. It is presumed that a party has a legitimate interest
in recovering its likely loss: *Cavendish Square* [2015] UKSC 67 at [32]. cf. a performance bond,
which is *not* an estimate of the damage which might be caused by a breach of contract: *Cargill*

International SA v Bangladesh Sugar & Food Industries Corp [1996] 4 All E.R. 563; *Comdel Commodities Ltd v Siporex Trade SA* [1997] 1 Lloyd's Rep. 424 CA.

[894] *Lordsvale Finance Plc v Bank of Zambia* [1996] Q.B. 752, 762–764; *United International Pictures v Cine Bes Filmcilik ve Yapimcilik AS* [2003] EWCA Civ 1669 at [15]; *Euro London Appointments Ltd v Claessens International Ltd* [2006] EWCA Civ 385, [2006] 2 Lloyd's Rep. 436 at [30]; *General Trading Co (Holdings) Ltd v Richmond Corp Ltd* [2008] EWHC 1479 (Comm), [2008] 2 Lloyd's Rep. 475; *Makdessi v Cavendish Square Holdings BV* [2013] EWCA Civ 1539. See further below, paras 26–193—26–194.

Effect of distinction. If the clause is not void as a penalty, it is enforceable   **26–178A** irrespective of the loss actually suffered, whether the actual loss is less or greater.[895] Courts of equity held that if the sum fixed was unenforceable as a penalty to ensure that the promise was not broken, the promisee should nevertheless receive by way of damages the sum which would compensate him for his actual loss.[896] The Court of Appeal has held that the strict legal position is that the innocent party can sue on the penal clause, but "it will not be enforced . . . beyond the sum which represents [his] actual loss".[897] Where there is provision for liquidated damages, the claimant may nevertheless, in appropriate cases, elect to ask for an injunction instead of enforcing the liquidated damages.[898]

[895] *Clydebank Engineering & Shipbuilding Co Ltd v Don Jose Ramos Yzquierdo y Castaneda* [1905] A.C. 6. This rule does not apply to deposits, though at least a deposit that it is larger than the customary amount may be a penalty: see below, paras 26–216Q and 26–216R.

[896] Story, *Equitable Jurisprudence*, para.1316. The assessment of damages is according to common law; there is no equitable rule on damages where a clause has been held to be penal: *AMEV-UDC Finance Ltd v Austin* (1986) 60 A.L.J.R. 741.

[897] *Jobson v Johnson* [1989] 1 W.L.R. 1026, 1040 (see also at 1038, 1039–1042, 1049). (cf. however, the dictum in *Scandinavian Trading Tanker Co AB v Flota Petrolera Ecuatoriana (The Scaptrade)* [1983] 2 A.C. 694, 702). ("The classic form of relief against such a penalty clause has been to refuse to give effect to it, but to award the common law measure of damages for the breach of the primary obligation instead.") In *Cavendish Square Holding BV v Makdessi* and *ParkingEye Ltd v Beavis* [2015] UKSC 67, [2015] 3 W.L.R. 1373 *Jobson v Johnson* was disapproved on other grounds, see below, para.26–216K. On whether the claimant may recover more than was provided for by the invalid penalty clause, see below, para.26–216L.

[898] See the cases cited in Main Work, Vol.I, para.26–007 n.48. Agreed damages clauses do not bar the remedy of rejection of the goods: *Benjamin's Sale of Goods*, 8th edn (2010), para.13–036.

Purpose of liquidated damage clauses. The purpose[899] of the parties in fixing   **26–179** a sum is to facilitate recovery of damages without the difficulty and expense of proving actual damage[900]; or to avoid the risk of under-compensation, where the rules on remoteness of damage might not cover consequential, indirect or idiosyncratic loss[901]; or to give the promisee an assurance that he may safely rely on the fulfilment of the promise[902]; or to deter a party from breaching the contract.[903] Often the parties to a contract fix a sum as liquidated damages in the event of one specific breach, and leave the claimant to sue for unliquidated damages in the ordinary way if other types of breach occur.[904]

[899] For an economic analysis of agreed damages clauses, see Goetz and Scott (1977) 77 Col. L.R. 554; Rea (1984) 13 J.Leg.Stud. 147. See also Harris, Campbell and Halson, *Remedies in Contract and Tort*, 2nd edn (2002) at Ch.9.

[900] *Clydebank Engineering & Shipbuilding Co Ltd v Don Jose Ramos Yzquierdo y Castaneda* [1905] A.C. 6, 11. Even where the consequences of a breach are precisely ascertainable after the event, a sum reserved by the contract may be intended by the parties as an agreed estimate of damage in order to avoid the expense and difficulty of assessment: *Diestal v Stevenson* [1906] 2 K.B. 345.

[901] *Robophone Facilities Ltd v Blank* [1966] 1 W.L.R. 1428, 1447–1448. See further below, para.26–186.

[902] The clause may also operate as a limitation on liability: below, para.26–180. The traditional legal test, which was restricted to expected *loss*, did not permit the promisee to justify the sum fixed as a reasonable incentive to the promisor to perform his promise, nor as a disincentive to the promisor not to commit a *deliberate* breach (see Harris, Campbell and Halson at pp.136–139); but giving an incentive to perform or deterring breach is now accepted as legitimate if the party to whom the sum must be paid has a legitimate interest is securing performance rather than relying on damages. See below, para.26–197.

[903] *Cavendish Square Holding BV v Makdessi* and *ParkingEye Ltd v Beavis* [2015] UKSC 67, [2015] 3 W.L.R. 1373.

[904] e.g. *Aktieselskabet Reidar v Arcos Ltd* [1927] 1 K.B. 352.

26–180   **"Underliquidated damages".** In practice, liquidated damages clauses frequently serve to limit one party's liability. In other words, the parties may agree that in the event of breach, the party in breach will pay a sum which is demonstrably less than a pre-estimate of the likely loss. A clause of this type is sometimes called an "underliquidated damages clause". This will not prevent it being a valid liquidated damages clause.[905] These clauses are often the basis of the insurance arrangements to be made by the parties. A clause of this type may operate as a limitation of the party's liability. For that reason it is likely to be construed in the same way as other clauses limiting liability.[906] It is possible that an underliquidated damages clause is not caught by the Unfair Contract Terms Act 1977[907] because it does not merely exclude or restrict one party's liability: the same amount is payable whether the actual loss is greater or less.[908] However, were such a clause to occur in a consumer contract, it would seem to fall within the Unfair Terms in Consumer Contract Regulations 1999 (if the contract was made before September 30, 2015 and if the term had not been individually negotiated[909]) or (if the contract was made after October 1, 2015) Pt 2 of the Consumer Rights Act 2015.[910]

[905] *Cellulose Acetate Silk Co Ltd v Widnes Foundry (1925) Ltd* [1933] A.C. 20; *Tullett Prebon Group Ltd v El-Hajjali* [2008] EWHC 1924 (QB), [2008] I.R.L.R. 760 at [83] ("a significantly smaller stipulated sum than the probable damages would be most unlikely to render a clause a penalty clause, though each case has to be decided on its own individual facts").

[906] cf. the rule that the effect of an exemption clause depends on the construction of the contract: *Suisse Atlantique Société d'Armement Maritime v NV Rotterdamsche Kolen Centrale* [1967] 1 A.C. 361; *Photo Production Ltd v Securicor Transport Ltd* [1980] A.C. 827 (see Main Work, Vol.I, paras 15–025 et seq.).

[907] See Main Work, Vol.I, paras 15–066 et seq., and in particular para.15–069.

[908] See Peel (ed.), *Treitel on The Law of Contract*, 14th edn (2015), paras 7–055 and 20–140.

[909] See Main Work, Vol.II, paras 38–201 et seq.

[910] See Main Work, Vol.II, paras 38–334 et seq.

26–181   **Similar types of clause.** In *Cavendish Square Holding BV v Makdessi*[911] a majority of the Supreme Court held that the penalty clause rules apply to provisions that would prevent a party who breaks the contract from receiving a sum to which it would otherwise be entitled,[912] and also to provisions that require a party in breach to transfer property to the other party at less than its full value.[913] The Supreme Court indicated that the penalty rules also apply to deposits[914] and forfeiture clauses[915] but not to sums that are payable on events other than a breach of contract, for example a sum that must be paid if a party exercises a right under the contract.[916]

911 [2015] UKSC 67, [2015] 3 W.L.R. 1373.
912 See below, para.26–216.
913 See below, para.26–216.
914 See below, para.26–216Q.
915 See below, paras 26–216S et seq.
916 See below, paras 26–216C et seq.

Reluctance to find clause penal. The rule against penalties has often been   **26–181A**
seen as anomalous because it applies even to clauses that were negotiated
between experienced parties of equal bargaining power.[917] In *Cavendish Square
Holding BV v Makdessi* and *ParkingEye Ltd v Beavis*[918] Lords Neuberger and
Sumption described it as "an edifice which has not weathered well".[919] The Privy
Council[920] has cited with approval[921] the view of Dickson J. in the Supreme
Court of Canada that:

> " . . . the power to strike down a penalty clause is a blatant interference with freedom
> of contract and is designed for the sole purpose of providing relief against oppression
> for the party having to pay the stipulated sum. It has no place where there is no
> oppression."[922]

Therefore, where there is no suggestion of oppression, "the court should not be
astute to decry a 'penalty clause'".[923] The:

> " . . . courts are predisposed . . . to uphold [liquidated damages clauses]. This predis-
> position is even stronger in the case of commercial contracts freely entered into
> between parties of comparable bargaining power."[924]

However, as it was put before the doctrine was modified by the *Cavendish Square*
case, the correct question is not whether one party secured the clause by the use
of unequal bargaining power or oppression, but whether or not the clause is a
genuine pre-estimate of the likely loss:

> " . . . whether a provision is to be treated as a penalty is a matter of construction to
> be resolved by asking whether at the time the contract was entered into the pre-
> dominant contractual function of the provision was to deter a party from breaking the
> contract or to compensate the innocent party for breach . . . . The question that has
> always had to be addressed is therefore whether the alleged penalty clause can pass
> muster as a genuine pre-estimate of loss."[925]

Similarly, in *Cavendish Square Holding BV v Makdessi* and *ParkingEye Ltd v
Beavis* the Supreme Court emphasised that where a party has a legitimate interest
in securing performance rather than damages, the test of validity is whether the
amount payable if the contract is broken is extravagant and unconscionable in
comparison to that interest.[926] A clause may be a penalty even though it was
freely negotiated between parties of equal bargaining power.[927]

917 For an early example see *Betts v Burch* (1859) 4 H & N 506, 509, cited by Lords Neuberger
and Sumption in *Cavendish Square Holding BV v Makdessi* and *ParkingEye Ltd v Beavis* [2015]
UKSC 67, [2015] 3 W.L.R. 1373 at [8]. See also their judgment at [33].
918 [2015] UKSC 67, [2015] 3 W.L.R. 1373.
919 The history of the rule in English law is summarised in the judgments of Lords Neuberger and
Sumption in the *Cavendish Square* case [2015] UKSC 67 at [4]–[8] and of Mason and Wilson JJ. in
the Australian case of *AMEV-UDC Finance Ltd v Austin* (1986) 162 C.L.R. 170 at [27]–[34]. See also
A. Simpson, "The Penal Bond with Conditional Defeasance" (1996) 82 L.Q.R. 392; D. Ibbetson, *A
Historical Introduction to the Law of Obligations* (1999), especially at pp.213 et seq. and 255 et seq.
Lord Hodge gives an account of the history in Scots law at [2015] UKSC 67 at [251]–[253].
920 *Philips Hong Kong Ltd v Att-Gen of Hong Kong* (1993) 61 Build. L.R. 49, 58.

[921] The view was also cited with approval in the High Court of Australia: *Esanda Finance Corp Ltd v Plessing* (1989) 166 C.L.R. 131, 140. See also Lord Neuberger and Lord Sumption's descriptions of the doubts as to the basis of the doctrine, *Cavendish Square Holding BV v Makdessi* [2015] UKSC 67 at [3].

[922] *Elsey v J.G. Collins Insurance Agencies Ltd* (1978) 83 D.L.R. (3d.) 1, 15.

[923] *Robophone Facilities Ltd v Blank* [1966] 1 W.L.R. 1428, 1447.

[924] *Alfred McAlpine Capital Projects Ltd v Tilebox Ltd* [2005] Build. L.R. 271 (TCC) at [48]. See also the *Cavendish Square* case [2015] UKSC 67 at [33].

[925] *Lordsvale Finance Plc v Bank of Zambia* [1996] Q.B. 752, 762–764, cited with approval in *Euro London Appointments Ltd v Claessens International Ltd* [2006] EWCA Civ 385, [2006] 2 Lloyd's Rep. 436 at [30].

[926] [2015] UKSC 67 at [32]. On the role of unconscionability in this context, see below, para. 26–214.

[927] *Makdessi v Cavendish Square Holdings BV* [2013] EWCA Civ 1539; [2015] UKHL 67, esp. at [257] (Lord Hodge).

26–181B   **A question of law.** The question whether a sum stipulated for in a contract is a penalty or liquidated damages is a question of law.[928]

[928] *Sainter v Ferguson* (1849) 7 C.B. 716, 727.

26–181C   **A question of construction.** In *Cavendish Square Holding BV v Makdessi* and *ParkingEye Ltd v Beavis*[929] a majority stated that whether a clause is a penalty is a question of construction. From this it follows, Lords Neuberger and Sumption said, that the test must be applied as of the date of the agreement, not when it falls to be enforced; a penalty clause is a species of agreement that is by its nature contrary to public policy. It also follows that the application of the test does not involve a discretion, and if the clause is penal it is wholly unenforceable. These points suggest that the question is one that other courts have preferred to call one of characterisation rather than of interpretation or construction.[930] However, construction in the normal sense may also be relevant. Though it is usually accepted that the words used by the parties are not determinative,[931] if the parties' intention was to compensate rather than to deter, it seems that the validity of the clause should be judged by whether it is extravagant by comparison to a "genuine pre-estimate" test, disregarding any interest that might have justified a deterrent.

[929] [2015] UKSC 67, [2015] 3 W.L.R. 1373 at [9] (Lords Neuberger and Sumption) and [243] (Lord Hodge).

[930] See the two-stage process (interpretation of the agreement to ascertain the parties' rights and obligations, followed by correct characterisation of the agreement) set out by Lord Millett in *Agnew v Inland Revenue Commissioners* [2001] UKPC 28, [2008] 2 A.C. 710 at [32].

[931] See Lord Dunedin's first proposition in *Dunlop Pneumatic Tyre Co Ltd v New Garage & Motor Co Ltd* [1915] A.C. 79, 86, quoted below, para.26–182 and n.934.

(b) *Genuine Pre-estimate of the Likely Loss*

26–182   **Genuine pre-estimate test.** What has been referred to above as the "traditional" test, which for many years was considered to have been the only test applicable,[932] was summed up by Lord Dunedin in delivering his opinion in *Dunlop Pneumatic Tyre Co Ltd v New Garage & Motor Co Ltd*[933] in the following propositions:

"(1) Though the parties to a contract who use the words 'penalty' or 'liquidated damages' may prima facie be supposed to mean what they say, yet the expression used is not conclusive. The court must find out whether the payment stipulated is in truth a penalty or liquidated damages . . . .[934]

(2) The essence of a penalty is a payment of money stipulated as *in terrorem* of the offending party; the essence of liquidated damages is a genuine pre-estimate of damage.[935]

(3) The question whether a sum stipulated is a penalty or liquidated damages is a question of construction to be decided upon the terms and inherent circumstances of each particular contract, judged of at the time of the making of the contract, not as at the time of the breach.[936]

(4) To assist this task of construction various tests have been suggested which, if applicable to the case under consideration, may prove helpful or even conclusive.[937] Such are:

(a) It will be held to be a penalty if the sum stipulated for is extravagant and unconscionable in amount in comparison with the greatest loss which could conceivably be proved to have followed from the breach.[938]

(b) It will be held to be a penalty if the breach consists only in not paying a sum of money, and the sum stipulated is a sum greater than the sum which ought to have been paid . . . .[939]

(c) There is a presumption (but no more) that it is a penalty when 'a single lump sum is made payable by way of compensation, on the occurrence of one or more or all of several events, some of which may occasion serious and others but trifling damage.'[940]

On the other hand:

(d) It is no obstacle to the sum stipulated being a genuine pre-estimate of damage, that the consequences of the breach are such as to make precise pre-estimation almost an impossibility. On the contrary, that is just the situation when it is probable that pre-estimated damage was the true bargain between the parties."[941]

In this case, dealers in tyres had agreed not to resell any tyres bought from the manufacturers to any private customers at less than the manufacturers' current list prices, not to supply them to persons whose supplies the manufacturers had decided to suspend, not to exhibit or export them without the manufacturers' consent, and to pay £5 by way of liquidated damages for every tyre sold or offered in breach of the agreement. It was held that the £5 was not a penalty and thus was recoverable as liquidated damages.

[932] In *Cavendish Square Holding BV v Makdessi* [2015] UKSC 67 at [22] Lords Neuberger and Sumption described it as having "achieved the status of a quasi-statutory code".

[933] [1915] A.C. 79, 86–88.

[934] "But no case . . . decides that the term used by the parties themselves is to be altogether disregarded, and I should say that, where the parties themselves call the sum made payable a 'penalty,' the onus lies on those who seek to show that it is to be payable as liquidated damages": *Willson v Love* [1896] 1 Q.B. 626, 630. See *Alder v Moore* [1961] 2 Q.B. 57, 65; *Robert Stewart & Sons Ltd v Carapanayoti & Co Ltd* [1962] 1 W.L.R. 34. cf. *Workers Trust & Merchant Bank Ltd v Dojap Investments Ltd* [1993] A.C. 573, 579.

[935] *Clydebank Engineering & Shipbuilding Co Ltd v Don Jose Ramos Yzquierdo y Castaneda* [1905] A.C. 6. See also *Bridge v Campbell Discount Co Ltd* [1962] A.C. 600, 622; *Photo Production Ltd v Securicor Transport Ltd* [1980] A.C. 827, 850; *Cameron-Head v Cameron & Co* (1919) S.C. 627; the *Workers Trust* case [1993] A.C. 573. It should be noted that by s.24 of the Agricultural Holdings Act 1986 "notwithstanding any provision in a contract of tenancy of an agricultural holding making the tenant liable to pay a higher rent or other liquidated damages" for breach of covenant, etc. the landlord may not recover for any such breach any sum "in excess of the damage actually suffered".

[936] *Commissioner of Public Works v Hills* [1906] A.C. 368, 376; *Webster v Bosanquet* [1912] A.C. 394. If the contract was varied in a way that will affect the likely loss, the validity of the clause should be judged by the time of the variation: *Unaoil Ltd v Leighton Offshore Pte Ltd* [2014] EWHC 2965 (Comm) at [75].

[937] *Pye v British Automobile Commercial Syndicate Ltd* [1906] 1 K.B. 425.

[938] *Clydebank Engineering & Shipbuilding Co Ltd v Don Jose Ramos Yzquierdo y Castaneda* [1905] A.C. 6, 17; *Webster v Bosanquet* [1912] A.C. 394; *Cooden Engineering Co Ltd v Stanford* [1953] 1 Q.B. 86; cf. *Bridge v Campbell Discount Co Ltd* [1962] A.C. 600 (below, para.26–216C).

[939] *Kemble v Farren* (1829) 6 Bing. 141. See also *Astley v Weldon* (1801) 2 B. & P. 346; *Wallis v Smith* (1882) 21 Ch. D. 243, 256–257. The breach may involve more than a failure to pay: *Thos. P. Gonzales Corp v F. R. Waring (International) Pty Ltd* [1986] 2 Lloyd's Rep. 160, 163. A discount for prompt payment, however, was held not make the undiscounted sum a penalty; nor was it a penalty where a loan agreement provides for a modest increase in the rate of interest, which operates only from the date of the borrower's default: *Lordsvale Finance Plc v Bank of Zambia* [1996] Q.B. 752 (a 1 per cent increase: if, however, the increase operated retrospectively, it might be a penalty. On this case see further below, paras 26–193—26–194); cf. *Jeancharm Ltd v Barnet Football Club Ltd* [2003] EWCA Civ 58, [2003] 92 Con. L.R. 26 (interest rate for late payment of 5 per cent per week held to be a penalty).

[940] *Lord Elphinstone v Monkland Iron & Coal Co Ltd* (1886) 11 App. Cas. 332, 342. See *Kemble v Farren* (1829) 6 Bing. 141, 148; *Magee v Lavell* (1874) L.R. 9 C.P. 107, 115; *Ford Motor Co v Armstrong* (1915) 31 T.L.R. 267 (see below, para.26–189); *Michel Habib Raji Ayoub v Sheikh Suleiman* [1941] 1 All E.R. 507, 510; *Cooden Engineering Co Ltd v Stanford* [1953] 1 Q.B. 86, 98; *Interoffice Telephones Ltd v Robert Freeman Co Ltd* [1958] 1 Q.B. 190, 194. The parties, in such a case, should fix separate sums for the various possible breaches: *Imperial Tobacco Co v Parslay* [1936] 2 All E.R. 515.

[941] See *Clydebank Engineering & Shipbuilding Co Ltd v Don Jose Ramos Yzquierdo y Castaneda* [1905] A.C. 6, 11; *Webster v Bosanquet* [1912] A.C. 394, 398; *English Hop Growers Ltd v Dering* [1928] 2 K.B. 174; *Imperial Tobacco Co v Parslay* [1936] 2 All E.R. 515, 519; *Philips Hong Kong Ltd v Att-Gen of Hong Kong* (1993) 61 Build. L.R. 49, 60 PC (the impact of delay by one contractor on other contracts). Some of the clauses that were justified under this category in particular, including the *Dunlop* case itself, may now be better viewed as cases of legitimate deterrence: see below, para.26–197.

26–183   The basis of the decision in the *Dunlop* case. The traditional approach treated Lord Dunedin's second proposition as an exhaustive dichotomy,[942] and had thus concentrated on whether the clause was a genuine pre-estimate of the loss that the payee was likely to suffer. A clause would be regarded as in terrorem if it provided for a greater sum, or at least an extravagantly greater sum, than the loss the payee was likely to suffer.[943] In *Cavendish Square Holding BV v Makdessi* and *ParkingEye Ltd v Beavis*[944] the Supreme Court pointed out that other judges in the *Dunlop* case had decided the case on a wider basis[945]; and as the result of the Supreme Court's decision in those cases, a clause may also be justified on the basis that the party who would benefit from it has a legitimate interest in securing performance rather than damages, and the amount payable or other consequence if the contract is broken is not extravagant and unconscionable in comparison to that interest.[946] However, as Lords Neuberger and Sumption said:

> "In the case of a straightforward damages clause, that interest will rarely extend beyond compensation for the breach, and we therefore expect that Lord Dunedin's four tests would usually be perfectly adequate to determine its validity."[947]

Thus if the party cannot demonstrate a legitimate interest in securing perform-ance rather than damages, or does not seek to do so, the clause may still be valid under the "genuine pre-estimate" test, and therefore that test is explored in more detail in this section.

942 cf. *United International Pictures v Cine Bes Filmcilik ve Yapimcilik AS* [2003] EWCA Civ 1669 at [15].
943 "That the contractual function is deterrent rather than compensatory can be deduced by comparing the amount that would be payable on breach with the loss that might be sustained if breach occurred". *Lordsvale Finance Plc v Bank of Zambia* [1996] Q.B. 752, 762, Colman J.
944 [2015] UKSC 67, [2015] 3 W.L.R. 1373.
945 See below, para.26–197.
946 See below, para.26–197.
947 [2015] UKSC 67 at [32].

An objective approach. Asking whether a clause was a genuine pre-estimate **26–184** of the loss might suggest a subjective approach, so that whether the clause is liquidated damages or a penalty depends on an assessment of what the parties thought they were agreeing on. However, there are clearly objective elements to a test which depends on whether the amount is "extravagant and unconscionable in comparison with the greatest loss"948; and it has been held that:

" . . . the test does not turn upon the genuineness or honesty of the party or parties who made the pre-estimate. The test is primarily an objective one."949

948 Lord Dunedin's proposition (4)(a) above, para.26–182.
949 *Alfred McAlpine Capital Projects Ltd v Tilebox Ltd* [2005] Build. L.R. 271 (TCC) at [48] (Jackson J.).

A substantial discrepancy. In *Murray v Leisureplay Plc*950 the Court of **26–185** Appeal emphasised that a clause will not be a penalty merely because it is not a precise pre-estimate of the loss.951 Arden L.J. said that a contractual provision does not become a penalty simply because it results in overpayment in particular circumstances: "The parties are allowed a generous margin".952

950 [2005] EWCA Civ 963, [2005] I.R.L.R. 946.
951 See also Jackson J. in *Alfred McAlpine Capital Projects Ltd v Tilebox Ltd* [2005] Build. L.R. 271 (TCC) at [48].
952 [2005] EWCA Civ 963 at [43]; see too the judgments of Clarke and Buxton L.JJ. at [105] and [114] respectively. See also *Cleeve Link Ltd v Bryla* [2014] I.R.L.R. 86 EAT.

Pre-estimate of damage. The word "damage" must mean "net loss" after **26–186** taking account of the claimant's expected ability to mitigate his loss. The comparison is to be made to the loss that the innocent party would be entitled to recover by way of damages, not to the possibly greater actual loss.953 If the clause is a genuine pre-estimate of the loss,954 there is no scope for arguing that the claimant could in fact have mitigated the loss: the purpose of the clause is to make proof of the actual loss unnecessary and irrelevant955; but the mitigation principle must be taken into account in deciding whether or not the clause was a genuine pre-estimate in the first place.956 A genuine pre-estimate may include loss that would be too remote957 unless notice of its possibility had been given to the party in breach at the time the contract was made.958 It has been suggested that a party may stipulate for liquidated damages in order to ensure it is compensated for some idiosyncratic loss that might not otherwise be recoverable, such as sentimental value attached to property.959 It must be the case that a genuine pre-estimate can include damages for loss of amenity or distress when the purpose of the contract is to provide that amenity or freedom from distress[960]; it seems unlikely that such loss be a legitimate part of a pre-estimate when the loss would not be recoverable by way of unliquidated damages,[961] but a genuine concern about such loss would presumably give rise to a legitimate interest that could be protected under the alternative basis set out in *Cavendish Square Holding BV v Makdessi* and *ParkingEye Ltd v Beavis*.[962] If, as it seems, "hypothetical bargain damages" allowing the innocent party to recover a share of the profit made by the other party through his breach of contract[963] may be recoverable in addition to other damages,[964] presumably a genuine pre-estimate of the loss may include such a figure if, at the time the contract was made, it is likely that the type of breach to which the agreed damages clause applies will lead to the party in breach making a profit from it. The claimant's chance to bargain with the defendant might constitute a legitimate interest[965] but it is probably unnecessary for the claimant to show this if the amount agreed falls within a genuine pre-estimate. On the traditional account of liquidated damages, the fact that the damage is difficult to assess with precision strengthened the presumption that a sum agreed between the parties represents a genuine attempt to estimate it and to overcome the difficulties of proof at the trial.[966] It seems that the risk of this kind of difficulty will now be treated as giving the claimant a legitimate interest in deterring breach.[967]

[953] *Lansat Shipping Co Ltd v Glencore Grain BV (The Paragon)* [2009] EWHC 551 (Comm), [2009] 1 Lloyd's Rep. 658 at [24]. See also para.26–197.

[954] Note that under the approach taken in the *Cavendish Square* and *ParkingEye* cases, a clause may be valid even if it is not a genuine pre-estimate of the loss: see below, para.26–197.

[955] *MSC Mediterranean Shipping Co SA v Cottonex Anstalt* [2015] EWHC 283 (Comm) at [70]–[71], referring to dicta in *Abrahams v Performing Rights Society Ltd* [1995] I.C.R. 1028, 1040–1041. However, in a contract in which the liquidated damages were only payable while the contract remained on foot, the innocent party was not entitled to ignore a repudiation and keep the contract alive so as to be able to continue to claim liquidated damages, as they would have no legitimate interest is doing so: at [94]–[105]. The Court of Appeal [2016] EWCA Civ 789 agreed (at [43]) though it decided the case on other grounds: see above, para.26–106.

[956] *MSC Mediterranean Shipping Co SA v Cottonex Anstalt* [2015] EWHC 283 (Comm) at [113]. If the relevant clause purported to give the innocent party an unfettered right to ignore the repudiation when it had no legitimate interest is doing so, the clause would be a penalty: [2015] EWHC 283 (Comm) at [116] (aff'd without reference to this point, [2016] EWCA Civ 789). In *Bunge SA v Nidera BV* [2015] UKSC 43 Lord Sumption said the Default Clause in a GAFTA sale contract differs from the common law paradigm in that the injured party is not required to mitigate by going into the market and buying or selling against the defaulter, but has a discretion whether to do so (at [28]). He did not discuss whether this might amount to a penalty, merely remarking that there is a difference between a clause prescribing a fixed measure of loss (such as a liquidated damages clause) and a clause providing a mechanical formula in place of the more nuanced and fact-sensitive approach of the common law (such as the GAFTA clause) (at [26]). With respect, a formula for measuring damages may also amount to a penalty if it produces results that are much greater than the damages that would be recoverable at common law: *Lombard North Central Plc v Butterworth* [1987] Q.B. 527. In contrast, Lord Toulson (with whom the other members of the Court agreed) did not think the GAFTA formula excluded the duty to mitigate (at [62]). In *Novasen SA v Alimenta SA* [2013] EWHC 345 (Comm), [2013] 1 Lloyd's Rep. 648 at [18], Popplewell J. said that the Default Clause did not constitute a penalty clause, applying his dicta in *Imam-Sadeque v Bluebay Asset Management (Services) Ltd* [2012] EWHC 3511 (QB).

[957] See Main Work, Vol.I, paras 26–107—26–134.

[958] *Robophone Facilities Ltd v Blank* [1966] 1 W.L.R. 1428, 1447–1448 (Diplock L.J.). The agreed sum may take account of loss likely to be suffered which may not fall within the normal remoteness

test: *Robert Stewart & Sons Ltd v Carapanayoti & Co Ltd* [1962] 1 W.L.R. 34, 39; *Philips Hong Kong Ltd v Att-Gen of Hong Kong* (1993) 61 Build. L.R. 49, 60–61 (the agreed sum may be justified by knowledge of "special circumstances").

[959] Goetz & Scott (1977) Columbia L.R. 554, 572–573.

[960] See Main Work, Vol.I, paras 26–144—26–146.

[961] The question whether the parties may give their own meaning to "loss" is mentioned below, para.26–192, text after n.994.

[962] [2015] UKSC 67, [2015] 3 W.L.R. 1373; see below, paras 26–196 et seq.

[963] See Main Work, Vol.I, paras 26–051—26–054.

[964] See Main Work, Vol.I, para.26–053, n.295.

[965] See below, para.26–197.

[966] *Dunlop Pneumatic Tyre Co Ltd v New Garage & Motor Co Ltd* [1915] A.C. 79; *English Hop Growers Ltd v Dering* [1928] 2 K.B. 174; *Imperial Tobacco Co v Parslay* [1936] 2 All E.R. 515; *Robophone Facilities Ltd v Blank* [1966] 1 W.L.R. 1428, 1447; *Philips Hong Kong Ltd v Att-Gen of Hong Kong* (1993) 61 Build. L.R. 49 (the loss to a governmental body caused by delay in construction was especially difficult to assess).

[967] See below, para.26–197.

Fluctuating sums. Although a valid agreed damages clause may specify a **26–187** graduated scale of sums payable according to the varying extent of the expected loss,[968] a sum which is liable to fluctuate according to extraneous circumstances will not be classified as liquidated damages.[969] In a railway construction contract it was provided that in the event of a breach by the contractor he should forfeit "as and for liquidated damages" certain percentages retained by the government of money payable for work done as a guarantee fund to answer for defective work, and also certain security money lodged with the government.[970] The Judicial Committee held that this was a penalty, since it was not a definite sum, but was:

" . . . liable to great fluctuation in amount dependent on events not connected with the fulfilment of this contract. It is obvious that the amount of retained money . . . depended entirely on the progress of those contracts, and that further, as those moneys are primarily liable to make good deficiencies in these contract works, the eventual sum available . . . could not in any way be estimated as a fixed sum."[971]

[968] See below, para.26–191, for graduated damages.

[969] *Commissioner of Public Works v Hills* [1906] A.C. 368, 376.

[970] On the question of the application of the penalty rules to this kind of clause, see below, para.26–216, esp. at n.1118m.

[971] *Commissioner of Public Works v Hills* [1906] A.C. 368, 376 (followed in *Jobson v Johnson* [1989] 1 W.L.R. 1026, 1036).

Minimum payment clause. A "minimum payment" clause in a hire-purchase **26–188** or hiring agreement that applies when the hirer is in breach of the contract by refusing to continue with it,[972] will usually be held to fail the genuine pre-estimate test if it provides for the same total sum to be payable by the hirer irrespective of how long the agreement has been in force.[973]

[972] Compare the situation where the hirer exercises an option, below, para.26–216C.

[973] *Lamdon Trust Ltd v Hurrell* [1955] 1 W.L.R. 391; *Bridge v Campbell Discount Co Ltd* [1962] A.C. 600. ("It is a sliding scale of compensation, but a scale that slides in the wrong direction": at 623.) See also *Anglo-Auto Finance Co Ltd v James* [1963] 1 W.L.R. 1042; *United Dominions Trust (Commercial) Ltd v Ennis* [1968] 1 Q.B. 54.

Single sum payable upon different breaches. The mere fact that the same **26–189** amount is made payable upon the breach of several undertakings of varying importance is by no means conclusive.[974] It may be that the amount is not disproportionate to the least important of these undertakings, and therefore represents a genuine attempt at an agreed estimate of real damage[975]; or, if the loss is hard to assess, the test seemed to be satisfied if a modest sum was used; but a clause setting a very high amount would not pass muster. Thus in *Dunlop Pneumatic Tyre Co Ltd v New Garage & Motor Co Ltd*,[976] the dealers had agreed not to resell any tyres bought from the manufacturers to any private customers at less than the manufacturers' current list prices, not to supply them to persons whose supplies the manufacturers had decided to suspend, not to exhibit or export them without the manufacturers' consent, and to pay £5 by way of liquidated damages for every tyre sold or offered in breach of the agreement. It was held that the £5 was not a penalty and thus was recoverable as liquidated damages.[977] The decision seems to fall within Lord Dunedin's last proposition:

> " . . . the damage caused by each and every one of those events, however varying in importance, may be of such an uncertain nature that it cannot be accurately ascertained"[978]

The clause may also be a genuine pre-estimate where the stipulated sum is taken as an average or mean figure of the losses probably incurred in the different events.[979] In *Ford Motor Co v Armstrong*,[980] in contrast, the retailer in a similar case agreed to pay £250 as "the agreed damage which the manufacturer will sustain" upon the breach of any one of several covenants (similar to those in the *Dunlop* case, above), and the Court of Appeal by a majority held that this (in 1915) was a penalty, since it was an arbitrary and substantial sum, and made payable for various breaches differing in kind, some of which might cause only trifling damage. The high amount of the agreed sum in this case showed that it could not be a genuine pre-estimate of loss.

---

[974] See r.4(c) in Lord Dunedin's propositions, above, para.26–182. See *Makdessi v Cavendish Square Holdings BV* [2013] EWCA Civ 1539 at [64]–[74].

[975] *Wallis v Smith* (1882) 21 Ch. D. 243; *Pye v British Automobile Commercial Syndicate Ltd* [1906] 1 K.B. 425; *Dunlop Pneumatic Tyre Co Ltd v New Garage & Motor Co Ltd* [1915] A.C. 79; *Philips Hong Kong Ltd v Att-Gen of Hong Kong* (1993) 61 Build. L.R. 49, 62–63 (Privy Council refers to: " . . . the error of assuming that, because in some hypothetical situation the loss suffered will be less than the sum quantified in accordance with the liquidated damage provision, that provision must be a penalty"). This suggests that the validity of a clause should be judged by its normal operation: Peel (ed.), *Treitel on The Law of Contract*, 14th edn (2015), para.20–131.

[976] [1915] A.C. 79.

[977] The House of Lords took the view that the £5 did not apply to the second and third obligations (not to sell to prohibited person, and not to exhibit without permission).

[978] *Dunlop Pneumatic Tyre Co Ltd v New Garage & Motor Co Ltd* [1915] A.C. 79, 95–96. See also *Galsworthy v Strutt* (1848) 1 Ex. 659, 666–667. Again, in some cases of this type the claimant may now be seen as having a legitimate interest in deterring breach, see below, para.26–197.

[979] *Dunlop Pneumatic Tyre Co Ltd v New Garage & Motor Co Ltd* [1915] A.C. 79, 99; *English Hop Growers Ltd v Dering* [1928] 2 K.B. 174, 182.

[980] (1915) 31 T.L.R. 267.

26–190   **Breach may cause varying loss.** A different case is where the sum is payable for any breach of a particular term of the contract, but the loss that follows may vary significantly from case to case. This seems to fall within Lord Dunedin's heading 4(a):

"It will be held to be penalty if the sum stipulated for is extravagant and unconscionable in amount in comparison with the greatest loss that could conceivably be proved to have followed from the breach."[981]

It is not clear that the converse proposition, that the sum will not be unconscionable if it is no more than the greatest possible loss, follows. Lord Parker said that loss caused by a breach of a non-solicitation covenant might vary according to where or not the solicitation was successful; nonetheless,

"whatever damage there is must be the same in kind for every possible breach, and the fact that it may vary in amount for each particular breach has never been held to raise any presumption or inference that the sum agreed to be paid is a penalty, at any rate in cases where the parties have referred to it as agreed or liquidated damages."[982]

That might be taken to suggest that provided the sum stipulated is not extravagant and unconscionable in relation to the greatest loss that might follow, it will not be a penalty even though the loss might well be much less and therefore the sum could not strictly be described as a genuine pre-estimate of the likely loss.[983] On occasion Lord Dunedin's statement has been applied literally,[984] and it was repeated by Lord Hodge in *Cavendish Square Holding BV v Makdessi* and *ParkingEye Ltd v Beavis*.[985] However, in the past it has been held a clause may be penal under the "genuine pre-estimate test" even though the sum does not exceed the greatest possible loss.[986] In *Bridge v Campbell Discount Co Ltd* a clause in a hire-purchase providing for a minimum payment if the hirer defaulted in paying was held to be a penalty because the loss to the finance company would differ according to how long the hirer kept the vehicle.[987] True, in that case the amount payable under the clause would also vary according to how much of the price the hirer had already paid, so that the two situations are technically distinguishable, but it is thought that the result in the *Bridge* case would have been the same if the clause had simply stated a fixed sum that the hirer must pay however much he had paid already. So it is better to treat Lord Dunedin's and Lord Parker's statements quoted above as no more than a presumption to be used when the genuine pre-estimate test is being applied[988]; and to note that when the claimant has a legitimate interest in obtaining performance rather than damages, an agreed sum that is not extravagant and unconscionable in relation to the greatest loss that might follow is likely to be treated as valid.[989]

[981] *Dunlop Pneumatic Tyre Co Ltd v New Garage & Motor Co Ltd* [1915] A.C. 79, 87.

[982] [1915] A.C. 79, 98.

[983] The cases on covenants in restraint of trade, such as *Crisdee v Bolton* (1827) 3 C. & P. 240; *Price v Green* (1847) 16 M. & W. 346, 354; *Reynolds v Bridge* (1856) 6 E. & B. 528, 541, have generally treated the sum payable for a breach as a sum stipulated for the breach of a single obligation, although it "is capable of being broken more than once, or in more ways than one": *Dunlop Pneumatic Tyre Co Ltd v New Garage & Motor Co Ltd* [1915] A.C. 79, 98 (see also at 92–93); *Law v Redditch Local Board* [1892] 1 Q.B. 127, 136.

[984] *Cleeve Link Ltd v Bryla* [2014] I.R.L.R. 86 (EAT) (clause upheld when not extravagant in relation to maximum loss, though loss would vary significantly depending on how soon breach occurred).

[985] [2015] UKSC 67, [2015] 3 W.L.R. 1373 at [255].

[986] *Makdessi v Cavendish Square Holdings BV* [2013] EWCA Civ 1539 at [73]–[74].

[987] [1962] A.C. 600. ("It is a sliding scale of compensation, but a scale that slides in the wrong direction": at 623.)

[988] See *Makdessi v Cavendish Square Holdings BV* [2013] EWCA Civ 1539 at [72], where Christopher Clarke L.J. added that "there may be some tension between" the two speeches.
[989] See further below, paras 26–196 et seq.

26–191 **Graduated damages.** In building contracts and other similar contracts the courts have upheld as liquidated damages a system of graduated sums which increase in proportion to the seriousness of the breach, e.g. so much per week for delay in performance,[990] or so much according to the number of items in question.[991] If in a building contract there is no such graduation the sum fixed is less likely to be held to be a genuine pre-estimate.[992] The sum must be graduated so that it changes in the right direction. Depreciation obviously increases over time, so a sum said to be compensation for depreciation is not a genuine pre-estimate of loss if it *decreases* over time as a hirer pays more instalments.[993]

[990] *Clydebank Engineering Co v Don Jose Ramos Yzquierdo y Castaneda* [1905] A.C. 6; *Philips Hong Kong Ltd v Att-Gen of Hong Kong* (1993) 61 Build. L.R. 49, 60 (PC); *Alfred McAlpine Capital Projects Ltd v Tilebox Ltd* [2005] Build. L.R. 271 (TCC). See also *Law v Redditch Local Board* [1892] 1 Q.B. 127; *Cellulose Acetate Silk Co Ltd v Widnes Foundry (1925) Ltd* [1933] A.C. 20 (above, para.26–180). The party entitled to the benefit of a liquidated damages clause in the event of failure to complete on time cannot take advantage of it if the delay is partly due to his own fault: *Peak Construction (Liverpool) Ltd v McKinney Foundations Ltd* (1971) 69 L.G.R. 1, 11, 16. Demurrage under a charterparty is a case of graduated liquidated damages: *President of India v Lips Maritime Corp* [1988] A.C. 395, 422–423.
[991] *Lord Elphinstone v Monkland Iron and Coal Co* (1886) 11 App. Cas. 332; *Diestal v Stevenson* [1906] 2 K.B. 345.
[992] e.g. *Commissioner of Public Works v Hills* [1906] A.C. 368 (above, para.26–188). See also *Re Newman* (1876) 4 Ch. D. 724.
[993] *Bridge v Campbell Discount Co Ltd* [1962] A.C. 600. ("It is a sliding scale of compensation, but a scale that slides in the wrong direction": at 623.) If it slides in the right direction, the clause is more likely to be held valid: *Phonographic Equipment (1958) Ltd v Muslu* [1961] 1 W.L.R. 1379. cf. *Lombank Ltd v Excell* [1964] 1 Q.B. 415.

26–192 **Damages following termination by the innocent party under an express term.** Where the hirer has neither repudiated the hiring (or hire-purchase) agreement, nor committed a "fundamental breach" of it, but the owner terminates it in the exercise of an express power to do so conferred by the agreement, the owner's damages are limited to loss suffered through any breaches up to the date of the termination.[994] This is, in effect, the measure of loss defined by law and the parties are not free to define it otherwise. A clause that provides for a larger sum to be paid, such as a "minimum payment" clause or one providing for recovery of the amount of future payments, even with deductions for any savings made,[995] will (under the genuine pre-estimate test) be void as a penalty.[996] It should be noted, however, that this principle does not apply where the contract made the broken term into a condition, any breach of which entitled the innocent party to terminate (e.g. a clause making compliance with time "of the essence"[997]). In this case the innocent party may both terminate the contract and recover damages for the loss of the bargain (viz in respect of all the outstanding obligations of the other party).[998] A clause that makes the hirer liable for a genuine pre-estimate of the owners' full loss in such a case will be valid.

[994] *Financings Ltd v Baldock* [1963] 2 Q.B. 104. The principle stated in the text has been regularly followed by the Court of Appeal: *Brady v St Margaret's Trust Ltd* [1963] 2 Q.B. 494; *Charterhouse Credit Co Ltd v Tolly* [1963] 2 Q.B. 683; *United Dominions Trust (Commercial) Ltd v Ennis* [1968]

1 Q.B. 54; *Capital Finance Co Ltd v Donati* (1977) 121 S.J. 270; *Lombard North Central Plc v Butterworth* [1987] Q.B. 527. See also the Australian cases cited, below, para.26–216A, n.1118p.

[995] In *Lombard North Central Plc v Butterworth* [1987] Q.B. 527 the contract contained a formula under which the owner was entitled to arrears, all future instalments that would have fallen due had and agreement not been terminated less a discount for accelerated payment. It omitted an allowance for the resale value of the repossessed goods. This would have prevented it being a genuine pre-estimate of the loss, but it was held that even had it provided for an allowance, the clause would have been a penalty for the reason stated in the text.

[996] *Lombard North Central Plc v Butterworth* [1987] Q.B. 527.

[997] See Main Work, Vol.I, paras 21–011 et seq.

[998] The *Lombard* case [1987] Q.B. 527. See Treitel [1987] L.M.C.L.Q. 143; Beale (1988) 104 L.Q.R. 355.

(c) *Commercially Justified but not a Deterrent*

"Genuine pre-estimate" and "whether imposed in terrorem". Before the   **26–193** decision of the Supreme Court in *Cavendish Square Holding BV v Makdessi* and *ParkingEye Ltd v Beavis*[999] there were a number of dicta to the effect that a clause that was not a genuine pre-estimate at all might nonetheless be valid if it was "commercially justifiable, provided always that its dominant purpose was not to deter the other party from breach".[1000] In *Makdessi v Cavendish Square Holdings BV*[1001] Makdessi had sold shares in his advertising and marketing business to another company, with payment to be made in stages. Ultimately Cavendish was substituted for the original purchaser by a novation agreement and ended up holding 60 per cent of the shares, Makdessi retaining 40 per cent. The purchaser had an option to buy the remaining shares. Makdessi entered various non-competition covenants. Clause 5.1 provided that if Makdessi was in breach of the non-competition clauses, he would not be entitled to further instalments of the price; and clause 5.6 provided that, in the same circumstances, the purchaser could require him to transfer his remaining shares at a price that was much lower than the option price, being based on asset value alone and ignoring any element of good will. Cavendish argued that Makdessi was in breach, refused to pay the outstanding instalments of the price and demanded that he transfer the remaining shares at the reduced value. Makdessi argued that clauses 5.1 and 5.6 were penalty clauses and unenforceable. Christopher Clarke L.J., with whom the other members of the court agreed, distinguished the traditional "genuine pre-estimate" approach from the "new approach" and said that the recent cases:

> " . . . show the court adopting the broader test of whether the clause was extravagant and unconscionable with a predominant function of deterrence; and robustly declining to do so in circumstances where there was a commercial justification for the clause. That this is a reversion to the foundation of the doctrine is apparent from the observations of Lord Halsbury in *Clydebank Engineering* when he asked of the relevant clause:
>> 'whether it is, what I think gave the jurisdiction to the Courts in both countries to interfere at all in an agreement between the parties, unconscionable and extravagant, and one which no Court ought to allow to be enforced'."[1002]

Christopher Clarke L.J. made it clear that in his view, deterrence is not recognised as a commercial justification.[1003] He then applied the two tests sequentially.[1004] The clauses, which would result in the seller of a business who had broken various undertakings not to compete receiving millions of dollars less in consideration, were held to be neither a genuine pre-estimate of the buyers' likely loss[1005] nor commercially justified. Although it had been argued that the clauses were part of a commercial bargain, reached after extensive negotiation, as to the price at which shares in the Company were to change hands:

> "The underlying rationale of the doctrine of penalties is that the Court will grant relief against the enforcement of provisions for payment (or the loss of rights or the compulsory transfer of property at nil or an undervalue) in the event of breach, where the amount to be paid or lost is out of all proportion to the loss attributable to the breach. If that is so, the provisions are likely to be regarded as penal because their function is to act as a deterrent.
>
> That seems to me the position here. The payment terms of clauses 5.1 and 5.6 do not serve to fulfil some justifiable commercial or economic function such as is exemplified in the cases—a modest extra interest in respect of a defaulting loan; a provision for the payment of the costs of earlier litigation; a generous measure of damages for wrongful dismissal; an allocation of credit risk; or the provision of capital which would be needed if a promised guarantee of a loan was not forthcoming . . . "[1006]

As will be seen in the next section, the Supreme Court[1007] reversed this decision, holding that a clause may be valid even if it clearly has a deterrent function, provided that the party to whom the sum will be paid has a legitimate interest in securing performance rather than damages, and the amount payable or other consequence if the contract is broken is not extravagant and unconscionable in comparison to that interest.[1008]

[999] [2015] UKSC 67, [2015] 3 W.L.R. 1373.
[1000] *Lordsvale Finance Plc v Bank of Zambia* [1996] Q.B. 752, 762–764; *United International Pictures v Cine Bes Filmcilik ve Yapimcilik AS* [2003] EWCA Civ 1669 at [15]; and semble, Arden L.J. in *Murray v Leisureplay Plc* [2005] EWCA Civ 963, [2005] I.R.L.R. 946 (Clarke and Buxton L.JJ. preferred to decide the case on the basis that given the difficulty of forecasting the possible effect on the claimant's employability and how quickly he would be able to obtain other employment, the sum payable was not, in the words of Lord Dunedin in the Dunlop case, "extravagant and unconscionable in amount in comparison with the greatest loss that could conceivably be proved to have followed from the breach" see [2005] EWCA Civ 963 at [105] and [114]–[115]). See also *Euro London Appointments Ltd v Claessens International Ltd* [2006] EWCA Civ 385, [2006] 2 Lloyd's Rep. 436 at [30]; *General Trading Co (Holdings) Ltd v Richmond Corp Ltd* [2008] EWHC 1479 (Comm), [2008] 2 Lloyd's Rep. 475.
[1001] [2013] EWCA Civ 1539; for an account of the Supreme Court decision in this case, [2015] UKSC 67, see below, para.26–197.
[1002] [2013] EWCA Civ 1539 at [104]. The reference is to *Clydebank Engineering & Shipbuilding Co Ltd v Don Jose Ramos Yzquierdo y Castaneda* [1905] A.C. 6.
[1003] [2013] EWCA Civ 1539 at [125].
[1004] [2013] EWCA Civ 1539 at [105]–[117] and [118]–[123].
[1005] [2013] EWCA Civ 1539 at [105]–[117].
[1006] [2013] EWCA Civ 1539 at [120]–[121].
[1007] [2015] UKSC 67, [2015] 3 W.L.R. 1373.
[1008] See below, para.26–197.

26–194   **"Commercial justifications" and "legitimate interests".** It seems likely that the "'commercial justifications" given in the cases referred to in this section and listed by Christopher Clarke L.J. in the passage cited in the previous paragraph, would also constitute legitimate interests[1009] within the meaning of the Supreme Court's new test.[1010] If that is correct, there is no further need to refer to "commercial justification" as a test of whether an agreed damages or similar clause is valid or a penalty.

[1009] On what constitutes a legitimate interest see below, para.26–198.
[1010] Lord Hodge said that the broader approach adopted in this group of cases "involves a correct analysis of the law" (at [225]; see also at [246]).

(d) Deterrence to Protect a Legitimate Interest

Permissible deterrence in protecting broader interests. The first modern **26–195** decision that a clause requiring a sum that is not a genuine pre-estimate of the loss that will be suffered by the other party, and which is clearly aimed at deterrence, may nonetheless be a valid liquidated damages clause was the decision of the Court of Appeal in *ParkingEye Ltd v Beavis*.[1011] The claimants operated a car park at a retail park on behalf of the owners. Motorists were allowed to park free of charge for up to two hours after which they should leave, but a "failure to comply" would result in a parking charge of £85. Moore-Bick L.J., with whom the other members of the court agreed, said the claimants would suffer no direct loss if the motorists overstayed the two hours; it had only an indirect commercial interest in that if it did not deliver the service required by the owners of the retail park it might lose its contract and its reputation.[1012] There was also a social interest,[1013] in that consumers and retailers would benefit from having free parking for limited periods.[1014] Although it was clear that the principal purpose of the parking charge was to deter motorists from overstaying, a charge designed to protect a combination of indirect commercial interests and social interests might be valid, provided that it was not manifestly excessive. The judge at first instance had taken the correct approach when he held that the charge was neither improper in its purpose nor manifestly excessive in its amount, having regard to the level of charges imposed by local authorities and others for overstaying in public car parks.[1015] While in a purely commercial context[1016] a "dominant purpose of deterrence" had been equated to extravagance and unconscionability, in the context of the case that was not the case.[1017] An appeal in the *ParkingEye* case was heard by the Supreme Court along with the appeal in the *Makdessi* case[1018]; as will be explained in the next paragraph, the Supreme Court[1019] rejected the appeal in the *ParkingEye* case, upholding the £85 charge on an even wider ground than had the Court of Appeal.

[1011] [2015] EWCA Civ 402.
[1012] [2015] EWCA Civ 402 at [25].
[1013] [2015] EWCA Civ 402 at [27].
[1014] [2015] EWCA Civ 402 at [30].
[1015] [2015] EWCA Civ 402 at [26].
[1016] Or, as Sir Timothy Lloyd put it, "where the transaction between the contracting parties can be assessed in monetary terms, as can the effects of a breach of the contract by one party or the other" (at [44]). To prohibit this provision would "fail to take account of the nature of the contract, with its gratuitous but valuable benefit of two hours' free parking, and of the entirely legitimate reason for limiting that facility to a two hour period" (at [49]).
[1017] [2015] EWCA Civ 402 at [27]. The Court also held that the term was not unfair under the Unfair Terms in Consumer Contracts Regulations 1999: see below, para.38–251A.

[1018] See above, para.26–193.
[1019] *Cavendish Square Holding BV v Makdessi* and *ParkingEye Ltd v Beavis* [2015] UKSC 67, [2015] 3 W.L.R. 1373

26–196   **Penalty doctrine confirmed.** The appeals from *Makdessi v Cavendish Square Holdings BV*[1020] and *ParkingEye Ltd v Beavis*[1021] were heard together by a seven-justice panel of the Supreme Court.[1022] The Court did not accept the argument made by counsel for Cavendish that the rule against penalty clauses should be abolished altogether[1023] or confined to cases in which the parties did not meet "on an equal playing field";[1024] although consumers are protected by the statutory power to strike down terms that are unfair, the doctrine serves a useful role in business to business contracts.[1025] In particular small businesses might need the protection offered by the doctrine.[1026] To abolish the doctrine would be inconsistent with the provisional recommendations of the Law Commission and the recommendations of the Scottish Law Commissions,[1027] and out of line with other jurisdictions both elsewhere in the common law world and in Europe.[1028]

[1020] [2013] EWCA Civ 1539; for the facts, see the account of the Court of Appeal decision in this case, above, para.26–193.
[1021] [2015] EWCA Civ 402; for the facts, see above, para.26–195.
[1022] *Cavendish Square Holding BV v Makdessi* and *ParkingEye Ltd v Beavis* [2015] UKSC 67, [2015] 3 W.L.R. 1373, noted by Conte (2016) 132 L.Q.R. 382 and Morgan [2016] C.L.J. 11.
[1023] See [2015] UKSC 67 at [36], [162] (Lord Mance), [218] and [256] (Lord Hodge).
[1024] See Lord Hodge [2015] UKSC 67 at [256] and [267].
[1025] [2015] UKSC 67 at [38], [260].
[1026] Lord Mance [2015] UKSC 67 at [167]; Lord Hodge at [263].
[1027] See Lord Mance [2015] UKSC 67 at [163]; Lord Hodge at [263].
[1028] See [2015] UKSC 67 at [164]–[167] (Lords Neuberger and Sumption) and [264]–[265] (Lord Hodge).

26–197   **Protecting legitimate interests.** However, the Supreme Court in *Cavendish Square* and *ParkingEye*[1029] was unanimous that the decision in *Dunlop Pneumatic Tyre Co Ltd v New Garage & Motor Co Ltd*,[1030] had been interpreted too narrowly. Lord Dunedin had not intended to lay down a strict code, and the other Lords had not adopted to his reasoning in full. In particular Lord Atkinson had upheld the clause requiring payment of £5 for every tyre sold at less than the list price not because it was hard to estimate the loss from the particular breach but because Dunlop had a broader interest to protect, namely its system of price maintenance.[1031] As Lord Mance put it[1032]:

> "It is clear . . . that a concern can protect a system which it operates across its whole business by imposing an undertaking on all its counterparties to respect the system, coupled with a provision requiring payment of an agreed sum in the event of any breach of such undertaking. The impossibility of measuring loss from any particular breach is a reason for upholding, not for striking down, such a provision. The qualification and safeguard is that the agreed sum must not have been extravagant, unconscionable or incommensurate with any possible interest in the maintenance of the system, this being for the party in breach to show."

A clause may be valid even if it does not represent a genuine pre-estimate of the loss, and even though it is aimed at deterring a party from breaking the contract, provided that the other party can show a legitimate commercial interest in deterring the breach rather than simply being entitled to damages[1033] and that the clause is not extravagant or unconscionable in proportion to that interest. Lords Neuberger and Sumption said:

> "The true test is whether the impugned provision is a secondary obligation which imposes a detriment on the contract-breaker out of all proportion to any legitimate interest of the innocent party in the enforcement of the primary obligation. The innocent party can have no proper interest in simply punishing the defaulter. His interest is in performance or in some appropriate alternative to performance. In the case of a straightforward damages clause, that interest will rarely extend beyond compensation for the breach, and we therefore expect that Lord Dunedin's four tests would usually be perfectly adequate to determine its validity. But compensation is not necessarily the only legitimate interest that the innocent party may have in the performance of the defaulter's primary obligations."[1034]

Cavendish had a legitimate interest in preserving the good will for which it was paying such a large amount[1035]; it would be hard to prove the loss flowing from any breach of the non-competition covenants; the seller's loyalty was critical and indivisible[1036] and therefore it was legitimate to deter Makdessi from any breach. Likewise, in the *ParkingEye* case there was clearly a legitimate interest in ensuring that motorists did not stay longer than two hours.[1037] Therefore Cavendish's appeal succeeded but Beavis' failed.

[1029] *Cavendish Square Holding BV v Makdessi* and *ParkingEye Ltd v Beavis* [2015] UKSC 67, [2015] 3 W.L.R. 1373.

[1030] [1915] A.C. 79.

[1031] [2015] UKSC 67 at [22]–[23], [135]–[139], referring to [1915] A.C. 79, 90–93. Lord Mance (at [132]–[134]) also referred to the words of Lord Robertson in *Clydebank Engineering & Shipbuilding Co Ltd v Yzquierdo y Castaneda* [1905] A.C. 6, 19.

[1032] [2015] UKSC 67 at [143].

[1033] [2015] UKSC 67 at [28]; cf. at [248]–[249] (Lord Hodge).

[1034] [2015] UKSC 67 at [32]. cf. Lord Hodge at [255], [275]. As Lord Carnwath and, on this point, Lord Clarke (see at [291]) agreed with Lords Neuberger and Sumption, this statement may be taken as the authoritative statement of the penalty rule. Lord Mance and Lord Hodge, with both of whom Lord Toulson agreed on this issue (see at [292]), each gave slightly different accounts but it is not thought that the differences between the judgments on this issue are substantial.

[1035] [2015] UKSC 67 at [75].

[1036] [2015] UKSC 67 at [75]; and see Lord Hodge at [272]. Lord Mance's analysis does not seem essentially different: he said that cl.5.1 should be judged in the light of the general interest being protected: at [179]–[180], and likewise cl.5.6 "must be viewed in nature and impact as a composite whole as well as in context".

[1037] [2015] UKSC 67 at [99] (Lords Neuberger and Sumption, with whom Lords Carnwath and, on this point, Clarke, agreed), [184] (Lord Mance) and [285]–[286] (Lord Hodge). Lord Toulson, who considered that the clause in the *ParkingEye* case was unfair within the meaning of the Unfair Terms in Consumer Contracts Regulations 1999 (see below, para.38–251A), declined to discuss whether it also amounted to a penalty at common law (at [316]).

"Legitimate interest". In *Makdessi v Cavendish Square Holdings BV* and **26–198** *ParkingEye Ltd v Beavis*[1038] the Supreme Court held that an agreed damages clause or other type of clause that falls within the scope of the penalty doctrine[1039] will be valid if it is designed to protect a legitimate interest of the innocent party and the amount involved is not extravagant or unconscionable in proportion to that interest.[1040] Punishment of the party in breach is not a legitimate purpose.[1041] The Supreme Court decided that when shares in a company that has been purchased will be of little value to the buyer if the seller is not loyal, as in the *Cavendish Square* case, or if a perfectly lawful scheme will not work unless there is an effective deterrent, as in the *ParkingEye* case, and damages will not provide an adequate sanction, there is a legitimate interest in deterrence and a sum that is designed to deter will not be penal, provided that it is not extravagant or unconscionable compared to the relevant legitimate interest.[1042] What general factors are relevant to whether the claimant has a legitimate interest for this purpose?

[1038] [2015] UKSC 67: see above, para.26–197.

[1039] See below, paras 26–216 et seq.

[1040] This test was applied in *Hayfin Opal Luxco 3 SARL v Windermere VII CMBS Plc* [2016] EWHC 782 (Ch) at [142].

[1041] See [2015] UKSC 67 at [13] and [30] (Lords Neuberger and Sumption), [148] (Lord Mance), [243] (Lord Hodge).

[1042] See [2015] UKSC 67 at [99].

26–199   **Difficulty of proving loss.** Lords Neuberger and Sumption referred to a legitimate interest in obtaining performance rather than merely damages[1043]; and, in support of their argument that in fashioning the rules on remedies the law takes into account legitimate interests, referred to the rule that specific performance may be available (subject to other constraints) if the innocent party has "a legitimate interest extending beyond pecuniary compensation for the breach".[1044] In each of the cases before the court, it seems that damages would not be adequate compensation, nor be adequate as a deterrent to breach, as it would be hard to prove what loss, if any, flowed from any particular breach.[1045] The same was true in the case of in *Dunlop Pneumatic Tyre Co Ltd v New Garage & Motor Co Ltd*,[1046] in which a payment of £5 per tyre sold at below the list price was upheld.

[1043] [2015] UKSC 67 at [28]

[1044] [2015] UKSC 67 at [30].

[1045] cf. Main Work, Vol.I, para.27–008 (difficulty in quantifying damages may mean damages inadequate).

[1046] [1915] A.C. 79.

26–200   **Difficulty in detection.** A related factor is that damages for each individual breach will not be an effective remedy if it will be hard for the claimant to detect breaches by the defendant.[1047]

[1047] See Lord Mance [2015] UKSC 67 at [172].

26–201   **Substitute not available.** The analogy drawn with specific performance indicates that it would also suffice that the contract was for a unique piece of property, so that the claimant would be unable to purchase a substitute.[1048] The case would presumably be even stronger if the claimant might suffer consequential loss (such as a reduction in trading profits that might have been made using a unique vessel[1049]) that is again hard to prove or quantify. It is submitted that a party may also have a legitimate interest in deterring the defendant from breaching a contract to provide services if it will be difficult for the claimant to obtain the services from a replacement contractor, even though specific performance of the contract might not be granted for other reasons, such as that because it would involve personal service[1050] or because it might require the court to supervise performance.[1051]

[1048] On the "adequacy of damages" test and the availability of a substitute, see Main Work, Vol.I, paras 27–010 et seq.
[1049] cf. Main Work, Vol.I, para.27–012 n.61.
[1050] See Main Work, Vol.I, paras 27–024 et seq.
[1051] See Main Work, Vol.I, paras 27–030 et seq.

Loss suffered by third party. In the *ParkingEye* case, there was an additional reason for damages being inadequate: the loss caused by the motorist overstaying the two hours free parking would be suffered not by ParkingEye Ltd but by the operator of the retail park and by members of the public who wished to use it. It is not only the legitimate interests of the contracting party that count for this purpose.[1052] It may be added that this appears to be a form of consequential loss that would not be recoverable under the principles that exceptionally permit a party to a contract to recover damages on the basis that the promisee has not received the benefit that he contracted for,[1053] nor to be within the cases that have permitted a promisee to recover for loss that is suffered by a third party.[1054] In *Beswick v Beswick*[1055] the majority considered that the promisee could recover only nominal damages, while the third party suffered the real loss, and that therefore specific performance was an appropriate remedy. It seems the presence of similar factors will mean that the promisee has a legitimate interest in securing performance rather than relying on the remedy of damages.

26–202

[1052] [2015] UKSC 67 at [99].
[1053] The "broader principle" suggested by Lord Griffiths in *Linden Gardens Trust Ltd v Lenesta Sludge Disposals Ltd* [1994] 1 A.C. 85. Further, even the cost of performance may be recoverable by the promisee only if he would be able and likely to remedy the breach: see Main Work, Vol.I, para.18–056 and paras 18–063—18–068.
[1054] e.g. when the parties contemplated that the property would be transferred to a third party, the ground of the majority decision in *Linden Gardens Trust Ltd v Lenesta Sludge Disposals Ltd* [1994] 1 A.C. 85: see Main Work, Vol.I, paras 18–057 et seq.
[1055] [1968] A.C. 58; see Main Work, Vol.I, paras 18–022 and 18–051 et seq.

Insolvency risk. The possible insolvency of either party may also be a relevant factor, at least when it is the claimant's solvency that is at risk. A factor that has sometimes been taken into account in deciding whether to grant specific performance (or, on the facts of the case, an injunction against breach) is that the defendant may not be able to pay any damages.[1056] It is not evident that the defendant's inability to pay damages can by itself[1057] give the claimant a legitimate interest in deterring breach by imposing liability for "deterrent" liquidated damages, which would mean the defendant paying even greater sums. Conversely, it has been said to be a relevant factor to specific performance that delay is likely to be encountered in securing the actual payment of any damages and that the claimant might become insolvent before they are paid.[1058] It is submitted that this may be relevant to an agreed damages clause. The claimant clearly has a legitimate interest in remaining solvent, and if the contract is sufficiently important to the claimant's financial state that non-performance by the defendant coupled with a likely delay in recovering the damages would put

26–203

the claimant's solvency at serious risk, the claimant seems to have a legitimate interest in performance rather than damages.

[1056] *Evans Marshall & Co v Bertola SA (No.1)* [1973] 1 W.L.R. 349, 367 (Kerr J. at first instance) and 385 (Edmund Davies L.J.)
[1057] Insolvency of the defendant is not a ground for refusing specific performance where the remedy is normally available as a matter of course: *AMEC Properties v Planning Research & Systems* [1992] 1 E.G.L.R. 70. See Main Work, Vol.I, para.27–013.
[1058] *Thames Valley Power Ltd v Total Gas and Power Ltd* [2006] 1 Lloyd's Rep. 441 at [64]; see Main Work, Vol.I, para.27–016 at n.95.

26–204   **Preference for performance.** Specific performance will not be awarded merely because the claimant would prefer performance to damages, if damages would be (or are likely to be) an adequate remedy. Equally, it is submitted that, despite another analogy which will be considered in the next paragraph,[1059] the decision in the *Cavendish Square* case[1060] does not mean that a party who simply has a preference for performance (which would presumably include most contracting parties, unless they have come to regret entering the contract) has a legitimate interest in deterring breach sufficient to justify an agreed damages clause that is aimed at deterring breach rather than being a genuine pre-estimate of the loss. To put the point another way, whether the claimant has a legitimate interest in performance rather than damages seems to be an objective test.[1061] It is submitted further that the claimant would not be able to overcome this by showing that it had paid a higher price to the defendant than it would have had to pay had the clause not been included in the contract.

[1059] See below, para.26–205.
[1060] *Cavendish Square Holding BV v Makdessi* and *ParkingEye Ltd v Beavis* [2015] UKSC 67, [2015] 3 W.L.R. 1373.
[1061] cf. above, para.26–184.

26–205   **Continuing performance after a repudiation.** Lords Neuberger and Sumption[1062] also referred to the line of cases, starting with a dictum of Lord Reid in *White & Carter (Councils) Ltd v McGregor*,[1063] to the effect that a party faced with a wrongful repudiation by the other party may, if he is able to continue to perform his part of the contract without the repudiating party's co-operation, ignore the repudiation, perform his part and sue for the agreed price unless he has no legitimate interest in doing so. The Court of Appeal has accepted the "no legitimate interest" restriction as part of the law.[1064] But in the context of repudiation, the concept of legitimate interest operates not as a reason for allowing an additional remedy but as a restriction on the right to keep the contract in force, a restriction that allows the right to be exercised except in fairly extreme cases. Facts that have been mentioned as possibly justifying an innocent party in continuing to perform and claiming the price despite the repudiation have included that the shipowner faced with a wrongful repudiation by the charterer would, if the owner could not claim the hire, be left with the burden of re-letting the ship rather than the charterer having to find a use for it[1065]; that the charter hire might have been assigned to a bank as security for a loan[1066]; that if the innocent party had to claim damages from a repudiating party who was in financial difficulties, the defendant's funds might have been directed elsewhere before the damages were paid[1067]; and the fact that an innocent ship owner would be left "in a difficult market where a substitute time charter was impossible, and trading on the spot market very difficult".[1068] The innocent party has been held to have a legitimate interest in performing "unless maintaining the contract can be described as 'wholly unreasonable',[1069] 'extremely unreasonable' or, as Popplewell J. put it after surveying the cases, "perhaps, in my words, 'perverse'".[1070] An arbitrator's decision that the shipowner had no legitimate interest in continuing to claim the hire under a charter because the owner could re-let the ship on the spot market and claim damages from the charter was held to be a misapplication of the law.[1071] So it is not clear that the analogy of the *White & Carter* cases will provide helpful guidance on the meaning of legitimate interest in the context of the penalty rule. The Supreme Court seemed to regard a legitimate interest in obtaining performance rather than recovering damages as exceptional,[1072] not as applying unless seeking to obtaining performance would be wholly unreasonable. It is submitted that the fact that the claimant would be faced with having to go into an uncertain market in order to mitigate its loss does not give it a legitimate interest sufficient to support a clause that is aimed at deterring breach rather than being a pre-estimate of loss. However, when the amount of loss is hard to predict the claimant will no doubt still be given a "generous margin"[1073] before the pre-estimate will be treated as extravagant or unconscionable and therefore a penalty.

[1062] [2015] UKSC 67 at [29].

[1063] [1962] A.C. 413, 431: see Main Work, Vol.I, para.26–106.

[1064] See Main Work, Vol.I, para.26–106.

[1065] *Gator Shipping Corp v Trans-Asiatic Oil SA (The Odenfeld)* [1978] 2 Lloyd's Rep. 357, 374. A similar point was made in respect of a landlord faced with a repudiation of a lease by a tenant: *Reichman v Beveridge* [2006] EWCA Civ 1659 at [31], though in that case the court also held it was reasonable for the landlord to continue to claim the rent given that there was uncertainty over whether English law permits a landlord who has terminated the lease to claim damages for loss of rent (at [28]), an uncertainty that does not arise in relation to contracts in general.

[1066] *Clea Shipping Corp v Bulk Oil International (The Alaskan Trader) (No.2)* [1984] 1 All E.R. 129, 137.

[1067] *Isabella Shipowner SA v Shagang Shipping Co Ltd (The Aquafaith)* [2012] EWHC 1077 (Comm), [2012] 2 Lloyd's Rep. 61 at [47].

[1068] *Isabella Shipowner SA v Shagang Shipping Co Ltd (The Aquafaith)* [2012] EWHC 1077 (Comm), [2012] 2 Lloyd's Rep. 61 at [56].

[1069] *Gator Shipping Corp v Trans-Asiatic Oil Ltd SA (The Odenfeld)* [1978] 2 Lloyd's Rep 357, 373.

[1070] *Isabella Shipowner SA v Shagang Shipping Co Ltd (The Aquafaith)* [2012] EWHC 1077 (Comm), [2012] 2 Lloyd's Rep. 61 at [44]. In *Attica Sea Carriers Corp v Ferrostaal Poseidon Bulk Reederei GmbH (The Puerto Buitrago)* [1976] 1 Lloyd's Rep. 250 the innocent party has been held to have no legitimate interest in claiming the hire of a chartered ship until it was returned fully repaired, when the vessel was beyond economic repair; and in *MSC Mediterranean Shipping Co SA v Cottonex Anstalt* [2016] EWCA Civ 789 the court said there would be no legitimate interest in claiming the demurrage in respect of containers that were being detained by a third party with no end in sight, so that the contractual venture had become frustrated (at [43]): see above, para.26–106.

[1071] *Isabella Shipowner SA v Shagang Shipping Co Ltd (The Aquafaith)* [2012] EWHC 1077 (Comm), [2012] 2 Lloyd's Rep. 61 at [42]. Popplewell J. seemed to doubt the decision of Lloyd J. in *Clea Shipping Corp v Bulk Oil International (The Alaskan Trader) (No.2)* [1983] 2 Lloyd's Rep. 645, of which Popplewell J. said: "Lloyd J found it impossible to interfere with the decision of the experienced commercial arbitrator who could not be shown to have applied the wrong test when finding that the owners' election to maintain the time charter (which had included 10 months of service, followed by six months of off-hire repairs) for a balance of eight months following premature re-delivery was a commercial absurdity".

[1072] It is probably for the claimant to show that it has a legitimate interest, whereas in the repudiation situation it is for the party in breach to show that the innocent party has no legitimate interest in performing: *Ocean Marine Navigation Ltd v Koch Carbon Inc (The Dynamic)* [2003] EWHC 1936 (Comm), [2003] 2 Lloyd's Rep. 693 at [23].

[1073] cf. above, para.26–185.

26–206   **Analogy to account of profits.** A further possible analogy, though not mentioned by the Supreme Court in the *Cavendish Square* case,[1074] are the cases in which a claimant is permitted to recover an account of the profit[1075] or, at least damages on the *"Wrotham Park"* basis,[1076] in other words, a share of the profit that the defendant has made through breaking the contract. An account of profit was awarded in *Att-Gen v Blake*[1077] after Blake had written and published a book in breach of the confidentiality agreement made by him when he entered the Secret Intelligence Service. The circumstances were said to be "exceptional", but Lord Nicholls said:

> "The court will have regard to all the circumstances, including the subject matter of the contract, the purpose of the contractual provision which has been breached, the circumstances in which the breach occurred, the consequences of the breach and the circumstances in which relief is being sought. A useful general guide, although not exhaustive, is whether the plaintiff had a legitimate interest in preventing the defendant's profit-making activity and, hence, in depriving him of his profit.
> It would be difficult, and unwise, to attempt to be more specific . . . "[1078]

Presumably the government would equally have had a sufficient legitimate interest to justify a clause requiring ex-employees who broke the confidentiality agreement to pay a sum that was designed to be a deterrent. Later cases have emphasised that for an account of profits to be appropriate the circumstances must be exceptional, and this has been taken to mean that an account of profits will not normally be appropriate in a commercial case,[1079] though it is certainly possible.[1080] To date an account of profits has been awarded in commercial circumstances only in one case at first instance. In *Esso Petroleum Co Ltd v Niad Ltd*[1081] the defendant had agreed to participate in a "Price Watch" scheme under which participating petrol stations agreed not to sell at above set prices. The defendant broke the agreement by selling at higher prices. The claimants were unable to show what loss this had caused them but it was held that they had a strong interest in performance and an account of profits was ordered. Though Esso's aim was to prevent dealers from selling petrol at higher prices than permitted by the scheme, rather than to prevent sales at less than a list price, in other respects the facts are quite similar to those of *Dunlop Pneumatic Tyre Co Ltd v New Garage & Motor Co Ltd*,[1082] and it seems clear that Esso would have had a sufficient legitimate interest to justify a clause requiring dealers who broke the agreement to pay a sum that was designed to be a deterrent, provided the sum set was not extravagant or unconscionable in proportion to Esso's interest. Moreover, it seems likely that an agreed damages clause that was calculated to take away any profit that the dealer might make by selling at higher than the set price would be proportionate to Esso's legitimate interest in deterring this kind of breach of contract by dealers.[1083] Beyond this, however, it is hard to gain much guidance from a class of cases that by definition are exceptional.

[1074] *Cavendish Square Holding BV v Makdessi* and *ParkingEye Ltd v Beavis* [2015] UKSC 67, [2015] 3 W.L.R. 1373.

[1075] See Main Work, Vol.I, para.26–055.

[1076] See Main Work, Vol.I, paras 26–046 et seq.

[1077] [2001] 1 A.C. 268. See Main Work, Vol.I, paras 26–055 et seq.

[1078] [2001] 1 A.C. 268, 285 (per Lord Nicholls). For a more detailed consideration of the relevant facts see Main Work, Vol.I. para.26–055.

[1079] See Main Work, Vol.I. para.26–055.

[1080] See the discussion in *Experience Hendrix LLC v PPX Enterprises Inc* [2003] EWCA Civ 323, [2003] 1 All E.R. (Comm) 830.

[1081] [2001] All E.R. (D) 324 (Nov).

[1082] [1915] A.C. 79.

[1083] See further below, para.26–208.

Analogy to *"Wrotham Park" damages*. In cases in which the claimant has found it impossible or difficult to show that it has suffered a loss as the result of the defendant's breach of contract, the courts have more often awarded what are often now called *"Wrotham Park"* or "hypothetical bargain" damages, in other words, damages measured by the sum that the claimant could reasonably have demanded as the price of releasing the defendant from its obligation.[1084] So where the defendant has failed to provide the services promised but the claimant cannot show a consequential loss, if damages cannot be awarded on the simple difference in value between the services promised and those provided,[1085] an award on the hypothetical bargain basis may be made instead.[1086] The facts do not have to be exceptional in the way required if an account of profits is to be ordered, nor is it necessary that to deny *Wrotham Park* damages would produce a manifest injustice; the question is whether an award would be a just response.[1087] Some of the factors taken into account in deciding whether to award *Wrotham Park* damages seem relevant to the question of whether the claimant has a legitimate interest in securing performance rather than damages.[1088] These include difficulty in showing loss, even if it would be possible for the court to make an award of general damages assessed "in a robust manner".[1089] Although it had been said that "the inability to demonstrate identifiable financial loss of the conventional sort is a pre-condition to the award of such damages",[1090] in *One Step (Support) Ltd v Morris-Garner* the Court of Appeal declined to follow this dictum and held that *Wrotham Park* damages may be awarded when it will be very difficult to prove the loss that has been caused by the breach.[1091] It may also be relevant that it would be difficult for the claimant to obtain interim relief.[1092] These factors seem to reflect similar ones that were suggested earlier. In any event, it was suggested earlier that loss of a hypothetical bargain is a kind of loss that may form part of a genuine pre-estimate of the loss.[1093] If that is correct, no further legitimate interest need be shown to justify an agreed damages clause that is designed to deter breach in circumstances in which *"Wrotham Park"* damages might be available.

26–207

[1084] See Main Work, Vol.I, paras 26–051 et seq.

[1085] See Main Work, Vol.I, para.26–041.

[1086] *Giedo van der Garde BV v Force India Formula One Team Ltd* [2010] EWHC 2373 (QB). Hamblen J. pointed out that an award was not "precluded by any of the following factors: (i) that the claimants advanced no claim for an injunction or specific performance, or the fact that there would have been no prospect of such an order being granted; (ii) the fact that damages are not claimed under Lord Cairns' Act in lieu of an injunction; (iii) the fact that the claim is not based on a breach of a restrictive covenant; and (iv) the fact that the claim is based on breach of contract rather than invasion of property rights" (at [533]). On the facts of the case, the loss assessed on this basis would be same amount as the difference in value (at [559]).

[1087] *One Step (Support) Ltd v Morris-Garner* [2016] EWCA Civ 180 at [122] and [145]–[146].

[1088] Other facts taken into account do not seem relevant. In *Experience Hendrix LLC v PPX Enterprises Inc* [2003] EWCA Civ 323, [2003] 1 All E.R. (Comm) 830 at [36], [44], [54] and [58] the Court of Appeal used some of the factors relevant to the granting of an account of profits as also relevant to their discretion to grant *Wrotham Park* damages, taking into account the fact that the defendant "did do the very thing it had contracted not to do"; that the defendant "knew that it was doing something which it had contracted not to do"; that it was a "deliberate breach", a "flagrant contravention" of the defendant's obligation. These factors do not seem relevant to whether or not the claimant had a legitimate interest in deterring the defendant from breach.

[1089] [2016] EWCA Civ 180 at [123].

[1090] *Abbar v Saudi Economic & Development Co (SEDCO) Real Estate Ltd* [2013] EWHC 1414 (Ch) at [225].

[1091] [2016] EWCA Civ 180 at [122] and [145]–[146]. It is submitted that *Wrotham Park* damages may also be awarded when the conventional measure of damages would leave the claimant under-compensated: see Main Work, Vol.I, para.26–053.

[1092] cf. Longmore L.J. in *One Step (Support) Ltd v Morris-Garner* [2016] EWCA Civ 180 at [151] (another wrongful competition case, in which the defendant's furtive conduct deprived claimant of opportunity to obtain interim relief).

[1093] See above, para.26–186.

26–208   **Capturing any profit from breach.** A further possible reason for including an agreed damages clause that fixes the sum to be paid at a sum much greater than the pre-estimated loss is that, even though damages will in other respects be an adequate remedy for the claimant's losses, the claimant considers that the defendant may break the contract in order to make a greater profit and wants to be able to claim the whole of the profit, not just a share of it as under the approach discussed in the last paragraph. If damages would be adequate,[1094] it seems unlikely that the claimant would be treated as having a legitimate interest in capturing the whole of the defendant's profit. In *Co-operative Insurance Society Ltd v Argyll Stores (Holdings) Ltd*[1095] Lord Hoffmann expressed the concern that in some circumstances an award of specific performance may allow "the plaintiff to enrich himself at the defendant's expense" by negotiating an excessive price for releasing the defendant from performance; one that "exceeds the value of performance to the plaintiff and approaches the cost of performance to the defendant".[1096] A similar concern would prevent a court holding that a claimant has a legitimate interest in a clause that is designed to capture the whole of, or a large share in, any profit that the defendant might make.[1097]

[1094] As opposed to a case like *Esso Petroleum Co Ltd v Niad Ltd* [2001] All E.R. (D) 324 (Nov), discussed above, para.26–206, in which the loss to the petrol supplier would be hard to prove.

[1095] [1998] A.C. 1.

[1096] [1998] A.C. 1, 15, citing Sharpe, "Specific relief for Contract breach" in Reiter and Swan (eds), *Studies in Contract Law* (1980), 129.

[1097] It should be noted that *"Wrotham Park"* damages, though they compensate the innocent party for its loss of opportunity to negotiate a price for releasing the defendant from the relevant contractual obligations, do not have the same effect of allowing the claimant to hold out for a large share of the profit, at least if the damages are fixed at a fairly modest share of the profit. In *Pell Frischmann Engineering Ltd v Bow Valley Iran Ltd* [2009] UKPC 45, [2011] 1 W.L.R. 2370 Lord Walker said that "Damages under this head . . . represent 'such a sum of money as might reasonably have been demanded by [the claimant] from [the defendant] as a *quid pro quo* for [permitting the continuation of the breach of covenant or other invasion of right]" (at [48]); the court should consider a hypothetical negotiation between a willing buyer (the contract-breaker) and a willing seller (the party claiming damages), both parties to be assumed to act reasonably, so that the fact that one or other would have refused to make a deal is to be ignored. But the fact that the alternative project could not proceed unless the negative rights were bought out can properly be taken into account (at [53]). See Main Work, Vol.I, paras 26–052—26–054.

Part of a legitimate scheme. The decision in the *ParkingEye* case[1098] may **26–209** also be explained, without having to show that a breach of the contract would cause the claimant to suffer a loss that would not be compensable (or indeed, any loss at all) on the basis that the charge was an essential part of a lawful scheme.[1099]

[1098] *ParkingEye Ltd v Beavis* [2015] UKSC 67, [2015] 3 W.L.R. 1373.
[1099] See [2015] UKSC 67 at [99], [199].

Conclusion on legitimate interest. It is submitted that a claimant will have a **26–210** sufficient legitimate interest in obtaining performance rather than damages to justify an agreed damages clause that is intended to deter breach, rather than as a pre-estimate of loss, in the following situations:

– if the claimant would face serious difficulties in proving what loss, if any, flowed from the breach[1100];
– if the claimant would face serious difficulties in detecting whether there has been a breach[1101];
– if damages will not be an adequate remedy because, if the defendant fails to perform, the claimant will not be able to obtain substitute goods, other property or services (irrespective of the fact that specific performance of the contract might not be available for other reasons)[1102];
– if loss will be suffered by a third party rather than by, or in addition to, the claimant[1103];
– if having to claim damages from the defendant would put the claimant's solvency at risk[1104];
– if that even though neither the claimant nor a third party will suffer any loss through the defendant's breach but the claimant has an exceptional interest in ensuring that defendant performs such that the court would award an account of profits, as in *Att-Gen v Blake*[1105]; or
– more generally, if deterrence is an essential element of a lawful scheme.[1106]

In contrast, the claimant does not have a legitimate interest in obtaining more than damages, or agreed damages that are substantially more than a genuine pre-estimate of the likely loss, merely because the claimant would have to incur time and expense in arranging a substitute transaction, or simply would prefer performance to claiming damages[1107]; nor because it hopes to secure a large share of any profit the defendant might make through breaking the contract, when damages would otherwise be an adequate remedy.[1108]

[1100] See above, para.26–199.
[1101] See above, para.26–200.

¹¹⁰² See above, para.26–201.
¹¹⁰³ See above, para.26–202.
¹¹⁰⁴ See above, para.26–203.
¹¹⁰⁵ See above, para.26–206.
¹¹⁰⁶ As in the *ParkingEye* case, see above, para.26–197.
¹¹⁰⁷ See above, para.26–205.
¹¹⁰⁸ See above, para.26–208.

26–211   **"Not extravagant or unconscionable".** Even if the claimant can show that it has a legitimate interest in obtaining actual performance instead of damages in lieu of performance, an agreed damages clause or other clause that is within the penalty clause rules will not be valid if it is extravagant or unconscionable compared to the legitimate interest. Lord Mance's reference to the sum being "not . . . incommensurate"[1109] and Lord Hodge's to whether it is "wholly disproportionate"[1110] to the interest to be protected are helpful to show what is meant.

[1109] [2015] UKSC 67 at [143].
[1110] [2015] UKSC 67 at [226]–[227], [255].

26–212   **Proportionate.** "Not extravagant or unconscionable compared to the legitimate interest", and "not incommensurate" or "not disproportionate", appears to mean that a sum agreed to be payable upon breach must not be substantially more than is required in order to deter the defendant from breach. How is this to be determined? Since the decision in *ParkingEye Ltd v Beavis*,[1111] there have been anecdotal reports[1112] of parking companies charging motorists who overstay the period of "free parking" as much as £300. Is that unconscionable or disproportionate? It does not seem to matter that the loss may vary from breach to breach. Though there is no necessary connection between deterrence and the amount of the loss caused by a breach, a motorist who overstays by ten minutes presumably causes less loss to the landowner and less inconvenience to the public, and is therefore less of a threat to the claimant's "legitimate interests" than one who overstays by six hours, but there is no suggestion in the case that the agreed sum needs to be gradated according to the length of the overstay in order to avoid being classed as a penalty.[1113] Some motorists will be more attentive than others to notices setting out charges for overstaying and other breaches of the rules, and some will be deterred more readily than others. Will a charge remain "proportionate" unless it is higher than is needed to make even the most inattentive motorist sufficiently aware of the charges to "stop and think" and to deter even the most thoughtless or perverse? This was not discussed in the *ParkingEye* case. Rather, there were references to proportionality in another sense, their Lordships pointing out that the £85 charge was not much greater than the fine for overstaying in many car parks operated by local authorities, and the latter do not usually allow a period of free parking.[1114] The difficulty of deciding what is not unconscionable or wholly disproportionate seems greater still when the breaches that will trigger the agreed damages or other clause[1115] may be quite various in nature. A seller of a business might breach a non-competition covenant by no more than continuing to make a few small transactions with no intent to compete further, which would probably pose no real threat to the buyer of the business; yet in the *Cavendish Square* case it was not treated as disproportionate to impose a price reduction of millions of dollars for any breach of the covenants. The Supreme Court's decision in *Cavendish Square* case may suggest that deterrent sums will only be disproportionate if they are excessive even for the "worst case scenario". However, it is submitted that the decision may be explained on the basis that the parties were of equal bargaining power and would not have agreed on a more draconian clause than was reasonably necessary to protect the buyer's interests.[1116] Had the parties been less equal, the "not extravagant or unconscionable" test might have been applied in a less generous way.

[1111] [2015] UKSC 67.

[1112] Information received during seminars on the case at the Judicial College.

[1113] Nor, according to the majority, to avoid it being unfair within the meaning of the Unfair Terms in Consumer Contracts Regulations 1999 (and now the Consumer Rights Act 2015), but see the dissent on this point by Lord Toulson. This aspect of the case is discussed below, para.38–251A.

[1114] [2015] UKSC 67 at [100].

[1115] For the kinds of clause that are within the penalty rule, see below, paras 26–215 et seq.

[1116] See below, para.26–214.

"Not ... extravagant". The word "extravagant" can be taken to mean that **26–213** disproportion will not be judged harshly; as in "pre-estimate" cases,[1117] the parties will be allowed "a generous margin of error". But otherwise it seems "usually to amount to the same thing" as "unconscionable".[1118]

[1117] See above, para.26–185.

[1118] Lords Neuberger and Sumption [2015] UKSC 67 at [31].

"Not ... unconscionable". It is not clear whether the word "unconsciona- **26–214** ble", which recurs in all the judgments, was intended to have any independent effect. Lord Toulson clearly thought "unconscionable" added nothing to "extravagant",[1118a] but Lord Hodge twice refers to it as a separate requirement.[1118b] Lords Neuberger and Sumption said[1118c]

> "the circumstances in which the contract was made are not entirely irrelevant. In a negotiated contract between properly advised parties of comparable bargaining power, the strong initial presumption must be that the parties themselves are the best judges of what is legitimate in a provision dealing with the consequences of breach."

Lord Mance also said that[1118d]

> " . . . the extent to which the parties were negotiating at arm's length on the basis of legal advice and had every opportunity to appreciate what they were agreeing must at least be a relevant factor."

These statements do not appear to mean that there is a separate requirement of procedural fairness. It seems more likely that all Lords Neuberger, Sumption and Mance meant was that if the parties meet on more-or-less equal terms, the non-breaching party is less likely to get away with a provision that is disproportionate to what it needs if there is no effective bargaining pressure from the other party. This may well be one reason[1118e] why the court did not question whether the provisions in the *Cavendish Square* case were proportionate to the buyer's legitimate interest.[1118f]

[1118] [2015] UKSC 67 at [293].

[1118b] Lord Hodge does not seem to have been referring to the general doctrine of unconscionable bargains, which normally requires claimants to show they were suffering from an identifiable bargaining weakness: see Main Work, Vol.I, paras 8–133 and 8–135. The possible application of the doctrine in cases like *Cavendish Square* is considered above, para.8–135.

[1118c] [2015] UKSC 67 at [35].

[1118d] [2015] UKSC 67 at [152].

[1118e] Lords Neuberger and Sumption's approach may also have been affected by their view that the clauses were not subject to the penalty rules at all because they were "primary obligations": see below, para.26–216H.

[1118f] See above, para.26–212.

(e) *Scope of the Law of Penalties*

26–215   **Sums payable on and other consequences of breach.** The penalty rules apply to sums that are payable on breach of contract by the defendant and to a variety of other clauses that will have an adverse consequence for a defendant who is in breach the contract, such as a clause that disentitles a defendant who is in breach from receiving the full amount of the price that would otherwise be paid.[1118g] The law on penalties is not applicable to many sums of money payable under a contract. Thus, it is not relevant where the claimant claims an agreed sum (a debt) which is due from the defendant in return for the claimant's performance of his obligations,[1118h] or which is due upon the occurrence of an event other than a breach of the defendant's contractual duty owed to the claimant,[1118i] though there have been suggestions that some such clauses may be "disguised penalties" that do fall within the rules.[1118j] It has also been said that some clauses, though "triggered" by a breach by the defendant, are exempt from the rules because they reflect the "primary obligations" of the defendant, whereas the penalty rules are said to apply only to "secondary obligations".[1118k]

[1118g] See below, para.26–216.

[1118h] *White & Carter (Councils) Ltd v McGregor* [1962] A.C. 413 (above, para.26–104). However, in a contract in which the liquidated damages were only payable while the contract remained on foot, the innocent party was not entitled to ignore a repudiation and keep the contract alive so as to be able to continue to claim liquidated damages, as they would have no legitimate interest is doing so: *MSC Mediterranean Shipping Co SA v Cottonex Anstalt* [2015] EWHC 283 (Comm) at [94]–[105]; the Court of Appeal [2016] EWCA Civ 789 agreed that there was no legitimate interest in continuing to perform but because the contractual venture had been frustrated: see above, para.26–106. The contrast between a debt and liquidated damages is drawn by the House of Lords in *President of India v Lips Maritime Corp* [1988] A.C. 395, 422–423, 424.

[1118i] See below, para.26–216C.

[1118j] See below, para.26–216G.

[1118k] See below, para.26–216H.

(i) *Types of Clause within the Penalty Doctrine*

26–216   **Types of clause within the penalty rules.** In *Cavendish Square Holding BV v Makdessi*[1118l] the Supreme Court held that the penalty clause rules apply not only to agreed damages clauses but also to provisions that would prevent a party who breaks the contract from receiving a sum to which it would otherwise be entitled,[1118m] and also provisions that require a party in breach to transfer property to the other party at less than its full value.[1118n] The Supreme Court also stated that the penalty rules also apply to deposits and forfeiture clauses; these will be considered in a separate section.[1118o]

[1118l] [2015] UKSC 67, [2015] 3 W.L.R. 1373.

[1118m] See [2015] UKSC 67 at [170] (Lord Mance); [226] (Lord Hodge); Lord Toulson agreed with both of them (at [292]). Lords Neuberger and Sumption were prepared to assume this without deciding it (at [73]); they considered that cl.5.1 of the agreement in the *Cavendish Square* case was part of the parties' primary obligations and therefore altogether outside the penalty rules: see below, para.26–216H. However, Lord Clarke preferred to leave this question open; he must therefore have held that the penalty rules do apply to clauses of this type. In *Gilbert Ash (Northern) Ltd v Modern Engineering (Bristol) Ltd* [1974] A.C. 689 the House of Lords had considered a clause entitling the contractor to "suspend or withhold" the payment of money due to the subcontractor on any breach of contract. It had been conceded that the clause fell within the doctrine, but a majority of the House appeared to consider that the concession was correct: see [2015] UKSC 67 at [70], [154] and [226].

[1118n] See at [170] and [183] (Lord Mance); [230] and [280] (Lord Hodge). On this point Lord Clarke (at [291]) agreed with Lord Hodge and Lord Toulson (at [292]) with both Lord Mance and Lord Hodge.

[1118o] See below, paras 26–216N et seq.

Acceleration clauses. An "acceleration" clause is often found in contracts providing for payment by instalments: on default in paying one instalment, all future instalments become immediately payable as one sum. Although the operation of these clauses produces results which may be "penal", the courts have usually enforced them on the ground that they do not increase the contract-breaker's overall obligation.[1118p] The Court of Appeal has held that it is not a penalty for an acceleration clause in a contract of loan to provide that, upon failure to pay an agreed instalment, the whole capital of the loan becomes immediately due and repayable.[1118q] But it might be held to be a penalty if it provided that, upon such failure, future interest (viz on payments not yet due) should be payable immediately.[1118r]   26–216A

[1118p] *Protector Endowment Loan Co v Grice* (1880) 5 Q.B.D. 592 (a loan case); *Wallingford v Mutual Society* (1880) 5 App. Cas. 685. See Goode [1982] J. Bus. L. 148; cf. *Wadham Stringer Finance Ltd v Meaney* [1981] 1 W.L.R. 39, 48 (see Main Work, Vol.II, para.39–272); *Edgeworth Capital (Luxembourg) Sarl v Ramblas Investments BV* [2015] EWHC 150 (Comm) at [67], citing this paragraph as it appeared in the 31st edition; the Court of Appeal, [2016] EWCA Civ 412, did not comment on this point. The High Court of Australia has sometimes upheld acceleration clauses (*IAC (Leasing) Ltd v Humphrey* (1972) 126 C.L.R. 131 (see also Main Work, Vol.II, para.39–353)) but sometimes not (holding them to be penalties): *O'Dea v Allstates Leasing Systems (WA) Pty Ltd* (1983) 152 C.L.R. 359; Muir (1985) 10 Sydney L.R. 503; *AMEV-UDC Finance Ltd v Austin* (1986) 162 C.L.R. 170; cf. *Esanda Finance Corp Ltd v Plessing* (1989) 166 C.L.R. 131.

[1118q] *The Angelic Star* [1988] 1 Lloyd's Rep. 122, 125, 127.

[1118r] *The Angelic Star* [1988] 1 Lloyd's Rep. 122. cf. *Lordsvale Finance Plc v Bank of Zambia* [1996] Q.B. 752 (see above, para.26–193).

Termination for breach of condition. As explained earlier,[1118s] where the hirer has neither repudiated the hiring (or hire-purchase) agreement, nor committed a "fundamental breach" of it, but the owner terminates it in the exercise of an express power to do so conferred by the agreement, the owner's damages are limited to loss suffered through any breaches up to the date of the termination.[1118t] It was noted, however, that this principle does not apply where the contract made the broken term into a condition, any breach of which entitled the innocent party to terminate (e.g. a clause making compliance with time "of the   26–216B essence"[1118u]). In this case the innocent party may both terminate the contract and recover damages for the loss of the bargain (viz in respect of all the outstanding obligations of the other party).[1118v] A clause that makes the hirer liable for a genuine pre-estimate of the owners' full loss in such a case will be valid. The Court of Appeal decided that the clause making prompt payment "of the essence" when it would not be so otherwise[1118w] is not itself subject to the law on penalties.[1118x] The difference between the two types of clause (viz an express power to terminate, and a clause making time of the essence) is "one of drafting form and wholly without substance".[1118y] The result is that the position of the parties may be changed by a simple, small change in the terminology of the contract which makes every term a "condition" in the sense of a term any breach of which entitles the promisee to terminate.[1118z] This follows, however, not from the law on penalties but from the firmly established rule that the parties are free to agree that any term of the contract is a condition.[1118aa]

[1118s] See above, para.26–192.

[1118t] *Financings Ltd v Baldock* [1963] 2 Q.B. 104. (A "minimum payment" clause specifying a larger sum will be held to be a penalty: see above, para.26–192.) The principle stated in the text has been regularly followed by the Court of Appeal: *Brady v St Margaret's Trust Ltd* [1963] 2 Q.B. 494; *Charterhouse Credit Co Ltd v Tolly* [1963] 2 Q.B. 683; *United Dominions Trust (Commercial) Ltd v Ennis* [1968] 1 Q.B. 54; *Capital Finance Co Ltd v Donati* (1977) 121 S.J. 270; *Lombard North Central Plc v Butterworth* [1987] Q.B. 527. See also the Australian cases cited, above, para.26–216A, n.1118p.

[1118u] See Main Work, paras 21 011 et seq.

[1118v] The *Lombard* case [1987] Q.B. 527. See Treitel [1987] L.M.C.L.Q. 143; Beale (1988) 104 L.Q.R. 355.

[1118w] In the *Lombard* case [1987] Q.B. 527, it was held that, according to common law principles, the hirer had not committed a repudiatory breach of the contract: at 543–545. The court nevertheless awarded as damages at common law almost the same sum which it had previously found not to be a genuine pre-estimate of loss (a penalty).

[1118x] The *Lombard* case [1987] Q.B. 527, 536–537.

[1118y] The *Lombard* case [1987] Q.B. 527, 546.

[1118z] Would the law uphold a clause providing expressly that for any breach, however trivial, the damages shall be assessed on the basis that the whole benefit of the contract has been lost by the other party? cf. decisions on mitigation, such as *The Solholt* [1983] 1 Lloyd's Rep. 605 (Main Work, Vol.I, para.26–093).

[1118aa] See Main Work, Vol.I, para.13–026.

(ii) *Events other than Breach*

26–216C   **Sum payable on event other than breach.** In *Cavendish Square Holding BV v Makdessi* and *ParkingEye Ltd v Beavis*[1118ab] the Supreme Court endorsed the view that the penalty clause rules apply only to sums payable, and equivalent consequences,[1118ac] that follow from a breach of contract. Previous authority was not wholly clear. In *Campbell Discount Co Ltd v Bridge*,[1118ad] a hire-purchase agreement permitted the hirer at his option to terminate the hiring during the period of the agreement, and provided that the hirer should thereupon pay a sum by way of agreed compensation for the depreciation of the chattel; the Court of Appeal held that the owner could recover the agreed sum, since being payable upon an event not constituting a breach of the agreement, it fell outside the scope of the law as to penalties. In the House of Lords[1118ae] the decision was based on a different view of the facts,[1118af] but four of their Lordships expressed obiter their views on the ruling of the Court of Appeal; two agreed that the law as to penalties was inapplicable, but two were prepared to hold that the hirer was entitled to some relief. The later decision of the House of Lords in the *Export Credits Guarantee* case[1118ag] appeared to support the restriction of the scope of the law on penalties to payments[1118ah] triggered by a breach of contract. The House held that the law did not apply to a clause providing for the contract-breaker (the defendant) to pay a specified sum to the plaintiff upon the happening of a certain event which was *not* the breach of a contractual duty owed by the defendant to the plaintiff. So it could not be a penalty where the defendant had agreed to reimburse the plaintiff the amount paid by the plaintiff to third parties under a guarantee (even where the plaintiff's obligation to meet the guarantee arose on the occasion of the defendant's breach of his contractual duties owed to other parties).[1118ai] Although the case concerned a guarantee in a complex commercial arrangement and the plaintiff was claiming only the sum it had actually lost, their Lordships' limitation on the scope of the law on penalties was expressed in such wide terms that it would prevent many other clauses from being subject to that law, for example a sum payable by one party should it exercise an option as to perform at a later date than anticipated (but not required).[1118aj] Although statutory protection is available in some cases[1118ak] the common law position has been thought unsatisfactory; for instance, an honest business hirer, who terminates his hire-purchase agreement when he finds that he cannot keep up the instalments, is in a worse position than the hirer who simply breaks his agreement by failing to pay the instalments.[1118al] The High Court of Australia had not followed the *Export Credits Guarantee* case,[1118am] holding that a clause may be a penalty:

> "if, as a matter of substance, it is collateral (or accessory) to a primary stipulation in favour of a second party and this collateral stipulation, upon the failure of the primary stipulation, imposes upon the first party an additional detriment, the penalty, to the benefit of the second party."[1118an]

However in *Cavendish Square Holding BV v Makdessi* and *ParkingEye Ltd v Beavis*[1118ao] the Supreme Court[1118ap] rejected this approach, which in any event they regarded as unworkable,[1118aq] and said that the penalty rules only come into play when a clause is triggered by a breach.[1118ar]

[1118ab] [2015] UKSC 67, [2015] 3 W.L.R. 1373.

[1118ac] See above, para.26–216.

[1118ad] [1961] 1 Q.B. 445 (following *Associated Distributors Ltd v Hall* [1938] 2 K.B. 83); see Main Work, Vol.II, paras 39–349—39–354. The decision is based on the non-statutory law. For statutory regulation of hire-purchase agreements, see Main Work, Vol.II, paras 39–356 et seq.

[1118ae] [1962] A.C. 600.

[1118af] viz that the hirer had committed a breach. The law on penalties applies to a minimum payment clause if the agreement is in fact terminated on the ground of the hirer's breach: *Cooden Engineering Co Ltd v Stanford* [1953] 1 Q.B. 86; *Lamdon Trust Ltd v Hurrell* [1955] 1 W.L.R. 391. See Main Work, Vol.II, paras 39–349—39–354.

[1118ag] *Export Credits Guarantee Department v Universal Oil Products Co* [1983] 1 W.L.R. 399. It is unfortunate that the short speech in this case made no attempt to discuss the opinions expressed in the *Campbell Discount* case [1962] A.C. 600. See also *Euro London Appointments Ltd v Claessens*

International Ltd [2006] EWCA Civ 385, [2006] 2 Lloyd's Rep. 436 (a condition precedent imposing no obligation).

[1118ah] And similar events: see above, para.26–216 and below, paras 26–216N et seq.

[1118ai] *Export Credits Guarantee Department v Universal Oil Products Co* [1983] 1 W.L.R. 399.

[1118aj] See also *Edgeworth Capital (Luxembourg) Sarl v Ramblas Investments BV* [2015] EWHC 150 (Comm); [2016] EWCA Civ 412. In *Berg v Blackburn Rovers Football Club & Athletic Plc* [2013] EWHC 1070 (Ch), [2013] I.R.L.R. 537 it was held that the penalty rules did not apply to a payment due when one party to a fixed-term employment contract exercised a right to terminate it early. In *M&J Polymers Ltd v Imerys Minerals Ltd* [2008] EWHC 344 (Comm), [2008] All E.R. (D) 445 (Feb) it was held that a "take or pay" clause is subject to the penalty rules (though it was held on the facts not to be a penalty). It is submitted that this will depend on the form of the clause. It will not be subject to the penalty rules if the buyer is simply obliged to pay for a minimum quantity with an option whether or not to take delivery of all the goods. On the facts of the case, however, it was held that the buyer was in breach of an obligation to order a certain quantity (at [41]). See also *E-Nik Ltd v Secretary of State for Communities and Local Government* [2012] EWHC 3027 (Comm) at [25] (clause requiring a customer to pay for a minimum amount of services was treated as being subject to the penalty rules but nonetheless upheld). In *Associated British Ports v Ferryways NV* [2008] EWHC 1265 (Comm), [2008] 2 Lloyd's Rep. 353 (affirmed on other grounds [2009] EWCA Civ 189, [2009] 1 Lloyd's Rep. 595) it was held that the penalty rules did not apply to sums due under a "minimum through-put" clause.

[1118ak] In particular under the Unfair Terms in Consumer Contracts Regulations 1999 or Consumer Rights Act 2015 s.62: see below, Main Work, Vol.II, paras 38–201 et seq. and 38–334 et seq. When the term provides for the forfeiture of a deposit or other sum, see below, paras 26–216N et seq.

[1118al] See the Law Commission's Working Paper No.61 (1975), paras 17–26; *Edgeworth Capital (Luxembourg) Sarl v Ramblas Investments BV* [2015] EWHC 150 (Comm) at [59] (rev'd on other grounds [2016] EWCA Civ 412).

[1118am] *Export Credits Guarantee Department v Universal Oil Products Co* [1983] 1 W.L.R. 399. It is unfortunate that the short speech in this case made no attempt to discuss the opinions expressed in the *Campbell Discount* case [1962] A.C. 600. See also *Euro London Appointments Ltd v Claessens International Ltd* [2006] EWCA Civ 385, [2006] 2 Lloyd's Rep. 436 (a condition precedent imposing no obligation); *Jervis v Harris* [1996] Ch. 195, 206–207.

[1118an] *Andrews v Australia and New Zealand Banking Group Ltd* (2012) 247 C.L.R. 205 at [10].

[1118ao] [2015] UKSC 67, [2015] 3 W.L.R. 1373.

[1118ap] Lords Neuberger and Sumption (with whom Lord Carnwath and, seemingly on this point, Lord Clarke agreed) [2015] UKSC 67 at [42]–[43]; Lord Hodge (with whom Lord Toulson agreed) at [241]. Note however the suggestion that a clause may be "a disguised penalty", discussed below, para.26–216G. Lord Mance said that the point concerning clauses that operate on events other than breach was not up for decision but the distinction is "not without rational or logical underpinning": at [130].

[1118aq] Lords Neuberger and Sumption [2015] UKSC 67 at [42].

[1118ar] If the sum is payable on one of several events, some of which are breaches and others are not, the penalty rule will apply if the event that in fact triggered the payment was a breach, but not otherwise, nor if, as on the facts of the case, it was a breach of a different contract by another party: *Edgeworth Capital (Luxembourg) Sarl v Ramblas Investments BV* [2015] EWHC 150 (Comm) at [60], [69]; the Court of Appeal confirmed that the penalty rule did not apply, [2016] EWCA Civ 412 at [7]. The death or bankruptcy of a party might be another event, not constituting a breach, upon which money is to be paid. cf. *Mount v Oldham Corp* [1973] Q.B. 309 (claim for a term's school fees in lieu of notice withdrawing a pupil).

26–216D   **Sums payable on exercise of an option under the contract.** Thus the law does not apply where one party to the contract is given an option to choose a particular method of performance, subject to his making a stipulated payment to the other[1118as]; or where a member of a pooling agreement failed to pay his levy to finance litigation and was excluded from sharing in the proceeds of the litigation.[1118at] It does not apply to an employee's loss of contingent future interests in fund units to which he would have been entitled had his employment continued.[1118au] In the Court of Appeal in the *ParkingEye* case it was said that the penalty rules would not apply to an £85 charge for overstaying in an otherwise free parking facility if the arrangement were expressed in terms of a licence to use the car park subject to conditions coupled with an agreement to pay the charge if the conditions are not adhered to.[1118av]

[1118as] *Fratelli Moretti SpA v Nidera Handelscompagnie BV* [1981] 2 Lloyd's Rep. 47, 53.
[1118at] *Nutting v Baldwin* [1995] 1 W.L.R. 201.
[1118au] *Imam-Sadeque v Bluebay Asset Management (Services) Ltd* [2012] EWHC 3511 (QB), citing the Australian case of *Interstar Wholesale Finance Pty Ltd v Integral Home Loans Pty Ltd* (2008) 257 A.L.R. 292. The provision was in any event commercially justifiable and not penal when read in the light of the contract as a whole: [2012] EWHC 3511 (QB) at [223]–[234].
[1118av] *ParkingEye Ltd v Beavis* [2015] EWCA Civ 402 at [23].

Reimbursement is not a penalty. If a contract provides that in a certain event a sum of money paid under the contract is to be repaid to the original payer, the reimbursement cannot be a penalty.[1118aw] So where the defendant received an insurance payment on the basis of his permanent disablement the insurers were able to enforce his undertaking to pay them "a penalty" of the same amount if he took part in a specified sport in future.[1118ax]   **26–216E**

[1118aw] *Alder v Moore* [1961] 2 Q.B. 57 (approving *Re Apex Supply Co Ltd* [1942] Ch. 108).
[1118ax] *Alder v Moore* [1961] 2 Q.B. 57. Although the defendant had agreed not to take part again in professional football, the majority considered that this was not a case in which the defendant was in breach by so doing but of a condition on the defendant retaining the insurance payment: see at 65 and 77.

Incentive payments. The reverse of an agreed damages clause is an incentive payment such as an extra payment for early completion. The law on penalties does not apply to a clause providing for an *increase* in the price if certain targets in the contract are bettered or if costs are reduced; similarly, the price for a specially-manufactured machine may be graduated according to its efficiency in operation. A Government report has recommended that in building contracts incentive payments should be preferred to agreed damages clauses.[1118ay]   **26–216F**

[1118ay] Banwell Report (Report of the Committee on Placing and Management of Contracts for Building and Civil Engineering Work) (HMSO, 1964), para.9.22.

Disguised penalties. Some doubt is thrown on the division between sums payable upon breach and sums payable on other events by the suggestion by some of their Lordships in *Cavendish Square Holding BV v Makdessi* and *ParkingEye Ltd v Beavis*[1118az] that certain clauses may amount to "disguised penalties". This follows a suggestion by Bingham L.J. in *Interfoto Picture Library Ltd v Stiletto Visual Programmes Ltd*[1118ba] that the clause in that case, which required a party who had hired photographic slides to pay a much higher charge if the slides were not returned within a fixed period, might be a "disguised penalty".[1118bb] It is hard to find any support for such a concept in earlier cases, and it is unclear how a disguised penalty differs from other sums payable if the party exercises an option under the contract. The only possible distinction seems to be that the amount of the payment is out of proportion to the claimant's interest in obtaining performance—in which case the "disguised penalty" rule would have the effect that the penalty clause rules (including the new "legitimate deterrent rule") would after all apply to a clause setting a price on an option that the defendant has chosen to exercise.   **26–216G**

1118az [2015] UKSC 67, [2015] 3 W.L.R. 1373 at [77] (Lords Neuberger and Sumption) and [258] (Lord Hodge).
1118ba [1989] Q.B. 433.
1118bb [1989] Q.B. 433, 439. The decision rested on the ground that the clause was not incorporated into the contract: see Main Work, Vol.I, para.13–015.

(iii) *"Primary Obligations"*

26–216H   **Primary obligations.** In *Cavendish Square Holding BV v Makdessi*[1118bc] Lords Neuberger and Sumption (with whom Lord Carnwath agreed) held that the clauses which provided that the seller of the business, if he was in breach of the non-competition covenants, would not receive the outstanding instalments of the price, and would require him to transfer further shares to the buyers at a much reduced value, were not subject to the penalty rules at all. Even if they were triggered by the seller's breach, clause 5.1 bore no relation to damages; it represented the reduced price that the buyer was prepared to pay for the business if it could not count on the loyalty of the seller, and so formed part of the "primary obligations" of the parties.[1118bd] The analysis of clause 5.6 was essentially similar: it represented the reduced price that the purchaser was prepared to pay when it could not count on the loyalty of Makdessi.[1118be] The law places controls over only the parties' secondary obligations, not their primary obligations,[1118bf] and both clauses belong among the primary obligations, even if the occasion of their operation was a breach of contract.[1118bg] In any event, both clauses were justified by the same legitimate interest in matching the price to the value that the seller was providing.[1118bh] Unlike an agreed damages clause, if the clauses did not stand there is no scale by which the court could make an award. The other members of the Supreme Court either decided the case on the ground that the clauses did not amount to penalties or preferred to leave the matter open.[1118bi] With respect, it is unclear how a payment (or other obligation that is within the doctrine[1118bj]) that is "triggered" by a breach of contract by the defendant but which is a primary obligation is to is to be distinguished from an agreed damages clause. The fact that the clause is in the form of a price reduction seems to emphasise form over substance; and while it is true that ex ante there is no alternative scale by which the court could fix appropriate prices, when an agreed damages clause is held to be unenforceable the court makes an ex post assessment of the actual loss suffered by the claimant. It seems that a court could equally assess damages in terms of the reduction in value in the shares caused by a breach by the seller of a non-competition covenant, and the valuation could include an element for the risk that the seller who had been disloyal once may be disloyal again.

1118bc [2015] UKSC 67, [2015] 3 W.L.R. 1373.
1118bd [2015] UKSC 67 at [74]–[75].
1118be [2015] UKSC 67 at [81].
1118bf [2015] UKSC 67 at [14] and [32].
1118bg [2015] UKSC 67 at [83].
1118bh [2015] UKSC 67 at [82].
1118bi Lord Mance said that cl.5.1 had the effect of revising the price payable for the shares but he clearly considered the clause to be subject to the penalty doctrine: see [2015] UKSC 67 at [181];

similarly, though cl.5.6 had the effect of reshaping of the parties' primary relationship (at [183]), it was valid because it was neither exorbitant or unconscionable (at [185]). Lord Hodge agreed that there were "strong arguments" for regarding each clause as primary obligations to which the doctrine does not apply: at [270] and [280]; but he decided the validity of cl.5.1 by applying the penalty doctrine, and held that cl.5.6 was a secondary obligation, adding that "if all such clauses were treated as primary obligations, there would be considerable scope for abuse". Lord Toulson agreed with the relevant parts of both Lord Mance's and Lord Hodge's judgments. Lord Clarke agreed with Lord Hodge rather than with Lords Neuberger and Sumption on these points: at [291].

[1118bj] See above, para.26–216.

"Core" obligations rather than primary obligations. One can understand   **26–216I**
the reluctance of judges to relieve a party from an obligation, whether it is correctly analysed as primary or secondary, that was negotiated with the assistance of experts and presumably agreed to in full knowledge of its possible implications, especially one that must have been seen as a central element of the agreement. Possibly a more useful distinction might be based on an approach suggested by Lord Toulson during argument, as a possible substitute for the penalty clause doctrine (which the Court had been invited to abandon[1118bk]). This was to borrow from the Directive on Unfair Terms in Consumer Contracts[1118bl] and ask whether the provision was a "core term".[1118bm] "Core" terms are likely to have been considered carefully by each party, even if the parties were not of equal sophistication or bargaining power, and therefore there is less reason to interfere than with more peripheral clauses that may not have been fully taken into account by both parties. The suggestion seems to be that if the change in price is so central to the deal that the party agreeing to it must have had it in mind, it would be exempt from control as a penalty. Lord Toulson did not, however, repeat this suggestion in his judgment.

[1118bk] See above, para.26–196.
[1118bl] 93/13/EC: see Main Work, Vol.II, paras 38–199 et seq.
[1118bm] In other words, it is the main subject matter or concerns the adequacy of the price or other remuneration and is therefore exempt from assessment for fairness provided that it is in plain and intelligible language, see art.4(2).

(iv) *"Invoicing back" Clauses*

"Invoicing back" clauses. The express terms of the contract may not only   **26–216J**
exclude or limit the innocent party's right to claim damages for breach of contract,[1118bn] but may also provide other provisions intended to apply in the event of a breach. Subject to the law as to penalties,[1118bo] and to the effect of the Unfair Contract Terms Act 1977[1118bp] or (if applicable) the Consumer Rights Act 2015,[1118bq] the courts will enforce these terms, despite the unexpected results which may occur. In one case,[1118br] a clause in a contract for the sale of goods provided that if the sellers made default in shipping, the contract should "be closed by invoicing back the goods" at the closing price fixed by the London Corn Trade Association. The sellers failed to ship, and the Association declared a closing price, which, because of a fall in market price, was lower than the contract price, so that a balance was due in favour of the sellers. Nevertheless, the Court of Appeal enforced the clause, despite the fact that the sellers were the

party in default.[1118bs] An "invoicing back" clause may not be interpreted as the exclusive remedy,[1118bt] e.g. the clause may not prevent the buyer obtaining damages for his loss of profits,[1118bu] and judges have interpreted such clauses restrictively.[1118bv] An "invoicing back" clause may also allow a percentage of the market price to be added to, or deducted from, the price, which if reasonable, will be upheld as liquidated damages covering items of loss not covered by the price alone.[1118bw]

[1118bn] On exemption clauses, see Main Work, Vol.I, Ch.15, above.
[1118bo] Above, paras 26–178 et seq.
[1118bp] See Main Work, Vol.I, paras 15–066 et seq.
[1118bq] See Main Work, Vol.II, paras 38–334 et seq.
[1118br] *Lancaster v J.F. Turner & Co Ltd* [1924] 2 K.B. 222 (Scrutton L.J. dissenting); followed in *J.F. Adair & Co Ltd v Birnbaum* [1939] 2 K.B. 149 (and the earlier case noted, 173); *Podar Trading Co Ltd v Tagher* [1949] 2 K.B. 277. cf. *James Laing, Son & Co Ltd v Eastcheap Dried Fruit Co Ltd* [1961] 2 Lloyd's Rep. 277.
[1118bs] Some clauses are drafted differently and avoid this difficulty, e.g. the clause may apply only to the defaulting buyer, and only if the market price has fallen: *Alexandria Cotton and Trading Co (Sudan) Ltd v Cotton Co of Ethiopia Ltd* [1963] 1 Lloyd's Rep. 576.
[1118bt] *Roth, Schmidt & Co v D. Nagase & Co Ltd* (1920) 2 Ll. L. Rep. 36 CA (the clause did not expressly exclude the right to reject the goods or to recover damages upon rejection).
[1118bu] *Re Bourgeois and Wilson Holgate & Co* (1920) 25 Com. Cas. 260 (the Court of Appeal decided in this case that the seller in these circumstances could not enforce the clause against the buyer).
[1118bv] One judge has held that the interpretation of a clause which requires damages to be paid *to* the defaulting party is contrary to "natural justice": *Cassir, Moore & Co Ltd v Eastcheap Dried Fruit Co* [1962] 1 Lloyd's Rep. 400, 402. See also the qualifications suggested in *Lancaster v J.F. Turner & Co Ltd* [1924] 2 K.B. 222, 231; *J.F. Adair & Co Ltd v Birnbaum* [1939] 2 K.B. 149, 169.
[1118bw] *Robert Stewart & Sons Ltd v Carapanayoti & Co Ltd* [1962] 1 W.L.R. 34.

(f) *Effect of Clause if a Penalty*

26–216K   **Penalty clause is not enforceable.** As mentioned earlier,[1118bx] if a clause is penal because it passes neither the "genuine pre-estimate" test[1118by] nor the "legitimate deterrent test,[1118bz] the clause will be wholly unenforceable.[1118ca] The court has no power to re-write the clause in order to make it valid.[1118cb]

[1118bx] See above, para.26–178A.
[1118by] See above, para.26–182.
[1118bz] See above, para.26–196.
[1118ca] *Cavendish Square Holding BV v Makdessi* and *ParkingEye Ltd v Beavis* [2015] UKSC 67, [2015] 3 W.L.R. 1373 at [9] and at [291], where Lord Clarke expressed his agreement with this part of the Lords Neuberger and Sumption's judgment.
[1118cb] [2015] UKSC 67 at [84]–[86], [283] and [292], disapproving *Jobson v Johnson* [1989] 1 W.L.R. 1026 on this point. Lord Mance preferred to leave this point for further argument (at [186]).

26–216L   **Can damages exceed the sum fixed in penal clause?** A clause which is not a genuine pre-estimate, e.g. because it stipulates for more than the likely loss, and which is therefore a penalty, may be ignored if it is for less than the actual damage suffered. Where a charterparty contained the following clause: "[p]enalty for non-performance of this agreement proved damages, not exceeding estimated amount of freight", it was held that the clause provided a penalty and not a limitation of liability, so that the party complaining of non-performance was entitled to recover damages for his actual loss although it exceeded the estimated amount of freight.[1118cc] It is unsettled whether this principle applies to penalty clauses in other types of contract, so as to entitle the claimant to ignore the sum stipulated as a penalty (where it was clearly not intended to limit liability) and to sue for damages for a greater amount to compensate him for his actual loss.[1118cd]

[1118cc] *Wall v Rederiaktiebolaget Luggude* [1915] 3 K.B. 66 (approved by the House of Lords in *Watts, Watts & Co Ltd v Mitsui & Co Ltd* [1917] A.C. 227). But this case may require reconsideration in the light of the *Suisse Atlantique* case [1967] 1 A.C. 361 (where a demurrage clause was held to be an agreed damages clause) and the *Photo Production* case [1980] A.C. 827.

[1118cd] In *Cellulose Acetate Silk Co Ltd v Widnes Foundry (1925) Ltd* [1933] A.C. 20, 26, the House left: " . . . open the question whether, where a penalty is plainly less in amount than the prospective damages, there is any legal objection to suing on it or, in a suitable case, ignoring it and suing for damages". cf. dicta to the effect that the penalty fixes the maximum recoverable: *Wilbeam v Ashton* (1807) 1 Camp. 78; *Elphinstone v Monkland Iron & Coal Co* (1886) L.R. 11 App. Cas. 332, 346; *Elsley v J.G. Collins Insurance Agencies Ltd* (1978) 83 D.L.R. (3d) 1, 14–16; *W.&J. Investments Ltd v Bunting* [1984] 1 N.S.W.L.R. 331, 335–336. See also Hudson (1974) 90 L.Q.R. 31; Gordon (1974) 90 L.Q.R. 296; Hudson (1975) 91 L.Q.R. 25; Barton (1976) 92 L.Q.R. 20; Hudson (1985) 101 L.Q.R. 480; Peel (ed.), *Treitel on The Law of Contract*, 14th edn (2016), para.20–140.

(g) *Consumer Contracts*

Sums payable on breach in consumer contracts.[1118ce] The Unfair Terms in Consumer Contracts Regulations 1999 provided that in a contract between a business and a consumer an "unfair term" that was not individually negotiated was not be binding on the consumer. For consumer contracts made after October 1, 2015, Pt 2 of the Consumer Rights Act 2015 provides that an unfair term[1118cf] in a consumer contract will not be binding on the consumer. The Regulations and the Act give illustrations of terms which may be regarded as unfair: relevant to clauses fixing damages is "requiring any consumer who fails to fulfil his obligation to pay a disproportionately high sum in compensation".[1118cg] So a consumer will be able to appeal to this standard, as well as to the common law on penalties; and it has been held that a term may be unfair even though on the facts it did not amount to a penalty at common law.[1118ch]   **26–216M**

[1118ce] SI 1999/2083.

[1118cf] Whether negotiated or not: s.62. See Main Work, Vol.II, para.38–358.

[1118cg] 1999 Regulations Sch.2 para.1(e); 2015 Act Sch.2 Pt 1 para.(6).

[1118ch] *Munkenbeck & Marshall v Harold* [2005] EWHC 356 (TCC), [2005] All E.R. (D) 227; see below, Vol.II, para.38–280. For clauses requiring a consumer to make a payment on some event that is not a breach of contract, see above, para.26–216C.

(h) *Deposits and Forfeiture of Sums Paid*

Deposits and forfeiture of sums paid.[1118ci] A contract may, instead of fixing a sum to be paid upon breach, provide that a sum already paid shall be forfeited[1118cj] upon breach by the party who paid it.[1118ck] Alternatively, a sum may be paid as a deposit, in which case the sum is forfeited if the payer breaks   **26–216N**

the contract.[1118cl] If the deposit has not been paid when the contract is terminated, but it was payable, it may be recovered as a debt[1118cm]; if the contract was repudiated and terminated before the deposit became payable, the innocent party may recover the amount of the deposit by way of damages.[1118cn] In *Cavendish Square Holding BV v Makdessi* and *ParkingEye Ltd v Beavis*[1118co] the Supreme Court said that both deposits and forfeiture clauses are subject to the penalty rules (though it will be submitted that to some extent the rules still differ[1118cp]). Many deposits and forfeiture provisions will also fall within the Law of Property Act 1925 s.49(2), the Consumer Credit Act 1974[1118cq] and the Consumer Rights Act 2015.[1118cr]

[1118ci] See Goff and Jones, *The Law of Unjust Enrichment*, 8th edn (2011), Ch.14; *McGregor on Damages*, 19th edn (2014), paras 15–096 et seq.; the Law Commission, Working Paper No.61 (1975) ("Penalty Clauses and Forfeiture of Moneys Paid"), paras 50, 65, 66; Smith [2001] C.L.J. 178; cf. *Commissioner of Public Works v Hills* [1906] A.C. 368 (recovery of amount deposited as "security" in a building contract; above, para.26–187).

[1118cj] The payee "forfeits" the sum where he retains it for his own beneficial use, having freed himself of any further obligations under the contract by terminating the contract on account of the payer's breach. It is then up to the payer to challenge the forfeiture if he has any legal ground for doing so.

[1118ck] If the sum is a deposit paid by the buyer (viz a sum intended to be received by the seller as a security for the completion of the purchase by the buyer) it will be assumed that it is intended to be forfeited to the seller if the buyer defaults: *Howe v Smith* (1884) 27 Ch. D. 89, 97–98 (Main Work, Vol.I, para.29–068); *Stockloser v Johnson* [1954] 1 Q.B. 476, 490 ("or the money is expressly paid as a deposit (which is equivalent to a forfeiture clause)"). The court has power to order the return of a deposit paid under a contract for the sale of land.

[1118cl] *Howe v Smith* (1889) 27 Ch. D. 89. If the payee claims damages from the payer, he must give credit for the amount of the deposit: see the dictum of Fry L.J. at 104 and *Ng v Ashley King (Developments) Ltd* [2010] EWHC 456 (Ch).

[1118cm] See above, Main Work, Vol.I, paras 24–053 and 26–008.

[1118cn] *Damon Compagnia Naviera SA v Hapag-Lloyd International SA* [1985] 1 W.L.R. 435 (see above, para.24–053); *Griffon Shipping LLC v Firodi Shipping Ltd (The Griffon)* [2013] EWCA Civ 1567, [2014] 1 C.L.C. 1. The contrary decision in *Lowe v Hope* [1970] Ch. 94 is no longer good law: see *Hardy v Griffiths* [2014] EWHC 3947 (Ch) at [102].

[1118co] [2015] UKSC 67, [2015] 3 W.L.R. 1373.

[1118cp] See below, para.26–216R.

[1118cq] See below, para.26–216AA.

[1118cr] See below, para.26–216AB.

26–216O   **Recovery of prepayments where no provision for forfeiture.** If in a contract of sale there is no express requirement that the buyer must pay a deposit or will, in the event of breach, forfeit sums paid, and the seller terminates the contract upon the buyer's default, the buyer may recover any prepayment or instalments paid in part payment of the price, subject to a cross-claim by the seller for damages for the breach of contract.[1118cs] Thus, in *Dies v British and International Mining and Finance Corp Ltd*,[1118ct] where a buyer repudiated his contract to purchase goods, he was nevertheless held to be entitled to recover a substantial prepayment (not in the nature of a deposit) made by him, subject to a deduction in respect of the actual damage suffered by the seller through the breach of contract: the court held that if it permitted the whole prepayment to be retained by the seller, it would be permitting the retention of a penalty, not liquidated damages.[1118cu] This decision has been distinguished by two of their Lordships in the House of Lords[1118cv] on the ground that it concerned a sale of existing goods where no expenditure was intended to be incurred by the seller in reliance on the advance payment. It has been persuasively argued[1118cw] that the question should depend on the construction of the clause in the contract requiring the advance payment: was the right to retain the payment intended to be conditional upon performance by the payee of his obligations, or was it intended to be a security for performance of the payer's obligations?

[1118cs] *Palmer v Temple* (1839) 9 A. & E. 508; *Mayson v Clouet* [1924] A.C. 980; *Dies v British and International Mining and Finance Corp Ltd* [1939] 1 K.B. 724; *Stockloser v Johnson* [1954] 1 Q.B. 476, 483, 489–490; Williams, *Vendor and Purchaser*, 4th edn (1936), p.1006.

[1118ct] [1939] 1 K.B. 724 (followed in *Rover International Ltd v Cannon Film Sales Ltd* [1989] 1 W.L.R. 912).

[1118cu] See also *RV Ward Ltd v Bignall* [1967] 1 Q.B. 534 (Main Work, Vol.II, para.44–358). It has been noted that the *Dies* case was decided on the basis that the buyer's payment of the price was conditional, but that now the case might be decided on the ground that there had been a total failure of consideration: *Cadogan Petroleum Holdings Ltd v Global Process Systems LLC* [2013] EWHC 214 (Comm) at [23]. On either approach, the payment is not recoverable if the contract provides otherwise: [2013] EWHC 214 (Comm) at [18] and [27].

[1118cv] *Hyundai Heavy Industries Co Ltd v Papadopoulos* [1980] 1 W.L.R. 1129, 1142–1143, 1147–1148. (The contract in this case was for work and material supplied in the course of building a ship, and so it was treated as analogous to a building contract: see Beatson (1981) 97 L.Q.R. 389, 401–404; *Stocznia Gdanska SA v Latvian Shipping Co* [1998] 1 W.L.R. 574 HL.) The *Dies* [1939] 1 K.B. 724 case was also distinguished in the *Hyundai* case 1134–1136, on the ground that there was a total failure of consideration in *Dies*: see Main Work, Vol.I, paras 29–057 et seq.

[1118cw] Beatson (1981) 97 L.Q.R. 389, 391–401. See also Dixon J. in *McDonald v Dennys Lascelles Ltd* (1933) 48 C.L.R. 457, 477 (following termination of the contract "rights are not divested or discharged which have already been *unconditionally* acquired" (italics supplied)); and the *Fibrosa* case [1943] A.C. 32, 65 ("[t]he condition of retaining it [the advance payment] is eventual performance"; cf. at 75).

(i) *Deposits*

Law of Property Act 1925 s.49(2). Perhaps the most common use of provisions for a deposit is in contracts for the sale of land, which normally fall within Law of Property Act 1925 s.49(2); this may account for the relative paucity of case law on deposits at common law. Section 49(2) provides: **26–216P**

> "Where the court refuses to grant specific performance of a contract, or in any action for the return of a deposit, the court may, if it thinks fit, order the repayment of any deposit."

This provision is restricted to contracts for the sale or exchange of any interest in land.[1118cx] Apart from this provision, the vendor would be obliged to return the deposit only where he was in breach of contract[1118cy]; the statutory discretion conferred on the court by s.49(2) enables the court to make an order where the justice of the case requires it.[1118cz] The scope of application of this section was for a time thought to be narrow. It was said that it:

> " . . . was passed to remove the former hardship which existed where a defendant had a good defence in equity to a claim for specific performance but no defence in law, and, therefore, the deposit was forfeited . . . outside that ambit [the jurisdiction] should only be exercised, if at all, sparingly and with caution."[1118da]

It now seems to be accepted that "repayment must be ordered in any circumstances which make this the fairest course between the two parties".[1118db] But an order will not be made in every case in which the purchaser defaults, even if the vendor does not suffer any loss: rather, the case must be somehow exceptional for an order to be made for the return of a standard 10 per cent deposit.[1118dc] The court's jurisdiction cannot be excluded by the parties.[1118dd]

[1118cx] Law of Property Act 1925 s.49(3).

[1118cy] *Best v Hamand* (1879) 12 Ch. D. 1; *Re Scott and Alvarez's Contract* [1895] 2 Ch. 603; *Beyfus v Lodge* [1925] Ch. 350; *James Macara Ltd v Barclay* [1945] K.B. 148, 156.

[1118cz] *Finkeilkraut v Monohan* [1949] 2 All E.R. 235, 237–238. (cf. *James Macara Ltd v Barclay* [1945] K.B. 148, 156).

[1118da] *Michael Richards Properties Ltd v Corp of Wardens of St Saviour's Parish, Southwark* [1975] 3 All E.R. 416, 424 (Goff J.).

[1118db] *Universal Corp v Five Ways Properties Ltd* [1979] 1 All E.R. 553, 555 (Buckley L.J.). See also *Schindler v Pigault* [1975] 30 P. C.R. 328; *County & Metropolitan Homes Survey Ltd v Topclaim Ltd* [1997] 1 All E.R. 254 (effect of exclusion of Law of Property Act 1925 s.49(2)); *Omar v El-Wakil* [2001] EWCA Civ 1090.

[1118dc] See *Omar v El-Wakil* [2001] EWCA Civ 1090, [2002] 2 P. & C.R. 3 at [37], [49] and [55]; *Tennaro Ltd v Majorarch Ltd* [2003] EWHC 2601 (Ch), [2003] 47 E.G. 154 (C.S.) at [84]; *Aribisala v St James Homes (Grosvenor Dock) Ltd* [2008] EWHC 456 (Ch), [2008] All E.R. (D) 201 (Mar); *Midill (97PL) Ltd v Park Lane Estates Ltd* [2008] EWCA Civ 1227, [2009] 2 P. & C.R. 6, citing the Privy Council case of *Bidaisee v Sampath* [1995] N.P.C. 59; *Cohen v Teseo Properties Ltd* [2014] EWHC 2442 at [57]. In the *Midill* case Carnwath L.J. said that "The critical point . . . is that the deposit is 'an earnest for the performance of the contract', which can be retained by the seller if the buyer defaults, without any necessary regard to the question of actual loss or its amount": [2008] EWCA Civ 1227 at [52].

[1118dd] *Aribisala v St James Homes (Grosvenor Dock) Ltd* [2007] EWHC 1694 (Ch), [2007] 37 E.G. 234, [2007] 2 P. & C.R. DG25.

26–216Q   **Penalty rules and deposits.** If the contract provides for one party to pay a deposit, and a breach of contract by the payor leads the payee justifiably to terminate the contract, then subject to the Law of Property Act 1925 s.49(2)[1118de] and what is said in the following paragraphs[1118df] the payee may retain the deposit provided that it does not exceed the amount that is customary (in contracts for the sale of land, normally 10 per cent of the purchase price). English courts have traditionally treated such deposits as somewhat different from a sum payable upon breach and have not required the seller to show that the amount is a genuine pre-estimate of the loss.[1118dg] In *Workers Trust & Merchant Bank Ltd v Dojap Investments Ltd* the Privy Council said, in general terms, that the law on penalties applies to:

" . . . a contractual provision which requires one party in the event of his breach of the contract to pay or forfeit a sum of money to the other party."[1118dh]

In that case a contract for the sale of land required a 25 per cent deposit. The Privy Council held that a larger deposit than the customary 10 per cent would be valid only if the seller could show that it was reasonable to demand one; and in the absence of that the whole deposit was invalid and must be repaid, subject to a cross-claim for any loss suffered by the seller. However, the Privy Council accepted that a customary 10 per cent deposit may be forfeited by the seller on the buyer's default, irrespective of the amount of the seller's loss. In *Cavendish Square Holding BV v Makdessi* and *ParkingEye Ltd v Beavis*[1118di] the Supreme Court again said that the penalty rules apply to deposits,[1118dj] but either explained the right to keep a customary 10 per cent deposit either on the grounds that this is to be seen as "earnest money" that is not subject to the penalty doctrine[1118dk] or, it is thought, on the basis of a legitimate interest of the seller in deterring breach by the buyer. This seems to rest on the fact that each piece of land is treated as unique, so that damages are not considered an adequate remedy. That justifies ordering specific performance[1118dl] and so it gives the either party a legitimate interest for the purposes of the penalty rules.[1118dm] A deposit in other types of contract, such as a deposit paid when goods are ordered, may not be treated in the same way[1118dn]: a seller of goods does not seem to have a legitimate interest in obtaining performance by the buyer rather than damages,[1118do] at least when the goods are readily re-saleable, so the deposit may be valid only if meets the genuine pre-estimate test.[1118dp]

[1118de] See above, para.26–216P.
[1118df] Especially para.26–216AB.
[1118dg] See *Cadogan Petroleum Holdings Ltd v Global Process Systems LLC* [2013] EWHC 214 (Comm) at [34].
[1118dh] [1993] A.C. 573, 578. Law of Property Act 1925 s.49(2) did not apply.
[1118di] [2015] UKSC 67, [2015] 3 W.L.R. 1373.
[1118dj] See [2015] UKSC 67 at [16] (Lords Neuberger and Sumption; see also at [35]); [238] (Lord Hodge; this was one of the paragraphs with which Lord Toulson (at [292]) said that he agreed); Lord Mance cited the *Workers Trust* case with apparent approval at [156] but left the application of the penalty rules to deposits open: at [170]). Lord Clarke referred to forfeiture clauses but not specifically to deposits.
[1118dk] Lord Hodge [2015] UKSC 67 at [238]. cf. above, para.26–216P n.1118dc.
[1118dl] See Main Work, Vol.I, para.27–007.
[1118dm] See above, para.26–198.
[1118dn] If the sale is to a consumer, the deposit might be challenged under the Unfair Terms in Consumer Contract Regulations 1999 or the Consumer Rights Act 2015 s.62, see below, para.26–216AB.
[1118do] See above, para.26–204.
[1118dp] See above, para.26–182.

Damages in addition to forfeiture of deposit. Although in *Cavendish Square*   **26–216R**
Holding BV v Makdessi and *ParkingEye Ltd v Beavis*[1118dq] the majority of the Supreme Court[1118dr] said that deposits are subject to the penalty rules, it is submitted that this is not so entirely. A valid agreed damages clause gives the claimant a right to the agreed sum, no less but also no more.[1118ds] In contrast it is well established that in contracts for a sale of land, a vendor who validly terminates the contract because of a breach by the purchaser may both forfeit the deposit and recover damages, giving due allowance for the amount of the deposit.[1118dt] It is not thought that the Supreme Court intended that this rule should be affected by its decision.

[1118dq] [2015] UKSC 67, [2015] 3 W.L.R. 1373.
[1118dr] Lord Hodge said that the customary 10 per cent deposit was exempt as "earnest money": see above, para.26–216Q. If this is the correct explanation, the issue discussed in the present paragraph does not arise.
[1118ds] See above, para.26–178.
[1118dt] *Lock v Bell* [1931] 1 Ch. 35. (In that case a separate clause requiring either party to pay the sum of £200 if it failed to perform any part of the contract. This was held to be a penalty clause and the court ordered an inquiry into the damages, if any, suffered by the vendor beyond the amount of the deposit: see [1931] 1 Ch. 35, 46.) See also *Behzadi v Shaftesbury Hotels Ltd* [1992] Ch. 1, 10.

(ii) *Forfeiture of Sums Paid*

Forfeiture provisions. As noted earlier, a contract may, instead of fixing a   **26–216S**
sum to be paid upon breach, provide that a sum already paid shall be forfeited[1118du] upon breach by the party who paid it. There has been considerable

doubt over whether, or to what extent, the penalty rules apply to provisions of this type and of the relationship between the penalty rules and the court's jurisdiction to give relief against forfeiture. In *Cavendish Square Holding BV v Makdessi* and *ParkingEye Ltd v Beavis*[1118dv] the Supreme Court said that the penalty rules do apply to forfeiture provisions of this type, and may render the provision invalid. Even if the provision is valid (as a genuine pre-estimate of the innocent party's loss or as a "legitimate deterrent"), in an appropriate case the court may still be able to grant relief against forfeiture.[1118dw]

[1118du] The payee "forfeits" the sum where he retains it for his own beneficial use, having freed himself of any further obligations under the contract by terminating the contract on account of the payer's breach. It is then up to the payer to challenge the forfeiture if he has any legal ground for doing so.
[1118dv] [2015] UKSC 67, [2015] 3 W.L.R. 1373.
[1118dw] Lord Mance [2015] UKSC 67 at [160].

26–216T **Purchase by instalments and pre-payment of price.** Traditionally, the courts were willing to grant relief against "forfeiture" clauses in only two situations; and, as will be seen below,[1118dx] the relief was of a limited form, which if the payee was entitled to terminate the contract, did not include ordering a return of the sums paid. The first type of case is of landlord and tenant. There has been a long history of equitable relief against forfeiture of leasehold interests, viz where a clause in the lease entitled the landlord to repossess the premises if the tenant failed to pay an instalment of the rent.[1118dy] The second situation was where the contract-breaker has been purchasing land by paying the price by instalments: it is clearly established that if, under a contract to purchase land by instalment payments, the purchaser defaults in payment of an instalment of the price, the court has jurisdiction in a proper case to relieve him against a clause providing for forfeiture of the instalments already paid, by granting him an extension of time within which he could pay the instalment now due.[1118dz] It is implicit in these cases that payment within the extended period would preserve the purchaser's contractual rights in the same way as payment by the time originally agreed would have done. In what follows it is primarily the second situation that will be addressed, as it is thought that this is what the Supreme Court had in mind. Lords Neuberger and Sumption stated that

> "Where a proprietary interest or a 'proprietary or possessory right' (such as a patent or a lease) is granted or transferred subject to revocation or determination on breach, the clause providing for determination or revocation is a forfeiture and cannot be a penalty."[1118ea]

Moreover, the first situation is equivalent termination of the contract by the landlord because of the tenant's breach of contract, and there is no sign that the Supreme Court intended to place any restrictions on the right to terminate, even when the right would not exist at common law and arises only because of an express term of the contract.[1118eb] The Court's remarks might apply, however, if the tenant has paid a premium that would not be returnable, so that in effect the tenant ends up paying in advance for occupation rights that he will not be able to exercise.[1118ec]

[1118dx] Below, paras 26–216V—26–216W.

[1118dy] See also the Law of Property Act 1925 s.146. See also n.1118ed, below.

[1118dz] *Re Dagenham (Thames) Dock Co* (1972-73) L.R. 8 Ch. App. 1022; *Kilmer v British Columbia Orchard Lands Ltd* [1913] A.C. 319; *Steedman v Drinkle* [1916] 1 A.C. 275; *Mussen v Van Diemen's Land Co* [1938] Ch. 253; *Starside Properties Ltd v Mustapha* [1974] 1 W.L.R. 816. (Time was not made "of the essence" in this contract: cf. above, para.26–216B.) The Privy Council has refused to extend this principle: *Union Eagle Ltd v Golden Achievement Ltd* [1997] A.C. 514 (see the comments by Heydon (1997) 113 L.Q.R. 385; and Stevens (1998) 61 M.L.R. 255). See Lang (1984) 100 L.Q.R. 427; Harpum [1984] C.L.J. 134.

[1118ea] [2015] UKSC 67 at [17]; relief against forfeiture is available (at [17]), though relief against forfeiture of leases may now be governed exclusively by the Law of Property Act 1925 s.146 (at [10], referring to *Official Custodian for Charities v Parway Estates Departments Ltd* [1985] Ch. 151).

[1118eb] See above, para.26–216B.

[1118ec] See below, para.26–216Z, n.1118fg.

It is only relatively recently that the courts began to grant a limited type of relief against forfeiture in a wider range of situations. A condition said to be necessary before equitable relief may be granted is that the forfeiture clause was inserted in order: **26–216U**

> " . . . to secure a stated result which can effectively be attained when the matter comes before the court, and where the forfeiture provision is added by way of security for the production of that result."[1118ed]

The wider development began in 1954 with *Stockloser v Johnson*[1118ee]: there was a provision, in a contract to purchase plant and machinery by instalment payments, that upon default by the buyer, the seller might terminate the contract and forfeit the instalments already paid. The majority of the Court of Appeal held that the court has an equitable jurisdiction to relieve against forfeiture of such instalments, even after termination of the contract, if in the actual circumstances of the case the clause was penal and it would be oppressive and unconscionable for the seller to retain all the instalments. In 1983, the House of Lords upheld the jurisdiction to relieve against forfeiture, but limited it to contracts concerning the transfer or creation of proprietary or possessory rights.[1118ef] Thus it did not apply to the facts of the case before the House, where a shipowner withdrew his ship (chartered under a time charter[1118eg]) on the ground of the charterer's failure to make punctual payment of an instalment of hire. Similarly, the House of Lords has refused relief against the forfeiture of "mere contractual licences" to use certain names and trade marks.[1118eh] But the principle is not limited to real property, so the Privy Council has granted relief in the case of a charge over shares.[1118ei] The Court of Appeal granted relief (in the form of an extension of time in which a payment could be made by the defendant) in a commercial contract which provided that his failure to pay a sum on time would entitle the plaintiff to claim an assignment of patent rights held by the defendant.[1118ej] The House of Lords[1118ek] has granted relief to the lessee of chattels from their forfeiture: the House held that the court's power to make an interim order for the sale of chattels (which formed the subject matter of the proceedings) did not prejudice the lessee's right to seek relief from forfeiture. The proceeds of sale stood in the place of the chattels and relief could be given by an order deciding the proportions in which the parties were entitled to the money; it did not matter that the lessee could not be restored to possession.

[1118ed] *Shiloh Spinners Ltd v Harding* [1973] A.C. 691, 723. (The case concerned the right to forfeit (re-enter upon) leasehold property for failure to repair fences and to maintain works for the protection of adjoining property.)

[1118ee] [1954] 1 Q.B. 476. (See also Main Work, Vol.II, para.39–343.)

[1118ef] *Scandinavian Trading Tanker Co AB v Flota Petrolera Ecuatoriana (The Scaptrade)* [1983] 2 A.C. 694 (followed in *Union Eagle Ltd v Golden Achievement Ltd* [1997] A.C. 514 PC, failure by 10 minutes to pay balance of purchase price on time, when time was "of the essence": see Heydon (1997) 113 L.Q.R. 385; Stevens (1998) 61 M.L.R. 255). See also *The Laconia* [1977] A.C. 850, 869–870, 873–874, 878, 887; cf. the High Court of Australia in *Legione v Hateley* (1983) 46 A.L.R. 1; *Ciavarella v Balmer* (1983) 153 C.L.R. 438; and in *Stern v McArthur* (1988) 165 C.L.R. 489.

[1118eg] A charter by demise would have given the charterer a possessory interest in the ship.

[1118eh] *Sport Internationaal Bussum BV v Inter-Footwear Ltd* [1984] 1 W.L.R. 776 (followed in *Crittall Windows Ltd v Stormseal (UPVC) Window Systems Ltd* [1991] R.P.C. 265). But it is not a purely contractual right where a hirer is entitled to indefinite possession of chattels so long as he makes hire payments: hence relief against forfeiture is available: *On Demand Information Plc v Michael Gerson (Finance) Plc* [2002] UKHL 13, [2003] 1 A.C. 368 at [29].

[1118ei] *Cukurova Finance International Ltd v Alfa Telecom Turkey Ltd* [2013] UKPC 2.

[1118ej] *BICC Plc v Burndy Corp* [1985] Ch. 232, 251–252. (The line drawn between this and the *Sport Internationaal* case [1984] 1 W.L.R. 776 is not justifiable in commercial terms.)

[1118ek] *On Demand Information Plc v Michael Gerson (Finance) Plc* [2002] UKHL 13.

26–216V **Form of relief: additional time to pay.** Under this equitable principle, the courts will seldom do more than give the contract-breaker more time in which to pay the sum he had failed to pay on time. This relief has the effect that the contract-breaker does not forfeit the rights which he had under the contract, provided he pays within the time fixed by the court.

26–216W **Return of payments subject to forfeiture clause.** If the contract-breaker is unable to pay, or if the contract has already been terminated, the position is less clear. Traditionally, the courts have been more reluctant[1118el] to allow recovery of money already paid by the contract-breaker (i.e. to grant affirmative relief)[1118em] than to deny recovery of a sum (a penalty) agreed to be payable upon breach by the contract-breaker (i.e. to grant negative relief) or to give more time to him to make a payment. In one case, the House of Lords directed the relief at the proceeds of sale where the court had made an interim order for sale pending the outcome of the litigation.[1118en] On the facts of *Stockloser v Johnson*, above, although the majority of the court were prepared to order that money paid be returned if it would be unconscionable for the seller to keep it, they did not think that the seller's conduct in retaining £4,750 out of the £11,000 price in one contract, and £3,500 out of the £11,000 price on another, was unconscionable, because the buyer had already received substantial benefits in the form of royalties.[1118eo] In any event, subsequent cases tended to follow the view of the third judge, Romer L.J., that there could be relief only if there had been fraud, sharp practice or unconscionable conduct on the part of the seller.[1118ep] In a Privy Council case in 1906, the contract-breaker obtained an order that the deposit he had paid in advance to the innocent party should, despite a forfeiture clause, be repaid to him (subject to his paying damages for the actual loss caused to the innocent party by the breach of contract),[1118eq] but this case has not to date been followed in England.[1118er] In *Cadogan Petroleum Holdings Ltd v Global Process Systems LLC* Eder J. held that it was unnecessary to resolve that debate because counsel accepted that in the circumstances the court did have jurisdiction to grant relief against forfeiture and that such jurisdiction went beyond simply giving the buyer more time to pay.[1118es] However, as the goods were of no use to the seller and their value was very uncertain, the court refused to order repayment of the sums already paid or that sums due before the date of termination should cease to be payable.[1118et]

[1118el] *Dies v British and International Mining and Finance Corp Ltd* [1939] 1 K.B. 724 (sale of goods); *Stockloser v Johnson* [1954] 1 Q.B. 476, 483, 489–490; *Mayson v Clouet* [1924] A.C. 980 (sale of land); *Galbraith v Mitchenall Estates Ltd* [1965] 2 Q.B. 473.

[1118em] cf. above, para.26–216Q.

[1118en] *On Demand Information Plc v Michael Gerson (Finance) Plc* [2002] UKHL 13.

[1118eo] [1954] 1 Q.B. 476, 484, 492.

[1118ep] See *Galbraith v Mitchenall Estates Ltd* [1965] 2 Q.B. 473.

[1118eq] *Commissioner of Public Works v Hills* [1906] A.C. 368 (above, para.26–187).

[1118er] Though the penalty rules were assumed to apply to a sum paid by way of deposit in *Pye v British Automobile Commercial Syndicate Ltd* [1906] 1 K.B. 425 (held not penal).

[1118es] [2013] EWHC 214 (Comm) at [38].

[1118et] [2013] EWHC 214 (Comm) at [41].

Provision for forfeiture may be a penalty. The Supreme Court has now **26–216X** expressed at least the provisional view that a clause providing for the forfeiture of sums already paid is subject to the penalty rules[1118eu]; and similarly[1118ev] a clause requiring the contract-breaker, upon breach, to re-transfer some property to the innocent party.[1118ew] Thus if the provision does not pass either the genuine pre-estimate test[1118ex] or the legitimate deterrent test,[1118ey] the sum that was to be forfeited will be subject to the normal rules on the repayment of sums already paid and the requirement to transfer the property at a reduced price will unenforceable.[1118ez]

[1118eu] *Cavendish Square Holding BV v Makdessi* and *ParkingEye Ltd v Beavis* [2015] UKSC 67, [2015] 3 W.L.R. 1373. Lord Mance said that it is "both logical and correct in principle under the current law" that a clause may both be subject to the penalty doctrine and the power of the court to give relief for forfeiture (at [160]) but said the application of the penalty doctrine to deposits and the forfeiture of money paid must await decision in due course (at [170]). Lord Hodge said that the court should determine whether a forfeiture clause was a penalty: at [227]. Lord Toulson agreed with what Lord Mance had said at [160] and with the relevant paragraphs of Lord Hodge's judgment; Lord Clarke was inclined to agree with them also. Lords Neuberger and Sumption said they could see the force in the arguments of Lords Mance and Hodge: at [18].

[1118ev] Lord Mance at [160]–[161], Lord Hodge at [230], [233]. Lords Neuberger and Sumption said there is no reason in principle "why an obligation to transfer assets (either for nothing or at an undervalue) should not be capable of constituting a penalty" (at [16]). At [84] they said that it was not necessary to decide whether it was open to the purchaser in *Jobson v Johnson* to argue that the obligation to transfer back shares he had received was a penalty: it may be subject only to the forfeiture rules but not the penalty rules, referring back to [18] of their judgment.

[1118ew] As in *Jobson v Johnson* [1989] 1 W.L.R. 1026. The order made in that case was disapproved: see below, para.26–216K.

[1118ex] See above, para.26–182.

[1118ey] See above, para.26–196.

[1118ez] See above, para.26–216.

Relief against forfeiture may also be given. In the *Cavendish Square* **26–216Y** case[1118fa] Lords Mance and Hodge said[1118fb] that even if the clause providing for the forfeiture of sums already paid is not void as a penalty from the outset, if the party who will be prejudiced by the clause defaults, the court may grant relief against forfeiture. The Supreme Court seemed to envisage this relief normally taking the form of giving the defaulting party extra time in which to pay,[1118fc] but

Lord Hodge at least indicated that it might also involve the purchaser recovering the payments made.[1118fd]

[1118fa] *Cavendish Square Holding BV v Makdessi* and *ParkingEye Ltd v Beavis* [2015] UKSC 67, [2015] 3 W.L.R. 1373.

[1118fb] *Cavendish Square Holding BV v Makdessi* and *ParkingEye Ltd v Beavis* [2015] UKSC 67, [2015] 3 W.L.R. 1373 at [160] (Lord Mance) and [227], [230] (Lord Hodge): Lord Toulson agreed, Lord Clarke was inclined to agree (see at [291]). Lords Neuberger and Sumption saw force in the argument but preferred not to express a view.

[1118fc] See Lord Mance [2015] UKSC 67 at [160], quoting the Privy Council in *Çukurova Finance International Ltd v Alfa Telecom Turkey Ltd (No.4)* [2013] UKPC 25, [2015] 2 W.L.R. 875 at [13] ("relief in equity will only be granted on the basis of conditions requiring performance, albeit late, of the contract in accordance with its terms as to principal, interest and costs"). This would not preclude relief in the form granted in *On Demand Information Plc v Michael Gerson (Finance) Plc* [2002] UKHL 13, [2003] 1 A.C. 368, see above, para.26–216U.

[1118fd] [2015] UKSC 67 at [229].

26–216Z **Forfeiture of leases and relief against termination clauses.** As stated earlier,[1118fe] a common situation in which relief against forfeiture may be given is where a lease entitles the landlord to repossess the premises because the tenant has failed to pay an instalment of the rent. It is not thought that the Supreme Court's statements in *Cavendish Square Holding BV v Makdessi* and *ParkingEye Ltd v Beavis*[1118ff] that forfeiture provisions are subject to the penalty rules were intended to address this situation. The tenant will normally not suffer the same "double loss"—loss of both their property rights and the money they have so far paid—as in, for example, cases in which the contract-breaker has been purchasing land by paying the price by instalments and the agreement provides that if he defaults in a payment, he will lose both the land and the sums he has paid.[1118fg] A similar situation occurs when a contract may provide that it may be terminated because of a default that at common law would not be sufficiently serious to justify termination. Although some such clauses have been held to confer only a right to terminate and not the further right to damages for non-performance,[1118fh] it has been held that the penalty rules are not relevant to this situation.[1118fi] There is nothing in the *Cavendish Square* case to indicate that the Supreme Court intended to change this position.

[1118fe] See above, para.26–216T.

[1118ff] [2015] UKSC 67, [2015] 3 W.L.R. 1373.

[1118fg] See above, para.26–216T. Possibly the penalty rule will apply if the tenant has paid a substantial premium in advance and will lose the benefit of that as well as losing the premises, but this suggestion is speculative.

[1118fh] See above, para.26–216T.

[1118fi] See above, para.26–216B.

(iii) *Deposits and Forfeiture of Money Paid in Consumer Contracts*

26–216AA **The Consumer Credit Act 1974.** Some of the problems created by contractual provisions requiring payments on the occurrence of specified events will be governed by the Consumer Credit Act 1974.[1118fj] For instance, s.100(1) provides that where a debtor under a regulated hire-purchase (or a regulated conditional sale) agreement[1118fk] has prematurely terminated the agreement, he shall be liable to pay the difference between the sums already paid or payable by him and one-half of the total price; but by s.100(3) the court may order payment of a smaller sum if that would be equal to the loss sustained by the creditor.[1118fl] The court is also empowered to intervene if it determines that the relationship between the creditor and the debtor is "unfair".[1118fm] It may determine that the relationship is unfair because of one or more of the following:

(a) any of the terms of the agreement or of any related agreement;
(b) the way in which the creditor has exercised or enforced any of his rights under the agreement or any related agreement;
(c) any other thing done (or not done) by, or on behalf of, the creditor (either before or after the making of the agreement or any related agreement).[1118fn]

The court may, for example, require the creditor, or any associate of his, to repay (in whole or in part) any sum paid by the debtor or by a surety, reduce or discharge any sum payable by the debtor or by a surety by virtue of the agreement, or alter the terms of the agreement or of any related agreement.[1118fo] The Act will therefore cover many of the situations which arise in practice, and the common law and equitable rules will not need to be applied. Thus, it is uncertain how far the principle discussed in paras 26–209—26–213, above, applies to hire-purchase[1118fp] or hiring[1118fq] agreements that fall within the Act so as to permit the court to grant relief to a hirer against a clause providing for the forfeiture of instalments already paid or for a "minimum payment" by the hirer upon his termination of the agreement.[1118fr] When a hire-purchase agreement is terminated by the owner upon the hirer's default, the common law as to penalties[1118fs] and the provisions of the Act will often protect the hirer against clauses requiring further payments, e.g. for "depreciation"; the common law rules apply to similar clauses in hiring agreements.[1118ft] The question whether a depreciation clause is a penalty or not depends on the construction of the clause in the light of all the circumstances surrounding the particular agreement.[1118fu]

[1118fj] See Main Work, Vol.II, paras 33–085 et seq. deal with hiring agreements, while paras 39–005 et seq. deal with the other agreements within the scope of the Act.

[1118fk] Definitions of these agreements are examined in Main Work, Vol.II, paras 39–356 et seq.

[1118fl] See Main Work, Vol.II, paras 39–368—39–369; cf. the similar power conferred on the court by s.132 in the case of a regulated consumer hire agreement.

[1118fm] Consumer Credit Act 1974 ss.140A–140C, inserted by Consumer Credit Act 2006 ss.19–22. These provisions replace ss.137–140 on "extortionate credit bargains", which are repealed by s.70 and Sch.4 of the 2006 Act. See further Main Work, Vol.II, paras 39–212 et seq.

[1118fn] s.140A(1).

[1118fo] s.140B(1). These powers can be exercised in relation to any credit agreement where the debtor is an individual (as defined in s.189(1), as amended: see Main Work, Vol.II, paras 39–016 et seq.) or any related agreement (as defined in s.140C(4)). The fact that the agreement is an exempt, and not a regulated, agreement is immaterial, except that no order can be made in connection with a credit agreement which is an exempt agreement by virtue of s.16(6C). These provisions came into force on April 6, 2007 (SI 2007/123 (c.6)).

[1118fp] *Campbell Discount Co Ltd v Bridge* [1961] 1 Q.B. 445 CA (on appeal, the case was decided on another point: [1962] A.C. 600); see Main Work, Vol.II, paras 39–349—39–353; Diamond (1956) 19 M.L.R. 498 and (1958) 21 M.L.R. 199; Prince (1957) 20 M.L.R. 620.

[1118fq] *Galbraith v Mitchenall Estates Ltd* [1965] 2 Q.B. 473; *Barton Thompson & Co Ltd v Stapling Machines Co* [1966] Ch. 499.

[1118fr] See the proposals for reform in the Law Commission's Working Paper No.61, *Penalty Clauses and Forfeiture of Moneys Paid* (1975).

[1118fs] *Bridge v Campbell Discount Co Ltd* [1962] A.C. 600, upholding the decision of the Court of Appeal in *Cooden Engineering Co Ltd v Stanford* [1953] 1 Q.B. 86; *Anglo Auto Finance Co Ltd v James* [1963] 1 W.L.R. 1042, 1049.

[1118ft] *Robophone Facilities Ltd v Blank* [1966] 1 W.L.R. 1428.

[1118fu] *Lombank Ltd v Excell* [1964] 1 Q.B. 415 (interpreting *Phonographic Equipment (1958) Ltd v Muslu* [1961] 1 W.L.R. 1379).

26–216AB   **Unfair Terms in Consumer Contracts Regulations 1999 and Consumer Rights Act 2015.**[1118fv] The Unfair Terms in Consumer Contracts Regulations 1999 provided that in a contract between a business and a consumer an "unfair term" will not be binding on the consumer.[1118fw] For contracts made after October 1, 2015, the Consumer Rights Act 2015 replaces the Regulations. The Regulations and the Act give illustrations of terms which will, prima facie, be regarded as unfair: relevant to clauses fixing damages is "requiring any consumer who fails to fulfil his obligation to pay a disproportionately high sum in compensation".[1118fx] This does not in so many words cover the case of a deposit or provision for forfeiture, but there seems no doubt that such a term may be declared to be unfair in an appropriate case.

[1118fv] SI 1999/2083.
[1118fw] See Main Work, Vol.II, paras 38–201 et seq.
[1118fx] cf. Main Work, Vol.II, para.38–280.

12. INTEREST

(b) *Damages for Loss of Interest at Common Law*

Loss of interest compensable if pleaded and proved

26–230   *[Add to note 1198, at the end: page* [1950]*]*
It has been held that "general evidence" that the claimant suffered loss from the delay will suffice: *Equitas Ltd v Walsham Bros & Co Ltd* [2013] EWHC 3264 (Comm) at [123], [2014] Lloyd's Rep. I.R. 398; *Sainsbury's Supermarkets Ltd v Mastercard Inc* [2016] CAT 11 at [521].

(d) *Statutory Rights to Interest*

Period of statutory interest: where a date for payment has been agreed

26–233   *[In paragraph, line 4, delete* "two" *and substitute: page* [1951]*]*
three

[Add to note 1218a, at the end: page [1952]*]*
The Late Payment of Commercial Debts Regulations 2002 (SI 2002/1674) reg.3, allow representative bodies to bring proceedings in the High Court on behalf of small and medium-sized enterprises to obtain an injunction preventing other

businesses using terms purporting to oust or vary the right to statutory interest in relation to qualifying debts created by those contracts. The Department of Business, Innovations and Skills has consulted on amendments to this regime: *Late Payment: challenging "grossly unfair" terms and practices: Consultation Paper* (2015).

CHAPTER 27

SPECIFIC PERFORMANCE AND INJUNCTION

1. Introduction

Scope of the remedy

27–003   *[Add to paragraph, after note 14: page* [1962]]
, and the court can, in principle, direct the defendant to take steps before the date
of performance in order to meet its obligations on that date.[14a]

> [14a] *Airport Industrial GP Ltd v Heathrow Airport Ltd* [2015] EWHC 3753 (Ch) at [113]. Morgan
> J. recognised that this would be applicable to many cases of anticipatory breach.

2. The "Adequacy" of Damages

Damages nominal, not recoverable, or excluded

27–009   *[Add to paragraph, at the end: page* [1967]]
Damages may also be inadequate where the infringement of the interest that a
party is trying to protect by way of an injunction is a person's privacy or reputation.[51a]

> [51a] *PJS v News Group Newspapers* [2016] UKSC 26 at [43]; *Kent Community Health NHS
> Foundation Trust v NHS Swale Clinical Commissioning Group* [2016] EWHC 1393 (TCC) at
> [15].

Discretion as to appropriate remedy to consumers

*[Delete heading, text and footnotes of paragraph and substitute: pages**27–022**
[1976]–[1978]]*

Discretion and consumer's choice between repair and replacement. The
2015 Act places restrictions on the consumer's rights of "repair or replacement"
relating to goods and digital content.[144] It also places restrictions on the consumer's right to "repeat performance" which applies to services,[145] but the restrictions are different. In the case of goods and digital content, ss.23(3) and 43(3) of
the 2015 Act provide that the consumer cannot require the trader to repair or
replace the goods or digital content if "that remedy" is (a) "impossible" or (b)
"disproportionate compared to the other of those remedies", i.e. if it "imposes
costs on the trader which, compared to those imposed by the other, are unreasonable".[146] It seems from the wording of these provisions that "repair" and
"replacement" are here treated as separate rights or remedies and that these
provisions are concerned with the power of the court to choose *between them*. By
contrast, where services do not conform to the contract, the consumer's right or
remedy that corresponds to "repair or replacement" is "the right to require repeat
performance"[147]; and since this is a single right there can be no question of its
being "disproportionate" to anything else. However, repeat performance cannot
be required where completing performance would be impossible.[148]

[144] Consumer Rights Act 2015 s.23(3) applies to goods and s.43(9) applies to digital content.
[145] Consumer Rights Act 2015 s.53(3).
[146] Taking into account a list of factors specified in the Consumer Rights Act 2015 ss.23(4) and
43(4).
[147] Consumer Rights Act 2015 ss.54(3)(a), 55(1).
[148] Consumer Rights Act 2015 s.55(3).

[Insert new paragraphs 27–022A and 27–022B: page [1978]]
Discretion to award price reduction: digital content and services. Where **27–022A**
ordering either repair or replacement (in the case of digital content[149]) or repeat
performance (in the case of services) would be disproportionate or even cause
severe hardship to the defendant,[150] the court can instead award a price reduction.[151] This is provided under s.58. When the customer claims to exercise any
of the above "rights"[152] (or "remedies"),[153] "on the application of the consumer,
the court may make an order requiring specific performance of"[154] the trader's
obligation to repair or replace goods[155] or digital content[156] or to repeat performances of services.[157] Further, s.58(3) and (4) provide that "if the exercise of
another right is appropriate"[158] then "the court may proceed as if the consumer
had exercised that other right"[159]; and the other rights are defined so as to
include, in each case, price reduction.[160] The effect is that if the consumer claims
repair or replacement, the court may instead order (if it is more appropriate than
either repair or replacement) another of the remedies provided by the Act. In
respect of digital content and services, that can only be a price reduction.[161]
These provisions differ from those discussed in the previous paragraph[162] by
which the consumer cannot require (for example) repair if that is "impossible"
or "disproportionate"[163] because it imposes unreasonable costs on the trader or

because the "other remedy" would cause "significant inconvenience to the consumer". The choice that the consumer is required to make under those provisions is between repair and replacement. In contrast, the "powers of the court"[164] are wider: under s.58 the court could, for example, refuse to order repair or replacement or repeat performance and instead order a price reduction.[164a] There is also no requirement under s.58[164b] that the remedy sought by the consumer must be "disproportionate", but it is hard to see on what other ground it would be appropriate for the court to do so. It would not be appropriate for the court to refuse to order repair or replacement or repeat performance, and instead order a price reduction, simply on the ground that damages would be an adequate remedy. That would render the provisions giving the consumer the right to repair or replacement or repeat performance nugatory.

[149] But not in the case of goods: see below, para.27–022B.

[150] cf. below, para.27–036.

[151] To which the consumer is entitled under ss.19(3)(c) (goods), 42(2)(b) (digital content) and 54(3)(b) (services) under the Consumer Rights Act 2015.

[152] i.e. "the right to repair or replacement of goods (s.19(3)(b)) or of digital content (s.42(2)(a)) or the "right to require repeat performance" of a service (s.54(3)(a)) Consumer Rights Act 2015. In addition, "specific performance" is listed among "other remedies" (ss.19(10), 42(7) and 54(7)) which the consumer may seek. In those situations, the word "other" suggests that the reference to "specific performance" is not to the right to repair or replacement, or repeat performance but is to cover the (unlikely) possibility that specific performance might be available under the normal principles governing that remedy.

[153] A term used in this context to mean the same thing as rights: see, for example, the use of the phrase "other remedies" in the Consumer Rights Act 2015 ss.19(10), 42(7) and 54(7).

[154] Consumer Rights Act 2015 s.58(2).

[155] Consumer Rights Act 2015 s.23.

[156] Consumer Rights Act 2015 s.43.

[157] Consumer Rights Act 2015 s.55.

[158] Consumer Rights Act 2015 s.58(3).

[159] Consumer Rights Act 2015 s.58(4). See below, paras 38–485, Main Work, Vol.II, paras 38–520, 38–543.

[160] Consumer Rights Act 2015 s.58(8).

[161] There is no right to treat a contract for digital content as at an end for non-conformity: s.42(8) (contrast the right to reject goods and treat the contract as at an end: see ss.19(3) and s.20(4)). In contracts for services the consumer's right to treat the contract as at an end is preserved, and in both contracts for digital content and for services so too is the right to damages (see ss.42(7) and 54(7)), but these are not "right[s] under the relevant remedies provisions" within s.58(3) and so cannot be ordered by the court instead of specific performance. See Main Work, Vol.II, para.38–486.

[162] Above, para.27–020.

[163] Consumer Rights Act 2015 ss.23(3) and (4), 43(3) and (4).

[164] Heading before Consumer Rights Act 2015 s.58.

[164a] See the references to Consumer Rights Act 2015 ss.24, 44 and 56 in s.58(8).

[164b] As there is under Consumer Rights Act 2015 ss.23(3)(b) and 43(3)(b).

27–022B **No discretion to award price reduction: goods.** In the case of goods, for the court to exercise its discretion under s.58 to order price reduction[164c] on the grounds that it is more appropriate than either repair or replacement would be inconsistent with the requirements of Directive 1999/44/EC,[164d] which Ch.2 of the Consumer Rights Act is designed to implement.[164e] The consumer's right to repair or replacement of goods under the Consumer Rights Act must be interpreted in the light of the interpretation of the Directive in *Weber and Putz*[164f] by the Court of Justice of the EU, at least while the United Kingdom remains in the

EU.[164g] The Court's assumption that the consumer's specific rights under the Directive were enforceable in kind against the seller has three consequences. First, on the facts of the case, it was decided that national law should not allow the trader to refuse replacement on the ground of disproportionality with the value of conforming goods and with the significance of the non-conformity, even though it meant that the trader had to bear the costs of the removing the goods installed by the consumer and the reinstallation of the replacement goods. Second, it suggests that English courts should not refuse specific performance in support of the consumer's right to repair or replacement because damages would be an adequate remedy, since this would then replace the consumer's "European rights" and so render them ineffective. Third, it suggests that, in the case of "sales contracts", use of the court's powers to substitute another "appropriate right" under s.58 is incompatible with the 1999 Directive except in the two situations referred to in the Directive: where the choice is between repair or replacement or where neither repair nor replacement is possible.[164h] The corollary is that courts should not apply other "bars" to specific performance not mentioned in the Directive itself.

[164c] Or equally to make an order as if the consumer had claimed to reject the goods and treat the contract as at an end, see s.19(3) and s.20(4).

[164d] Directive on certain aspects of the sale of consumer goods and associated guarantees [1999] O.J. L171/99, p.12, art.3(2). See Main Work, Vol.II, paras 44–006—44–013.

[164e] See below, para.38–485. And see Whittaker (2017) 133 L.Q.R. (forthcoming). On the Consumer Sales Directive 1999 generally, see Main Work, Vol.II, para.38–400. On "sales contracts" see Main Work, Vol.II, paras 38–452—38–454.

[164f] *Gebr Weber GmbH v Wittmer, Putz v Medianess Electronics GmbH* (C-65/09 and C-87/09) [2011] 3 C.M.L.R. 27, [63]–[78].

[164g] See above, paras 1–013A et seq.

[164h] The Directive only mentions impossibility and disproportionality compared to the other specific remedy. Directive 1999/44/EC art.3(3) is reflected in 2015 Act s.23(3)–(4) and see Main Work, Vol.II, para.38–482.

4. OTHER GROUNDS FOR REFUSING SPECIFIC PERFORMANCE

Severe hardship to defendant

[*Add to paragraph, at the end: page* [1990]]   27–036
, or the loss of its entire interest in a joint venture.[265a]

[265a] *Man UK Properties Ltd v Falcon Investments Ltd* [2015] EWHC 1324 (Ch).

[*Add new paragraph 27–036A: page* [1990]]
Adjustments to mitigate harshness. The court may, instead of denying   27–036A
specific performance, make adjustments to the specific performance order to mitigate its harshness, taking into account the proportionality between the adverse consequences of specific performance without adjustment, the defendant's degree of fault, and the adequacy of damages to compensate the claimant for any variation to its entitlement. In *Airport Industrial GP Ltd v Heathrow Airport Ltd*[265b] Morgan J. permitted a two-year delay on the time of performance

in the context of an obligation of 999 years duration, subject to damages being paid to the claimant for the delay, to allow the defendant time to implement a method of performance that was more advantageous for it but would take longer compared with a more immediate method which was likely to render it insolvent. However,

> "the court's order should seek to specify milestones to be achieved with provision for a default position [i.e. an obligation to revert to the immediate method] to apply if the defendant does not achieve a milestone."[265c]

[265b] [2015] EWHC 3753 (Ch) at [133]–[134].
[265c] [2015] EWHC 3753 (Ch) at [133].

8. Injunction

Interim injunctions

27–066   [*Add to note 443, at the end: page* [2009]]
And see *Kent Community Health NHS Foundation Trust v NHS Swale Clinical Commissioning Group* [2016] EWHC 1393 (TCC) on what is meant by the adequacy of damages for a not-for-profit organisation and on the role of the public interest in assessing the balance of convenience; *Allfiled UK Ltd v Eltis* [2015] EWHC 1300 (Ch) on the effect of the claimant's delay.

[*Add to paragraph, at the end: page* [2010]]
Damages may also be inadequate where the infringement of the interest that a party is trying to protect by way of an injunction is a person's privacy or reputation.[447a]

[447a] *PJS v News Group Newspapers Ltd* [2016] UKSC 26 at [43]; *Kent Community Health NHS Foundation Trust v NHS Swale Clinical Commissioning Group* [2016] EWHC 1393 (TCC) at [15].

27–067   [*Add to note 449, at the end: page* [2010]]
See also *RSM International Ltd v Harrison* [2015] EWHC 2252 (QB).

Injunction against refusal to contract

27–079   [*Add to paragraph, line 2, after* "refusing to contract with another": *page* [2020]]
, particularly if it would force an entity to engage in a long-term contract with another[524a]

[524a] Although it may do so exceptionally: *Woods Building Services v Milton Keynes Council* [2015] EWHC 2172 (TCC) at [9]–[11].

CHAPTER 28

LIMITATION OF ACTIONS

1. PERIODS OF LIMITATION

Latent damage in actions in the tort of negligence

[Add to note 59, at the end: page [2035]] **28–011**
; *Schumann v Veale Wasbrough* [2015] EWCA Civ 441, [2015] P.N.L.R. 25.

Carriage by sea

[In note 99, delete last sentence, starting "In Feest . . . " and substitute: page **28–023**
[2039]]
In *Feest v South West Strategic Health Authority* [2015] EWCA Civ 708, [2016]
Q.B. 503 it was held that the two-year limitation period under the Athens
Convention does not bar a claim by an alleged tortfeasor for contribution against
the carrier, under the Civil Liability (Contribution) Act 1978, in respect of
personal injury to a passenger.

2. ACCRUAL OF THE CAUSE OF ACTION

Successive and continuing breaches

[Add to note 159, at the end: page [2046]] **28–035**
Although not involving any question of limitation, as regards the apparent
conflict regarding whether there was a continuing breach of contract between

[197]

Midland Bank Trust Co Ltd v Hett, Stubbs and Kemp [1979] Ch. 384 and *Bell v Peter Browne & Co* [1990] 2 Q.B. 495, the majority of the Court of Appeal in *Capita (Banstead 2011) Ltd v RFIB Group Ltd* [2015] EWCA Civ 1310, [2016] P.N.L.R. 17, indicated that they preferred (and indeed, as a matter of precedent, were bound to apply) the latter case rather than the former.

Money lent

28–036   *[Add to note 164, at the end: page* [2046]]
; *Goldsmith v Chittell* [2016] EWHC 630 (Ch).

5. EXTENSION OF THE PERIOD

(b) *Fraud, Concealment or Mistake*

Concealment

28–087   *[Add to note 333, at the end: page* [2063]]
See also *Gresport Finance Ltd v Battaglia* [2016] EWHC 964 (Ch) (s.32(1)(b) was applied in the context of breach of contract and breach of fiduciary duty by the defendant who had concealed his lack of authority).

7. COMMENCEMENT OF PROCEEDINGS

Legal proceedings

28–117   *[In note 461, delete the second sentence, starting* "See also ... " *and substitute: page* [2075]]
On the relevance, to the commencement of proceedings for limitation purposes, of the non-payment of the correct court fee, see *Page v Hewetts Solicitors* [2012] EWCA Civ 805; *Bhatti v Ashgar* [2016] EWHC 1049 (QB); *Glenluce Fishing Co Ltd v Watermota Ltd* [2016] EWHC 1807 (TCC).

Part Nine

RESTITUTION

CHAPTER 29

RESTITUTION

1. INTRODUCTION

(a) *Nature of Restitution*

Classification

[*Add to note 17, at the end: page* [2096]]
and Havelock (2016) L.Q.R. 470.

29–004

(c) *The Theoretical Basis of the Law of Restitution*

Two main theories

29–010   [*Add to note 46, line 2, after* [2013] Ch. 156.": *page* [2101]]
See also *Bank of Cyprus UK Ltd v Menelaou* [2015] UKSC 66, [2016] A.C. 176
at [37] (Lord Clarke); [98] (Lord Neuberger); [108] (Lord Carnwath).

The principle of unjust enrichment

29–011   [*Add to note 50, penultimate line, after* "[2013] UKSC 50, [2014] A.C. 938": *page*
[2101]]
Bank of Cyprus UK Ltd v Menelaou [2015] UKSC 66, [2016] A.C. 176; *Patel v
Mirza* [2016] UKSC 42, [2016] 3 W.L.R. 399.

The state of the unjust enrichment principle

29–015   [*Add to note 77, at the end: page* [2104]]
Also in Malaysia: *Dream Property v Atlas Housing* [2015] 2 M.L.J. 441.

Different claims within the law of restitution

29–016   [*Add to note 85, line 3, after* "[2013] Ch. 156": *page* [2105]]
However, in *Bank of Cyprus UK Ltd v Menelaou* [2015] UKSC 66, [2016] A.C.
176 a majority of the Supreme Court recognised that the proprietary remedy of
subrogation could be awarded to reverse the defendant's unjust enrichment. See
Watterson [2016] C.L.J. 209.

2. UNJUST ENRICHMENT

(a) *The Content of the Unjust Enrichment Principle*

The elements of unjust enrichment

29–017   [*Add to note 87, penultimate line, after* "[2014] EWCA Civ 361, [52] (Etherton
C.).": *page* [2105]]
See also *Bank of Cyprus UK Ltd v Menelaou* [2015] UKSC 66, [2016] A.C. 176
at [80] where Lord Neuberger described the remedy as "financial compensation".

[*Add to note 89, penultimate line, after* "if they had statutory force": *page* [2106]]
This was confirmed by Lord Clarke in *Bank of Cyprus UK Ltd v Menelaou*
[2015] UKSC 66, [2016] A.C. 176 at [19]. But failing to consider the distinct
elements of the unjust enrichment claim will result in a loss of rigour in the
analysis and application of the law.

[*Add to note 90, at the end: page* [2106]]
See also *Patel v Mirza* [2016] UKSC 42, [2016] 3 W.L.R. 399 at [246] (Lord Sumption).

(b) *Enrichment*

The nature of the enrichment

[*Add to note 108, at the end. page* [2108]] 29–019
See also *Richards v Worcestershire County Council* [2016] EWHC 1954 (Ch) (discharge of defendant's statutory liabilities).

[*In paragraph, lines 9–11, delete from* "In Menelaou" *to* "belonging to the defendant." *and substitute: page* [2108]]
In *Bank of Cyprus UK Ltd v Menelaou*[112] the Supreme Court recognised that the transfer of freehold property without a charge, when the property should have been subject to a valid charge, constituted an enrichment to the extent of the amount with which the property should have been charged.

[112] [2015] UKSC 66, [2016] A.C. 176.

Valuing enrichment

[*Add to paragraph, at the end: page* [2112]] 29–025
In *Bank of Cyprus UK Ltd v Menelaou*[136a] Lord Neuberger suggested that if the valuation of the enrichment resulted in a sum which was "unfair or oppressive" it was open to the court to adjust it, although he identified no basis for the court to make such an adjustment.

[136a] [2015] UKSC 66, [2016] A.C. 176 at [81].

(c) *At the Expense of the Claimant*

Direct and indirect enrichment

[*Add to note 150, at the end: page* [2114]] 29–028
See now *Bank of Cyprus UK Ltd v Menelaou* [2015] UKSC 66, [2016] A.C. 176.

[*In paragraph, lines 31–38, delete from* "In Menelaou" *to* "purchase the other property." *(including note): page* [2114]]

[*Add to paragraph, at the end: page* [2115]]
In *Bank of Cyprus UK Ltd v Menelaou*[156a] Lord Clarke[156b] recognised that the function of the "at the expense of" requirement was to ensure that there was a transfer of value between the claimant and the defendant which needed to be reversed. On the facts of the case there was what was considered to be a direct transfer of value from the respondent bank to the appellant, since the bank had agreed to release £785,000 of the sum which it was owed on one property to

enable another property to be purchased, but subject to a charge in favour of the bank on that property. In the end that property was received by the appellant without a valid charge, who was consequently enriched to the extent that the property had not been charged. Lords Clarke and Neuberger[156c] considered this to involve one single scheme which directly benefited the appellant. Nevertheless, the Supreme Court recognised that an enrichment might be indirectly transferred and still be at the expense of the claimant. Lord Clarke[156d] considered that this "at the expense of" requirement turned on whether there was a sufficient causal connection between the claimant's loss and the benefit received by the defendant. The analysis of Henderson J. in *Investment Trust Companies v Revenue and Customs Commissioners* was approved by Lord Clarke,[156e] with particular endorsement of the relevance of having regard to the economic or commercial reality, although he left open whether it is better to adopt a narrow test of direct enrichment subject to exceptions or a broader approach recognising indirect enrichment, because he considered that the result is likely to be the same.[156f] His focus on causation being at the heart of the "at the expense of" inquiry suggests that he was willing to adopt the broader approach, although this was not significant on the facts of the case because the causation test was clearly established. In fact, *Menelaou* illustrates that it is not helpful to distinguish between direct and indirect enrichment and it is preferable instead to focus on a test of causation. This is because the enrichment in *Menelaou* was negative, in the sense that the appellant had received the property without a charge. It was the absence of a valid charge that constituted the enrichment and this did not involve a direct or even an indirect transfer of any value via a third party from the bank to the appellant, but simply the obtaining of a valuable benefit as a consequence of the bank's agreement to allow the property to be purchased subject to a charge.

[156a] [2015] UKSC 66, [2016] A.C. 176.
[156b] [2015] UKSC 66 at [23].
[156c] [2015] UKSC 66 at [25] and [73].
[156d] [2015] UKSC 66 at [27].
[156e] [2015] UKSC 66 at [31].
[156f] [2015] UKSC 66 at [32].

(d) *The Grounds of Restitution*

Absence of basis

29–032   [*Add to note 171, at the end, page* [2117]]
; *Patel v Mirza* [2016] UKSC 42, [2016] 3 W.L.R. 399 at [246] (Lord Sumption); *Richards v Worcestershire County Council* [2016] EWHC 1954 (Ch) at [34] (Newey J.)

(e) *Mistake*

Personal and proprietary remedies

29–050   [*Add to note 303, at the end: page* [2132]]
See also *Angove's Pty Ltd v Bailey* [2016] UKSC 47, [2016] 1 W.L.R. 3179.

Mistaken voluntary dispositions

[*Add to note 308, at the end: page* [2133]]
; *Freedman v Freedman* [2015] EWHC 1457 (Ch).

29–052

(f) *Failure of Basis*

General principles

[*Add to note 328, line 8, after* "endeavour between the parties.".: *page* [2136]]
cf. *Bank of Cyprus UK Ltd v Menelaou* [2015] UKSC 66, [2016] A.C. 176 where
it was accepted that the ground of total failure of consideration applied (Lord
Clarke at [21]) without analysis of whether there was a joint endeavour between
respondent and appellant, which could not have been established because the
appellant was unaware of the basis for the transfer of the enrichment.

29–057

Payments made under a void contract

[*Add to note 505, at the end: page* [2157]]
See also *Marlbray Ltd v Laditi* [2016] EWCA Civ 476 (no recovery of deposit
where no failure of consideration).

29–080

Money paid under illegal contracts

[*Delete text of paragraph and substitute: page* [2159]]
If money is paid under a contract which is illegal it has been recognised that
restitution should not be awarded because of the taint of illegality.[518] However,
following the decision of the Supreme Court in *Patel v Mirza*,[519] as a general rule
restitution will be awarded if the elements of the unjust enrichment claim can be
established, which will usually be possible because an illegal transaction will
always involve a failure of consideration since the basis for the transaction will
be void, save where the court considers that the taint of illegality should defeat
the claim for restitution. In determining whether the defence of illegality should
operate the court should have regard to a "trio of considerations", namely
examination of the reason for making the conduct illegal; identification of the
policies which would be adversely affected by denying the claim; and proportionality.[520] Lord Toulson recognised that various factors will be relevant to
determine whether it is disproportionate to refuse relief, although he did not
consider that it was possible to produce a definitive list because of the infinite
variety of cases which might raise illegality. Factors he identified include the
seriousness of the conduct, its centrality to any contract, whether the conduct was
intentional and whether there was a marked disparity in the parties' respective
culpability.[521]

29–083

[518] e.g. *Parkinson v College of Ambulance Ltd* [1925] 2 K.B. 1.
[519] [2016] UKSC 42, [2016] 3 W.L.R. 399. See also above, paras 16–014A et seq.

[520] [2016] UKSC 42 at [101].
[521] [2016] UKSC 42 at [107].

[Add new paragraph 29–083A: page [2159]]

29–083A   In *Patel v Mirza*[521a] itself the respondent had transferred £620,000 to the appellant to be used by the latter to bet on share price movements based on inside information. Such insider dealing is a crime under Pt V of the Criminal Justice Act 1993. The inside information was not forthcoming and so the agreement was not carried out. The respondent sought restitution of the money paid on the ground that the appellant had been unjustly enriched at his expense, the ground of restitution being that the basis for the transfer had failed totally. In the Supreme Court the nine Justices unanimously held that the respondent should recover the money he had paid to the appellant. The general approach of the Supreme Court was that it was appropriate to return the parties to the status quo ante despite the illegality of the transaction because, as Lord Sumption recognised,[521b] "an order for restitution would not give effect to the illegal act or to any right derived from it". It follows that there is only a very limited role for the defence of illegality in the law of restitution, since the courts will be willing to unwind the transaction because the claimant will not profit from it, save perhaps where the illegality is considered to be particularly serious.[521c] The old rule[521d] that the defence of illegality would apply whenever the claimant needs to rely on the illegality to establish a claim was rejected by the Supreme Court in *Patel v Mirza*.[521e] The majority did not examine the old doctrine of *locus poenitentiae*, by virtue of which a claim will not be defeated by illegality if the claimant has voluntarily withdrawn from the transaction before any part of the illegal purpose has been achieved,[521f] but it is likely that this doctrine will be considered to have been subsumed into the new "trio of considerations" approach of the majority.[521g]

[521a] [2016] UKSC 42, [2016] 3 W.L.R. 399. See also above, paras 16–014A et seq.
[521b] [2016] UKSC 42 at [268].
[521c] [2016] UKSC 42 at [116] (Lord Toulson).
[521d] See *Tinsley v Milligan* [1994] 1 A.C. 340.
[521e] [2016] UKSC 42, [2016] 3 W.L.R. 399 at [110] (Lord Toulson).
[521f] See *Tribe v Tribe* [1996] Ch. 107.
[521g] [2016] UKSC 42 at [101]; see above, para.29–083.

Services provided under illegal contracts

29–084   *[Add to note 522, at the end: page* [2159]]
This was confirmed in *Patel v Mirza* [2016] UKSC 42, [2016] 3 W.L.R. 399 at [119] (Lord Toulson).

Minors' contracts

29–087   *[Add to note 532, at the end: page* [2161]]
See Häcker in *Defences in Unjust Enrichment* (ed. Dyson, Goudkamp and Wilmot-Smith) (2016), Ch.9.

(g) *Ultra vires Receipts by the Revenue and Public Authorities*

Scope of right

[*Add to note 569, line 16, after* "restitution against public bodies.".*: page* [2165]]   **29–091**
In *Richards v Worcestershire County Council* [2016] EWHC 1954 (Ch) the
claimant was allowed to pursue a private law claim for restitution arising from
the claimant discharging the defendant's statutory obligations, even though this
raised questions as to whether the defendant had performed public law duties.
This conclusion was reached both because the claimant only sought financial
redress rather than any other relief and because the strict time limit for judicial
review proceedings was inappropriate for a private law claim for restitution.

(h) *Compulsion*

Compulsory payments to a third person

[*Add to note 655, at the end: page* [2175]]   **29–105**
In *Angove's Pty Ltd v Bailey* [2016] UKSC 47, [2016] 1 W.L.R. 3179 at [16(4)]
(Lord Sumption) *Moule v Garett* was specifically approved and was explicitly
justified by reference to the law of unjust enrichment.

[*Add to note 658, at the end: page* [2175]]
See also *Angove's Pty Ltd v Bailey* [2016] UKSC 47, [2016] 1 W.L.R. 3179 at
[16(4)] (Lord Sumption).

The right to contribution

[*Add to note 743, at the end: page* [2187]]   **29–127**
In New Zealand the award of equitable contribution depends on there being
liability for the same damage and a judicial assessment of what is just and
reasonable: *Hotchin v New Zealand Guardian Trust Co Ltd* [2016] NZSC 24.

4. PROPRIETARY RESTITUTIONARY CLAIMS

(a) *Establishing Proprietary Rights*

Identifying a proprietary interest

[*Add to note 976, line 2, after* "decision on unjust enrichment"*: page* [2213]]   **29–167**
applied in *Re Hampton Capital Ltd* [2015] EWHC 1905 (Ch), [2016] 1 B.C.L.C.
374.

Constructive trusts

[*Add to note 980, line 10, after* "(Lord Neuberger MR)"*: page* [2214]]   **29–168**
; *Keown v Nahoor* [2015] EWHC 3418 (Ch) at [41] (D Halpern QC).

[Add to note 981, penultimate line, after "[2006] 1 B.C.L.C. 66": page [2214]]
; *Angove's Pty Ltd v Bailey* [2016] UKSC 47, [2016] 1 W.L.R. 3179 at [30] (Lord Sumption).

[Add to note 982, at the end: page [2214]]
See also *Angove's Pty Ltd v Bailey* [2016] UKSC 47, [2016] 1 W.L.R. 3179 at [30] (Lord Sumption) and *Fistar v Riverwood Legion and Community Club Ltd* [2016] NSWCA 81.

[Add to note 984, at the end: page [2214]]
In *Angove's Pty Ltd v Bailey* [2016] UKSC 47, [2016] 1 W.L.R. 3179 the Supreme Court did not accept that a constructive trust would be recognised where the recipient of money knew that imminent insolvency would prevent him from performing the corresponding obligation. In doing so the reasoning in *Nesté Oy v Lloyd's Bank Plc*, namely that a constructive trust was triggered because a reasonable and honest person would have repaid the money which had been received after the directors had concluded that the company was insolvent, was rejected. The justification for this appears to turn on what good conscience requires and that, just because a reasonable person would have returned a payment, it does not follow that it should have been returned. But this misses the point about the basis for recognising the constructive trust on the ground of unconscionable retention. The prior question is whether the defendant is liable to make restitution to the claimant by virtue of unjust enrichment. If there is such a liability and the defendant is aware of the circumstances which establish the claim then the money will be held on constructive trust. That is why money paid by mistake may be held on constructive trust, as was acknowledged by Lord Sumption, although he described this as a fundamental mistake, thus confusing mistakes which prevent legal title from passing with mistakes which may trigger a constructive trust. But if the defendant is liable to make restitution by virtue of a total failure of consideration and is aware of the circumstances amounting to this, that should be sufficient to justify the recognition of the constructive trust. The key question should then be whether a total failure of consideration can be identified. Despite this, the Supreme Court asserted that neither an actual nor a potential total failure of consideration will give rise to a proprietary restitutionary right, but is simply a matter of contractual readjustment.

[Add to note 991, at the end: page [2215]]
; *Angove's Pty Ltd v Bailey* [2016] UKSC 47, [2016] 1 W.L.R. 3179 at [27] (Lord Sumption).

(c) *Proprietary Restitutionary Claims*

Subrogation

29–180   *[Delete the text of the first sub-paragraph (ending at note 1078) and substitute: page [2224]]*
By virtue of "subrogation" a person may, in certain situations, "step into the shoes" of another so as to enjoy the latter's legal position or his rights against a third person. Subrogation may arise from the express or implied agreement of the

parties or by operation of law. In the latter situation subrogation may be triggered by the defendant's unjust enrichment.[1074] It follows that it will be necessary to establish that the defendant was enriched at the expense of the claimant and that a ground of restitution can be identified.[1075] In *Bank of Cyprus UK Ltd v Menelaou*[1076] a bank was subrogated to a vendor's unpaid lien where the bank had released charges on one property which enabled funds to become available to purchase another property, with the bank incorrectly assuming that it would have a valid charge over the second property. The majority in the Supreme Court justified the award of subrogation on the basis that the owner of the second property was unjustly enriched at the Bank's expense. Lord Neuberger considered that it would be hard to find a more appropriate remedy to award in this case,[1077] since it would give to the bank what it should have had if the charge over the second property had been valid. The Supreme Court's recognition of the award of subrogation to reverse the defendant's unjust enrichment involves the award of a proprietary remedy as a response to unjust enrichment, since the effect of subrogation is to give the claimant the benefit of a security interest to gain priority over the defendant's unsecured creditors, even though, as Lord Clarke said, "a claim in unjust enrichment does not need to show a property right".[1078] But, where it is possible to establish that the claimant's value has been used to discharge a secured debt, it is preferable to analyse the award of the remedy of subrogation without necessary recourse to the unjust enrichment principle but with reference to the vindication of equitable property rights, such that the identification of a recognised ground of restitution need not be considered.[1078a] Indeed, this was how Lord Carnwath in *Menelaou* justified the award of the subrogation remedy,[1078b] with the bank being able to establish the necessary proprietary interest in the money which had been used to discharge the unpaid vendor's lien by virtue of a *Quistclose* resulting trust.[1078c]

[1074] *Bank of Cyprus UK Ltd v Menelaou* [2015] UKSC 66, [2016] A.C. 176. See also *Banque Financière de la Cité SA v Parc (Battersea) Ltd* [1999] 1 A.C. 221, where the claimant sought a personal remedy against a third party by means of subrogation; *Cheltenham & Gloucester Plc v Appleyard* [2004] EWCA Civ 291; *Anfield (UK) Ltd v Bank of Scotland* [2010] EWHC 2374 (Ch), [2011] 1 W.L.R. 2414 at [10] (Proudman J.); *Sandher v Pearson* [2013] EWCA Civ 1822; *Re Beppler & Jacobson Ltd* [2016] EWHC 20 (Ch) at [122] (Hildyard J.). In *Niru Battery Manufacturing Co v Milestone Trading Ltd (No.2)* [2004] EWCA Civ 487, [2004] 2 All E.R. (Comm) 289, the remedy of subrogation was ordered to prevent the defendant's unjust enrichment arising from the discharge of a liability owed by the defendant. It is unclear, however, why this remedy was sought or obtained since the claimant had a direct restitutionary claim to recover the value of the benefit obtained by the defendant and did not need to step into the shoes of any other party to bring such a claim. The High Court of Australia rejected unjust enrichment as the doctrinal foundation of subrogation in Australia: *Bofinger v Kingsway Group Ltd* [2009] HCA 44; Ridge (2010) 126 L.Q.R. 188.

[1075] See *Adams v Moore* Unreported, May 12, 2016 QBD where subrogation was awarded as a remedy to reverse the defendant's unjust enrichment where the claimants had paid money to discharge the defendant's mortgage in circumstances where the claimants understood that they had lent the money to the defendant. Subrogation was justified on the ground that it would be unjust for the claimants not to recover their money, although it is not obvious what the ground of restitution would be. cf. *Re Beppler & Jacobson Ltd* [2016] EWHC 20 (Ch) where it was recognised that subrogation to reverse unjust enrichment will not lie if there is a subsisting contract between the parties.

[1076] [2015] UKSC 66, [2016] A.C. 176.

[1077] [2015] UKSC 66 at [79].

[1078] [2015] UKSC 66 at [38].

[1078a] See also *Lehman Commercial Mortgage Conduit Ltd v Gatedale Ltd* [2012] EWHC 848 (Ch).

[1078b] [2015] UKSC 66, [2016] A.C. 176 at [107]. Lord Neuberger acknowledged that this route to subrogation was also available, and he considered this would have been simpler and less controversial: [100].

[1078c] *Barclays Bank Ltd v Quistclose Investments Ltd* [1970] A.C. 567.

Personal restitutionary remedies

29–181   *[Add to note 1101, at the end: page* [2227]]]
In *Fistar v Riverwood Legion and Community Club Ltd* [2016] NSWCA 81 the New South Wales Court of Appeal recognised that a strict liability claim in unjust enrichment for money had and received relating to stolen money lay even though the claimant alternatively had a claim in unconscionable receipt which required proof of fault.

5. DEFENCES

(b) *Change of Position*

Bad faith

29–191   *[Add to paragraph, at the end: page* [2237]]]
In *Re Hampton Capital Ltd*[1182a] George Bompas Q.C. sitting as a Deputy High Court Judge acknowledged that the test of bad faith for change of position was the same as the test of knowledge for the claim in knowing receipt, namely whether what was known to the defendant was sufficient to make it unconscionable for the defendant to refuse to repay the money. In that case it was held that the defendant knew enough to have reasonable grounds to suspect that the money he had received had been stolen.

[1182a] [2015] EWHC 1905 (Ch), [2016] 1 B.C.L.C. 374.

CHAPTER 30

CONFLICT OF LAWS

1. PRELIMINARY CONSIDERATIONS

[Add new paragraph 30–002A: page [2248]]

"Brexit". As noted above,[6a] the future legal relationship of the UK to the EU   **30–002A** remains to be determined. In the absence of any arrangements which include the UK remaining bound by EU law, the impact on conflict of laws is potentially very significant. Key European private international law instruments, notably the Brussels I Regulation (recast) (which governs jurisdiction in European cases) and the Rome II Regulation (which governs choice of law in non-contractual cases) would cease to have effect. Most significantly for the purposes of this chapter, the Rome I Regulation, which applies to all contracts entered into on or after December 17, 2009, and whose rules form the main subject matter of this chapter, would no longer be directly effective EU law. One possibility is that the UK would return to the position under the Contracts (Applicable Law) Act 1990, which implemented the Rome Convention into English law. However, the status of those rules following the UK's exit from the EU raises difficult issues of international law and UK statutory law. Alternatively, as choice of law rules are unilateral (not requiring reciprocity, unlike rules of jurisdiction) it would be possible for the UK to enact national legislation which substantially mirrors the Rome I Regulation. All of these issues remain to be determined and this Supplement to Chapter 30, and particularly the discussion of conflict of laws, remains written on the premise that the status of EU law in UK law remains unchanged.[6b]

[6a] See above, paras 1–013A—1–013E.
[6b] For a discussion see A. Dickinson, "Back to the future: the UK's EU exit and the conflict of laws" [2016] JPIL 195.

3. THE ROME CONVENTION

(a) *In General*

Interpretation: the European Court

30–018   [*Add to note 109, at the end: page* [2261]]
; *ERGO Insurance SE v If P&C Insurance AS* (Joined cases C-359/14 and C-475/14).

(b) *Exclusions*

Wills, succession, etc.

30–036   [*Add to note 165, at the end: page* [2268]]
Following the failure to reach a political agreement on these proposals, on March 2, 2016, the European Commission adopted a proposal for a Council decision authorising enhanced cooperation in the area of jurisdiction, applicable law and the recognition and enforcement of decisions on the property regimes of international couples, covering both matters of matrimonial property regimes and the property consequences of registered partnerships (COM(2016) 108 final). The Commission also published proposals for two new Regulations, a Council Regulation on jurisdiction, applicable law and the recognition and enforcement of decisions in matters of matrimonial property regimes (COM(2016) 106 final) and

a proposal for a Council Regulation on jurisdiction, applicable law and the recognition and enforcement of decisions in matters of the property consequences of registered partnerships (COM(2016) 107 final).

Insurance

[*In note 214, delete from* "However, the implementation date" *in last line to the end and substitute: page* [2274]]   **30–044**
The Solvency II Directive came into force on January 1, 2016.

(c) *Choice of Law by the Parties*

Mandatory rules

[*Add to note 296, at the end: page* [2284]]   **30–060**
There is no need to show evasiveness or bad faith: *Banco Santander Totta SA v Cia de Carris de Ferro de Lisboa SA* [2016] EWHC 465 (Comm) at [373].

[*Add to note 299, at the end: page* [2284]]
In *Banco Santander Totta SA v Cia de Carris de Ferro de Lisboa SA* [2016] EWHC 465 (Comm) the judge confirmed that the test was "deliberately general" (at [390]) and that it was enough that the case involved "international elements" (at [411]).

"Mandatory rules"

[*Add to note 308, at the end: page* [2286]]   **30–062**
In *Banco Santander Totta SA v Cia de Carris de Ferro de Lisboa SA* [2016] EWHC 465 (Comm) the judge confirmed that it was sufficient to take a rule outside the scope of art.3(3) if the rule could be disapplied by agreement between the parties whether *ex ante* or *ex post* (at [506]).

(d) *Applicable Law in the Absence of Choice by the Parties*

Specific applications

[*Add to note 368, at the end: page* [2294]]   **30–076**
By analogy, the supplier of bunkers in the type of *sui generis* supply contract identified by the Supreme Court in *PST Energy 7 Shipping LLC v OW Bunker Malta Ltd (The Res Cogitans)* [2016] UKSC 23 (see para.44–174A) will also be the characteristic performer.

"Other contracts" involving carriage of goods

[*In note 434, update the reference to Scrutton on Charterparties to: page* [2302]]   **30–085**
23rd edition (2015), paras 1.013 et seq.

(e) *Certain Consumer Contracts and Individual Employment Contracts*

Article 5(2): first condition: advertising

30–096   [*Add to note 503, line 6, after* "within the scope of those activities"": *page* [2312]]
and also with art.17(1)(c) of the recast Regulation, which is identical

EU consumer protection legislation

30–102   [*Add to note 519, at the end: page* [2315]]
For contracts entered into after October 1, 2015, the Unfair Terms in Consumer
Contracts Regulations 1999 are replaced by the Consumer Rights Act 2015,

"Employment": autonomous meaning

30–109   [*Add to note 550, line 10, after* "[2007] I.L.Pr. 706"*: page* [2319]]
; *Petter v EMC Europe Ltd* [2015] EWCA Civ 828; [2016] I.L.Pr. 3

[*Add to note 550, at the end: page* [2319]]
In *Holterman Ferho Exploitatie BV v Spies von Bullesheim* (C-47/14) [2015]
I.L.Pr. 44 the Court of Justice of the EU adopted an autonomous meaning in the
context of Section 5 of the Judgments Regulation.

Territorial limitations

30–114   [*Add to note 573, at the end: page* [2322]]
; *Olsen v Gearbulk Services Ltd* [2015] I.R.L.R. 818 (EAT); Merrett (2015) I.L.J.
53.

4. THE ROME I REGULATION

(b) *Exclusions*

Matrimonial property regimes, etc.

30–154   [*Add to note 708, at the end: page* [2339]]
Following the failure to reach a political agreement on these proposals, on March
2, 2016, the European Commission adopted a proposal for a Council decision
authorising enhanced cooperation in the area of jurisdiction, applicable law and
the recognition and enforcement of decisions on the property regimes of international couples, covering both matters of matrimonial property regimes and the
property consequences of registered partnerships (COM(2016) 108 final). The
Commission also published proposals for two new Regulations, a Council Regulation on jurisdiction, applicable law and the recognition and enforcement of
decisions in matters of matrimonial property regimes (COM(2016) 106 final) and
a proposal for a Council Regulation on jurisdiction, applicable law and the

recognition and enforcement of decisions in matters of the property consequences of registered partnerships (COM(2016) 107 final).

(e) *Applicable Law in the Absence of Choice*

Principles

[Add to note 783, at the end: page [2349]]   **30–187**
See generally on choice of law governing commercial disputes in the absence of
express choice Arzandeh [2015] L.M.C.L.Q. 525

Sale of goods

[Add to note 786, at the end: page [2349]]   **30–189**
The autonomous Community meaning of "sale of goods" is likely to be broad
enough to encompass the *sui generis* supply contracts of the sort considered in
PST Energy Shipping LLC v OW Bunker Malta Ltd (The Res Cogitans) [2016]
UKSC 23, given that such contracts are "in commercial terms" regarded as
contracts for the sale of goods ([2015] EWCA Civ 1058 at [33], [2016] 2 W.L.R.
1072). In *Molton Street Capital LLP v Shooters Hill Capital Partners LLP* [2015]
EWHC 3419 (Comm) it was disputed whether a sale of junk bonds was a sale of
"goods" within the meaning of art.4(1)(a) but it was unnecessary to decide the
point as the seller of the bonds was also the characteristic performer under the
default in art.4(2).

Contract concluded within multilateral system

[Add to note 803, at the end: page [2351]]   **30–196**
The original Directive has been replaced by Directive 2014/65/EU (MiFID 2)
although the deadline for compliance with the new Directive has been extended
to January 2018 (COM(2016) 56 final).

Rule of displacement

[Add to note 826, line 4, after "displace the primary rule")": page [2354]]   **30–203**
; *Molton Street Capital LLP v Shooters Hill Capital Partners LLP* [2015] EWHC
3419 (Comm) at [94] ("The new language and structure suggests a higher
threshold, which requires that the cumulative weight of the factors connecting the
contract to another country must clearly and decisively outweigh the desideratum
of certainty in applying the relevant test in Article 4.1 or 4.2")

Relevant factors

[Add to note 828, penultimate line, after "[2012] EWCA Civ 265": page [2354]]   **30–204**
; *Aquavita International SA v Ashapura Minechem Ltd* [2015] EWHC 2807 (QB)
and Enonchong [2015] L.M.C.L.Q. 194

(f) *Contracts of Carriage*

[Add to note 832, at the end: page [2355]]
; Okoli [2015] L.M.C.L.Q. 512.

(g) *Consumer Contracts*

Contract of carriage

30–235   *[Add to note 899, at the end; page* [2363]]
A new Package Travel Directive (2015/2302/EU) entered into force on December 31, 2015 and must be implemented by July 1, 2018.

Rights and obligations constituting a financial instrument, etc.

30–237   *[Add to note 906, at the end: page* [2364]]
The original Directive has been replaced by Directive 2014/65/EU (MiFID 2) although the deadline for compliance with the new Directive has been extended to January 2018 (COM(2016) 56 final).

[Add to note 907, at the end: page [2364]]
In July 2012, the European Commission formally adopted a reform of the UCITS Directive, commonly referred to as UCITS V, which was enacted and published in July 2014. UCITS V (Directive 2014/91/EU) amends the previous version of the UCITS Directive, known as UCITS IV (Directive 2009/65/EC). The UCITS V Directive has an implementation deadline of March 18, 2016. Unlike the UCITS IV Directive, the UCITS V Directive does not recast the UCITS Directive. Instead, it amends and stands alongside the UCITS IV Directive.

Choice of law by the parties

30–249   *[Add to note 961, at the end: page* [2371]]
On click-wrapping and jurisdiction agreements under the Judgments Regulation see *El Majdoub v CarsOnTheWeb.Deutschland GmbH* (C-322/14) [2015] 1 W.L.R. 3986, and see *Verein für Konsumenteninformation v Amazon EU Sarl* (C-191/15) on standard terms.

(i) *Individual Employment Contracts*

[Add to note 1028, line 5, after "Merrett (2010) I.L.J. 355": *page* [2381]]
; Merrett (2015) I.L.J. 53.

Meaning of individual employment contract

30–279   *[Add to note 1040, at the end; page* [2382]]
In *Holterman Ferho Exploitatie BV v Spies von Büllesheim* (C-47/14) [2015] I.L.Pr. 44, the Court of Justice of the EU adopted an autonomous meaning in the context of Section 5 of the Judgments Regulation.

[*Add new note 1042a, after* "framework of the counterparty" *in line 13: page*
[2382]]

[1042a] Each of these three criteria was referred to by the Court of Justice in *Holterman Ferho Exploitatie BV v Spies von Büllesheim* (C-47/14) [2015] I.L.Pr. 44 when considering the meaning of employment contract under the Judgments Regulation.

(j) *Voluntary Assignment and Contractual Subrogation*

Background

[*In note 1065, penultimate line, after* "Mollman [2011] L.M.C.L.Q. 262" *add: page*   **30–289**
[2385]]
; Goode [2015] L.M.C.L.Q. 289.

(k) *Legal Subrogation*

Background

[*Add to note 1080, at the end: page* [2388]]   **30–294**
Article 15 is discussed in *ERGO Insurance SE v If P&C Insurance AS* (Joined Cases C-359/14 and C-475/14).

(m) *Set-off*

Set-off in insolvency proceedings

[*Add to note 1099, at the end: page* [2390]]   **30–302**
The Insolvency Regulation is to be replaced by Regulation (EU) 2015/848 of the European Parliament and of the Council of 20 May 2015 on insolvency proceedings (recast) (Recast Insolvency Regulation). The Recast Insolvency Regulation will apply to insolvency proceedings commencing on or after June 26, 2017.

5. Scope of the Applicable Law

(e) *Burden of proof*

Burden of proof and presumptions

[*Add to note 1329, line 4, after* "negotiated to show that it was)"*: page* [2419]]   **30–354**
(for contracts entered into after October 1, 2015, the Unfair Terms in Consumer Contracts Regulations 1999 are replaced by the Consumer Rights Act 2015).

[*Add to note 1334, at the end: page* [2420]]   **30–355**
For contracts entered into after October 1, 2015, the Unfair Terms in Consumer Contracts Regulations 1999 are replaced by the Consumer Rights Act 2015.

(g) *Foreign Currency Obligations*

Scope of discussion

30–371   [*In note 1398, update the reference to Mann on the Legal Aspect of Money to: page [2429]*]
7th edn (2012).

VOLUME II

SPECIFIC CONTRACTS

CHAPTER 31

AGENCY

1. AGENCY IN GENERAL

Foreign law

31–004   [*Add to note 15, at the end: page* [4]]
; Kortmann and Kortmann, "Undisclosed Indirect Representation—Protecting the Principal, the Third Party, or Both?", Ch.6 in Busch, Macgregor and Watts (eds), *Agency Law in Commercial Practice* (OUP, 2016).

Relationship of principal and agent

31–006   [*Add to note 30, at the end: page* [6]]
In *Plevin v Paragon Personal Finance Ltd* [2014] UKSC 61, [2014] 1 W.L.R. 4222, Lord Sumption said, in the context of s.140A of the Consumer Credit Act 1974, that "In their ordinary and natural meaning the words 'on behalf of' import agency": at [30]. The effect was to narrow the broad protective discretion in respect of liability of a lender for acts of others given by s.140A. See comment by McMeel, "Agency and the Retail Distribution of Financial Products", Ch.10 in Busch, Macgregor and Watts (eds), *Agency Law in Commercial Practice* (2016) paras 10.25 et seq.

2. EXAMPLES OF TYPES OF AGENT

Solicitors

31–013   [*Add new note 77a, after* "be easily inferred today" *in line 13: page* [10]]
    [77a] The modern position regarding solicitor's authority to bind his or her client, at any rate in Australia, is discussed at length in *Pavlovic v Universal Music Australia Pty Ltd* [2015] NSWCA 313.

3. COMMERCIAL AGENTS

Commercial agents

31–017   [*In note 93, update reference to Singleton, Commercial Agency Agreements: Law and Practice to: page* [12]]
4th edn (2015).

[*Add to note 99, at the end: page* [13]]
See also *Software Incubator Ltd v Computer Associates Ltd* [2016] EWHC 1587 (QB).

The Commercial Agents Regulations: conflict of laws

31–020   [*Add to note 120, at the end: page* [15]]
; Carruthers, Ch.13 in Busch, Macgregor and Watts (eds), *Agency Law in Commercial Practice* (2016).

4. Creation of Agency

(c) *Ratification*

General rule

[*Add to note 148, at the end: page* [18]]
See in general Krebs, "Ratification", Ch.2 in Busch, Macgregor and Watts (eds), *Agency Law in Commercial Practice* (2016).

31–027

Proof of ratification

[*Add to note 152, at the end: page* [19]]
See also *Sino Channel Asia Ltd v Dana Shipping and Trading Pte Singapore* [2016] EWHC 1118 (Comm) (no ratification of arbitration held without valid service (because of lack of authority to receive it), and hence without participation, by inactivity after award made).

31–028

(d) *Agency of Necessity*

Agency of necessity

[*In note 197, update reference to Scrutton on Charterparties to: page* [24]]
23rd edn (2015), Arts 134–142.

31–035

6. Principal's Relations with Third Parties

(a) *General Rule*

General rule: identified and unidentified principal

[*Add to note 313, at the end: page* [36]]
These dicta are doubted by Leggatt J. in *Magellan Spirit ApS v Vitol SA* [2016] EWHC 454 (Comm) at [19], but no reasons are given.

31–054

Cases where contract required to be in writing

[*Add to note 320, at the end: page* [37]]
In *Rabiu v Marlbray Ltd* [2016] EWCA Civ 476 a husband signed a land contract on behalf of himself and his wife but without her authority. He was held severally liable on the contract.

31–055

(b) Apparent Authority

Apparent authority

31–056   [*In note 329, line 1, delete* "to others": *page* [38]]

[*In note 329, update reference to Handley, Estoppel by Conduct and Election to: page* [38]]
2nd edn (2016), p.30.

[*Add to note 338, at the end: page* [39]]
In *Galaxy Aviation v Sayegh Group Aviation* [2015] EWHC 3478 (Comm) it is said that "in practice this is I think relatively unusual". But that may not be so: see McMeel, "Agency and the Retail Distribution of Financial Products", Ch.10 in Busch, Macgregor and Watts (eds), *Agency Law in Commercial Practice* (2016), paras 10.28 et seq.

Agents of companies

31–058   [*Add to note 361, at the end: page* [42]]
See also Watts, "Directors as Agents—Some Aspects of Disputed Territory", Ch.7 in Busch, Macgregor and Watts (eds), *Agency Law in Commercial Practice* (2016).

(c) Undisclosed Principal

Doctrine of the undisclosed principal

31–063   [*Add to note 396, at the end: page* [45]]
cf. Kortmann and Kortmann, above, para.31–004, n.15; Fridman, "Undisclosed Principals and the Sale of Goods", Ch.5 in Busch, Macgregor and Watts (eds), *Agency Law in Commercial Practice* (2016).

Meaning of "undisclosed principal"

31–065   [*Add to note 403, at the end: page* [46]]
In *Magellan Spirit ApS v Vitol SA* [2016] EWHC 454 (Comm) such a proposition appears to be doubted by Leggatt J., but he may be referring to the initial creation of the agency (which obviously cannot be created by mere subjective intention) rather than the intention to act for the principal in a particular instance, which when the principal is not named is certainly required over and above the basic authority. The matter is considered at more length in the *Bowstead and Reynolds on Agency*, 1st Supplement of the 20th edition, para.8–072 (modifying the text and adding to a footnote).

[*Add to note 404, at the end: page* [46]]
The *Yukong* case is considered by Leggatt J. in *Magellan Spirit ApS v Vitol SA* [2016] EWHC 454 (Comm) at [27], [28].

(f) *Agent's Torts*

Agent's torts

[*Add to note 503, at the end: page* [55]]   **31–075**
For a recent example see *Mohamud v Wm Morrison Supermarkets Plc* [2016]
UKSC 11, [2016] A.C. 677 (assault by employee).

7. AGENT'S RELATIONS WITH THIRD PARTIES

(a) *On the Main Contract*

Where principal is company not yet in existence

[*Add to note 623, line 4, after* "(1979) 11 U. Queensland L.J. 53.".: *page* [68]]   **31–097**
For a more recent example in respect of an unincorporated association see *Davies
v Barnes Webster & Sons* [2011] EWHC 2560 (Ch), [2012] B.P.I.R. 97 (service
on President of Rugby Club valid).

8. OBLIGATIONS OF PRINCIPAL AND AGENT INTER SE

(a) *Duties of Agents*

(i) *Common Law: Carrying Out Instructions*

Authority

[*Add to note 703, at the end: page* [77]]   **31–113**
See further for wider discussion DeMott, "The Poseur as Agent", Ch.3 in Busch,
Macgregor and Watts (eds), *Agency Law in Commercial Practice* (2016).

(ii) *Common Law: Exercise of Care and Skill*

Exercise of care and skill

[*Add to note 704, at the end: page* [77]]   **31–114**
And it has recently been held that where the action is in substance one for breach
of contract the contractual rules for the calculation of damages apply: *Wellesley
Partners LLP v Withers LLP* [2015] EWCA Civ 1146, [2016] 2 W.L.R. 1351.

Due care for principal's interests

[*Add to note 710, at the end: page* [78]]   **31–115**
; *Khouj v Acropolis Capital Partners Ltd* [2016] EWHC 2120 (Comm) (right to
inspect agent's documents).

(iii) *Equity: Fiduciary Duties and Duties of Loyalty*

Fiduciary duties and duties of loyalty

31–118 [*Add to note 724, line 8, after "[2003] Eu. L.R. 874": page* [79]]
See in general Tosato, "Commercial Agency and the Duty to Act in Good Faith"
[2016] O.J.L.S. 661.

Exclusion of liability

31–126 [*Add to note 775, at the end: page* [84]]
; *Barnsley v Noble* [2016] EWCA Civ 799 (trustee under will).

[*Add to note 777, at the end: page* [85]]
See discussion of the general topic by McMeel, "Agency and the Retail Distribu-
tion of Financial Products", Ch.10 in Busch, Macgregor and Watts (eds), *Agency
Law in Commercial Practice* (2016), paras 10.25 et seq., paras 10.19 et seq.

(iv) *Remedies*

Equity: duty to account and restitution of the trust estate

31–129 [*Add to note 792a, at the end: page* [86]]
; Gummow (2015) 41 Aust. Bar Rev. 5; Millett (2015) *UK Supreme Court
Yearbook* 193; Turner [2015] C.L.J. 188; Davies (2015) 78 M.L.R. 681.

(b) *Rights of Agents*

General

31–136 [*Add to note 833, at the end: page* [91]]
; Tosato, "Commercial Agency and the Duty to Act in Good Faith" [2016]
O.J.L.S. 661.

(i) *Remuneration*

Termination: where Commercial Agents Regulations applicable

31–152 [*Add to note 946, at the end: page* [104]]
This is so also where the agent's agreement is terminated during a trial period
agreed at first appointment: *Fadin Habitat (Société) v Constructions Tradi-
tionnelles du Val de Loire* [2015] E.C.C. 27 (Cour de Cassation, France); *Monk
v Largo Foods Ltd* [2016] EWHC 1837 (Comm) (similar facts: duty of good faith
does not impact on absolute right to terminate irrespective of breach).

Indemnity and compensation: indemnity

31–153 [*Add new note 954a, after "the cessation of the contract." in line 5: page* [104]]
[954a] "New customers" includes persons brought in by the agent, notwithstanding that the customers
had already had relations with the principal in relation to other goods: *Marchon Germany GmbH v
Karaszkiewicz* (C-315/14) [2016] Bus. L.R. 694.

[*Add to note 960, at the end: page* [105]]
In *Quenon K SPRL v Beobank SA* (C-338/14) [2016] Bus. L.R. 264 the CJEU
held that the Directive permitted Member States who had chosen the indemnity
option to provide for recovery of additional loss, provided that "the award of
damages may not result in double recovery by combining the indemnity for
customers with the compensation for loss resulting, in particular, for the loss of
commission following termination of the contract": at [32].

Compensation

[*Add to note 962, at the end: page* [105]]   **31–154**
In the result, the normal compensation regime applied by default: contrast *Brand
Studio Ltd v St John Knits Inc* [2015] EWHC 3143 (QB), [2015] Bus. L.R. 1421,
where a similar clause was held severable from a choice of indemnity, which
therefore remained valid.

[*Add to note 968, at the end: page* [105]]
; *Alan Ramsay Sales and Marketing Ltd v Typhoo Tea Ltd* [2016] EWHC 486
(Comm), [2016] 4 W.L.R. 59; *Software Incubator Ltd v Computer Associates Ltd*
[2016] EWHC 1587 (QB).

[*Add new note 969a, at end of paragraph: page* [106]]
969a For an example of the two methods operating together see *Software Incubator Ltd v Computer
Associates Ltd* [2016] EWHC 1587 (QB).

Calculation of compensation

[*Add to note 982, at the end: page* [107]]   **31–155**
; *Alan Ramsay Sales and Marketing Ltd v Typhoo Tea Ltd* [2016] EWHC 486
(Comm), [2016] 4 W.L.R. 59 (food sector, especially cash and carry and wholesale); *Software Incubator Ltd v Computer Associates Ltd* [2016] EWHC 1587
(QB); *Monk v Largo Foods Ltd* [2016] EWHC 1837 (Comm) (consultant to food
manufacturer; contract likely to have been terminated: not decisive on compensation but uncertainties taken into account).

Commercial agents

[*Add to note 992, line 2, after* "[2003] Eu.L.R. 189": *page* [108]]   **31–157**
; *Monk v Largo Foods Ltd* [2016] EWHC 1837 (Comm).

9. TERMINATION OF AUTHORITY

How authority terminated

[*Add to note 1053, at the end: page* [113]]   **31–166**
See in general Wee and Tan, "The Agency of Liquidators and Receivers", Ch.8
in Busch, Macgregor and Watts (eds), *Agency Law in Commercial Practice*

(2016), stressing that it must be understood that agency notions, as often, apply in flexible ways in this area.

Irrevocable authority

31–167 *[Delete text of paragraph and substitute: pages* [114]–[115]]
Though an agent's authority is, as stated above, normally revocable at will (without prejudice to his right, if any, to damages for breach of contract), there are some cases where this is not so. These are cases where

> "the agent has a relevant interest of his own in the exercise of his authority. This requires first, an agreement that the agent's authority shall be irrevocable, and secondly that the authority is given to secure an interest of the agent, being a proprietary interest (for example a power of attorney given to enable the holder of an equitable interest to perfect it[1065]) or a liability (generally in debt) owed him personally. In these cases, the agent's authority is irrevocable while the interest subsists."[1066]

This involves use of the format of agency at least in part to enable the agent to act in his own interest. But it is not necessary that the sole purpose of the arrangement is to secure the agent's financial interest: an agent can remain an agent owing the fiduciary and other duties to act in the principal's interest, while having a personal interest in the exercise of his authority sufficient to make it irrevocable.[1067] The authority to sell goods is not irrevocable merely because the agent has made advances to his principal; but it would be if the arrangement was specifically made to secure such advances.[1068] The mere right to commission is not sufficient to create irrevocable authority,[1069] but an interest in recovering a debt in respect of commission already earned may be. By an extension of this reasoning it has been held that in a sub-underwriting contract, the authority given by a sub-underwriter to apply for shares such as he is bound by his contract to take up is an authority coupled with an interest and as such irrevocable.[1070] The scope of this extension is still not clear.[1070a]

[1065] *Walsh v Whitcomb* (1797) 2 Esp. 565, 566; *Gaussen v Morton* (1830) 10 B. & C. 731 (powers of attorney to sell to satisfy existing debt).
[1066] *Bailey v Angove's Pty Ltd* [2016] UKSC 47 at [7] per Lord Sumption. See also *Frith v Frith* [1906] A.C. 254, 261; *Restatement, Third, Agency* (2006), para.3.12; Powers of Attorney Act 1971 s.4(1), below, para.31–168.
[1067] *Bailey v Angove's Pty Ltd* [2016] UKSC 47 at [9].
[1068] *Smart v Sandars* (1848) 5 C.B. 895, 917.
[1069] *Doward, Dickson & Co v Williams & Co* (1890) 6 T.L.R. 316.
[1070] *Re Olympic Fire & General Reinsurance Co Ltd* [1920] 2 Ch. 341. See also *Re Hartt Group and Land Securities Ltd* (1984) 7 D.L.R. (4th) 89 (power of landlord to re-enter as agent of tenant); *Slatter v Railway Commissioners for New South Wales* (1931) 45 C.L.R. 68 (power to apply for licence for premises); *Schindler v Brie* [2003] EWHC 1804 (Ch), [2003] W.T.L.R. 1361 (no intention to make authority irrevocable); *Temple Legal Protection Ltd v QBE Insurance (Europe) Ltd* [2009] EWCA Civ 453, [2010] 1 All E.R. (Comm) 903 at [79]; *Despot v Registrar-General of New South Wales* [2013] NSWCA 313. In *Bailey v Angove's Pty Ltd* [2016] UKSC 47 no view was expressed about the basis of these and related cases beyond saying that their results were "undoubtedly convenient": see at [10].
[1070a] The general principle of revocability of authority can cause difficulty when applied to arrangements at Lloyd's, which to a considerable extent depend on irrevocable agency and passivity of the principal. See Reynolds in Cranston (ed.), *Making Commercial Law* (1997), Ch.10. In *Society of Lloyd's v Leigh* [1997] C.L.C. 759 Colman J. was prepared to uphold irrevocability of authority outside the context of security: but the Court of Appeal decided the case on grounds connected with

the Lloyd's Act 1982 and Bylaws made thereunder: sub nom. *Society of Lloyd's v Lyon* [1997] C.L.C. 1398. In *Temple Legal Protection Ltd v QBE Insurance (Europe) Ltd* [2009] EWCA Civ 453, [2010] 1 All E.R. (Comm) 703 it was held that a broker's interest in maintaining and developing his business was not sufficient to render the authority to conduct a run-off irrevocable.

Apparent authority

[*Add to note 1075, at the end: page* [116]]   **31–169**
; and *DVB Bank SE v Isim Amin Ltd* [2014] EWHC 2156 (Comm) (valid service on agent after actual authority had expired).

Chapter 32

ARBITRATION

2. The Arbitration Agreement

Agreements to be in writing

32–023   [*Add to note 99, at the end: page* [130]]
; *Barrier Ltd v Redhall Marine Ltd* [2016] EWHC 381 (QB)

Separability of arbitration agreement

32–028   [*Add new note 115a, after* "that, unless otherwise agreed," *in line 7: page* [133]]
      115a In *National Iranian Oil Co v Crescent Petroleum Co International Ltd* [2016] EWHC 510 (Comm), [2016] 2 Lloyd's Rep. 146, at [7]–[14], the Court held that a contractual choice of law clause, on its own, will not operate as an agreement to the contrary for the purposes of s.7.

3. Stay of Legal Proceedings

Foreign proceedings outside the EU

32–053   [*Add to note 214, at the end: page* [144]]
For the view that the jurisdiction resides only in s.37, see *Southport Success SA v Tsingshan Holding Group Co Ltd* [2015] EWHC 1974 (Comm), [2015] 2 Lloyd's Rep. 578.

[*Add to note 219, line 6, after* "[2013] 1 Lloyd's Rep. 285.".*: page* [145]]
; *Crescendo Maritime Co v Bank of Communications Co Ltd* [2015] EWHC 3364
(Comm), [2016] 1 Lloyd's Rep. 414. In *ADM Asia-Pacific Trading Pte Ltd v PT
Budi Semesta Satria* [2016] EWHC 1427 (Comm) the Court declined to grant an
anti-suit injunction because of the delay in making the application. See also
Essar Shipping Ltd v Bank of China Ltd [2015] EWHC 3266 (Comm), [2016] 1
Lloyd's Rep. 427; *Ecobank Transnational Inc v Tanoh* [2015] EWCA Civ 1309,
[2016] 1 W.L.R. 2231 (anti-enforcement injunction).

[*Add to note 219, at the end: page* [145]]
Where a third party seeks to exercise rights under a contract containing an
arbitration clause, see *Shipowners' Mutual Protection and Indemnity Association
(Luxembourg) v Containerships Denizcilik Nakliyat ve Ticaret AS* [2016] EWCA
Civ 386, [2016] 1 Lloyd's Rep. 641.

Mandatory stay

[*Add to note 270, at the end: page* [154]]   32–068
; [2015] EWCA Civ 1171, (2015) 163 Con. L.R. 259 at [31]–[34] (reversing the
judge's decision in exercising his discretion to order a stay).

4. COMMENCEMENT OF ARBITRAL PROCEEDINGS

Power of court to extend time for beginning arbitral proceedings

[*Add to note 304, at the end: page* [158]]   32–076
; *Expofrut SA v Melville Services Inc* [2015] EWHC 1950 (Comm) at
[12]–[14]

Commencement of arbitral proceedings

[*Add to note 319, at the end: page* [160]]   32–081
; *Glencore International AG v PT Tera Logistic Indonesia* [2016] EWHC 82
(Comm), [2016] 1 Lloyd's Rep. 527 (arbitral proceedings were held to have been
commenced in respect of counterclaims by reason of the reference to *"claims"*
and *"all disputes arising under the contract"* in the arbitration notices).

5. THE ARBITRAL TRIBUNAL

Removal of arbitrator

[*Add to note 378, line 22, after* "s.68(2)(a) application failed)".*: page* [167]]   32–096
; *Cofely Ltd v Bingham* [2016] EWHC 240 (Comm); [2016] 2 All E.R. (Comm)
129 at [98]–[116] (arbitrator removed on the ground of apparent bias where 18
per cent of his appointments and 25 per cent of his arbitrator/adjudicator income

over the previous three years had come from cases involving the defendant as a party or as a claims consultant and where the Chartered Institute of Arbitrators acceptance of nomination form calls for disclosure of "*any involvement, however remote, with either party over the last five years*"); *W Ltd v M Sdn Bhd* [2016] EWHC 422 (Comm), [2016] 1 Lloyd's Rep. 552 at [27]–[44] (the IBA Guidelines 2014 are of assistance to the Court, but they are not a statement of English law; the Court noted some "*weaknesses*" in the IBA Guidelines 2014).

[*Add to note 378, line 28, after* "above, at [39]"*: page* [167]]
; *Cofely Ltd v Bingham* [2016] EWHC 240 (Comm), [2016] 2 All E.R. (Comm) 129 at [72]

6. JURISDICTION OF THE ARBITRAL TRIBUNAL

Tribunal can rule on its own jurisdiction

32–101   [*Add to note 412, at the end: page* [171]]
In *C v D1* [2015] EWHC 2126 (Comm) at [135] the Court said that s.30 is likely to contain an exhaustive definition of jurisdictional matters.

Objection to substantive jurisdiction of tribunal

32–102   [*Add to note 423, line 7, after* "[2005] 1 Lloyd's Rep. 192 at [66]"*: page* [172]]
; *Frontier Agriculture Ltd v Bratt Bros* [2015] EWCA Civ 611, [2015] 2 Lloyd's Rep. 500.

32–103   [*Add to paragraph, at the end: page* [172]]
By contrast, a party asserting the existence of an arbitration agreement will not be able to seek a declaration from the Court that the arbitration exists other than pursuant to the procedures laid down in the Arbitration Act 1996 (unless the declaration is sought in support of other relief, such as an anti-suit injunction).[429a]

[429a] *HC Trading Malta Ltd v Tradeland Commodities SL* [2016] EWHC 1279 (Comm), [2016] 1 W.L.R. 3120 at [16]–[20], [40].

7. THE ARBITRAL PROCEEDINGS

Peremptory orders

32–121   [*Add new note 504a, after* "with that peremptory order." *in line 8: page* [180]]
[504a] There is no obligation on the arbitral tribunal to exercise these powers: *Enterprise Insurance Co Plc v U-Drive Solutions (Gibraltar) Ltd* [2016] EWHC 1301 (QB) at [47]–[59].

32–122   [*Add to note 510, line 1, after* "the parties: s.42(1)"*: page* [180]]
; *Pearl Petroleum Co Ltd v Kurdistan Regional Government of Iraq* [2015] EWHC 3361 (Comm), [2016] 4 W.L.R. 2 at [17]–[27].

8. POWERS OF THE COURT

Power of court to extend time limits

[*Add to note 546, line 5, after "[2011] 2 Lloyd's Rep. 159": page [185]]*   **32–129**
; *Xstrata Coal Queensland Pty Ltd v Benxi Iron & Steel (Group) International Economic & Trading Co Ltd* [2016] EWHC 2022 (Comm).

Anti-arbitration injunction

[*Add to note 552, at the end: page [186]]*   **32–130**
; *AmTrust Europe Ltd v Trust Risk Group SpA* [2015] EWHC 1927 (Comm), [2015] 2 Lloyd's Rep. 231.

9. THE AWARD

Correction of award or additional award: the "slip rule"

[*Add to note 622, at the end: page [192]]*   **32–143**
; *Union Marine Classification Services LLC v Government of the Union of Comoros* [2016] EWCA Civ 239, [2016] 2 Lloyd's Rep. 193.

[*Add to note 624, line 2, after "Naval Gijon SA, above": page [192]]*
; *Xstrata Coal Queensland Pty Ltd v Benxi Iron & Steel (Group) International Economic & Trading Co Ltd* [2016] EWHC 2022 (Comm).

11. POWERS OF THE COURT IN RELATION TO THE AWARD

[*Insert new paragraph 32–155A before para.32–156: page [197]]*
Introduction. The Court's powers to review an arbitration award are set out   **32–155A**
in ss.67–69 of the Arbitration Act 1996. An application under ss.67–69 must conform to the requirements of those provisions and the procedural requirements set out in s.70. The mere fact that the parties agree that the Court should hear a challenge or appeal against an award will not confer jurisdiction on the Court unless the requirements of the Act are satisfied.[677a] In order that ss.67–69 may apply, there must have been an "*award*" made by the arbitral tribunal.[677b] An "*award*" is a formal written record of the arbitral tribunal's decision, in an arbitral reference made pursuant to an arbitration agreement,[677c] which disposes of or resolves an issue or dispute between the parties.[677d]

[677a] *Enterprise Insurance Co Plc v U-Drive Solutions (Gibraltar) Ltd* [2016] EWHC 1301 (QB) at [34].
[677b] In *Enterprise Insurance Co Plc v U-Drive Solutions (Gibraltar) Ltd* [2016] EWHC 1301 (QB) at [39]–[40], [116] the Court held that an order refusing to strike out a claim and an order for security for costs were not "*awards*" for the purposes of ss.68 and 69.

677c s.5 of the Arbitration Act 1996. A decision by the secretariat of the arbitral institution, as opposed to the tribunal, will not be an award unless the arbitral institution's rules provide otherwise.

677d s.52 of the Arbitration Act 1996 makes provision for the form of the award. See above, para.32–139.

Challenging the award: substantive jurisdiction

32–156 [Add to note 684, at the end: page [198]]
; *Emirates Trading Agency LLC v Sociedade de Fomento Industrial Private Ltd* [2015] EWHC 1452 (Comm), [2015] 2 Lloyd's Rep. 487.

32–157 [Add to note 690, at the end: page [198]]
In *Sino Channel Asia Ltd v Dana Shipping and Trading Pte Singapore* [2016] EWHC 1118 (Comm), [2016] 2 Lloyd's Rep. 97 at [4]–[5], the Court said that there was no time limit applicable to proceedings under s.72 and such an action may be brought after the making of an arbitration award.

32–158 [Add to note 691, line 9, after "[2014] 1 Lloyd's Rep. 479": page [199]]
; *Frontier Agriculture Ltd v Bratt Bros* [2015] EWCA Civ 611, [2015] 2 Lloyd's Rep. 500

Challenging the award: serious irregularity

32–162 [Add to note 708, penultimate line, after "[2015] 1 Lloyd's Rep. 67": page [201]]
; *BV Scheepswerf Damen Gorinchem v Marine Institute* [2015] EWHC 1810 (Comm), [2015] 2 Lloyd's Rep. 351; *W Ltd v M Sdn Bhd* [2016] EWHC 422 (Comm), [2016] 1 Lloyd's Rep. 552.

[Add to note 709, at the end: page [202]]
; *C v D1* [2015] EWHC 2126 (Comm) at [136]–[147].

32–163 [Add to note 719, at the end: page [204]]
; *BV Scheepswerf Damen Gorinchem v Marine Institute* [2015] EWHC 1810 (Comm), [2015] 2 Lloyd's Rep. 351.

[Add to note 722, at the end: page [205]]
Maass v Musion Events Ltd [2015] EWHC 1346 (Comm), [2015] 2 Lloyd's Rep. 383 at [40]–[42]

Appeal on point of law

32–167 [Add to note 738, line 3, after "(consent in advance).": page [207]]
cf. *ST Shipping and Transport Pte Ltd v Space Shipping Ltd* [2016] EWHC 880 (Comm), [2016] 2 Lloyd's Rep. 17.

Challenge or appeal: restrictions and time limits

32–175 [Add to note 780, at the end: page [213]]
In *S v A* [2016] EWHC 846 (Comm), [2016] 1 Lloyd's Rep. 604, at [26], the Court applied the test laid down in *Terna Bahrain Holding Company WLL v Al*

Shamsi, because it was common ground that it should do so, but questioned whether such a test should continue to apply in light of the Court's more recent decision in *Denton v TH White Ltd* [2014] EWCA Civ 906, [2014] 1 W.L.R. 3926.

[Update note 783: page [213]]   **32–176**
Frontier Agriculture Ltd v Bratt Bros [2015] EWCA Civ 611 is reported at [2015] 2 Lloyd's Rep. 500

Challenge or appeal: appeals to the Court of Appeal

[Add to note 796, penultimate line, after "[2007] 2 Lloyd's Rep. 548"*: page* [215]]   **32–181**
; *Integral Petroleum Ltd v Melars Group Ltd* [2016] EWCA Civ 108, [2016] 2 Lloyd's Rep. 141.

[Add to note 808, at the end: page [216]]   **32–184**
In *Michael Wilson & Partners Ltd v Emmott* [2015] EWCA Civ 1285, [2016] 1 W.L.R. 857 the Court explained the nature of the Court's jurisdiction. See also *Integral Petroleum Ltd v Melars Group Ltd* [2016] EWCA Civ 108, [2016] 2 Lloyd's Rep. 141 at [25]–[31].

Foreign awards

[Add to note 843, line 8, after "CPR r.62.18."*: page* [219]]   **32–189**
In *Pencil Hill Ltd v US Citta Di Palermo SpA* Unreported, January 19, 2016 at [30], the Court said that there is a strong leaning towards the enforcement of foreign arbitral awards and the circumstances in which the English Court may refuse enforcement are narrow. In this case, the Court allowed the enforcement of an award which included a penalty.

[Add to note 848, at the end: page [219]]
See also *LR Avionics Technologies Ltd v Federal Republic of Nigeria* [2016] EWHC 1761 (Comm), [2016] 4 W.L.R. 120 at [24]–[27].

[In note 850, lines 24–25 and 35–36, delete "[2014] EWHC 576 (Comm), [2014] 1
    Lloyd's Rep. 625" *(both instances) and substitute: page* [220]]
[2015] EWCA Civ 1144, [2016] 1 Lloyd's Rep. 5; [2015] EWCA Civ 1145, [2016] 1 Lloyd's Rep. 36 (supplementary judgment)

[Add to note 853, line 6, after "[2014] 1 All E.R. (Comm) 942"*: page* [221]]   **32–191**
; *Gold Reserve Inc v Bolivarian Republic of Venezuela* [2016] EWHC 153 (Comm), [2016] 1 W.L.R. 2829; *LR Avionics Technologies Ltd v Federal Republic of Nigeria* [2016] EWHC 1761 (Comm), [2016] 4 W.L.R. 120.

[Add to note 853, at the end: page [221]]
See above para.12–021.

12. Miscellaneous

Adjudication

32–199   *[Add to note 880, at the end: page* [224]]
In *RMC Building & Civil Engineering Ltd v UK Construction Ltd* [2016] EWHC
241 (TCC), [2016] B.L.R. 264 at [56], the Court said that the provisions
introduced by the 1996 Act and the Scheme are all about maintaining cash
flow.

Chapter 33

BAILMENT

2. Possession and Related Matters

Conversion of the chattel by the bailee

[*Add to note 75, line 4, after* "(2002) 118 L.Q.R. 544)": *page* [236]] **33–014**
; *Sang Stone Hamoon Jonoub Co Ltd v Baoyue Shipping Co Ltd (The Bao Yue)*
[2015] EWHC 2288 (Comm), [2016] 1 Lloyd's Rep. 320 (although goods may
be converted by a person who creates a lien without the authority of the owner,
an owner who authorises a bailee to deliver goods into storage must be taken to
authorise the creation of a lien where that is a reasonable and foreseeable incident
of the storage contract which the bailee is authorised to conclude).

4. Bailments for Valuable Consideration

(b) *Custody for Reward*

(i) *In General*

Custody for reward

33–049   [*Add to note 261, at the end: page* [255]]
; *Rana v Tears of Sutton Bridge* [2015] EWHC 2597 (QB).

The onus of proof and the scope of the duty

33–050   [*Add to note 269, at the end: page* [256]]
and *Rana v Tears of Sutton Bridge* [2015] EWHC 2597 (QB).

(f) *Pledge*

(i) *Pledge at Common Law*

Delivery essential for pledge

33–123   [*Add to note 768, line 1, after* "[1935] A.C. 53, 58–59": *page* [297]]
; *Impala Warehousing and Logistics (Shanghai) Co Ltd v Wanxiang Resources (Singapore) Pte Ltd* [2015] EWHC 811 (Comm), [2015] 2 All E.R. (Comm) 234 at [54]–[59].

CHAPTER 34

BILLS OF EXCHANGE AND BANKING

1. Negotiable Instruments

(b) *Bills of Exchange*

(i) *Definitions and Requirements*

Unconditional order in writing

34–010   [*Add to note 41, line 10, after* "December 2001, para.9.5": *page* [316]]
; cf. Practice Note on Execution of Documents Using an Electronic Signature (July 21, 2016) issued by a joint working party of the Law Society Company Law Committee and the City of London Law Society Company Law and Financial Law Committees, which suggests (at para.4.2) that an "electronic" promissory note can be "in writing" and "signed by the maker" for the purposes of s.83(1) of the Bills of Exchange Act 1882 (but without any mention of bills of exchange)

(ii) *Capacity and Authority of Parties*

Sufficient signature

34–042   [*Add to note 172, at the end: page* [332]]
See also Practice Note on Execution of Documents Using an Electronic Signature (July 21, 2016) issued by a joint working party of the Law Society Company Law Committee and the City of London Law Society Company Law and Financial Law Committees which, inter alia, considers Regulation (EU) No.910/2014 (the eIDAS Regulation) that has direct effect in EU Member States from July 1, 2016 (and see above, para.34–010, n.41).

(iv) *Transfer of Bills*

Negotiation of a bill

34–085   [*Add to note 290, line 1, after* "s.31(2).": *page* [352]]
"Delivery" is defined in s.2 as the "transfer of possession, actual or constructive, from one person to another". Contrast the narrower definition of delivery in

s.61(1) of the Sale of Goods Act 1979: "*voluntary* transfer of possession from one person to another . . . ".

Rights of mere holder

[*Add to note 333, at the end: page* [357]]   **34–094**
, distinguished in *Cassa di Risparmio di Parma e Piacenza SpA v Rals International Pte Ltd* [2015] SGHC 264.

(vii) *Discharge of Bill*

Assessment

[*Add to note 457, line 24, after* "commercially unacceptable conduct)"*: page* [378]]   **34–134**
; *T & L Sugars Ltd v Tate & Lyle Industries Ltd* [2015] EWHC 2696 (Comm) at [137] (on anticipatory reliance)

Tracing order

[*Add to note 461, line 6, after* "[1997] Q.B. 85"*: page* [379]]   **34–135**
; *FHR European Ventures LLP v Mankarious* [2016] EWHC 359 (Ch); *Bainbridge v Bainbridge* [2016] EWHC 898 (Ch)

2. Aspects of Banking Law

(a) *Bank Regulation*

(i) *Overview*

The Prudential Regulation Authority (PRA) and the Financial Conduct Authority (FCA)

[*In note 654, line 1, delete* "is set to replace" *and substitute: page* [410]]   **34–217**
has now replaced

Banking Conduct of Business Sourcebook (BCOBS)

[*Add to note 656, at the end: page* [411]]   **34–219**
Directive 2007/64/EC has recently been replaced by a revised Directive on payment services in the internal market (2015/2366/EU), also known as the second Payment Services Directive or PSD2. EU Member States have until January 13, 2018 to implement the requirements of PSD2. See further, J. Chertkow, J. Patient and V. Montgomery, "New Payment Services Regime: Preparing for a Revised Landscape" [2016] PLC (August) 21.

[*In note 660, line 2, delete* "with the current revision published in October 2014" *and substitute: page* [411]]
with revisions published in October 2014 and September 2015

[*Add to note 660, at the end: page* [411]]
On July 21, 2016, the Lending Standards Board published a new Standards of Lending Practice, which come into force on October 1, 2016. The Standards of Lending Practice will replace the Lending Code. The Standards of Lending Practice apply to personal customers and cover loans, credit cards and current account overdrafts. The new Standards represent a move away from the Lending Code, which was focused more on compliance with provisions than customer outcomes. It is anticipated that new standards for business lending, which will include small and medium-sized businesses (SMEs), will be published in 2017. In the interim the existing protections of the Lending Code will continue to apply to micro-enterprises (Standards of Lending Practice, p.3).

34–221   [*Add to note 672, line 5, after* "[2014] EWHC 2882 (QB) at [44]": *page* [412]]
; *Thornbridge Ltd v Barclays Bank Plc* [2015] EWHC 3430 (QB) at [138]–[141]

[*Add to note 672, at the end: page* [412]]
In *Sivagnanam v Barclays Bank Plc* [2015] EWHC 3985 (Comm), it was held (at [8]–[15]) that the claimant, the sole director/shareholder of a company that entered into an interest rate hedging product with the defendant bank, could not bring a claim for loss said to have been suffered as a private person as a result of breach of the conduct of business rules under FSMA 2000 s.138D(2), as he did not fall within the category of person intended to be protected by the FSMA 2000 or the relevant conduct of business rules. It was also held (at [16]–[21]) that his loss, as a shareholder, was irrecoverable due to the rule against reflective loss.

The Lending Code

34–222   [*In note 673, line 2, delete* "with the current revision published in October 2014" *and substitute: page* [413]]
with revisions published in October 2014 and September 2015

[*Add to note 673, at the end: page* [413]]
On July 21, 2016, the Lending Standards Board published a new Standards of Lending Practice, which come into force on October 1, 2016. The Standards of Lending Practice will replace the Lending Code. The Standards of Lending Practice apply to personal customers and cover loans, credit cards and current account overdrafts. The new Standards represent a move away from the Lending Code, which was focused more on compliance with provisions than customer outcomes. It is anticipated that new standards for business lending, which will include small and medium-sized businesses (SMEs), will be published in 2017. In the interim the existing protections of the Lending Code will continue to apply to micro-enterprises (Standards of Lending Practice, p.3).

[*In note 674 delete* "2nd edn" *and substitute: page* [413]]
September 28, 2015

Payment Services Regulations

[*In note 676, delete from* "On July 24, 2013 . . . " *in line 2 to the end and*   **34–223**
substitute: page [413]]
Directive 2007/64/EC has recently been replaced by a revised Directive on
payment services in the internal market (2015/2366/EU), also known as the
second Payment Services Directive or PSD2. EU Member States have until
January 13, 2018 to implement the requirements of PSD2. See further, J.
Chertkow, J. Patient and V. Montgomery, "New Payment Services Regime:
Preparing for a Revised Landscape" [2016] PLC (August) 21.

(iii) *EU Harmonisation Measures*

Single payment market

[*Delete text of note 732 and substitute: page* [420]]   **34–243**
Directive 2007/64/EC has been replaced by a revised Directive on payment
services in the internal market (2015/2366/EU), also known as the second
Payment Services Directive or PSD2. EU Member States have until January 13,
2018 to implement the requirements of PSD2. See further, J. Chertkow, J. Patient
and V. Montgomery, "New Payment Services Regime: Preparing for a Revised
Landscape" [2016] PLC (August) 21.

(b) *The Relationship of Banker and Customer*

(iv) *Fiduciary Relationship and Duty of Care*

Limitations of general principle defined

[*In note 766, line 4, delete* "2nd edn (2014)" *and substitute: page* [428]]   **34–257**
September 28, 2015

[*Add to note 766, at the end: page* [428]]
See also the *Standards of Lending Practice* (above, para.34–222, n.673) at pp.4
(Principles for lending), 6 (Product sale) and 8 (Money Management).

Effect of contractual documents on duty of care

[*Add to note 778, line 23, after* "a form of estoppel at all)": *page* [431]]   **34–260**
; *Thornbridge Ltd v Barclays Bank Plc* [2015] EWHC 3430 (QB) at [111]

[*Add to note 778, five lines from the end, after* "[2012] 1 B.C.L.C. 317 at [54]":
page [432]]
; *Thornbridge Ltd v Barclays Bank Plc* [2015] EWHC 3430 (QB) at [96]; *Finch
v Lloyds TSB Bank Plc* [2016] EWHC 1236 (QB) at [52]–[58]

[*Add to note 779, line 21, after* "at [115]–[117], [119]–[121]": *page* [432]]
; *Thornbridge Ltd v Barclays Bank Plc* [2015] EWHC 3430 (QB) at [97]–[121]
(HH Judge Moulder, sitting as a judge of the High Court, said "the test is not

whether the clause attempts to rewrite history or parts company with reality. The first step is to determine as a matter of construction whether the terms define the basis upon which the parties were transacting business or whether they were clauses inserted as a means of evading liability" [105]); *Sears v Minco Plc* [2016] EWHC 433 (Ch) at [74]–[84] (HH Judge Hodge, sitting as a judge of the High Court, said "I respectfully agree with Judge Moulder's analysis and conclusions [in *Thornbridge*]": at [80]).

(v) *Banks and Undue Influence*

O'Brien guidelines in practice

34–268   [*In note 807, line 5, delete* "2nd edn (2014)" *and substitute: page* [436]]
September 28, 2015

[*Add to note 807, at the end: page* [436]]
See also the *Standards of Lending Practice* (above, para.34–222, n.673) at pp.7 (Account maintenance and servicing) and 11 (Customer vulnerability).

Relationship between surety and debtor

34–271   [*In note 814, update reference to Treitel on The Law of Contract to: page* [437]]
14th edn (2015), paras 10–026 and 10–039

Nature of the transaction

34–272   [*Add to note 819, line 2, after* "loan to mother and son)": *page* [438]]
; *Bradley v Governor of the Bank of Ireland* [2016] NICh 11 (joint loan to mother and son)

[*Add to note 821, at the end: page* [438]]
For loan made to family partnership, see *O'Neill v Ulster Bank Ltd* [2015] NICA 64, [2016] B.P.I.R. 126 at [17] (arguable that situation analogous to where wife stands surety for loan made to company in which she is a shareholder).

Future transactions

34–274   [*In note 832, line 1, delete* "2nd edn (2014)" *and substitute: page* [440]]
September 28, 2015

[*Add to note 832, at the end: page* [440]]
See also the *Standards of Lending Practice* (above, para.34–222, n.673) at p.7 (Account maintenance and servicing).

(vi) *Banks as Constructive Trustees*

(iv) Dishonesty

[Add to note 892, at the end: page [449]]   **34–291**
Recklessness is not equivalent to dishonesty but it can be a sign of dishonesty:
see Lord Nicholls at 389–391, as interpreted by Lewison L.J. in *Clydesdale Bank
Plc v Workman* [2016] EWCA Civ 73, [2016] P.N.L.R. 18 at [48]–[53].

Knowing receipt

[Add to note 908, at the beginning: page [453]]   **34–297**
Arthur v Att-Gen of the Turks and Caicos Islands [2012] UKPC 30 at [37].

Unconscionability as the test of liability

[Add to note 923, at the end: page [456]]   **34–306**
; and, following agreement of the parties, by the Privy Council in *Arthur v Att-
Gen of the Turks and Caicos Islands* [2012] UKPC 30 at [33]–[36] (stressing the
difference between proprietary and personal remedies)

[Add to note 929, at the end: page [457]]   **34–307**
In *Arthur v Att-Gen of the Turks and Caicos Islands* [2012] UKPC 30 at [40], Sir
Terence Etherton, delivering the advice of the Privy Council, said "Knowing
receipt in the *Akindele* sense is . . . not merely absence of notice but unconscionable conduct amounting to equitable fraud. It is a classic example of lack of *bona
fides*".

(vii) *Duty of Secrecy*

Duty of secrecy

[In note 937, line 9, delete "2nd edn (2014)" *and substitute: page [459]]*   **34–310**
September 28, 2015

[Add to note 937, line 10, after "treated as private and confidential)": *page [459]]*
; the *Standards of Lending Practice* (above, para.34–222, n.673) at pp.7 (Account
maintenance and servicing: "Firms will maintain the security of customers' data
but may share information about the day-to-day running of a customer's
account(s), including positive data, with credit reference agencies where the firm
has agreed to follow the principles of reciprocity. [CONC 5]").

[Add to note 940, at the end: page [460]]
; *Santander UK Plc v Royal Bank of Scotland Plc* [2015] EWHC 2560 (Ch) at
[11]–[17], but with criticism of the ruling in *Santander UK Plc v National
Westminster Bank Plc*, above, that a claim in unjust enrichment was a wrong
capable of justifying a *Norwich Pharmacal* order (noted by M. Campbell [2016]
L.M.C.L.Q. 42).

[*Add to note 943, at the end: page* [460]]
For examples where legislation allows disclosure but only with customer consent, see the Small and Medium Sized Business (Credit Information) Regulations 2015 (SI 2015/1945) regs 3(2), 6(1)(b); the Small and Medium Sized Business (Finance Platforms) Regulations 2015 (SI 2015/1946) regs 3(4), 6(3)(b).

[*Add to note 945, line 10, after* "of giving banker's references.": *page* [461]]
(See also the *Standards of Lending Practice* (above, para.34–222, n.673) at p.7 (Account maintenance and servicing), with the relevant paragraph set out in n.937 above.)

[*Add to note 945, at the end: page* [461]]
For the duty imposed on designated banks to provide information about their small and medium-sized business customers to designated credit reference agencies ("CRAs"), and the duty on designated CRAs to provide credit information about small and medium-sized businesses to finance providers, see the Small and Medium Sized Business (Credit Information) Regulations 2015 (SI 2015/1945).

(viii) *Termination of Relationship*

Termination of relationship by consent

34–314   [*Add to note 957, at the end: page* [463]]
cf. *N v S* [2015] EWHC 3248 (Comm) at [12]–[13], where Burton J. held that the customer had an arguable case that the bank was not entitled to terminate the banking relationship without notice under its contractual terms, and went on to grant an interim mandatory injunction requiring the bank to comply with the customer's instructions in relation to existing transactions, while the customer sought to move its account to a new bank (for the money-laundering aspects of this case, see below, para.34–325A).

(c) *The Current Account*

(i) *Rights and Duties of the Banker*

Overdrafts

34–319   [*Add to note 981, three lines from the end, after* "Mason [2013] L.M.C.L.Q. 233).": *page* [466]]
The Supreme Court of the UK reviewed the law relating to penalty clauses in *Cavendish Square Holding BV v Makdessi* [2015] UKSC 67, [2015] 3 W.L.R. 1373, which is now the leading authority on the subject (see above, paras 26–178 et seq.). The Supreme Court (at [40]–[43]) declined to follow the approach taken in Australia and retained the requirement the penalty doctrine is only triggered by breach. The different approaches to the breach requirement in the two jurisdictions has been confirmed by the High Court of Australia in *Paciocco v ANZ Banking Group Ltd* [2016] HCA 28 at [7]–[10] and [119]–[127], which is now the leading authority in relation to the test to be applied in Australia in determining where a clause is penal.

Combining accounts

[*In note 985, penultimate line, delete* "2nd edn (2014)" *and substitute: page* [467]]   **34–320**
September 28, 2015

[*Add to note 985, at the end: page* [467]]
The *Standards of Lending Practice* (above, para.34–222, n.673) has no detailed provisions about the use of the right of set off.

Proceeds of Crime Act 2002

[*Insert new para.34–325A: page* [472]]
In *N v S*,[1020a] the defendant bank, suspicious about eight accounts held by the   **34–325A**
claimant foreign exchange dealer (an authorised payment institution), which related to particular customers of the claimant, froze all 160 of the claimant's accounts and gave notice to close all of its accounts with immediate effect. This left 476 individual transactions in limbo and the claimant in danger of going out of business. Buxton J., recognising the exceptional nature of the case, granted an interim mandatory injunction requiring the bank to comply with the customer's instructions in relation to the 476 transactions, and made an interim declaration protecting the defendant bank against any related criminal liability that might arise under the Proceeds of Crime Act 2002. The judge held that the claimant had an arguable case that the bank had no contractual right to terminate the banking relationship without notice and that the balance of convenience and justice required the claimant be given this protection. No express consent had been sought from the NCA by the bank in respect of the transactions and the judge accepted that if consent was now sought the resultant moratorium period would almost certainly have disastrous consequences for the claimant. The judge stated that "[t]he significant fact" was that there was no evidence known to the NCA that the monies being transferred were criminal property or suspected of being so.[1020b]

[1020a] [2015] EWHC 3248 (Comm).
[1020b] At [17].

(ii) *Termination of Duty to Pay*

Bankruptcy

[*Add to note 1042, at the end: page* [475]]   **34–332**
See also *Thomas v D'Eye* [2016] B.P.I.R. 883 at [49], per Baister R., who said of s.284, "we are not dealing with unjust enrichment generally but a particular statutory regime which gives rise to an account for money had and received to which there are limited defences".

(e) *The Giro System and Electronic Transfer of Funds*

Paper-based and electronic system

[*In paragraph, line 11, delete* "and VocaLink ("BACS") and" *and substitute: page*   **34–387**
[507]]
, called BACS,

[*Add to paragraph, line 12, after* "and the Faster Payments Service": *page* [507]]
operated by the Faster Payments Scheme Ltd

Clearing house rules

34–392   [*In paragraph, lines 2–4, delete from* "that operate with the administrative support"
to "of the Payments Council,": *page* [508]]

[*Delete text of note 1223 and substitute: page* [508]]
The Financial Services (Banking Reform) Act 2013 creates a new competition-
focused, economic regulator of retail payment systems in the UK: the new
Payment Systems Regulator became fully operational on April 1, 2015. In 2015
the Payments Council was replaced by Payments UK, which is the trade association representing the UK payments industry.

[*Add to note 1226, at the end: page* [508]]
(the judgments, even of the majority, are not easy to reconcile, but all three Lord
Justices appear to agree that there can be reliance on banking practice for the
purposes of interpretation where the practice is known or reasonably available to
both the bank and its customer).

[*Delete text of note 1228 and substitute: page* [509]]
As occurs, e.g. with the CHAPS Scheme Rules, Version 13 (May 2016),
r.11.1.11.

UK clearing systems

34–393   [*In paragraph, lines 2–4, delete from* "operating with the administrative" *to* "of the
Payments Council." *and substitute: page* [509]]
supported by Payments UK, which is the trade association representing the UK
payments industry.

[*In paragraph, line 8, delete* "and VocaLink Ltd": *page* [509]]

[*In paragraph, lines 14–15, delete* "also operated by the CHAPS . . . " *to* "Faster
Payment System" *and substitute: page* [509]]
operated by Faster Payments Scheme Ltd, is called the Faster Payments Service

[*Add to note 1232, at the end: page* [509]]
It is now possible to send individual payments of up to £250,000 using the Faster
Payments Service, but individual banks and building societies set their own
limits depending on how the payment is sent and the type of account their
customer is sending from (*www.fasterpayments.org.uk*).

Cancellation of a direct debit

34–402   [*Add to note 1246, at the end: page* [513]]
In some cases there may be an issue as to whether the 1977 Act is engaged in the
first place, see *African Export-Import Bank v Shebah Exploration and Production*

Co Ltd [2016] EWHC 311 (Comm), [2016] 2 All E.R. (Comm) 307 (no set-off clause in facilities agreement based on industry standard form).

Statutory controls

[In note 1252, delete from "On July 24, 2013 . . . " to the end and substitute: page [514]] **34–404**
Directive 2007/64/EC has itself recently been replaced by a revised Directive on payment services in the internal market (2015/2366/EU), also known as the second Payment Services Directive or PSD2. EU Member States have until January 13, 2018 to implement the requirements of PSD2. See further, J. Chertkow, J. Patient and V. Montgomery, "New Payment Services Regime: Preparing for a Revised Landscape" [2016] PLC (August) 21.

Non-execution or defective execution

[In paragraph, line 13, delete "Where the payment transaction is initiated" and substitute: page [516]] **34–407**
Where the payment order is initiated

Position of the paying banker at common law

[In note 1288, lines 1–2, delete "[2014] EWCA Civ 2780 (QB)" and substitute: page [518]] **34–409**
[2014] 2 Lloyd's Rep. 549

(g) *Giving Information on Financial Transactions*

Scope

[Add to note 1361, line 10, after "person", see n.672 above.": page [532]] **34–438**
In *Sivagnanam v Barclays Bank Plc* [2015] EWHC 3985 (Comm), it was held (at [8]–[15]) that the claimant, the sole director/shareholder of a company that entered into an interest rate hedging product with the defendant bank, could not bring a claim for loss said to have been suffered as a private person as a result of breach of the conduct of business rules under FSMA 2000 s.138D(2), as he did not fall within the category of person intended to be protected by the FSMA 2000 or the relevant conduct of business rules. It was also held (at [16]–[21]) that his loss, as a shareholder, was irrecoverable due to the rule against reflective loss.

[Add to note 1361, at the end: page [532]]
In *Suremime Ltd v Barclays Bank Plc* [2015] EWHC 2277 (QB) the judge, when granting the claimant permission to amend its particulars of claim, held (at [31]–[37]) that it was sufficiently arguable that the claimant had a claim in the tort of negligence against the defendant bank for its conduct of a review of swaps it had agreed with the FCA. But it has subsequently been said that the judge in *Suremime* "did not have the benefit . . . of having the full regulatory picture

painted before him" and (obiter) that if the judge "had before him all necessary matters, then I would respectfully conclude that the decision was wrong and one which I should not follow": *CGL Group Ltd v Royal Bank of Scotland* [2016] EWHC 281 (QB) at [53]–[54], per HH Judge Bird, sitting as a judge of the High Court.

Advising on investments

34–439   *[Add to paragraph, at the beginning: page* [532]*]*
In general a bank is not under a legal obligation to provide advice but if it gives advice then it must do so using reasonable care and skill.[1361a]

[1361a] *Finch v Lloyds TSB Bank Plc* [2016] EWHC 1236 (QB) at [52].

[In paragraph, lines 4–5, delete "The duty is based on the" *to* "banker and the customer." *and substitute: page* [532]*]*
The duty will be contractual where the claimant can prove a contract under which the defendant bank has agreed to provide a service including the provision of advice,[1362a] otherwise the claimant must establish a tortious duty to advise, and such a duty will arise only in exceptional circumstances.

[1362a] Supply of Goods and Services Act 1982 s.13; Consumer Rights Act 2015 s.49.

[Add to note 1363, at the beginning: page [532]*]*
See *Finch v Lloyds TSB Bank Plc* [2016] EWHC 1236 (QB) at [47]–[59] (borrower's claim that lender owed a contractual or tortious duty to advise it about a potentially onerous clause in a loan agreement failed because there was no contract whereby the lender was to provide advice and there was nothing exceptional about the relationship to justify the imposition of a tortious duty to advise, especially where borrower represented by professional advisers and giving of advice might have been contrary to lender's best interests). See also *Worthing v Lloyds Bank Plc* [2015] EWHC 2836 (QB) (investors' claim that bank was in breach of a strict obligation to correct an error in its original investment advice failed because the original advice had not been given in error and, even if it had been, there was no strict contractual obligation to correct that advice).

[Add to end of note 1363: page [532]*]*
In *Finch v Lloyds TSB Bank Plc* [2016] EWHC 1236 (QB), above, at [58], the judge saw no significance in the fact that the defendant lender had used the phrase "trusted advisor" in its marketing and training material, finding that the phrase was merely part of a marketing strategy to differentiate the lender from its competitors.

[Add to note 1369, at the end: page [533]*]*
But contrast the doubts as to the existence of such an intermediate duty expressed by the judge in *Thornbridge Ltd v Barclays Bank Plc* [2015] EWHC 3430 (QB) at [118]–[131].

Banking references

[*In note 1375, lines 4–6, delete from* "[2014] EWHC 2613 (QB)... " *to* **34-441**
"contributory negligence and loss)." *and substitute: page* [534]]
[2016] EWCA Civ 457, [2016] 1 W.L.R. 3169 (defendant bank did not owe a
duty of care to casino for negligent misstatement as to gambler's creditworthi-
ness when request for reference came from associated company of casino: there
was no assumption of responsibility or proximity, because neither the true
purpose of the reference nor the existence of the casino was revealed and the
reference was "given in strict confidence", and it was not fair, just and reasonable to impose liability on the bank).

(i) *Bankers Commercial Credits*

(i) *The UCP*

Modern practice

[*In paragraph, lines 6–7, delete from* "conditional undertaking to pay given from **34-446**
one bank to another." *and substitute: page* [537]]
undertaking given by an obligor bank (usually the buyer's bank) to a recipient
bank (which must be the seller's bank) to pay a specified sum under the condition
of a successful electronic matching of data or acceptance of mismatches.

[*Add to note 1391, at the end: page* [537]]
See also *The ICC Guide to the Uniform Rules for Bank Payment Obligations*
(ICC Publication No.751E).

[*Add to paragraph, line 13, after* "SWIFT Trade Services Utility"*: page* [537]]
; and, unlike the beneficiary of a letter of credit, the seller does not receive a
payment undertaking directly from the obligor bank (the seller's claim is against
the recipient bank, i.e. the seller's bank, according to the terms of any separate
contractual agreement that the seller will usually have entered into with that
bank, but this bilateral agreement is not part of the BPO itself).

[*Add to note 1392, at the end: page* [537]]
See also K. Vorpeil, "Bank payment obligations: alternative means of settlement
in international trade" [2014] I.B.L.J. 41.

Construction of the UCP

[*In note 1409, line 2, delete* "arbitration awards" *and substitute: page* [541]] **34-452**
decisions

[*Add to note 1410, line 4, after* "interpretation and implication is"*: page* [541]]
Marks & Spencer Plc v BNP Paribas Securities Services Trust Co (Jersey) Ltd
[2015] UKSC 72, [2016] A.C. 742, commenting upon

[*Add to note 1410, at the end: page* [541]]
In the context of performance bonds, the courts have consistently emphasised
that it will be rare for a term to be implied into such a contract, see below,
para.34–548, n.1611.

(ii) *Types of Documentary Credits*

Negotiation credits

34–483   *[Delete paragraph, including heading and footnotes, and substitute: pages [551]–[552]]*

Credits "available by negotiation" and negotiation credits. The credit may be available by negotiation with a bank nominated in the credit (or with any bank if the credit so provides). UCP 600 art.2 defines "negotiation" to mean the purchase by the nominated bank of bills of exchange ("drafts") drawn on a bank other than the nominated bank (e.g. the issuing bank), and/or documents under a complying presentation, by advancing or agreeing to advance funds to the beneficiary on or before the banking day on which reimbursement is due to the nominated bank. This enables the beneficiary to obtain funds without delay by selling the documents to the nominated bank (and so it is only of practical use to the beneficiary where payment under the credit is not immediate). A nominated bank that has honoured or negotiated a complying presentation and forwarded the documents to the issuing bank is entitled to reimbursement from the issuing bank under UCP 600 art.7(c).[1445] In *Société Générale SA v Saad Trading*,[1446] Teare J. held that (i) if the documents forwarded to the issuing bank are not compliant, the issuing bank is not obliged to reimburse the confirming bank under art.7(c) (and that the issuing bank is not bound by the view of the confirming bank that the documents are compliant)[1447]; and (ii) under art.7(c) the documents to be forwarded to the issuing bank must be the documents presented to the confirming bank under the credit (discretion on the part of the confirming bank as to which documents to forward would be contrary to the principle of strict compliance).[1448] In this case the confirming bank did not forward bills of exchange required to be presented under the letter of credit to the issuing bank, but as there was no dispute that the documents presented by the beneficiary to the confirming bank were compliant, the judge held that the issuing bank was not entitled to refuse to reimburse the confirming bank.[1449]

[1445] UCP 600 art.7(c), adds that "[r]eimbursement for the amount of a complying presentation under a credit available by acceptance or deferred payment is due at maturity, whether or not the nominated bank prepaid or purchased before maturity". See UCP 600 art.8(c) for a similar undertaking of a confirming bank to reimburse another nominated bank that has honoured or negotiated a complying presentation and forwarded the documents to the confirming bank.

[1446] [2011] EWHC 2424 (Comm), [2011] 2 C.L.C. 629.

[1447] At [44].

[1448] At [45]–[46].

[1449] At [47].

[Insert new paragraph 38–483A: page [552]]

34–483A   **"Negotiation credits".** The term "negotiation" is sometimes used in a different sense, namely where the undertaking contained in the credit is extended to third parties (including a negotiating bank) as well as the beneficiary, so that the third party may purchase the documents and present them to the issuing bank in its own right. Credits of this type are called "negotiation credits" and should be contrasted with credits "available by negotiation" in the sense described above (and also contrasted with "straight credits" where the issuing bank's payment undertaking is directed solely to the seller). UCP 600 has made the practice of using "negotiation credits" virtually redundant for if, under a credit incorporating UCP 600, it is intended that the beneficiary should be able to obtain payment by selling the documents to any bank, then the credit should be made freely available by negotiation.[1449a]

[1449a] A. Malek and D. Quest, *Jack: Documentary Credits*, 4th edn (2009), para.2.19.

(iv) *The Relationship of Issuing Banker and Buyer*

Deposit of security

[*Add new note 1503a, after* "recoverable in full by the buyer." *in line 5: page* [563]]
[1503a] See also S. Connelly, "Bank recovery and resolution: the case of contingent letters of credit under bail-in" (2016) 2 J.I.B.F.L. 78.

34–502

(v) *The Relationship of Banker and Seller*

The autonomy of an irrevocable credit

[*In note 1524, line 20, delete* "where Wuhan/Paget principles applied." *and substitute: page* [567]]
, and in *South Lanarkshire Council v Aviva Insurance Ltd* [2016] CSOH 83 at [26] (Outer House of Court of Session). The presumption that an instrument gives rise to independent, primary liability seems to apply "[w]here ... the granter is a bank or other financial institution whose business includes the granting of financial instruments for a fee", e.g. an insurance company: *South Lanarkshire Council v Aviva Insurance Ltd*, above, at [25], per Lord Doherty, citing *Meritz Fire & Marine Insurance Co Ltd v Jan de Nul NV* [2010] EWHC 3362 (Comm), [2011] 1 All E.R. (Comm) 1049 at [65]–[66], per Beatson J.; *Caterpillar Motoren GmbH & Co KG v Mutual Benefits Assurance Co*, above, at [20], per Teare J.; *Spliethoff's Bevrachtingskantoor BV v Bank of China Ltd*, above, at [83], per Carr J.

34–507

Obtaining an injunction against a bank

[*In note 1539, line 7, delete* "[2001] EWCA Civ 1041" *and substitute: page* [570]]
[2001] EWCA Civ 1059

34–510

The measure of damages

[*Add to note 1590, at the end: page* [579]]
For position on insolvency of issuing bank or confirming bank, see S. Connelly, "Bank recovery and resolution: the case of contingent letters of credit under bail-in" (2016) 2 J.I.B.F.L. 78.

34–522

(vii) *The Tender of Documents*

Construction of terms of credit

34–528   [*Add to note 1608, at the end: page* [582]]
Whether the strict compliance rule applies to performance bonds and demand
guarantees has been the subject of some uncertainty: but see *IE Contractors Ltd
v Lloyds Bank Plc* [1990] 2 Lloyd's Rep. 496 at 500–501, per Staughton L.J.
("[i]t is a question of construction of the bond"), applied in *Sea-Cargo Skips AS
v State Bank of India* [2013] EWHC 177 (Comm), [2013] 2 Lloyd's Rep. 477 at
[30], *Lukoil Mid-East Ltd v Barclays Bank Plc* [2016] EWHC 166 (TCC) at [17]
and *South Lanarkshire Council v Coface SA* [2016] CSIH 15 at [12].

> [*In note 1611, lines 1–2, delete from* ", which, through dealing . . . " *to* "letters of
> credit." *and substitute: page* [582]]
> ; *Uzinterimpex JSC v Standard Bank Plc* [2007] EWHC 1151 (Comm), [2007] 2
> Lloyd's Rep. 187 at [157]–[158]; *South Lanarkshire Council v Aviva Insurance
> Ltd* [2016] CSOH 83 at [29], which cases, although dealing with performance
> bonds, ought to apply also to letters of credit.

The ISBP

34–534   [*Add to paragraph, line 3, after "Examination of Documents": page* [585]]
under UCP 600

CHAPTER 35

CARRIAGE BY AIR

4. European Legislation

European Parliament and Council Regulation 889/2002

An EU carrier, still referred to in the legislation as a "Community air carrier", is one holding an air operating certificate issued by the authorities of a Member State. Pre-requisites for the issue of a licence include the carrier having a principal place of business in the Member State and that nationals of a Member State own or effectively control the carrier. On the UK withdrawing from the EU, and subject to any contrary provision in the withdrawal agreement, Regulation 889/2002 will cease to apply to carriers based in and owned by nationals of the UK. The Montreal Convention will continue to apply on the basis of the UK's earlier ratification. For the effect of the Regulation on non-international carriage, see below, para.35–074). **35–018**

> [*Add to note 82, at the end: page* [607]]
> ; *Air Baltic Corp AS v Lietuvos Respublikos specialiųjų tyrimų tarnyba* (C-429/14) [2016] 1 Lloyd's Rep. 407 at [23]

5. Liability of the Carrier

(d) *Delay to Passengers, Baggage or Cargo*

Liability for delay

There can be liability to persons other than the delayed passenger. The CJEU held (*Air Baltic Corp AS v Lietuvos Respublikos specialiųjų tyrimų tarnyba* **35–069**

(C-429/14) [2016] 1 Lloyd's Rep. 407) that art.19 of the Montreal Convention applies not only to the damage suffered by a passenger but also to the damage suffered by a person in its capacity as an employer who had concluded a contract of international carriage with an air carrier for the purpose of carriage of passengers who were its employees.

Delay is to be distinguished from "non-performance", the latter falling outside the scope of the Montreal Convention (see *Shawcross and Beaumont on Air Law*, para.VII1003.1 and the very full judgment in *Chaing v Air Canada* Unreported, January 22, 2016 (Cty Ct at Kingston-upon-Thames)).

European Parliament and Council Regulation 261/2004

35–071   For commentary on many aspects of the Regulation, see Bobek and Prassl (eds), *Air Passenger Rights: Ten Years On* (2016).

Regulation 261/2004 only applies (Regulation 261/2004 art.3) to passengers who have a confirmed reservation on the flight concerned (*Kupeli v Sirketti* [2016] EWHC 930 (QB)) and, except in the case of cancellation, present themselves for check-in by a time specified by the air carrier, the tour operator or an authorised travel agent, or, if no time is indicated, not later than 45 minutes before the published departure (see *Caldwell v easyJet Airline Co Ltd*, 2015 GWD 34-546 (Sheriff Court (Lothian and Borders) (Edinburgh)) (arrival two hours before scheduled departure but unable to check-in before 45 minute deadline owing to slow-moving queues; held within the Regulation).

Difficult issues have arisen in cases involving connecting flights. The European Commission has proposed a new provision that where a passenger misses a connecting flight as a result of a delay to a preceding connecting flight, the passenger is to have a right to compensation by the Community air carrier operating that preceding flight; for this purpose, the delay would be calculated by reference to the scheduled time of arrival at the final destination (COM/ 2013/0130 final).

Remedies

35–072   *[Add to note 335, at the end: page [639]]*
; *Van der Lans v Koninklijke Luchtvaartmaatschappij NV* (C-257/14); *Pešková* (C-315/15) (bird strike not an extraordinary circumstance).

[Add to note 340, at the end: page [639]]
and, for a defence of the decision by Judge Malinovský, Bobek and Prassl (eds), *Air Passenger Rights: Ten Years On* (2016), p.25. "Arrival time" is the time at which at least one of the aircraft doors is opened to allow passengers to disembark: *Germanwings GmbH v Henning* (C-452/13) [2015] C.E.C. 661.

6. Non-international Carriage

Applicable rules

35–074   Regulation 889/2002 applies only to "air carriers" defined by art.2(1)(a) to mean air transport undertakings with valid operating licences, and to "Community air carriers" defined by art.2(1)(b) to mean air carriers with valid operating licences granted by a Member State; carriage within a single Member State to view a property from the air by a carrier not required to have a valid operating licence was held not to be within the Regulation or (as it was not international carriage; see Main Work, Vol.II, para.35–012) the Montreal Convention (see *Pruller-Frey v Brodnig* (C-240/14)).

CHAPTER 36

CARRIAGE BY LAND

3. INTERNATIONAL CARRIAGE

(a) *Introduction*

Multi-modal or combined transport

36–084   [*Add to note 459, at the end: page* [693]]
As to defining the modes of carriage, see Clarke, "The Shape of the Conventions on the Carriage of Goods" (2015) 50 E.T.L. 371, 375–376.

(d) *Goods by Road*

The carrier's exemptions from liability: art.17(4)

[*Add to note 707, line 6, after* "by the sender.": *page* [720]]   **36–128**
See, e.g. *Anon.*, Bundesgerichtshof, March 19, 2015, (2016) 51 E.T.L. 99.

Upper financial limits of liability and measure of damages

[*Add to note 724, line 1, after* "and Road Act 1979 s.4(2).": *page* [722]]   **36–130**
See *Topdanmark Forsikring A/S v DSV Road A/S* (2016) 51 E.T.L. 93 (SC Denmark).

Wilful misconduct: an exception to limitation

[*Add to note 740, at the end: page* [725]]   **36–131**
See also *Topdanmark Forsikring A/S v DSV Road A/S* (2016) 51 E.T.L. 93 (SC Denmark).

Successive carriers

[*Add new note 759a, after* "takes possession of the goods." *in line 10: page* [728]]   **36–136**
[759a] See *Anon.*, Hoge Raad der Nederlanden, September 11, 2015, (2016) 51 E.T.L. 109; Laurijssen (2016) 51 E.T.L. 121.

Contribution proceedings

[*Add to note 784, line 3, after* "exclusive jurisdiction in disputes.": *page* [732]]   **36–141**
See *British American Tobacco Switzerland SA v Exel Europe Ltd* [2015] UKSC 65, [2016] A.C. 262 at [36]–[37], [68].

Jurisdiction

[*In note 814, lines 1–8, delete* "A carrier who did not agree ... " *to* "at [97]   **36–146**
(subject to appeal)." *and substitute: page* [736]]
A carrier who did not agree to a particular jurisdiction, and had no notice of a particular jurisdiction agreement, would not be bound by that agreement: *British American Tobacco Switzerland SA v Exel Europe Ltd* [2012] EWHC 694 (Comm), [2012] 2 Lloyd's Rep. 1 at [46]–[51]; [2015] UKSC 65, [2016] A.C. 262 at [26]. Accordingly, a successive carrier cannot be sued in proceedings brought against the primary carrier pursuant to a jurisdiction agreement between the claimant and the primary carrier, if the successive carrier did not agree to that clause and if the jurisdiction agreement is not in the consignment note, subject to the other heads of jurisdiction in CMR: *British American Tobacco Switzerland SA v Exel Europe Ltd* [2015] UKSC 65, [2016] A.C. 262.

[*Add to note 814, line 9, after* "extends to extra-contractual claims.": *page* [736]]
See also *Anon.*, Oberster Gerichtshof Österreich, February 25, 2015, (2015) 50 E.T.L. 700.

[In note 816, lines 3–6, delete from "British American Tobacco Switzerland SA v Exel Europe Ltd" to "(subject to appeal to the Supreme Court)" and substitute: page [737]]
British American Tobacco Switzerland SA v Exel Europe Ltd [2015] UKSC 65, [2016] A.C. 262

[In note 817, lines 2–4, delete from "See British American Tobacco Switzerland SA v Exel Europe Ltd" to "(subject to appeal to the Supreme Court)." and substitute: page [737]]
See *British American Tobacco Switzerland SA v Exel Europe Ltd* [2015] UKSC 65, [2016] A.C. 262, at [48]–[58].

[Delete text of note 819 and substitute: page [738]]
Sch. art.36. However, art.36 is not a provision stipulating in which jurisdiction proceedings by cargo claimants may be brought; that is a matter for art.31. See *British American Tobacco Switzerland SA v Exel Europe Ltd* [2015] UKSC 65, [2016] A.C. 262 at [19]–[20], [34]–[47], [67], [69].

[In paragraph, lines 22–29, delete from "Article 31(1) is to be construed" to "against the primary carrier.⁸²²" and substitute: page [738]]
Article 39(2) is concerned only with actions among carriers and not claims by cargo interests (whose claims are governed by art.31).[821–822]

[821–822] *British American Tobacco Switzerland SA v Exel Europe Ltd* [2015] UKSC 65, [2016] A.C. 262 at [36]–[37], [62], [68].

CHAPTER 37

CONSTRUCTION CONTRACTS

3. CONTRACT TERMS

(c) *Implied Terms*

General principles

37–072   [*Add to note 198, at the end: page* [782]]
In *Marks & Spencer Plc v BNP Paribas Securities Services Trust Co (Jersey) Ltd*
[2015] UKSC 72, the Supreme Court reaffirmed the applicability of these five
principles and provided further guidance as to their usage: see above, para.
14–007.

[*Add to note 200, at the end: page* [782]]
In *Walter Lilly & Co Ltd v Clin* [2016] EWHC 357(TCC), [2016] B.L.R. 247 it
was held that in order to make a Design Portion JCT Contract work effectively
the employer, who had the responsibility for obtaining planning permission,
should provide in good time to the local authority the information that its
planning officers require and are lawfully entitled to expect in order to grant the
necessary consents.

(e) *Tort in Construction*

Tort and contract

37–094   [*Add new note 303a, at the end of paragraph: page* [793]]
[303a] Following the Court of Appeal decision in *Wellesley Partners LLP v Withers LLP* [2015]
EWCA Civ 1146 the contractual rules on remoteness, and possibly also causation, would continue to
apply even where there are concurrent duties of care in contract and tort. See above,
para.1–195A.

4. Particular Features

(d) *Extension of Time and Liquidated Damages*

Concurrent delay

[*Add to note 428, at the end: page* [808]]   **37–120**
; and also approved in *Saga Cruises BDF Ltd v Fincantieri SpA* [2016] EWHC
1875 (Comm) at 249–251.

[*Add new paragraph 37–121A: page* [809]]
Revised rule on penalty clauses. In *Cavendish Square Holding BV v Mak-*   **37–121A**
dessi the Supreme Court held that the true test for a penalty is whether the
impugned provision is a secondary obligation which imposes a detriment on the
contract-breaker out of all proportion to any legitimate interest of the innocent
party in the enforcement of the primary obligation.[439a] This test is likely to be
more permissive of liquidated damages clauses and any cases pre-dating this
decision must be treated with care.

[439a] [2015] UKSC 67 at [32], [255] and [291]. See above, paras 26–178 et seq.

5. Payment

(b) *Interim Payment and Milestones*

Right to interim payment

[*Add new note 511a, after* "performed, or to the contract sum." *in line 22: page*   **37–145**
[819]]
[511a] *Grove Developments Ltd v Balfour Beatty Regional Construction Ltd* [2016] EWHC 168
(TCC) at [33].

10. Disputes

(e) *Adjudication*

The enforcement of adjudicator's awards

[*Add to paragraph, at the end: page* [878]]   **37–267**
Whilst adjudicators' decisions are binding until finally determined, it is possible
and permissible for the losing party to seek final determination of legal issues in
Court prior to, or at the same time as, any enforcement steps are taken by the
successful party.[896a] This can have the effect that the outcome of the adjudication
is overturned before it can be enforced.

[896a] *Caledonian Modular Ltd v Mar City Developments Ltd* [2015] EWHC 1855 (TCC) at [13].

Some procedural aspects of adjudication

37–268   [*Add to note 901, at the end: page* [879]]
However, it is possible that in cases where statutory interest runs, s.5A(2A) of the
Late Payment of Commercial Debts (Interest) Act 1998 would permit a party to
recover its reasonable legal costs of pursing a debt claim by adjudication. This is
a new provision brought in by the Late Payment of Commercial Debts Regulations 2013 and there are no decided cases on whether s.5A(2A) is intended to
cover legal costs of proving a contested debt and, if so, whether this new
provision which was only brought in by way of secondary legislation can survive
s.108A of the Housing Grants Act referred to above.

[*Add to note 906, at the end: page* [879]]
cf. *Paice v Harding (t/a MJ Harding Contractors)* [2015] EWHC 661 (TCC)

[*Add to note 907, at the end: page* [879]]
See also *Cofely Ltd v Bingham* [2016] EWHC 240 (Comm), [2016] B.L.R. 187,
where it was held by Hamblen J. that an arbitrator's scale of prior appointments
as an adjudicator and arbitrator in disputes involving the claimant, either as a
party or party representative, together with his conduct of the arbitration and his
reaction to questions concerning his relationship with the claimant, generated the
required basis for a finding of apparent bias.

Effect of an adjudicator's decision

37–270   [*Add to note 913, at the end: page* [880]]:
; approved by the Supreme Court at [2015] UKSC 38.

CONSUMER CONTRACTS

1. Introduction

Legislative protection for consumer contractors

[*In notes 10, 11 and 12 delete* "1979" *and substitute: page* [886]]
1893

38–002

The growing importance of European law

[*Add new note 16a, at end of paragraph title: page* [887]]
[16a] See general note on the announcement that the United Kingdom will leave the European Union, above, para.1–013A.

38–003

[*Add to note 22, at the end: page* [887]]
The 1990 Directive is repealed by Directive (EU) 2015/2302 on package travel and linked travel arrangements [2015] O.J. L326/1.

2. The Relationship of EU And UK Consumer Contract Law

(a) *The Continuing Interpretative Significance of EU Directives*

EU regulations and directives

[*Add new note 77a, at end of paragraph title: page* [887]]
[77a] See general note on the announcement that the United Kingdom will leave the European Union, above, para.1–013A.

38–012

Significance of EU source of English consumer contract law for its interpretation

[*Add to note 87, at the end: page* [896]]
; *United States of America v Nolan* [2015] UKSC 63, [2016] A.C. 463 where Lord Mance J.S.C. (with whom Lord Neuberger of Abbotsbury P.S.C., Baroness

38–013

Hale of Richmond D.P.S.C. and Lord Reed J.S.C. agreed) at [14] described the principle of conforming interpretation as "a cardinal principle of European Union and domestic law".

"Autonomous" and national interpretations

38–014   [*Add to note 99, at the end: page* [898]]
Identical provision to art.3(5) of the 2011 Directive is found in Directive (EU) 2015/2302 on package travel and linked travel arrangements [2015] O.J. L326/1 art.2(3) (this Directive repeals and replaces Directive 90/314/EEC on package travel, package holidays and package tours [1990] O.J. L158/59).

The duty of national courts to intervene of their own motion to protect EU consumer rights

38–018   [*Add to note 121, at the end: page* [901]]
; *Bucura v SC Bancpost SA* (C-348/14) July 9, 2015 para.44. On the possibility that a Member State may incur liability for a court's failure to protect a consumer's EU law rights see *Tomášová v Republic of Slovakia* (C-168/15) July 28, 2016, below, para.38–304.

[*Add to note 127, at the end: page* [901]]
; *Radlinger v Finway a.s.* (C-377/14) April 21, 2016 at paras 62–74 (information duties) and see below, para.38–063A.

[*Add to note 135, at the end: page* [902]]
cf. *Radlinger v Finway a.s.* (C-377/14) April 21, 2016 at paras 62–74 where the CJEU recognised an obligation on the national court to consider whether the information duties of the trader under the Consumer Credit Directive 2008 had been complied with simply by reference to the need to ensure the protection of the consumer and to its earlier case-law.

(b) *The Intensity of Harmonisation Required by EU Legislation*

Examples of "minimum harmonisation" directives

38–022   [*Add to note 158, at the end: page* [906]]
The 1990 Directive is repealed by Directive (EU) 2015/2302 on package travel and linked travel arrangements [2015] O.J. L326/1, art.4 of which sets a general principle of full harmonisation. The Directive must be implemented by the UK by January 1, 2018.

Examples of "full harmonisation" and "partial full harmonisation": Unfair Commercial Practices Directive 2005

38–024   [*Add new note 166a, at end of paragraph title: page* [907]]
[166a] Directive (EU) 2015/2302 on package travel and linked travel arrangements [2015] O.J. L326/1 art.4 sets a general principle of full harmonisation, with certain exceptions which the Directive itself sets out.

3. Definitions Of Consumer Contract

(b) *"Consumer"*

"Consumer" in EU law

[*Add to note 197, at the end: page* [911]]   **38–030**
However, the 1990 Directive is repealed (as of January 1, 2018) by Directive
(EU) 2015/2302 on package travel and linked travel arrangements [2015] O.J.
L326/1 which substitutes for "consumer" a new category of "traveller" which
"means any person who is seeking to conclude a contract, or is entitled to travel
on the basis of a contract concluded, within the scope of [the] Directive":
art.3(6). As recital 7 explains, the majority of travellers buying packages or
linked travel arrangements are "consumers within the meaning of Union consumer law", but the Directive's protections should extend to "business travellers
including members of liberal professions, or self-employed or other natural
persons where they do not make travel arrangements on the basis of a general
agreement".

European case-law

[*Add to paragraph, at the end: page* [913]]   **38–032**
The Court of Justice has recently held that, in order to determine whether a
person was acting as a consumer for the purposes of the Directive on unfair terms
in consumer contracts, a national court should take into account "all the circumstances of the case, particularly the nature of the goods or service covered by the
contract in question, capable of showing the purpose for which those goods or
that service is being acquired",[214a] this being a "functional criterion".[214b] However, the concept of "consumer" is "objective in nature and is distinct from the
concrete knowledge the person in question may have, or from the information
that person actually has".[214c] As a result, while lawyers may constitute "traders"
in their contracts with their own clients,[214d] they may, even if they are technically
knowledgeable, nonetheless act as consumers in other transactions as they may
be weaker parties compared to the traders with whom they deal.[214e]

[214a] *Costea v SC Volksbank România SA* (C-110/14) April 23, 2015 at para.23.
[214b] *Tarcău v Banca Comercială Intesa Sanpaolo România SA* (C-74/15) Order of CJEU November
19, 2015 at para.27.
[214c] *Costea v SC Volksbank România SA* (C-110/14) April 23, 2015 at para.21. See similarly,
Tarcău v Banca Comercială Intesa Sanpaolo România SA (C-74/15) Order of CJEU November 19,
2015 para.27 on which see below, paras 38–207 and 45–156.
[214d] *Šiba v Devėnas* (C-537/13) January 15, 2015 [2015] Bus. L.R. 291 paras 23 and 24.
[214e] *Costea v SC Volksbank România SA* (C-110/14) April 23, 2015 at paras 20–27.

The Consumer Rights Directive and its possible wider influence

[*Add to note 225, line 6, after* "2011 Directive recital 17": *page* [915]]   **38–034**
A similar pattern is found in Directive 2014/17/EU of 4 February 2014 on credit
agreements for consumers relating to immovable property [2014] O.J. L60/34

(the "Mortgage Credit Directive") recital 12 and art.4(1), referring to the definition of "consumer" in Directive 2008/48/EC of 23 April 2008 on credit agreements for consumers [2008] O.J. L133/66 art.3(1).

[In note 227, delete "The CJEU . . . " to "time of writing" and substitute: page [915]]
The CJEU in its judgment of September 3, 2015 did not address this issue.

United Kingdom case-law on earlier definition

38–037 *[Add to note 238, line 4, after "Brussels I bis Regulation") art.17.": page [917]]*
In commenting on the contrast between the *Apostolakis* and *Rouvroy* decisions, the HC in *AMT Futures Ltd v Mazillier, Dr Meier & Dr Guntner Rechtsanwaltsgesellschaft mbH* [2014] EWHC 1085 (Comm), [2015] 2 W.L.R. 187 at [58] considered that the dividing line between investors who count as "consumers" and those who do not "is likely to be heavily dependent on the circumstances of each individual and the nature and pattern of investment". (This point was not discussed on appeal: [2015] EWCA Civ 143, [2015] Q.B. 699; an appeal is pending before the SC.)

[Add to note 238, line 22, after "Regulations 2008 (SI 2008/1816)": page [917]]
; *R. (on the application of Bluefin Insurance Services Ltd) v Financial Ombudsman Service Ltd* [2014] EWHC 3413 at [121]–[128] (director of company taking out a Directors and Officers Insurance Policy was not a "consumer" for the purposes of the Financial Ombudsman Service's jurisdiction (which was defined by reference, inter alia, to the definition of "consumer" in the 1993 Directive) as the insurance concerned his liability for acts in the course of his trade, business, or profession).

Consumers as the supplier of goods or services?

38–044 *[In note 277, update reference to Treitel on The Law of Contract to: page [922]]*
14th edn (2015), para.7–054

[In paragraph, lines 41–46, delete from "On the other hand, . . . " to "traders is more arguable.²⁹²" and substitute: page [923]]
And while the wording of the Unfair Terms in Consumer Contracts Directive 1993 (formerly implemented in UK law by the Unfair Terms in Consumer Contracts Regulations 1999 and now by the Consumer Rights Act 2015)[292] is not completely clear, the Court of Justice has recently held that there is no requirement that the "consumer" be the recipient of goods or services and so may apply to a contract under which a natural person acting other than in the course of business guarantees a loan made by a creditor to a commercial company.[292a]

[292] See Main Work, Vol.II, paras 38–192 et seq.
[292a] *Tarcău v Banca Comercială Intesa Sanpaolo România SA* (C-74/15) Order of CJEU November 19, 2015, on which see below, para.38–207.

(c) *The Other Party to Consumer Contracts—"Traders"*

EU legislation

[*Add to note 319, line 4, after* "("organizer" and "retailer")": *page* [926]]   **38–048**
(this approach is amended by Directive (EU) 2015/2302 on package travel and
linked travel arrangements [2015] O.J. L326/1, which revokes and replaces the
1990 Directive. Article 3 of the new Directive defines "organiser" and "retailer"
as categories of "trader", which is itself defined and which extends to persons
facilitating a "linked travel arrangement")

[*Add new paragraph 38–052A: page* [930]]
Traders as "intermediaries" of non-traders. In *Wathelet v Garage Bietheres*   **38–052A**
& Fils SPRL[342b] the question arose whether a trader which acts "in the name of
and on behalf" of a private individual (who is therefore not a trader) with the
latter's authority can count as a "seller" within the meaning of the Consumer
Sales Directive 1999.[342c] According to Advocate General Saugmandsgaard Øe,
in principle such a trader does not "sell" the goods to the consumer by virtue of
a contract but instead acts only as an intermediary in a contract of sale between
two individuals, but he distinguished from this general position the case where
the trader gives the consumer the impression that he contracts as a seller: this is
similar to the situation where a trader acts in his own name where (as a general
rule in national laws) the trader is treated as the seller.[342d] As a result, the
Advocate General recommended that where a trader gives such an impression to
the consumer, the trader should count as a "seller" as a matter of its uniform EU
law meaning even if national law does not consider him to be a party to the
contract of sale itself.[342e] In English law, it would seem that in these circumstances the trader would be considered to be an undisclosed principal,[342f] and so
could be sued on the contract.[342g] The judgment of the Court of Justice of the EU
is pending at the time of writing.

[342b] C-149/15.
[342c] 1999 Directive art.1(1)(c) ("*seller*: shall mean any natural or legal person who, under a
contract, sells consumer goods in the course of his trade, business or profession"). On the significance
of the 1999 Directive and its implementation in English law see Main Work, Vol.II, paras 38–400 et
seq. cf. the position under the Sale of Goods Act 1979 s.14(5), according to which s.14's provisions
on implied terms as to quality and fitness for purpose apply to a sale by a person who in the course
of a business acts as agent for another as they apply to a sale by a principal in the course of a business
except where that other is *not* selling in the course of a business and either the buyer knows that fact
or reasonable steps are taken to bring it to the notice of the buyer before the contract is made: see
Main Work, Vol.II, para.44–097. However, s.14 of the 1979 Act does not apply to contracts made on
or after October 1, 2015 which fall within Ch.2 of Pt 1 of the Consumer Rights Act 2015, i.e.
contracts for a trader to supply goods to a consumer, which include "sales contracts": 1979 Act
s.14(5) as inserted by the 2015 Act, Sch.1 para.13(3); 2015 Act s.3(2). There is no equivalent
provision to s.14(5) of the 1979 Act in the provisions governing "goods contracts" in the 2015 Act
(on which see Main Work, Vol.II, paras 38–446 et seq.); the definition of "trader" in s.2(2) of that
Act concerns the different case where the *trader* acts "through another person acting in the trader's
name or on the trader's behalf", on which see Main Work, Vol.II, para.38–053.
[342d] Opinion of A.G. Saugmandsgaard Øe April 7, 2016 (available only in French) paras 50–51.
[342e] Opinion of A.G. Saugmandsgaard Øe April 7, 2016, paras 60–63.
[342f] There is a degree of uncertainty here as the A.G.'s Opinion refers to an intermediary acting *in
the name of* as well as on behalf of the individual and the former suggests that the agency is dis-
closed.

342g See Main Work, Vol.II, para.31–063. The general law of agency applies to contract for the sale of goods: Sale of Goods Act 1979 s.62(2); *Benjamin's Sale of Goods*, 9th edn (2014), para.3–002.

4. Information Requirements and Consumers' Rights of Cancellation

(a) *Introduction*

Rationale

38–055 [*Add to note 359, at the end: page* [932]]
Directive (EU) 2015/2302 on package travel and linked travel arrangements [2015] O.J. L326/1 repeals and replaces the 1990 Directive: see below, para. 38–132.

Consumer Contracts (Information, Cancellation and Additional Charges) Regulations 2013

38–057 [*In paragraph, line 5, delete* "revoked and"*: page* [934]]

[*Add to note 376, line 1, after* "SI 2013/3134"*: page* [934]]
(in force June 13, 2014)

[*Add to note 377, at the end: page* [934]]
The 2008 Regulations (SI 2008/1816) therefore do not apply to contracts entered into on or after June 13, 2014, being the date of coming into force of the 2013 Regulations: 2013 Regulations reg.2(b).

[*Add to note 378, at the end: page* [934]]
The 2000 Regulations (SI 2000/2334) therefore do not apply to contracts entered into on or after June 13, 2014, being the date of coming into force of the 2013 Regulations: 2013 Regulations reg.2(a).

[*Add new paragraph 38–063A: page* [939]]
38–063A   **Duty of court in relation to compliance with information duties.** The Court of Justice of the EU has held that the purpose of consumer protection pursued by a number of directives requires national courts to raise of their own motion issues relating to possible rights for the consumer under national laws implementing those directives.[408a] In *Radlinger v Finway a.s.*[408b] the Court of Justice of the EU followed this case-law in the context of the information requirements imposed on traders to consumers by the Consumer Credit Directive 2008. The particular justification for such a duty as regards information requirements was that the consumer is in "a weak position vis-à-vis the seller or supplier, as regards both his bargaining power and his level of knowledge, which leads to the consumer agreeing to terms drawn up in advance by the seller or supplier without being able to influence the content of those terms".[408c] The Court of Justice continued:

"In that regard, information, before and at the time of concluding a contract, on the terms of the contract and the consequences of concluding it is of fundamental importance for a consumer. It is, in particular, on the basis of that information that the consumer decides whether he wishes to be bound by the conditions drafted in advance by the seller or supplier."[408d]

There is a real risk, moreover, that the consumer may not rely on a legal rule protecting him owing to lack of awareness.[408e] Effective consumer protection therefore requires national courts to consider whether the information duties in the 2008 Directive have been complied with and, if that have not, they must draw all the consequences provided by national law, in the context, as regards penalties imposed as required by that directive.[408f] It is submitted that this reasoning applies by analogy to other information requirements imposed on traders by EU directives for the benefit of consumers and, therefore, that the Court of Justice would equally require national courts to raise the question whether these other information requirements have been fulfilled and, if not, with what effect. This special role of the court in relation to information duties must be borne in mind when considering the range of legal consequences of non-compliance with the information requirements under the 2013 Regulations.[408g]

[408a] See Main Work, Vol.II, paras 38–018—38–019.
[408b] C-377/14, April 21, 2016 ("*Radlinger* (C-377/14)").
[408c] *Radlinger* (C-377/14) at para.63, referring to *ERSTE Bank Hungary Zrt v Sugár* (C-32/14) October 1, 2015 at para.39 (which concerned the 1993 Directive).
[408d] *Radlinger* (C-377/14) at para.64, referring to *Constructora Principado SA v Menéndez Álvarez* (C-226/12) January 16, 2014 at para.25 (which concerned the 1993 Directive).
[408e] *Radlinger* (C-377/14) at paras 65, 70 and 74 (an obligation and not merely a power).
[408f] *Radlinger* (C-377/14) at para.73.
[408g] See Main Work, Vol.II, paras 38–099 et seq.

(b) *Contracts Covered by the 2013 Regulations*

Distinctions according to the subject matter of the contract

[*Add to note 418, at the end: page* [940]]   **38–067**
cf. *Software Incubator Ltd v Computer Associates UK Ltd* [2016] EWHC 1587 (QB) at [35]–[69] (contract for the supply of software may constitute a "sale of goods" for the purposes of the Commercial Agents (Council Directive) Regulations 1993 (SI 1993/3053), the court distinguishing the position in the law of sale of goods).

Exclusions from the scope of the 2013 Regulations

[*Add to note 449, line 2, after* "reg.6(1)(g)": *page* [945]]   **38–071**
(as amended by the Consumer Contracts (Amendment) Regulations 2015 (SI 2015/1629) art.3)

[*Add to note 449, at the end: page* [945]]
The scope of this exclusion will change on implementation of Directive (EU) 2015/2302 on package travel and linked travel arrangements [2015] O.J. L326/1, which repeals and replaces the 1990 Directive (see below, para.38–132) and

which excludes only the provisions in the 2015 Directive governing "packages" (and not therefore "linked travel arrangements") from the scope of the 2011 Directive: 2015 Directive art.3(2), (3) and (5) and art.27(2) (amending the 2011 Directive art.3(3)).

(c) *Information Requirements*

(iv) *The Effects of the Information Requirements*

General

38–099   [*Add to paragraph, at the end: page* [962]]
As has earlier been noted, the Court of Justice has held that the effectiveness of the protection provided by information requirements for consumers in the Consumer Credit Directive 2008 means that a national court must raise the issue whether these requirements have been fulfilled and, if not, must "draw all the consequences provided for under national law".[577a]

[577a] *Radlinger v Finway a.s.* (C-377/14) April 21, 2016 at paras 62–74 and see above, para. 38–063A.

The contractual significance of information supplied

38–100   [*In paragraph, line 3, delete* "2013 Regulations provide" *and substitute: page* [962]]
2013 Regulations (as made) provided

[*Add to paragraph, at the end: page* [963]]
After the enactment of these provisions in the 2015 Act, the 2013 Regulations were amended so that their own broad provisions governing the contractual significance of information are replaced with a residual provision to similar effect but applicable only to contracts for the supply of digital content *other than* for a price paid by the consumer.[585a]

[585a] Consumer Contracts (Amendment) Regulations 2015 (SI 2015/1629) arts 4–6 (replacing 2013 Regulations reg.9(3) (on-premises contracts), reg.10(5) (off-premises contracts) and reg.13(6) (distance contracts)). The intention was that the 2013 Regulations should still apply to contracts under which digital content is supplied which do not fall within the definition of "digital content contracts" in the 2015 Act: Explanatory Note to SI 2015/1629, which states that the amendments are "in consequence of the Act and revoke provisions of the 2013 Regulations to the extent they are replicated in the Act". The retention of the residual category of contracts for the supply of digital content in the 2013 Regulations as amended is required by their broad scope following in this respect the Consumer Rights Directive 2011: see Main Work, Vol.II, para.38–067. However, under the 2015 Act Pt 1 Ch.3, "a contract for a trader to supply digital content to a consumer" is of two types: where digital content "is supplied for a price paid by the consumer" (s.33(1)) and where "(a) it is supplied free with goods or services or other digital content for which the consumer pays a price, and (b) it is not generally available to consumers unless they have paid a price for it or for goods or services or other digital content" (s.33(2)). This being the case, it would appear that the second type of digital content contract defined by s.33(2) would also count as a "contract for the supply of digital content other than for a price paid by the consumer" under the new 2013 Regulations (regs 9(3), 10(5) and 13(6), thus retaining (apparently by mistake) a degree of regulatory overlap. (The amendments to the 2013 Regulations apply to contracts entered into on or after October 1, 2015: SI 2015/1629 art.1).

Effect on the contract of failure to provide information

[*Add to note 587, at the end: page* [963]]   **38–101**
; *Allproperty Claims Ltd v Tang* [2015] EWHC 2198 (QB) at [45] and cf. *Kell v Department of Energy and Climate Change* (Newcastle upon Tyne County Ct, July 23, 2015).

Criminal law: off-premises contracts

[*Delete text of note 596 and substitute: page* [964]].   **38–102**
2013 Regulations regs 20–23; regs 24–26 (powers of investigation, obstruction of authorised officers, and freedom from self-incrimination, respectively) were revoked by the Consumer Rights Act 2015 (Consequential Amendments) Order 2015 (SI 2015/1726) art.2, Sch. Pt 2, para.7; the 2015 Act is amended so as to include the 2013 Regulations in the list of legislation to which the investigatory powers in that Act (Sch.5) applies: SI 2015/1726 art.2, Sch. Pt 1 para.6.

Misleading omissions

[*Add to note 601, line 5, after* "2013 Regulations regs 13 and 14."*: page* [965]]   **38–105**
For the "complementary nature" of information obligations under specific EU legislation and the provision in art.7(5) of the 2005 Directive (implemented by reg.6(3)(b) of the 2013 Regulations), see *Abcur AB v Apoteket Farmaci, Apoteket AB and Apoteket Farmaci AB* (C-544/13 and C-545/13) July 16, 2015 at paras 78–82 (medicinal products for human use).

Misleading actions

[*Add to note 609, at the end: page* [966]]   **38–106**
In *Abcur AB v Apoteket Farmaci, Apoteket AB and Apoteket Farmaci AB* (C-544/13 and C-545/13) July 16, 2015 the CJEU held that art.3(4) of the 2005 Directive "applies only in so far as there are no specific EU law provisions regulating specific aspects of unfair commercial practices, such as information requirements and rules on the way the information is presented to the consumer" in relation to medical products for human use (at para.79) and that, where the specific provisions conflict with the provisions in the 2005 Directive, the former "take precedence and apply to those specific aspects of unfair commercial practices" (at para.81), but in the result, this allowed advertising practices relating to such medical products to fall within the scope of the 2005 Directive "provided that the conditions for the application of that directive are satisfied" (at para.83). Moreover, it is submitted that the line of argument in the Main Work is not contradicted by the later judgment in *Citroën Commerce GmbH v Zentralvereinigung des Kraftfahrzeuggewerbes zur Aufrechterhaltung lauteren Wettbewerbs eV (ZLW)* (C-476/14) July 7, 2016 at paras 44–46. There, the CJEU held that the provision in the 2005 Directive regarding the materiality of certain information in invitations to purchase for the purposes of misleading omissions (which included "the price inclusive of taxes" (art.7(4)(c))) could not apply to the case before them "as the aspect relating to the selling price referred to in an

advertisement", as that issue was governed by Directive 98/6/EC on consumer protection in the indication of the prices of products offered to customers [1998] O.J. L80/27 art.3(1)'s provision on "selling price": the 1998 Directive governed this "specific aspect" within the meaning of art.3(4) of the 2005 Directive, which therefore "cannot apply as regards that aspect": (C-476/14 judgment at para.45). This case therefore provides an example of where the "special provision" must prevail, as explained in the Main Work.

(d) *The Consumer's Right of Cancellation or Withdrawal*

(i) *The Situations in Which the Right Arises and its Duration*

No effective waiver of right by consumer

38–115   *[Add to note 670, at the end: page* [973]]
cf. *Salat v Barutis* [2013] EWCA Civ 1499, [2014] E.C.C. 2 at [22] (CA "inclined to agree" that under the Cancellation of Contracts made in a Consumer's Home or Place of Work etc. Regulations 2008 (SI 2008/1816) (which were replaced by the 2013 Regulations) a consumer cannot affirm a contract that would otherwise be unenforceable against him).

(ii) *The Effects of Cancellation or Withdrawal*

Reimbursement by the trader of payments received from the consumer

38–118   *[In note 689, delete from* ". Regulation 34(6) refers" *in line 1 to the end and substitute: page* [975]]
(as amended by SI 2015/1629 art.7).

(f) *Special Rules for Financial Services Contracts, Timeshare Contracts, Package Travel Contracts, Contracts Concluded by Electronic Means and ADR*

(i) *Introduction*

Special rules governing particular contracts in EU law

38–130   *[Add to note 764, at the end: page* [983]]
The 1990 Directive is repealed and replaced by Directive (EU) 2015/2302 on package travel and linked travel arrangements [2015] O.J. L326/1. At the time of writing, this directive has not been implemented in UK law.

(ii) *Package Travel, Package Holidays and Package Tours*

Introduction

38–132   *[Add to note 788, at the end: page* [986]]
The 1990 Directive is repealed and replaced by Directive (EU) 2015/2302 on package travel and linked travel arrangements [2015] O.J. L326/1, which must be implemented by January 1, 2018. (At the time of writing, it has not been

implemented in UK law.) The 2015 Directive requires significant changes to the law governing package travel, creating a new category of "linked travel arrangements" and in principle requiring "full harmonisation".

Liability for proper performance of the contract

[*Add to note 806, at the end: page* [988]]   **38–134**
, applied in *Evans v Kosmar Villa Holidays Plc* [2007] EWCA Civ 1003, [2008] 1 W.L.R. 297 at [21] and *Committeri v Club Mediterranee SA* [2016] EWHC 1510 (QB) at [29], where it was also held (at [49]–[53]) that liability arising from national law implementing the 1990 Directive and therefore arising in respect of "the proper performance of the obligations arising from the contract" is contractual rather than non-contractual for the purposes of the EU private law instruments on applicable law, i.e. Regulation 593/2008 on the law applicable to contractual obligations ("Rome I") [2008] O.J. L177/6 (on which see Main Work, Vol.I, paras 30–129 et seq.) and Regulation 864/2007 of the European Parliament and of the Council law applicable to non-contractual obligations ("Rome II Regulation") [2007] O.J. L199/40.

(iii) *Timeshare and Related Contracts*

Exclusion by agreement or choice of law

[*Add to paragraph, at the end: page* [994]]   **38–141**
Finally, it would appear that an express choice of law clause in a contract falling within the scope of the 2010 Regulations may be assessed for its fairness under the general controls on unfair contract terms implementing the Unfair Terms in Consumer Contracts Directive 1993, i.e. the Unfair Terms in Consumer Contracts Regulations 1999 or the Consumer Rights Act 2015 Pt 2.[876a]

[876a] cf. *Verein für Konsumenteninformation v Amazon EU Sàrl* (C-191/15) July 28, 2016, see below, para.38–295A. For the relevant controls, see Main Work, Vol.II, paras 38–192 et seq.

(iv) *Trader's Information Duties in Relation to ADR*

EU law and ADR

[*In note 891, lines 2–3, delete* "(in force July 9, 2015)" *and substitute: page* [995]]   **38–143**
(the amendment came into force on July 9, 2015 but could not take effect until the commencement of SI 2015/542 reg.19 on October 1, 2015).

5. UNFAIR COMMERCIAL PRACTICES AND THE CONSUMER'S RIGHTS TO REDRESS

(b) *The Unfair Commercial Practices Directive 2005*

Relationship with other EU legislation

[*Add to note 932, at the end: page* [1000]]   **38–149**
See also above, para.38–106, discussing *Citroën Commerce GmbH v Zentralvereinigung des Kraftfahrzeuggewerbes zur Aufrechterhaltung lauteren Wettbewerbs eV (ZLW)* (C-476/14) July 7, 2016 at paras 44–46.

(c) *The General Scheme of the 2008 Regulations*

Enforcement by authorities

38–159   [*Add to note 1000, at the end: page* [1008]]
From that date, the enforcement authorities instead enjoy the investigatory
powers set out under the general regime in the 2015 Act, Sch.5 (as specified by
Pt 2 para.10 referring to the 2008 Regulations reg.19(1) and (1A)): SI 2015/1630
art.3(h).

(d) *The New Rights to Civil Redress for Consumers*

(ii) *General Conditions for the Availability of the Rights to Redress*

Misleading omissions

38–172   [*In note 1077, line 2, delete* "option" *and substitute: page* [1017]]
invitation

6. The Control of Unfair Contract Terms

(a) *Introduction*

Consumer Rights Act 2015

38–196   [*Add to note 1238, at the end: page* [1037]]
See also Conway, *Consumer Rights Act, Briefing Paper* (House of Commons
Library, SN 6588, October 1, 2015).

[*Delete text of note 1248 and substitute: page* [1038]]
2015 Act ss.31(7), 47(5), 57(7), 70 and Sch.3, on which see Main Work, Vol.II,
para.38–343. In addition, the provisions in Pt 2 of the 2015 Act which implement
the 1993 Directive have been designated as a specified UK law for the purposes
of s.212 of the Enterprise Act 2002 ("Community infringements"), and acts or
omissions in respect of any provision in Pt 2 of the 2015 Act are specified as
possible "domestic infringements" for the purposes of s.211 of the Enterprise
Act 2002. For the details and more general discussion of these powers see Main
Work, Vol.II, paras 38–388—38–394 (as amended by this Supplement).

Temporal application of the 2015 Act's provisions on unfair terms

38–197   [*In note 1249, line 4, delete* "April 6, 2015: 2015 Order art.4)." *and substitute: page*
[1038]]
October 1, 2016: 2015 Order arts 4 and 6(2) as amended by the Consumer Rights
Act 2015 (Commencement No.3, Transitional Provisions, Savings and Consequential Amendments) (Amendment) Order 2016 (SI 2016/484) art.2). But see
further below, para.38–403.

[*Add to paragraph, line 7, after* "Parts 1 and 2 of the Act were brought into force"*:
page* [1039]]
generally

[*Add to note 1250a, penultimate line, after* "Regulations by the 2015 Act."*: page*
[1039]]
Similarly, the provisions brought into force on October 1, 2016 in Pt 1 of the
2015 Act in relation to any "contract to supply a consumer transport service" do
not apply to contracts entered before that date and the provisions in the Unfair
Contract Terms Act 1977 therefore still apply to those contracts until that date:
SI 2015/1630 arts 4 and 6(2) (as amended by SI 2016/484 art.2(3)).

(c) *The Old Law: the Unfair Terms in Consumer Contracts Regulations 1999*

Summary of impact of the 1999 Regulations

[*Add to note 1270, at the end: page* [1042]]   **38–202**
See also CMA, *Consumer law compliance review: cloud storage, Findings
report* (May 27, 2016), esp. Ch.5, available at *https://www.gov.uk/government/
uploads/system/uploads/attachment_data/file/526447/cloud-storage-findings-
report.pdf.*

(i) *The Types of Contracts Governed by the 1999 Regulations*

All types of consumer contracts

[*Add to paragraph, after note 1285: page* [1044]]   **38–203**
In *Tarcău v Banca Comercială Intesa Sanpaolo România SA,* the Court of Justice
followed this earlier case-law and therefore held that the 1993 Directive could
apply to a contract of guarantee undertaken by a natural person acting other than
in the course of business under which he or she guaranteed the obligations of a
debtor company to a commercial lender.[1285a] According to the Court of Justice
"[t]he purpose of the contract is . . . subject to the exceptions listed in the recital
10 of the Directive . . . , irrelevant in determining the scope of the directive".[1285b]

[1285a] C-74/15 Order of CJEU November 19, 2015 (*"Tarcău* (C-74/15)") (an "order" is made by the
CJEU where it considers that the question for a preliminary ruling admits of no reasonable doubt).
See similarly *Bucura v SC Bancpost SA* (C-348/14) July 9, 2015 (available only in French) paras
35–38 (1993 Directive may apply where the alleged "consumer" contracted as "co-debtor" to a
person concluding a contract of consumer credit).
[1285b] *Tarcău* (C-74/15) at para.22. On the status of these "exceptions" see Main Work, para.38–203
n.1280.

"Consumers" as "suppliers"?

[*In note 1308, update reference to Treitel on The Law of Contract to: page* [1046]]   **38–207**
14th edn (2015), para.7–054

[*Delete text of note 1314 and substitute: page* [1047]]
The view taken by this paragraph that the 1993 Directive can apply to contracts
under which "consumers" supply persons acting in the course of business was

recently confirmed explicitly by the Court of Justice in its decision in *Tarcău v Banca Comercială Intesa Sanpaolo România SA* (C-74/15) Order of CJEU November 19, 2015 (*"Tarcău* (C-74/15)"). In that case, the national court had considered that the 1993 Directive applied only to contracts for the supply of goods or services to consumers, but the Court of Justice held the Directive applies to "all contracts" between consumers and sellers or suppliers and that "[t]he purpose of the contract is thus, subject to the exceptions listed in the recital 10 of the Directive . . . , irrelevant in determining the scope of the directive": *Tarcău* (C-74/15) at para.22 and on the status of these "exceptions" see Main Work, para.38–203 n.1280. According to the Court of Justice:

> "It is therefore by reference to the capacity of the contracting parties, according to whether or not they are acting for purposes relating to their trade, business or profession, that the directive defines the contracts to which it applies" (*Tarcău* (C-74/15) at para.23).

The Court therefore further held that whether a natural person who agrees to secure the contractual obligations owed by a commercial company to a banking institution under a credit agreement is to be regarded as a "consumer" depends on whether he "acted for purposes relating to his trade, business or profession or because of functional links he has with that company, such as a directorship or non-negligible shareholding" or whether instead "he acted for purposes of a private nature": *Tarcău* (C-74/15) at para.29.

[*Delete text of note 1316 and substitute: page* [1047]]
See *Tarcău v Banca Comercială Intesa Sanpaolo România SA* (C-74/15) Order of CJEU November 19, 2015 (discussed above, para.38–207, n.1314).

Third parties and consumers

38–209   [*Add to note 1322, at the end: page* [1048]]
For the position of a third party assignee of the consumer's rights in relation to contract terms "not binding" on the consumer as unfair, see below, para. 38–315.

An autonomous view of "contract"?

38–211   [*Add new note 1327a, after* "considered non-contractual." *in line 5: page* [1049]]
[1327a] On the other hand, some legal relationships which involve elements of agreement in one or both parties may nevertheless be properly characterised as "non-contractual" owing to the nature or extent of their regulation: e.g. the relationship between a student on the Bar Professional Training Course and the Bar Council: *R. (on the application of Prescott) v General Council of the Bar* [2015] EWHC 1919 (Admin) at [79].

[*Add to note 1335, at the end: page* [1050]]
cf. *Roundlistic Ltd v Jones* [2016] UKUT 325 (LC) at [100], where it was held that a lease of residential premises granted by a landlord to its tenant was a contract concluded between those parties, despite the fact that it was concluded within the context of the obligation on the landlord to grant a new lease pursuant to the Leasehold Reform, Housing and Development Act 1993, though it was further held that these terms of the new lease were excluded from the scope of the 1999 Regulations on the basis that they reflected "mandatory statutory

provisions" within the meaning of reg.4(2), on which see below, para.38–217A.

(ii) *Contract Terms Excluded From the 1999 Regulations*

[Add new paragraph 38–217A: page [1056]]

Statutory obligation to grant contract on same terms. In *Roundlistic Ltd v Jones*,[1377a] a new lease had been granted to a tenant by her landlord under its obligation imposed by the Leasehold Reform, Housing and Development Act 1993.[1377b] The Upper Tribunal (Lands Chamber) noted that the terms upon which the landlord was obliged to grant the new lease were provided by the Act and that, while there was scope for some alternations in the terms, the Act's starting-point was that the new lease was to be on the same terms as the existing lease subject to certain limited modifications.[1377c] In these circumstances, the Upper Tribunal concluded that the 1999 Regulations did not apply to the terms of the new lease as they fell within the exclusion in reg.4(2) concerning "mandatory statutory provisions".[1377d] It is submitted, however, that this decision extends the scope of application of reg.4(2) beyond the likely interpretation by the Court of Justice of the EU of art.1(2) of the 1993 Directive which reg.4(2) implements[1377e]: art.1(2) is to be strictly construed[1377f] and there is a difference between contract terms required by legislation itself (where "it may legitimately be supposed that the national legislature struck a balance between all the rights and obligations of the parties to certain contracts"[1377g]) and contract terms which reflect an earlier contract between the parties whose content has not been the object of any legislative consideration or imposition.

38–217A

[1377a] [2016] UKUT 325 (LC).
[1377b] i.e. ss.43, 56 and 57.
[1377c] [2016] UKUT 325 (LC) at [101].
[1377d] [2016] UKUT 325 (LC) at [101]. It had been held that the new lease was a "contract" for the purposes of the 1999 Regulations despite its compulsory elements: see above, para.38–321.
[1377e] See notably *RWE Vertrieb AG v Verbraucherzentrale Nordrhein-Westfalen eV* (C-92/11) March 21, 2013 ("*RWE Vertrieb AG* (C-92/11)") discussed in the Main Work, Vol.II, para. 38–215.
[1377f] *Kušionová v SMART Capital a.s.* (C-34/13) September 10, 2014 para.77.
[1377g] *RWE Vertrieb AG* (C-92/11) at para.29. See also the explanation of the exclusion in art.1(2) in recital 13 of the 1993 Directive that "the statutory or regulatory provisions of the Member States which directly or indirectly determine the terms of consumer contracts are presumed not to contain unfair terms".

(iii) *The Requirement of Fairness*

(bb) *The "Core Exclusion"*

The condition that the "terms are in plain intelligible language"

[Add to note 1484, at the end: page [1072]]
See similarly *Bucura v SC Bancpost SA* (C-348/14) July 9, 2015 at paras 57–63.

38–239

(cc) *The Composite Test of Unfairness*

[Add new paragraph 38–251A: page [1085]]

38–251A   ***ParkingEye Ltd v Beavis.*** In *ParkingEye Ltd v Beavis*[1571a] the Supreme Court considered how the test of unfairness in the 1999 Regulations would apply to a term in a contract under which a consumer could park for free in a car park for up to two hours, but would incur a charge of £85 for overstaying this permitted period or for breaking other rules set by the management company of the car park, such as parking only within marked bays.[1571b] A notice to this effect in "large, prominent and legible" print was displayed on signs at the entrance of the car park and around it.[1571c] A user of the car park (the "consumer") overstayed the two-hour limit by nearly an hour and the management company sought to recover the charge from him. The Supreme Court considered that contract was a licence to park cars on the terms posted at its entrance, that the charge was not a charge for the right to park or even to overstay at the car park, but arose only on certain breaches of the contract by the user.[1571d] The car park was operated in this way as its owner was concerned to ensure that motorists should park for free to attract customers for the retailers to which it had leased other parts of its site, but that these customers should not overstay their parking period so as to increase the potential number of customers. The purposes of the charge were therefore to manage the efficient use of parking spaces in the interests of the owner, the retailers and other would-be customers and to provide an income stream for the car park's managers to meet its costs and make a profit.[1571e] In considering the fairness of the term imposing the charge under the 1999 Regulations, the Supreme Court followed the guidance of the Court of Justice of the EU in *Aziz*,[1571f] which it saw as the "leading case on the topic" provided by that court.[1571g] It noted Advocate General Kokott's advice in *Aziz*, which was followed by the Court of Justice, that the requirement that the "significant imbalance" in the contracting parties' rights and obligations to the detriment of the consumer should be contrary to good faith allows account to be taken of the legitimate interests of the parties to organise their own legal relationship even in a way which derogates from national legal rules otherwise applicable.[1571h] In this respect, the Supreme Court noted the formula used by the Court of Justice to assess good faith by reference to the hypothetical test of whether the seller or supplier "could reasonably assume that the consumer would have agreed to such a term in individual negotiations" and the views of Advocate General Kokott on the relevant circumstances for this purpose, such as whether or not the term would be surprising.[1571i] A majority of the Supreme Court therefore held that the contract term on which the £85 charge was based was fair within the meaning of the Regulations. While the term did create an imbalance in the parties' rights and obligations to the detriment to the consumer, both the management company and the owners of the car park had a legitimate interest in imposing a liability on consumers in excess of any damages recoverable in inducing them to observe the two-hour time limit: indeed "charging overstayers £85 underpinned the business model which enabled members of the public to park free of charge for two hours" and was "fundamental to the contractual relationship created by [consumers'] acceptance of the terms of the notice, whose whole object was the efficient management of the car park".[1571j] In the view of the majority of the Supreme Court, the hypothetical test was objective:

> "the question is not whether [the defendant consumer] himself would in fact have agreed to the term imposing the £85 charge in a negotiation, but whether a reasonable motorist in his position would have done so. In [its] view, a reasonable motorist would have agreed."[1571k]

Motorists generally and the defendant in particular *did* accept the term and while this would not usually have much weight as regards standard terms, the term in question "could not have been briefer, simpler or more prominently proclaimed".[1571l] Moreover, objectively, they had every reason to accept the terms, as they were allowed to park free for two hours in return for the risk of the £85 charge if they overstayed.[1571m] The terms were beneficial to motorists themselves as they freed up parking spaces, as well as being beneficial to the management company, the site owner and the retailers and the level of the charge was not exorbitant: the terms were therefore "objectively reasonable".[1571n] In this respect, Lord Mance's view was more nuanced, considering that the Court of Justice of the EU in *Aziz* could not be taken to have identified the hypothetical test as conclusive, but rather relevant to the assessment of fairness of a term, given that the Directive requires a court to take into account all circumstances for these purposes.[1571o] Lord Mance found the argument that the management company could not reasonably have assumed that customers in the defendant's position would have agreed to the scheme in individual contractual negotiation "less easy to address", as such a customer, if asked, would have been satisfied with the proposal of two hours of free parking, but would probably have asked for "some form of gradated payment in the event of overstaying".[1571p] Nevertheless, Lord Mance concluded that the term was not unfair within the meaning of the Regulations, as a term of this sort is simple and familiar and clear notice was given; there is no significant imbalance in the parties' rights and obligations given that the consumer is given a valuable privilege (the free parking) in return for a promise to pay a sum in the event of overstaying; and, finally, the charge is not disproportionately high.[1571q] By contrast, Lord Toulson dissented on this issue, and would have held the term unfair under the 1999 Regulations. In his view, the term on which the charge was based did create a significant imbalance in the parties' rights and obligations to the detriment of the consumer as the charge far exceeded any amount which was otherwise likely to be recoverable as damages.[1571r] Moreover, he considered that the hypothetical test which *Aziz* used to explain the requirement of good faith is "significantly more favourable to the consumer" than is the general common law governing penalty clauses, as its starting point is the special protection of consumers rather than that parties should be kept to their bargains.[1571s] In his view, no assumption can fairly be made that a consumer would have agreed to the term in individual negotiations and the burden of proof is on the trader to establish that he or she would have done as it makes no allowance for circumstances, allows period of grace and provides no room for adjustment.[1571t] He therefore concluded that the term was unfair.[1571u]

[1571a] [2015] UKSC 67, [2015] 3 W.L.R. 1373. Subsequent to the decision of the SC (but without reference to it) it has been said that a term of a new lease granted pursuant to the landlord's obligation

under the Leasehold Reform, Housing and Development Act 1993 and therefore replicating a term in an earlier lease not subject to the 1999 Regulations, was not "contrary to the requirement of good faith", though it had earlier been held that that the 1999 Regulations did not apply to the term as it fell within the exclusion in reg.4(2): *Roundlistic Ltd v Jones* [2016] UKUT 325 (LC) at [101] and [104]; see above, para.38–217A.

[1571b] [2015] UKSC 67 at [90] and [123].
[1571c] [2015] UKSC 67 at [91].
[1571d] [2015] UKSC 67 at [94].
[1571e] [2015] UKSC 67 at [97]–[98].
[1571f] *Aziz v Caixa d'Estalvis de Catalunya, Tarragona i Manresa* (C-415/11) March 14, 2013 discussed in the Main Work, Vol.II, para.38–247.
[1571g] [2015] UKSC 67 at [105] (Lord Neuberger of Abbotsbury P.S.C., Lord Sumption and Lord Carnwath JJ.S.C.) (with whom Lord Hodge J.S.C. (at [289]) and Lord Clarke of Stone-cum-Ebony J.S.C. (at [291]) agreed on these points); [204] and [208] (Lord Mance J.S.C.); Lord Toulson J.S.C. agreed on the importance of the *Aziz* decision (at [306]–[308]), but dissented on its significance on the facts of *ParkingEye Ltd*: see below. The SC also held that the term imposing the charge was not a penalty clause at common law as the management company had a legitimate interest in imposing these charges which could not be satisfied by damages even though the amount did not represent any loss caused to them by the breaches by the user and, secondly, the sum was *not* out of all proportion to its interest or the owner's interests: [2015] UKSC 67 at [99]–[101] (Lord Neuberger, Lord Sumption and Lord Carnwath); [197]–[199] (Lord Mance); Lord Toulson did not express a decided view on this issue: at [316]. *ParkingEye Ltd v Beavis* was joined with *Cavendish Square Holding BV v Makdessi* which concerned the common law regarding contractual penalty clauses in a commercial context, on which see above, paras 26–178 et seq.
[1571h] [2015] UKSC 67 at [106], referring to A.G. Kokott's Opinion at paras 73 and 87. Recital 16 of the 1993 Directive itself explains the requirement of good faith as allowing "an overall evaluation of the different interests involved" as noted in the Main Work, Vol.II, para.38–244.
[1571i] [2015] UKSC 67 at [106]; A.G. Kokott's Opinion, *Aziz v Caixa d'Estalvis de Catalunya, Tarragona i Manresa* (C-415/11) at para.75 quoted in Main Work, Vol.II, para.38–247.
[1571j] [2015] UKSC 67 at [106] (Lord Neuberger, Lord Sumption and Lord Carnwath, with whom Lord Hodge (at [289]) and Lord Clarke (at [291]) agreed on this point).
[1571k] [2015] UKSC 67 at [108] (referring for this purpose to A.G. Kokott's Opinion in *Aziz* at para.75, though her reference was to "an objective reason for the term" rather than specifically an objective approach to the hypothetical test).
[1571l] [2015] UKSC 67 at [108].
[1571m] [2015] UKSC 67 at [109].
[1571n] [2015] UKSC 67 at [109]. See also at [111]–[113] rejecting further arguments as to the unfairness of the term.
[1571o] [2015] UKSC 67 at [208], having noted (at [202]–[203]), the 1999 Regulations reg.6(1) and the 1993 Directive recital 16 to this effect.
[1571p] [2015] UKSC 67 at [209].
[1571q] [2015] UKSC 67 at [212], adopting the conclusions of Judge Maloney Q.C. at trial.
[1571r] [2015] UKSC 67 at [307].
[1571s] [2015] UKSC 67 at [308].
[1571t] [2015] UKSC 67 at [309]–[310].
[1571u] [2015] UKSC 67 at [314].

Potential for unfairness

38–255 [*Add to note 1592a, penultimate line, after* "binding" on the consumer": *page* [1088]]
See similarly *Radlinger v Finway a.s.* (C-377/14) April 21, 2016 at para.95 (potential cumulative effect of all penalty clauses on consumer the basis for assessment of fairness).

[*Add to paragraph, at the end: page* [1088]]
And, as Advocate General Szpunar has observed, reasonable behaviour on the part of the trader under an unfair contract cannot deprive a term of its unfair character.[1592b]

1592b *Banco Primus SA v Gutiérrez Garcia* (C-421/14) A.G. Opinion February 2, 2016 para.85 (paraphrase from the French by the editor) (judgment of the CJEU pending at the time of writing).

The significance of imbalance

[*Add to note 1597, at the end: page* [1089]]   **38–256**
cf. *Roundlistic Ltd v Jones* [2016] UKUT 325 (LC) at [103] where it was held that the fact that the terms of a new long lease (subject to the 1999 Regulations) granted on the same terms as a lease for which it was substituted (which had 80 years remaining and which was not subject to the 1999 Regulations) meant that a term of the new lease could not be said to "cause" a significant imbalance in the rights and obligations of the contracting parties: "[i]f there was a significant imbalance it already existed".

"All the circumstances attending the conclusion of the contract"

[*Add to note 1603, at the end: page* [1090]]   **38–259**
The CJEU has held that national legislation cannot therefore apply a restricted legal standard for the assessment of a contract term, such as a restriction on the rate of default interest to three times the interest otherwise owed under the contract: *Ibercaja Banco SAU v Cortés González* (C-613/15) March 17, 2016 (available only in French) at para.33.

[*Add new note 1603a, after* "conclusion of the contract" *in line 4: page* [1090]]
1603a In *Banco Primus SA v Gutiérrez Garcia* (C-421/14), A.G. Szpunar in his Opinion of February 2, 2016 at para.70 advised the CJEU that the "circumstances attending the conclusion of the contract" can include circumstances that were easily foreseeable by the parties at the time of its conclusion even though they occur afterwards and circumstances already existing but known only to one of the contracting parties (for example, likely market changes known to the trader but unknown to the consumer). At the time of writing, the CJEU had not given judgment in this case.

[*In note 1610, update reference to* Treitel on The Law of Contract *to: page* [1090]]
14th edn (2015), paras 7–004—7–010.

Lack of plainness or intelligibility sufficient?

[*Add to paragraph, at the end: page* [1092]]   **38–260**
On the other hand, in *Verein für Konsumenteninformation v Amazon EU Sàrl*,1624a the Court of Justice of the EU came close to saying that an express choice of law clause in a consumer contract *will* be unfair if the trader does not explain that its effect is limited by the restrictions imposed by art.6(2) of the Rome I Regulation on the law applicable to contractual obligations, on the basis that this means that the term fails the requirement of plain intelligible language.1624b

1624a C-191/15, July 28, 2016 ("*Amazon EU Sàrl* (C-191/15)").
1624b *Amazon EU Sàrl* (C-191/15) at para.68 and see further below, para.38–295A.

Procedural issues

38–272   [*Add to note 1663, at the end: page* [1098]]
See also below, para.38–306A in relation to *Sales Sinués v Caixabank SA, Drame Ba v Catalunja Caixa SA* (Joined Cases C-381/14 and C-385/14) April 14, 2016 concerning stays of individual claims by consumers.

(dd) *The "Indicative List" of Terms*

Exclusion or limitation clauses

38–275   [*Add to note 1674, at the end: page* [1100]]
See also CMA, *Consumer law compliance review: cloud storage, Findings report* (May 27, 2016), paras 5.59–5.66 (on exclusions or limitations of liability in contract for the provision of "cloud computing" services), available at *https:// www.gov.uk/government/uploads/system/uploads/attachment_data/file/526447/ cloud-storage-findings-report.pdf.*

Choice of jurisdiction clauses

38–277   [*Add new note 1693a at end of paragraph title: page* [1103]]
[1693a] cf. the position as regards choice of law clauses discussed below, para.38–395A.

[*Add to paragraph, at the end: page* [1104]]
However, the decision in *Apostolakis (No.2)* was distinguished in *Chopra v Bank of Singapore Ltd* on the basis that the clause in the latter case conferred only non-exclusive jurisdiction, the contract was in a language (English) known to the consumers and was "fairly simple and straightforward": there was, moreover, no evidence that if they had known about the clause they would not have entered the contract.[1697a]

[1697a] [2015] EWHC 1549 (Ch) at [139]–[140].

Penalty clauses

38–280   [*Add new note 1701a, line 7, after* "(valid) liquidated damages clause"*: page* [1105]]
[1701a] See, however, the reformulation of the common law of penalty clauses in *Cavendish Square Holding BV v Makdessi, ParkingEye Ltd v Beavis* [2015] UKSC 67, [2015] 3 W.L.R. 1373, discussed above, para.26–197. The decision of the SC in *ParkingEye Ltd* in relation to the 1999 Regulations is noted below, para.38–281 and also above, para.38–251A.

38–281   [*Add to note 1708, at the end: page* [1106]]
The CJEU has held that where more than one term in a consumer contract requires the consumer to pay sums in compensation for failure to perform his obligation, the national court should assess the cumulative effect of all such terms in assessing their disproportionate effect, whether or not the trader actually insists on their enforcement: *Radlinger v Finway a.s.* (C-377/14) April 21, 2016 at paras 92–95.

[In paragraph, delete text and notes after note 1710a to the end and substitute: pages [1106]–[1107]]
For example, as earlier noted, in *ParkingEye Ltd v Beavis*[1710b] the Supreme Court held that a term in a contract under which a consumer parked for free in a car park for up to two hours, but who incurred a charge of £85 for overstaying this permitted period was not unfair even though this amount did not reflect the potential loss caused by its breach to the managers of the car park,[1710c] as the amount was not disproportionate to the legitimate interest of the managers of the car park, its owners and its other users in the efficient management of the car park.[1710d]

[1710b] [2015] UKSC 67, [2015] 3 W.L.R. 1373 on which see above, para.38–251A.
[1710c] [2015] UKSC 67, [2015] 3 W.L.R. 1373 at [97] (concession by the car park's managers).
[1710d] See above, para.38–251A.

"Automatic extension clauses"

[Add to note 1717, at the end: page [1108]]   **38–284**
See also CMA, *Consumer law compliance review: cloud storage, Findings report* (May 27, 2016), paras 5.50–5.58 (on terms which automatically renew fixed-term contract for the provision of "cloud computing" services), available at *https://www.gov.uk/government/uploads/system/uploads/attachment_data/file/ 526447/cloud-storage-findings-report.pdf.*

Variation clauses

[Delete text of note 1721 and substitute: page [1109]]   **38–286**
cf. the position under the Consumer Rights Act 2015, which provides that certain categories of information provided by the trader about goods or digital content are to be treated as included as a term of the relevant contract and that "any change to any of that information, made before entering into the contract or later, is not effective unless expressly agreed between the consumer and the trader" (2015 Act ss.11(4)–(5) and 12(2)–(3) (goods contracts); ss.36(3)–(4) and 37(2)–(3) (digital content contracts)) and which makes similar provision in respect of information provided by the trader in respect of a services contract (2015 Act s.50(2) and (3)). On these provisions see Main Work, Vol.II, para. 38–100.

[Add to note 1722, at the beginning: page [1109]]
The CMA has expressed concern as to the fairness of contract terms under which the provider of "cloud computer" services reserves to itself broad powers of unilateral variation of the terms of the contract or the characteristics of the services: see CMA, *Consumer law compliance review: cloud storage, Findings report* (May 27, 2016), paras 5.24–5.38, available at *https://www.gov.uk/govern-ment/uploads/system/uploads/attachment_data/file/526447/cloud-storage-findings-report.pdf.*

"Unequal opt out clauses"

[Add to note 1762, at the end: page [1115]]   **38–293**
cf. CMA, *Consumer law compliance review: cloud storage, Findings report* (May 27, 2016), paras 5.39–5.49 available at *https://www.gov.uk/government/*

uploads/system/uploads/attachment_data/file/526447/cloud-storage-findings-report.pdf (terms allowing the trader to suspend or terminate the service in the context of cloud computing).

[Add new paragraph 38–296A: page [1118]]

38–296A   **Choice of law clauses.** In *Verein für Konsumenteninformation v Amazon EU Sàrl* the question arose as to the fairness under the 1993 Directive of a standard contract term in an online trader's contracts which designated the law of Luxembourg (which was the place of the trader's "seat") as "applicable to the exclusion of the United Nations Convention on the international sale of goods".[1782a] While arts 3(1) and 6(1) of the Rome I Regulation recognise that in principle the parties to a consumer contract may choose the law applicable to it, art.6(2) provides that, subject to certain conditions, any such choice of law does not "have the result of depriving the consumer of the protection afforded to him by provisions that cannot be derogated from by agreement" under the law of his habitual residence[1782b] and this may include national law implementing the 1993 Directive even where they ensure a higher level of protection for the consumer than the Directive requires.[1782c] In *Amazon EU Sàrl*, the Court of Justice of the EU noted the position governing choice of law clauses in consumer contracts under the Rome I Regulation, and that therefore:

> "a pre-formulated term on the choice of the applicable law designating the law of the Member State in which the seller or supplier is established is unfair only in so far as it displays certain specific characteristics inherent in its wording or context which cause a significant imbalance in the rights and obligations of the parties."[1782d]

For this purpose, the Court noticed that the unfairness of a such a term may result from its failure to conform to the requirement of plain and intelligible language by the trader failing to inform the consumer that the effects of a term are affected by mandatory statutory provisions for the consumer's protection (as in the case of art.6(2) of the Rome I Regulation).[1782e] And if the national court finds that the trader has failed to do so and "so leads the consumer into error by giving him the impression that only the law of [the Member State chosen] applies to the contract", then the choice of law clause would itself be an unfair term.[1782f]

[1782a] C-191/15, July 28, 2016 ("*Amazon EU Sàrl* (C-191/15)").
[1782b] Regulation (EC) 593/2008 on the law applicable to contractual obligations ("Rome I") [2008] O.J. L177/6.
[1782c] *Amazon EU Sàrl* (C-191/15) at para.59 (noting art.8 of the Directive).
[1782d] *Amazon EU Sàrl* (C-191/15) at para.67.
[1782e] *Amazon EU Sàrl* (C-191/15) at paras 68–70.
[1782f] *Amazon EU Sàrl* (C-191/15) at para.71.

(ff) *The Relative Roles of the Court of Justice of the EU, National Courts and the Parties*

Judicial discretion and domestic appeals

38–303   *[In note 1813, update reference to Treitel on The Law of Contract to: page* [1122]]
14th edn (2015), para.7–082

The power and duty of national courts to intervene of their own initiative

[Add to note 1823, at the end: page [1123]]   **38–304**
; *Bucura v SC Bancpost SA* (C-348/14) July 9, 2015 para.44. In *Tomášová v
Republic of Slovakia* (C-168/15) July 28, 2016 at paras 33–34 (available only in
French), the CJEU held that only on its decision in *Pannon* had it made clear that
national courts have an *obligation* to consider the fairness of terms in consumer
contracts and that therefore before the date of this decision a national court could
not be said to have committed a sufficiently serious breach of EU law by its
failure to do so for the purpose of State liability under the *Francovich* principle
(on which see Craig and de Búrca, *EU Law*, 6th edn (2015) pp.251 et seq.).

"National procedural autonomy" and its limits

[Add to note 1839, line 10, after "credit: C-618/10 at paras 45, 49–57)"*: page*   **38–306**
[1126]]
; see similarly, *Finanmadrid EFC SA v Albán Zambrano* (C-49/14) February 18,
2016.

[Add to note 1839, at the end: page [1126]]
; *ERSTE Bank Hungary Zrt v Sugár* (C-32/14) October 1, 2015 (effectiveness of
the protection of consumers in context of national law governing notaries); *BBVA
SA v Peñalva López* (C-8/14) October 29, 2015 (time-limit for relying on
unfairness of terms specified by transitional legislation); *Radlinger v Finway a.s.*
(C-377/14) April 21, 2016 at paras 51–59 (court's duty applies to insolvency
proceedings).

[Add new paragraph 38–306A: page [1128]]
Collective actions and stays of proceedings. Under the Civil Procedure   **38–306A**
Rules, the courts possess a power to stay the whole or part of any proceedings or
judgment either generally or until a specified date or event.[1846b] This power was
used to stay the many thousands of proceedings relating to "bank charges" which
had been brought by consumers against their banks until the general legal issues
relating to the contract terms on the basis of which these charges were imposed
were resolved by the courts in proceedings between the OFT against eight major
banks for a declaration as to the ambit of the "core exclusion" allowed by
art.4(2) of the 1993 Directive.[1846c] However, in *Sales Sinués and Drame Ba*[1846d]
the Court of Justice of the EU considered the lawfulness of the staying of
individual actions brought by consumers pending the outcome of "collective
proceedings" on a preliminary reference from a Spanish court. There, individual
proceedings had been brought by consumers for the annulment of a particular
category of allegedly unfair terms ("interest rate floor clauses") in their contracts
of consumer credit with banks, and the latter had asked the courts seized of these
proceedings to stay them under a national provision allowing the staying of
proceedings with the same subject-matter pending the outcome of "collective
proceedings" brought by a consumers' association under art.7 of the 1993
Directive. Under Spanish law, the individual consumers could join the collective
proceedings, but only subject to various constraints not imposed in respect of the

individual proceedings. The Court of Justice explained the different purposes and legal effects of individual actions by consumers and collective actions under art.7, and that the principle of procedural autonomy allows national laws to establish the rules applicable to those collective actions subject to the principles of equivalence and effectiveness.[1846e] As regards the latter, the Court held that it was clear from the national court's reference that the provision of national law under which the consumers' individual actions may be stayed would lead to the consumer no longer being able individually to assert the rights which the 1993 Directive recognises other than by joining the collective proceedings.[1846f] This

> "is liable to undermine the effectiveness of the protection intended by that directive, in view of the differences in the purpose and nature of the consumer-protection mechanisms given specific expression by those actions."[1846g]

For if the consumer joins the collective proceedings, national civil procedure rules would prevent the court hearing them from considering the circumstances relating to the individual consumer contract, the individual consumer would be dependent on the period set for the collective proceedings without consideration of his particular circumstances and he or she would be subject to further procedural constraints: these rules therefore do not constitute an adequate or effective means of bringing the continued use of unfair terms to an end contrary to art.7[1846h]; and as regards the consumer's individual proceedings that would be stayed,

> "the need to ensure consistency between judicial decisions cannot justify such a lack of effectiveness since . . . the difference in nature between judicial control exercised in the context of a collective action and that exercised in the context of an individual action should, in principle, prevent the risk of incompatible judicial decisions."[1846i]

Moreover, the "need to avoid overburdening the courts" cannot justify the effective exercise of a consumer's own individual ("subjective") rights.[1846j] While the decision in *Sales Sinués and Drame Ba* has no direct application in the English context, it does emphasise that any power under the English Civil Procedure Rules to stay consumers' individual proceedings must not be exercised in a way which undermines the practical exercise of their own individual rights under the UK legislation implementing the 1993 Directive.

[1846b] CPR r.3.1(f).

[1846c] *Office of Fair Trading v Abbey National Plc* [2009] UKSC 6, [2010] 1 A.C. 696 at [17] and [61]. For general discussion of this case, see Main Work, Vol.II, paras 38–226—38–227 and 38–241.

[1846d] *Sales Sinués v Caixabank SA, Drame Ba v Catalunja Caixa SA* (Joined Cases C-381/14 and C-385/14) April 14, 2016.

[1846e] Joined Cases C-381/14 and C-385/14 at paras 30–32.

[1846f] Joined Cases C-381/14 and C-385/14 at para.35.

[1846g] Joined Cases C-381/14 and C-385/14 at para.36.

[1846h] Joined Cases C-381/14 and C-385/14 at paras 37–39.

[1846i] Joined Cases C-381/14 and C-385/14 at para.41.

[1846j] Joined Cases C-381/14 and C-385/14 at para.42. The judgment of the Court of Justice is expressed in terms of the precluding of a national provision which *requires* the national court *automatically* to suspend the consumer's individual action without considering its effect on the protection of the consumer and without that consumer being able to dissociate himself from the collective proceedings, even though (as A.G. Szpunar made clear at paras 29, 45 and 74) the national provision itself appears to provide a discretion rather than impose a duty. This is apparently explained

by the existence of uncertainty at the national level of the proper force of the provision in question.

(gg) *The Effects of a Finding That a Term is Unfair*

"The contract shall continue to bind the parties upon those terms if it is capable of continuing in existence without the unfair terms"

[*In note 1880a, update reference to Treitel on The Law of Contract to: page* [1133]] **38–313**
14th edn (2015), para.7–120

No application of national "supplementary rules" more generally

[*Add to note 1880n, at the end: page* [1135]] **38–313A**
And see *Cavendish Square Holding BV v Makdessi, ParkingEye Ltd v Beavis* [2015] UKSC 67, [2015] 3 W.L.R. 1373 at [9].

Restitution of money paid by the consumer

[*Add to note 1885a, at the end: page* [1136]] **38–314**
The position adopted in the Main Work appears to be reflected in the Opinion of A.G. Mengozzi in *Gutiérrez Naranjo v Cajasur Banco SAU* (C-154/15, C-307/15 and C-308/15) July 13, 2016 (decision of CJEU pending at time of writing). The background to this case is that in 2013 the Spanish Supreme Court had held contract terms providing that the variable interest rate in a mortgage loan would not go below a certain threshold ("floor clauses") were not transparent and were unfair under Spanish law implementing the 1993 Directive. In a later decision, the same court held that the effect of this unfairness was to render the terms invalid, but restricted claims for restitution of monies paid under the clauses to money paid *after* the date of its earlier judgment on unfairness, on the basis of "considerations of legal certainty, good faith and risk of serious economic difficulties": Opinion at para.21. As to the lawfulness of this approach as a matter of EU law, A.G. Mengozzi noted that the language of art.6(1) of lack of binding effect of unfair terms was "entirely neutral" and does not specify that its effect is retroactive (at para.54), as is explained by its express reference to national law. Having reviewed the case-law of the CJEU on art.6(1) (discussed in the Main Work, Vol.II, paras 38–311—38–313), the A.G. concluded that the requirement of non-bindingness of an unfair term does *not* require that term to be held *invalid*, noting that the CJEU has not "peremptorily remedied the imprecision of Article 6(1)" by holding that a "national court must declare them invalid and create a corresponding right to restitution *in integrum*": Opinion at paras 63 and 64. He noted that in general under Spanish law the "general penalty for unfair terms is invalidity" but that the Spanish Supreme Court had limited the temporal effects of its own earlier judgment, reflecting the principle of the procedural autonomy of national legal orders: this is permitted by EU law, subject to the principles of equivalence and effectiveness: Opinion at para.68. In the view of A.G. Mengozzi, the limitation of the temporal effect of its judgment did not breach the principle of effectiveness, as the national court was entitled (exceptionally) to balance the

purposes of the 1993 Directive (including its deterrent effect) and "the macro-economic challenges to the already weakened banking system of a Member State": Opinion at para.72 and see further paras 73–76.

[*Add to note 1889, at the end: page* [1136]]
See also *Re Welcome Financial Services Ltd* [2015] EWHC 815 (Ch) at [106], where the court accepted (in the context a scheme of arrangement under Pt 26 of the Companies Act 2006) that a consumer who had paid money under a contract term held unfair under the 1999 Regulations could recover it.

Terms "not binding" on consumer and third parties

38–315   [*In note 1890, last line, delete* "(not in force at the time of writing)" *and substitute: page* [1137]]
(in force on May 26, 2015: 2015 Act s.100(4) and see the Consumer Rights Act 2015 (Consequential Amendments) Order 2015 (SI 2015/1726) arts 2–4; Sch. paras 2–5).

[*Add to paragraph, at the end: page* [1137]]
Finally, more difficult is the position of a person who, while not party to the original contract, enjoys rights under the contract by way of assignment or grant. For example, a landlord (the "trader") may grant a long lease to a tenant (the "consumer"), the contract of tenancy constituting a "consumer contract" for the purposes of the 1999 Regulations.[1895a] If the tenant sells the lease to a third party, the question could arise as to whether that third party can claim the benefit of the controls of the 1999 Regulations on the fairness of its terms, even though not party to the original contract and, in some situations, even though not himself a "consumer".[1895b] It could be argued that the protections which the 1993 Directive (and therefore the 1999 Regulations) provide are personal to the consumer party to the contract with the trader and therefore cannot be enjoyed by a third party. However, it is submitted that in principle where under the contract of transfer the third party enjoys the *contractual* rights of the consumer, then he should also be able to claim the benefit of the protections of the 1999 Regulations which his own transferor would have enjoyed: the purpose of the requirement of fairness under the 1999 Regulations is to "re-balance" the parties' rights and obligations under the consumer contract and it is these "rebalanced" rights which the third party acquires.[1895c]

[1895a] *London Borough of Newham v Khatun* [2004] EWCA Civ 55, [2005] Q.B. 37 and see Main Work, Vol.II, paras 38–203—38–204.
[1895b] cf. the position in *Roundlistic Ltd v Jones* [2016] UKUT 325 (LC) where, however, these points were not raised: on this case, see above, para.38–211.
[1895c] On the idea that the purpose of the requirement of fairness is to re-balance the parties' rights, see *Aziz v Caixa d'Estalvis de Catalunya, Tarragona i Manresa* (C-415/11) March 14, 2013 at paras 44–45, on which see Main Work, Vol.II, para.38–247.

(iv) *The Requirement of Plain and Intelligible Language*

The place of the requirement in the Regulations

38–319   [*Add to note 1904, at the end: page* [1139]]
; *Allproperty Claims Ltd v Tang* [2015] EWHC 2198 QB) at [45].

Broad approach to the requirement of transparency in the CJEU

[*Add to note 1915, at the end: page* [1140]]   **38–320**
See also *Verein für Konsumenteninformation v Amazon EU Sàrl* (C-191/15) July
28, 2016 at paras 67–71 and above, para.38–260.

(v) *Choice of Law Clauses*

Choice of law clauses ineffective

[*In paragraph, line 10, delete* "allows" *and substitute: page* [1141]]   **38–322**
does not control

[*Add to paragraph, at the end: page* [1141]]
However, an express choice of law clause may be held unfair under the national
law applicable to its assessment under the Rome I Regulation, as explained
earlier.[1924a]

[1924a] See above, para.38–295A.

(d) *The New Law: The Consumer Rights Act 2015*

(i) *Introduction and Overview*

Temporal application of the 2015 Act's provisions on unfair terms

[*Add to paragraph, line 3, after* "contract terms were brought into force": *page*   **38–335**
[1152]]
generally

[*Add to note 2005a, line 3, after* "arts 3(a)–(c), 6(1), (3) and (4)": *page* [1152]]
The exception to this general position is found in relation to "consumer transport
services" where the relevant provisions in the Act apply only from October 1,
2016: 2015 Order arts 4 and 6(2) as amended by the Consumer Rights Act 2015
(Commencement No.3, Transitional Provisions, Savings and Consequential
Amendments) (Amendment) Order 2016 (SI 2016/484) art.2; and for further
likely future qualifications, see above, para.38–403.

The strategies of the 2015 Act in relation to contract terms

[*Add new note 2014a, at the end of paragraph: page* [1153]]   **38–339**
[2014a] The CMA has published guidance on the unfair contract terms provisions in the 2015 Act:
*Unfair contract terms guidance, Guidance on the unfair terms provisions in the Consumer Rights Act
2015* (CMA37, July 2015).

[*In note 2035, lines 1–6, delete* "The question whether . . . " *to* "under s.212 of the   **38–343**
Enterprise Act 2002." *and substitute: page* [1156]]
In addition, acts or omissions in respect of any provision in Pts 1 and 2 of the
2015 Act are specified as possible "domestic infringements" for the purposes of

s.212 of the Enterprise Act 2002: Enterprise Act 2002 (Part 8 Domestic Infringements) Order 2015 (SI 2015/1727) art.2.

(iv) *Contract Terms and Notices Not Binding on the Consumer Where Assessed as Unfair*

(aa) *Terms of Consumer Contracts*

General test of unfairness

38–359   [*In paragraph, replace final full stop with comma after* "found in the Consumer Rights Act" *and before note 2123 in line 21: page* [1165]]

[*Add to paragraph, after note 2123: page* [1165]]
with the following qualification. As explained in the Main Work, the Court of Justice in *Aziz* advised that, under the requirement of good faith, the national court must assess whether the trader "dealing fairly and equitably with the consumer, could reasonably assume that the consumer would have agreed to such a term in individual contract negotiations".[2123a] However, there is a particular difficulty in applying this approach to the test of unfairness in the Consumer Rights Act 2015, as the latter can apply to terms which *have been* individually negotiated as well as to terms which have not.[2123b] Where it does, explaining the requirement of good faith by reference to a hypothetical test of what the trader could objectively have assumed the (reasonable) consumer would have agreed in individual negotiations would make little sense, given that, ex hypothesi, the consumer had in fact agreed to the term in question.[2123c] It is submitted that this difficulty disappears if the hypothetical test is treated as *relevant* to the assessment of good faith but not conclusive of it,[2123d] as this allows a court to be able to interpret the requirement of good faith in the context of an individually negotiated term on other and broader grounds, as is indeed suggested by recital 16 of the 1993 Directive itself.[2123e] This is apparently the view taken by the CMA, which has observed that the "requirement of good faith . . . allows for proper account to be taken of the significance of any real negotiation that has actually taken place", but considers that

> "any contention that a particular consumer has actually influenced the substance of a term has to be tested against a detailed consideration of the circumstances existing at the time the contract was concluded. In [the CMA's] view, individual consumers rarely in practice have the required knowledge and bargaining power to ensure that contractual negotiations involving them are effectively conducted on equal terms."[2123f]

[2123a] *Aziz v Caixa d'Estalvis de Catalunya, Tarragona i Manresa* (C-415/11) March 14, 2013 at para.69, and see Main Work, para.38–247.
[2123b] 2015 Act s.62 and see Main Work, para.38–358.
[2123c] cf. the discussion of the hypothetical test in *Aziz* in *ParkingEye Ltd v Beavis* [2015] UKSC 67, [2015] 3 W.L.R. 1373 above, para.38–251A.
[2123d] This view was taken by Lord Mance in *ParkingEye Ltd v Beavis* [2015] UKSC 67 at [208].
[2123e] See Main Work, Vol.II, paras 38–244—38–245.
[2123f] CMA, *Unfair contract terms guidance, Guidance on the unfair terms provisions in the Consumer Rights Act 2015* (CMA37, July 2015), para.2.30.

The "indicative list of terms"

[*Add to note 2126, at the end: page* [1166]]   **38–360**
While the list of terms in Sch.2 applies to "contract terms" rather than to
"consumer notices", the CMA's view is that its "indicative list" also serves to
illustrate the forms that unfairness can take in non-contractual notices: CMA,
*Unfair contract terms guidance, Guidance on the unfair terms provisions in the
Consumer Rights Act 2015* (CMA37, July 2015), para.1.25 and Pt 5 (which
considers the practical significance of the examples in the list more generally).

[*Add to note 2128, at the end: page* [1166]]
For discussion of these new examples of terms in the list see CMA, *Unfair
contract terms guidance, Guidance on the unfair terms provisions in the
Consumer Rights Act 2015* (CMA37, July 2015), paras 5.15.1–5.15.7,
5.22.11–5.22.12 and 5.23.1–5.23.7.

Comments; relationship to recent case-law of the CJEU

[*Add to note 2179, at the end: page* [1172]]   **38–368**
See also the guidance in CMA, *Unfair contract terms guidance, Guidance on the
unfair terms provisions in the Consumer Rights Act 2015* (CMA37, July 2015),
paras 3.20–3.32.

(bb) *Certain Types of Term of "Secondary Contracts"*

Extending the controls of Pt 2 to certain types of term in "secondary contracts"

[*In note 2203, update reference to Treitel on The Law of Contract to: page* [1175]]   **38–370**
14th edn (2015), para.7–084

[*In note 2208, update reference to Treitel on The Law of Contract to: page* [1176]]
14th edn (2015), para.7–084

(vii) *Choice of Law*

Special rule governing choice of law

[*Add to paragraph, after note 2275: page* [1185]]   **38–386**
Be that as it may, the Court of Justice of the EU has held that where a consumer
contract contains a choice of law clause which designates the law of another
Member State, that term may itself be an unfair term within the meaning of the
1993 Directive.[2275a]

[2275a] *Verein für Konsumenteninformation v Amazon EU Sàrl* (C-191/15) July 28, 2016, above,
para.38–295A.

(viii) *Enforcement*

Summary of position before the enactment of the Consumer Rights Act 2015

38–387 [*Add to note 2281, line 1, after* "paras 38–323—38–333": *page* [1185]]
(where the qualifications on this general position are noted)

[*Add to note 2284, at the end: page* [1186]]
cf. the position as regards "domestic infringements" under Pt 8 of the 2002 Act, which extend, inter alia, to the Unfair Contract Terms Act 1977: Enterprise Act 2002 (Part 8 Domestic Infringements) Order 2003 (SI 2003/1593) art.2 and Sch. Pt 1.

Enforcement measures under the Consumer Rights Act 2015

38–388 [*In paragraph, after note 2303, delete* "The Act" *and substitute: page* [1187]]
For this purpose, the relevant provisions in Pt 2 of the 2015 Act which implement the 1993 Directive have been designated as a specified UK law for the purposes of s.212 of the 2002 Act[2303a] and in addition, acts or omissions in respect of any provision in Pt 2 of the 2015 Act are specified as possible "domestic infringements" for the purposes of s.211 of the Enterprise Act 2002.[2303b] The 2015 Act

[2303a] Enterprise Act 2002 s.212(3); Enterprise Act 2002 (Part 8 Community Infringements Specified UK Laws) Order 2003 art.3; Sch., as amended by the Enterprise Act 2002 (Part 8 Community Infringements and Specified UK Laws) (Amendment) Order 2015 (SI 2015/1628) art.2(2)(a), listing 2015 Act ss.2, 61–64, 67–70, 72–74, Schs 2 and 3 and Sch.5 Pt 3.
[2303b] Enterprise Act 2002 s.211(2); Enterprise Act 2002 (Part 8 Domestic Infringements) Order 2015 (SI 2015/1727) art.2.

The impact of "full harmonisation" under the Unfair Commercial Practices Directive 2005

38–390 [*Add to note 2311, at the end: page* [1188]]
The 1990 Directive is repealed and replaced by Directive (EU) 2015/2302 on package travel and linked travel arrangements [2015] O.J. L326/1.

[*Add to note 2312, at the end: page* [1188]]
And see *Citroën Commerce GmbH v Zentralvereinigung des Kraftfahrzeuggewerbes zur Aufrechterhaltung lauteren Wettbewerbs eV (ZLW)* (C-476/14) July 7, 2016 at paras 44–46, noted above, para.38–106.

(e) *Special Rules Governing Consumer Payments*

Payment surcharges

38–396 [*Add to note 2339, line 1, after* "(the "2012 Regulations")": *page* [1193]]
(as amended by the 2013 Regulations (SI 2013/3134))

7. CONTRACTS FOR THE SUPPLY OF GOODS, DIGITAL CONTENT OR SERVICES

(a) *Introduction*

Temporal application of Pt 1 of the 2015 Act

[*In note 2395, lines 3–4, delete* "do not apply to . . . " *to* "2015 Order art.4." *and*   **38–403**
substitute: page [1199]]
do not apply to certain "consumer transport services" (certain rail passenger
services, carriage by air, and sea and inland waterway transport, all as specially
defined by the 2015 Order art.2) until October 1, 2016: 2015 Order arts 4 and
6(2) as amended by the Consumer Rights Act 2015 (Commencement No.3,
Transitional Provisions, Savings and Consequential Amendments) (Amendment)
Order 2016 (SI 2016/484) art.2. The main reason for this delay in the bringing
into force of the provisions of the 2015 Act in this area was a concern that the
Act's provisions (especially s.57's controls on the exclusion or restriction of
liability in the carrier) would risk complexity and duplication with sectoral
transport schemes: Department of Transport, *Applying the Consumer Rights Act
2015 to the rail, aviation and maritime sectors, Response to Consultation,
Moving Britain Ahead* (July, 2016). However, the Department of Transport
(para.2.4) has announced that the exemption from the application of s.57(3) of
the 2015 Act (governing *restrictions* on liability, as noted by the Main Work,
Vol.II, para.38–546) will continue to apply to passenger services operated by EU
licensed rail passenger operators until October 1, 2017: see *draft* Consumer
Rights (Rail Passenger Service Exemption, Enforcement and Amendments)
Order 2016 (laid before Parliament, July 7, 2016).

[*Add new paragraph 38–403A: page* [1199]]
  Proposed EU directives on distance contracts for the sale of goods and on   **38–403A**
contracts for the supply of digital content. The EU Commission has published
two proposals for directives which would, if enacted and implemented in UK
law, require the amendment of the 2015 Act's provisions governing contracts of
sale of goods and contracts for the supply of digital content. Both proposed
directives would require "full harmonization"[2395a] and this would make their
implementation within the existing frameworks of English law particularly difficult. The first is a proposal for a directive on aspects of the law governing
"distance contracts" for the sale of goods[2395b]: if enacted, this directive would
disapply the Consumer Sales Directive 1999 from distance contracts for the sale
of goods[2395c] and could require the UK either to amend Ch.2 of Pt 1 of the 2015
Act so as to follow the scheme of the new directive even beyond its scope of
"distance contracts" or to disapply Ch.2 from distance contracts of sale of goods
and enact a dedicated regime for this purpose. The second is a proposal for a
directive on aspects of the law governing the distance supply of digital content.[2395d] If enacted, this could require the amendment of Ch.3 of Pt 1 of the 2015
Act.[2395e]

[2395a] Distance sales directive proposal 2015 art.3; Digital content directive proposal 2015 art.4.

2395b Proposal for a Directive of the European Parliament and of the Council on certain aspects concerning contracts for the online and other distance sales of goods COM(2015) 635 final ("Distance sales directive proposal 2015").

2395c Distance sales directive proposal 2015 art.19.

2395d Proposal for a Directive of the European Parliament and of the Council on certain aspects concerning contracts for the supply of digital content COM(2015) 634 final ("Digital content directive proposal 2015").

2395e On this law, see Main Work, Vol.II, paras 38–496—38–526.

(c) *The New Law: Consumer Rights in Respect of Goods Contracts, Digital Content Contracts and Services Contracts*

(ii) *"Goods Contracts"*

(aa) *The Four Types of "Goods Contracts"*

"Sales contracts"

38–452   [*Add to note 2593, at the end: page* [1221]]
cf. *Software Incubator Ltd v Computer Associates UK Ltd* [2016] EWHC 1587 (QB) at [35]–[69] where it was held that a contract for the supply of software could constitute a "sale of goods" for the purposes of the Commercial Agents (Council Directive) Regulations 1993 (SI 1993/3053), distinguishing (at [47]) the position under the Consumer Rights Act 2015.

[*Add to note 2594, at the end: page* [1221]]
And see above, para.38–052A, which discusses *Wathelet v Garage Bietheres & Fils SPRL* (C-149/15) (Opinion of A.G. Saugmandsgaard Øe April 7, 2016, decision of CJEU pending) on the question when a trader who acts on behalf of a private individual is to be treated as a "seller" of goods under the Consumer Sales Directive 1999.

(cc) *The Scheme of Remedies for the Consumer*

The right to reject: general provisions

38–478   [*In note 2757, update reference to Treitel on The Law of Contract to: page* [1240]]
14th edn (2015), para.18–001

Discretion as to appropriate remedy

38–485   [*In paragraph, line 13, delete* "These powers" *and substitute: page* [1245]]
It is submitted, though, that in the case of contracts for the *sale* of goods ("sales contracts"), the consumer's right to repair or replacement of goods in the Act reflects requirements of the Consumer Sales Directive 1999 and so the provisions of the Act relating to them must be interpreted with this in mind and in the light of the principle of effectiveness, here, of the consumer's protection.[2799a] For this purpose, in *Weber and Putz* the Court of Justice of the EU assumed that the consumer's specific rights under the Directive were enforceable in kind against

the seller, holding that national law must not allow replacement to be refused by a trader on the ground of disproportionality with regard to the value of the goods as conforming and the significance of the non-conformity, even though in the circumstances this meant that the trader had to bear the costs of the removal of goods installed by the consumer and the reinstallation of the replacement goods.[2799b] This suggests that an English court should not refuse specific performance in support of the consumer's right to repair or replacement of goods sold on the ground that damages would be an adequate remedy, as this would to this extent replace the consumer's "European rights" with damages and so render them ineffective and that the court should not take into account other traditional elements governing the availability of specific performance stemming from its equitable nature on the basis that the Directive itself provides only two circumstances (impossibility and disproportionality compared to the other specific remedy) where the trader is entitled to refuse to repair or replace.[2799c] It also suggests that, in the case of "sales contracts", the court's powers to substitute another "appropriate right" under s.58 is incompatible with the 1999 Directive. Finally, on their terms, the court's powers under s.58

[2799a] See Whittaker (2017) 133 L.Q.R. (forthcoming). On the Consumer Sales Directive 1999 generally, see Main Work, Vol.II, para.38–400. On "sales contracts" see Main Work, Vol.II, paras 38–452—38–454.

[2799b] *Gebr Weber GmbH v Wittmer, Putz v Medianess Electronics GmbH* (C-65/09 and C-87/09) [2011] 3 C.M.L.R. 27 at [63]–[78].

[2799c] 1999 Directive art.3(3), reflected in 2015 Act s.23(3)–(4) and see Main Work, Vol.II, para. 38–482.

(dd) *Other Rules About Goods Contracts*

Delivery of goods in sales contracts

[*Add to note 2833, at the end: page* [1249]]   **38–489**
(revoked by SI 2015/1629 art.8).

Passing of risk

[*Add to note 2858, at the end: page* [1251]]   **38–490**
The 2015 Act s.29 implements the Consumer Rights Directive 2011 art.20 and replaces its earlier implementation by the 2013 Regulations reg.43 (which was itself revoked by the Consumer Contracts (Amendment) Regulations 2015 (SI 2015/1629) art.8 as regards contracts entered into on or after October 1, 2015).

(ee) *Exclusion of Liability and Choice of Law*

Enforcement of Pt 1 more generally

[*In paragraph, delete from* "However, what is less clear . . . " *in line 7 to the end*   **38–495**
and substitute: page [1255]]
As a result, the relevant provisions in Ch.2 of the 2015 Act, which implement the 1999 Directive or the 2011 Directive or which "provide additional permitted

protections",[2894] have been designated as specified UK laws for the purposes of s.212 of the 2002 Act.[2894a] In addition, acts or omissions in respect of any provision in Pt 1 of the 2015 Act are specified as possible "domestic infringements" for the purposes of s.211 of the Enterprise Act 2002.[2894b]

[2894] Enterprise Act 2002 s.212(1)(b).
[2894a] Enterprise Act 2002 s.212(3); Enterprise Act 2002 (Part 8 Community Infringements Specified UK Laws) Order 2003 art.3; Sch., as amended by the Enterprise Act 2002 (Part 8 Community Infringements and Specified UK Laws) (Amendment) Order 2015 (SI 2015/1628) art.2(2)(b) listing 2015 Act ss.2, 3, 9–11, 13–15, 19, 23, 24, 30–32, 58 and 59 (1999 Directive); art.3(2) listing 2015 Act ss.5, 11(4)–(6), 12, 19, 28, 29, 36(3)–(4), 37, 38, 42, 50 and 54 (2011 Directive).
[2894b] Enterprise Act 2002 s.211(2); Enterprise Act 2002 (Part 8 Domestic Infringements) Order 2015 (SI 2015/1727) art.2.

(iv) *Digital Content Contracts*

Introduction

38–496   [*Add new note 2894c, after* "defines for these purposes." *in line 3: note* [1255]]
[2894c] On the Proposal for a Directive of the European Parliament and of the Council on certain aspects concerning contracts for the supply of digital content COM(2015) 634 final, see above, para.38–403A.

[*Add to note 2895, at the end: page* [1256]]
cf. *Software Incubator Ltd v Computer Associates UK Ltd* [2016] EWHC 1587 (QB) at [35]–[69] (a contract for the supply of software could constitute a "sale of goods" for the purposes of the Commercial Agents (Council Directive) Regulations 1993 (SI 1993/3053), distinguishing (at [47]) the position under the Consumer Rights Act 2015).

(ee) *Exclusion of Liability*

Enforcement

38–526   [*Add to paragraph, at the end: page* [1277]]
As a result, the relevant provisions in Ch.3 of Pt 1 of the 2015 Act which implement the 2011 Directive or which "provide additional permitted protections"[3066a] have been designated as specified UK laws for the purposes of s.212 of the 2002 Act.[3066b] In addition, acts or omissions in respect of any provision in Pt 1 of the 2015 Act are specified as possible "domestic infringements" for the purposes of s.211 of the Enterprise Act 2002.[3066c]

[3066a] Enterprise Act 2002 s.212(1)(b).
[3066b] Enterprise Act 2002 s.212(3); Enterprise Act 2002 (Part 8 EU Infringements) Order 2014 (SI 2014/2908) art.4; Schedule (as amended by the Enterprise Act 2002 (Part 8 Community Infringements and Specified UK Laws) (Amendment) Order 2015 (SI 2015/1628) art.3(2)) listing, inter alia, 2015 Act ss.36(3)–(4), 37, 38 and 42.
[3066c] Enterprise Act 2002 s.211(2); Enterprise Act 2002 (Part 8 Domestic Infringements) Order 2015 (SI 2015/1727) art.2.

(v) *Services Contracts*

(aa) *Introduction*

Background

[*Add new note 3066d, after* "governing "services contracts"" *in line 2: page* [1278]]   **38–527**
3066d The 2015 Act's substantive provisions on "services contracts" generally came into force on October 1, 2015, but exceptions have been made as regards certain categories of "consumer transport service" as explained in the Main Work, Vol.II, para.38–403, esp. at n.2395 as amended by this Supplement.

(bb) *The statutory terms*

Express terms; relation of statutory terms to other law on contract terms

[*Add to note 3112, at the end: page* [1284]]   **38–539**
An example may be found in relation to contracts of services governed by the carriage of air conventions (notably, the Warsaw Convention and the Montreal Convention, on which see Main Work, Vol.II, paras 35–002 et seq.) which, in the view of the UK government, will remain the exclusive basis of liability on the routes to which they apply even after the 2015 Act applies to them: Department of Transport, *Applying the Consumer Rights Act 2015 to the rail, aviation and maritime sectors, Response to Consultation, Moving Britain Ahead* (July 2016), para.2.8.

(ee) *Enforcement*

Enforcement of provisions on exclusion of trader's liabilities

[*Add to paragraph, at the end: page* [1290]]   **38–547**
Secondly, the relevant provisions in Ch.4 of the 2015 Act which implement the 2011 Directive or which "provide additional permitted protections"[3153] (notably, the provisions in s.50 giving contractual effect to certain categories of information provided by the trader to the consumer) have been designated as specified UK laws for the purposes of s.212 of the 2002 Act.[3154] And, thirdly, acts or omissions in respect of any provision in Pt 1 of the 2015 Act are specified as possible "domestic infringements" for the purposes of s.211 of the Enterprise Act 2002.[3155]

[3153] Enterprise Act 2002 s.212(1)(b).
[3154] Enterprise Act 2002 s.212(3); Enterprise Act 2002 (Part 8 Community Infringements Specified UK Laws) Order 2003, art.3; Sch., as amended by the Enterprise Act 2002 (Part 8 Community Infringements and Specified UK Laws) (Amendment) Order 2015 (SI 2015/1628) art.3, listing 2015 Act ss.50 and 54.
[3155] Enterprise Act 2002 s.211(2); Enterprise Act 2002 (Part 8 Domestic Infringements) Order 2015 (SI 2015/1727) art.2.

CHAPTER 39

CREDIT AND SECURITY

1. THE REGULATION OF CONSUMER CREDIT

The Mortgage Credit Directive

This Directive came into force on March 21, 2016 and hence most residential
mortgages (and so called "MCD art.3(1)(b) agreements", see n.11, below) are
now no longer regulated under the Consumer Credit Act 1974 (being "exempt
agreements", see para.38–038, above) but are within the FSMA 2000 regime.

39–003

The future of consumer credit regulation

[*Add new note 14a, at the end of the paragraph: page* [1293]]
[14a] The FCA has begun the review process: see *Call for Input: Review of retained provisions of the Consumer Credit Act*, February 2016.

39–004

Consumer Credit Directive

[*Note 46: page* [1296]]
The Mortgage Credit Directive (and hence the relevant amendment) came into
force on March 21, 2016.

39–011

Lending Code

[*Add to note 56, line 1, after* "March 2011": *page* [1297]]
(revised September 2015)

39–013

Other EU Directives

The Mortgage Credit Directive came into force on March 21, 2016 and hence the
relevant changes were effected then.

39–014

[*In note 65, delete* "Ch.37" *and substitute: page* [1298]]
paras 38–334 et seq.

(a) *Terminology*

"Regulated" consumer credit agreement

[*Note 85: page* [1300]]
The Mortgage Credit Directive (and hence the relevant amendment) came into
force on March 21, 2016.

39–017

"Credit"

[*Add to note 98, at the end: page* [1301]]
; *Burrell v Helical (Bramshott Place) Ltd* [2015] EWHC 3727 (Ch) (no defer-
ment of any obligation to pay hence no credit).

39–019

The Consumer Credit Directive: "credit exceeding £60,260"

39–022 [*Note 113: page* [1302]]
The Mortgage Credit Directive (and hence the relevant amendment) came into force on March 21, 2016.

"Debtor-creditor agreement"/"borrower-lender agreement"

39–033 [*In note 168, line 1, delete* "16(2),": *page* [1308]]

Exempt land mortgages

39–039 The Mortgage Credit Directive (and hence the relevant amendments noted in the footnotes) came into force on March 21, 2016 and resulted in significant changes to the three types of mortgages that are exempt from the 1974 Act. In relation to the first type of exempt mortgage mentioned, this now results in most land mortgages (as well as any loans to acquire or retain property rights in residential property (so called "MCD art.3(1)(b) agreements": see CCA 1974 s.8(3)(b), added on March 21, 2016 by the Mortgage Credit Directive Order 2015 (SI 2015/910) art.3 and Sch.1 para.2(2)) being "exempt agreements", the majority of residential mortgages now being regulated under the Financial Services and Markets Act 2000. And note that none of the three types of exemption mentioned apply in so far as they are incompatible with that Directive (see the list of mortgage contracts that are not "regulated mortgage contracts" in the new RAO art.60HA, added by the Mortgage Credit Directive Order 2015 (SI 2015/910) art.3 and Sch.1 para.4(19), mentioned in nn.223 and 228 in relation to the second and third types of exempt mortgages).

"Investment mortgages" exemption

39–040 The Mortgage Credit Directive (and hence the relevant amendments noted in the footnotes) came into force on March 21, 2016.

[*Add to note 234, at the end: page* [1314]]
But such so-called "MCD art.3(1)(b) agreements" (see para.39–039, above) are not regulated by the CCA 1974 by reason of CCA 1974 s.8(3)(b), added on March 21, 2016 by the Mortgage Credit Directive Order 2015 (SI 2015/910) art.3 and Sch.1 para.2(2).

Exempt credit agreements: number of payments

39–041 [*Note 238: page* [1314]]
The Mortgage Credit Directive (and hence the relevant amendment) came into force on March 21, 2016.

[*Add to note 244, line 1, after* "RAO art.60F(4)": *page* [1315]]
Note (see n.238) that art.60F(4) does not apply in so far as it is incompatible with the Mortgage Credit Directive.

Exempt credit agreements: low-cost of credit

[*Note 246: page* [1315]] 39–042
The Mortgage Credit Directive (and hence the relevant amendment) came into
force on March 21, 2016.

High net worth "opt-out" exemption

[*Note 259: page* [1316]] 39–045
The Mortgage Credit Directive (and hence the relevant amendment) came into
force on March 21, 2016.

[*Note 260: page* [1316]]
The Mortgage Credit Directive (and hence the relevant amendment) came into
force on March 21, 2016.

(b) *Authorisation of Credit and Hire Businesses*

Trading whilst unauthorised

[*Add to note 400, at the end: page* [1328]] 39–064
Special provision for the specific funding of teams detecting illegal money
lenders (so-called "loan sharks") has been made in the Bank of England and
Financial Services Act 2016 (new Pt 20B added to the Financial Services and
Markets Act 2000).

(c) *Seeking Business*

Canvassing

[*In note 426, line 4, delete* "para.39–247" *and substitute: page* [1330]] 39–068
para.39–252

(e) *The Agreement*

Pre-contract disclosure

[*Note 460: page* [1333]] 39–076
The Mortgage Credit Directive (and hence the relevant amendments) came into
force on March 21, 2016.

Copy of draft agreement

[*Note 478: page* [1335]] 39–079
The Mortgage Credit Directive (and hence the relevant amendment) came into
force on March 21, 2016.

Form and content of agreement: general

39–080   [*Note 488: page* [1336]]
The Mortgage Credit Directive (and hence the relevant amendment) came into force on March 21, 2016.

Form and content of agreement: the 2010 Agreements Regulations

39–082   [*Note 500: page* [1337]]
The Mortgage Credit Directive (and hence the relevant amendment) came into force on March 21, 2016.

Supply of copies: two regimes

39–085   [*Note 524: page* [1339]]
The Mortgage Credit Directive (and hence the relevant amendment) came into force on March 21, 2016.

(f) *Withdrawal and Cancellation*

14-day "right of withdrawal"

39–101   [*Note 607: page* [1345]]
The Mortgage Credit Directive (and hence the relevant amendment) came into force on March 21, 2016.

Consumer Contracts (Information, Cancellation and Additional Charges) Regulations 2013

39–125   [*Add to note 764, at the end: page* [1357]]
and *Allproperty Claims v Tang* [2015] EWHC 2198 (lack of notification of cancellation right rendered agreement unenforceable).

(g) *Supply of Information*

Statement of account to debtor under fixed-sum credit agreement on request

39–130   [*Note 816: page* [1361]]
The Mortgage Credit Directive (and hence the relevant amendment) came into force on March 21, 2016.

[*In note 817, line 2, delete* "s.16B(2)–(5)" *and substitute: page* [1361]]
RAO art.60(3)–(7)

(h) *Variation of Agreements*

Unilateral variation under a power in agreement: the general rule

[*In note 947, line 5, delete* "para.38–201" *and substitute: page* [1371]]
para.39–201

39–146

(m) *Unfair Relationships*

[*Add to note 1295, at the end: page* [1401]]
Brown (2016) 36(2) L.S. 230-257.

Extortionate credit bargains

[*Add to note 1304, at the end: page* [1403]]
; *Barclays Bank Plc v McMillan* [2015] EWHC 1596 (Comm) (loan to finance US law firm's partner's capital subscription on usual terms); *Bluestone Mortgages Ltd v Momoh* [2015] EW Misc B4 (CC) (refusal of permission to appeal the decision of the county court that failure to notify in advance that mortgagee would invoke usual clause in buy-to-let mortgage permitting him to pay outstanding lease charges if mortgagor failed to do so, did not give rise to an unfair relationship); *Nelmes v NRAM Plc* [2016] EWCA Civ 491 (borrower's broker secret commission rendered buy-to-let mortgage "unfair").

39–212

Wide application of "unfair relationship" provisions

[*Add to note 1306, at the end: page* [1403]]
And note the "buy-to-let" loans considered in *Paragon Mortgages Ltd v McEwan-Peters* [2011] EWHC 2491 (Comm); *Graves v Capital Home Loans Ltd* [2014] EWCA Civ 1297; *Bluestone Mortgages Ltd v Momoh* [2015] EW Misc B4 (CC) and *Nelmes v NRAM Plc* [2016] EWCA Civ 491.

39–213

[*Note 1310: page* [1403]]
The Mortgage Credit Directive came into force on March 21, 2016 and hence the relevant protection has been lost.

Exercise or enforcement of rights by creditor

[*Add to note 1360, at the end: page* [1408]]
See also *Bluestone Mortgages Ltd v Faith Momoh* [2015] EW Misc B4 (CC) (refusal of permission to appeal the decision of the county court that failure to notify in advance that mortgagee would invoke usual clause in buy-to-let mortgage permitting him to pay outstanding lease charges if mortgagor failed to do so, did not give rise to an unfair relationship).

39–221

Any other action by creditor

[*In paragraph, line 13, delete* "Harrison v Black Horse Ltd" *and substitute: page* [1409]]
Plevin v Paragon Personal Finance Ltd

39–222

[*Add to note 1378, line 1, after* "[2012] J.B.L. 713 at 727": *page* [1409]]
and Lomnicka, "The impact of rule-making by financial services regulators on the common law: the lessons of PPI", in Gullifer and Vogenauer (eds) *English and European Perspectives on Contract and Commercial Law: Essays in Honour of Hugh Beale* (Hart, 2014), Ch.4.

Onus of proof

39–224   [*Add to note 1400, at the end: page* [1411]]
Bevin v Datum Finance Ltd was noted in *Bluestone Mortgages Ltd v Momoh* [2015] EW Misc B4 (CC) but the Court of Appeal nevertheless refused permission to appeal a summary judgment that the relationship was not unfair even though no evidence was adduced by the creditor to discharge the burden of proof.

[*Add to note 1401, line 3, after* "prospects of success)": *page* [1411]]
as was the case in *Bluestone Mortgages Ltd v Momoh* [2015] EW Misc B4 (CC), see previous note.

Nature of relief

39–225   [*In note 1407, delete from* "For orders to repay . . . " *in line 3 to the end and substitute: page* [1412]]
For orders to repay premiums of mis-sold PPI policies see *Scotland v British Credit Trust Ltd* [2014] EWCA Civ 790 and *Plevin v Paragon Personal Finance Ltd* [2016] C.C.L.R. 5, March 2, 2015, Manchester Cty Ct (the sequel to *Plevin v Paragon Personal Finance Ltd* [2014] UKSC 61), where the amount of commission received by the PPI seller was, on the facts, regarded as the appropriate remediation. In *Nelmes v NRAM Plc* [2016] EWCA Civ 491 the court ordered the repayment of a secret commission paid by the lender to the borrower's broker.

(n) *Ancillary Credit Businesses*

Credit broking: exclusions

39–233   [*Note 1451: page* [1415]]
The Mortgage Credit Directive (and hence the relevant new version of art.36E) came into force on March 21, 2016.

Debt-counselling: exclusions

39–237   [*In note 1470, delete* "art.39K" *and substitute: page* [1417]]
art.39KA

Seeking business: promotion

39–251   [*Add new note 1529a, at the end of the paragraph: page* [1422]]
[1529a] See above, paras 38–153 et seq.

(o) *Operating an electronic system in relation to lending*

Operating an electronic system in relation to lending

[*Add to note 1553, at the end: page* [1424]]   **39–256**
See the exclusions in arts 36I and 36IA.

2. LOANS AND INTEREST

(a) *Loans of Money*

Term loans

[*Add to note 1610, at the end: page* [1430]]   **39–268**
Note *Alexander v West Bromwich Mortgage Co Ltd* [2016] EWCA Civ 496.

"No set-off" clauses

[*Add to note 1624, line 1, after* "para.15–104 n.541.".: *page* [1432]]   **39–271**
As noted above at para.38–334, for consumer contracts made on or after October
1, 2015, the 1977 Act is replaced by provisions in the Consumer Rights Act 2015
Pt 2, see above paras 38–334 et seq.

[*Add to note 1624, at the end: page* [1432]]
See the unsuccessful attempt to invoke that Act in *African Export-Import Bank
v Shebah Exploration and Product Co Ltd* [2016] EWHC 311 (Comm) (syndi-
cated loan).

(b) *Interest*

Variation of interest rate

[*Add to note 1721, at the end: page* [1441]]   **39–293**
See *Alexander v West Bromwich Mortgage Co Ltd* [2016] EWCA Civ 496
(power to vary interest inconsistent with mortgage offered as "tracker mortgage").

Default interest

[*In note 1734, line 2, delete* "Vol.I, para.26–182" and substitute : *page* [1443]]   **39–294**
; *Cavendish Square Holdings BV v Makdessi* [2015] UKSC 67, see above, paras
26–178 et seq.

[*Add to note 1735, line 1, after* "[1996] Q.B. 752".: *page* [1443]]
(approved in *Cavendish Square Holdings BV v Makdessi* [2015] UKSC 67 at
[26]–[28], [146]–[148], [222] and [239]–[241])

(c) *Effect of Consumer Credit Regulation*

Additional "connected lender liability"

39–305   [*Note 1809: page* [1448]]
The Mortgage Credit Directive (and hence the relevant amendment) came into
force on March 21, 2016.

3. HIRE-PURCHASE AGREEMENTS

(b) *At Common Law*

Sums paid by hirer

39–344   [*Add to note 1950, at the end: page* [1463]]
See also *Cadogan Petroleum Holdings Ltd v Global Process Systems LLC* [2013]
2 Lloyd's Rep. 26 (*Stockloser v Johnson* not followed and forfeiture allowed in
relation to repayments towards acquisition of gas plants).

[*Add to note 1952, at the end: page* [1463]]
The relationship between the doctrines of "penalties" and "relief against forfeiture" was discussed by the Supreme Court in *Cavendish Square Holdings BV
v Makdessi* [2015] UKSC 67, approving *BICC Plc v Bundy Corp* [1985] Ch. 232.
See above, paras 26–216X et seq.

[*Add to paragraph, at the end: page* [1464]]
In *Cavendish Square Holdings BV v Makdessi*[1954a] the Supreme Court declined
to opine at length on forfeiture clauses (as the allegation was that the relevant
clauses were penalty not forfeiture clauses) and hence only referred to *Stockloser
v Johnson* in passing.

[1954a] [2015] UKSC 67. See above, paras 26–216S et seq.

Operative on events other than breach

39–350   [*Add to paragraph, at the end: page* [1466]]
In *Cavendish Square Holdings BV v Talal El Makdessi*[1981a] the Supreme Court
declined to follow Australian authority extending the doctrine of penalties to
clauses operative on events other than breach.[1981b]

[1981a] [2015] UKSC 67 at [41]–[43], [129]–[130], [163]–[165].
[1981b] See above, para.26–216C.

Bridge v Campbell Discount Co Ltd

39–351   See now the new the Supreme Court decision on penalties in *Cavendish Square
Holdings BV v Makdessi* [2015] UKSC 67, in particular that the general test is
not whether the clause is not a genuine estimate of the respondents' loss (a

liquidated damages clause) but whether it comprises "a secondary obligation which imposes a detriment on the contract breaker out of all proportion to any legitimate interest of the innocent party in the enforcement of the primary obligation" (per Lord Neuberger J.S.C. at [32]; see also Lord Mance J.S.C. at [152] and Lord Hodge J.S.C. at [255]). Hence where the legitimate interest is in performance (and hence compensation) the approach in *Dunlop Pneumatic Tyre Co Ltd v New Garage and Motor Co Ltd* was regarded as "usually . . . perfectly adequate to determine [the clause's] validity" (at [32]).

6. Credit and Other Payment Cards, and Checks

The consumer credit regulatory regime

[*Add to note 2453, line 1, after* "Supply of Goods and Services Act 1982,":*page* **39–485**
[1512]]
or under the Consumer Rights Act 2015,

8. Mortgages of Land

Consumer credit regulation

[*Add to note 2647, at the end: page* [1526]] **39–529**
Article 61 was further amended on March 21, 2016 by the Mortgage Credit Directive Order 2015 (SI 2015/910) art.3 and Sch.1 para.4(21) so as to include second charge residential mortgages previously regulated by the CCA 1974.

[*Note 2651: page* [1527]]
The Mortgage Credit Directive (and hence the relevant amendments) came into force on March 21, 2016.

[*Note 2652: page* [1527]]
The Mortgage Credit Directive (and hence the relevant amendments) came into force on March 21, 2016.

[*Note 2653: page* [1527]]
The Mortgage Credit Directive (and hence the relevant amendments) came into force on March 21, 2016.

The Mortgage Credit Directive

The Mortgage Credit Directive came into force on March 21, 2016 and hence the **39–531**
proposed changes noted in this paragraph have come into force, reducing the number of CCA-regulated mortgages. As a result (and see above, para.39–529) the Consumer Credit Act 1974 provisions considered below only apply to a small number of land mortgages.

Chapter 40

EMPLOYMENT

[Add to note 1, at the beginning: page [1533]]   **40–001**
Freedland (ed.), *The Contract of Employment* (2016);

1. Introduction

The contract of service or personally to execute any work or labour: "workers" and "persons employed"

[In note 58, delete "[2014] I.R.L.R. 914 EAT" and substitute: page [1541]]   **40–009**
[2016] EWCA Civ 459, [2016] I.R.L.R. 628.

[Add to note 58, at the end: page [1541]]
In the case of personal service companies, another avenue for recourse could be found in *EAD Solicitors LLP v Abrams* [2015] I.R.L.R. 978 EAT.

2. The Factors Identifying a Contract of Employment

Special cases: (2) agency workers

[Add to note 188, at the end: page [1554]]   **40–027**
Compare now also *Smith v Carillion (JM) Ltd* [2015] EWCA Civ 209, [2015] I.R.L.R. 467.

[Add to note 190, at the end: page [1555]]
See now also the Conduct of Employment Agencies and Employment Businesses (Amendment) Regulations 2016 (SI 2016/510).

[Add to note 192, at the end: page [1555]]
In *Coles v Ministry of Defence* [2015] I.R.L.R. 872 EAT the confinement of the equal treatment obligation to basic working and employment conditions was emphasised in the context of recruitment to jobs.

Special cases: (6) zero-hours contracts

[Add to note 207, at the end: page [1557]]   **40–031**
See now also the Exclusivity Terms in Zero Hours Contracts (Redress) Regulations 2015 (SI 2015/2021).

3. Formation of the Contract

Formation and variation of the contract

40–032   [*Add to note 212, at the end: page* [1157]]
or the contractual check-off mechanism which was held not to be derogable in *Cavanagh v Secretary of State for Work and Pensions* [2016] EWHC 1136, [2016] I.R.L.R. 591.

[*Add to paragraph, at the end: page* [1557]]
In *Sparks v Department for Transport*,[213a] the High Court held that in the absence of an explicit agreement, the employer could only make unilateral changes to terms and conditions if they were not detrimental to employees. Moreover, any explicit contractual power to vary must be stated in express and clear terms.[213b]

[213a] [2015] EWHC 181 (QB), [2015] I.R.L.R. 641.
[213b] *Norman v National Audit Office* [2015] I.R.L.R. 634 (EAT).

5. Rights and Duties Under and Associated with a Contract of Employment

(b) *Duties of the Employer*

(i) *Remuneration*

The national minimum wage

40–080   [*Add to note 535, at the end: page* [1591]]
Different considerations may apply where the worker's home was her place of work: *Shannon v Rampersad (t/a Clifton House Residential Home)* [2015] I.R.L.R. 982 EAT.

Holidays and holiday pay

40–081   [*In note 548, delete* "[2015] I.R.L.R. 438 EAT" *and substitute: page* [1592]]
[2016] I.R.L.R. 316 EAT

Opportunity to earn and the right of lay-off

40–089   [*Add to note 613, at the end: page* [1598]]
Compare, however, *Craig v Bob Lindfield & Son Ltd* [2016] I.C.R. 527 EAT.

(ii) *Other Duties*

The Working Time Regulations

[*Add to paragraph, after note 820: page* [1616]]   **40–112**
"Working time" is to be interpreted widely and purposively, including for
example travel from a worker's place of residence to customer premises,[820a] or
the attendance of meetings as a trade union or health and safety representative.[820b]

[820a] *Federación de Servicios Privados del sindicuto Comisiones obreras (CC OO) v Tyco Inte-
grated Security SL* (C-266/14) EU:C:2015:578, [2016] 1 C.M.L.R. 22.
[820b] *Edwards v Encirc Ltd* [2015] I.R.L.R. 528 EAT.

Further applications and extensions of the implied obligation of trust and confidence

[*Add to note 1014, at the end: page* [1637]]   **40–152**
and *Patural v DB Services (UK) Ltd* [2015] EWHC 3659 (QB), [2016] I.R.L.R.
286.

[*Add to note 1016, at the end: page* [1637]]
Compare now also *Stevens v University of Birmingham* [2015] EWHC 2300
(QB), [2015] I.R.L.R. 899.

[*Add to paragraph, at the end: page* [1637]]
The Court opined in *Bradbury v BBC*[1016a] that an employer's several actions
might cumulatively amount to a breach of the implied term.

[1016a] [2015] EWHC 1368 (Ch), [2015] Pens. L.R. 457.

Disclosures of information in the public interest

[*Add to note 1030, at the end: page* [1639]]   **40–154**
Though cf. *Day v Lewisham and Greenwich NHS Trust* [2016] I.R.L.R. 415
EAT.

[*Add to paragraph, after note 1030: page* [1639]]
Claims can be brought both against a worker's employer, an end-user of agency
services, or both if the exercise of employer functions is shared.[1030a]

[1030a] *McTigue v University Hospital Bristol NHS Foundation Trust* [2016] UKEAT/0354/15, [2016]
I.R.L.R. 742.

7. REMEDIES, AND RIGHTS INCIDENTAL TO THE TERMINATION OF EMPLOYMENT

(b) *Recovery of Remuneration*

Apportionment of wages or salary

[*Add to note 1373, at the end: page* [1674]]   **40–196**
A similar approach was followed in *Hartley v King Edward VI College* [2015]
EWCA Civ 455, [2015] I.R.L.R. 650.

8. Unfair and Discriminatory Dismissal

(a) *Unfair Dismissal*

(iv) *Remedies*

Introduction

40–236 [*Add to note 1690, after* "ss.112–117": *page* [1704]]
See now generally *McBride v Scottish Police Authority* [2016] UKSC 27, [2016] I.R.L.R. 633.

9. Redundancy Payments and Procedure

(b) *Redundancy Procedure*

Consultation with the representatives of recognised trade unions or of employees

40–260 [*In note 1893, delete from* "The restriction to . . . " *to the end and substitute: page* [1722]]
The restriction to "at one establishment" had been placed in doubt by *USDAW v Ethel Austin Ltd (In Administration)* [2014] EWCA Civ 142, [2014] 2 C.M.L.R. 45, but was subsequently confirmed by the CJEU in *USDAW v Ethel Austin Ltd* (C-80/14) EU:C:2015:291, [2015] 3 C.M.L.R. 32.

CHAPTER 41

GAMBLING CONTRACTS

1. INTRODUCTION

"Gambling" and "wagering"

[*Add to note 36, at the end: page* [1729]]   **41–006**
cf. WW Properties Investments Ltd v National Westminster Bank plc [2016]
EWHC 378 (QB), where interest rate swap agreements were said at [17] not to
be betting contracts regulated by the Gambling Act 2005; nor were they wagers
(at common law) as they had a "genuine commercial purpose" (at [30], following *Morgan Grenfell v Welwyn Council* [1995] 1 All E.R. 1). In *Banco Santander
Totta SA v Companjia de Carris de Ferro de Lisboa SA* [2016] EWHC 465
(Comm), [2016] 4 W.L.R. 49 interest rate swaps were likewise found not to be
void under Portuguese law as "games of chance", though that finding was not
strictly necessary to the outcome in that case.

2. Enforceability of Gambling Contracts

(c) *Exceptions to Enforceability under the Gambling Act 2005*

(i) *"Unlawfulness"*

Failure to comply with other provisions of the Act

41–019   [*Add to note 102, at the end: page* [1736]]
See also *Ritz Hotel Casino Ltd v Al Geabury* [2015] EWHC 2294 (QB), [2015]
L.L.R. 860 where an action on a dishonoured cheque given by a gambler in
exchange for chips (which he gambled away) succeeded as there had been *no*
breach of the casino's licence condition or of the Gambling Commission's Code
of Practice, and hence no illegality by reason of any violation of s.33 or 82 of the
Gambling Act 2005.

(e) *Related Transactions*

(ii) *Enforceability*

Related transactions in general enforceable

41–026   [*Add to paragraph, at the end: page* [1744]]
This provision can, of course, only apply if the transaction relied upon by the
person seeking enforcement has contractual force; and this requirement was held
not to have been satisfied in *Ritz Hotel Casino Ltd v Al Geabury*[172a] where a
persistent gambler had entered into a "voluntary self-exclusion agreement"
(VSE) with the casino by which he had excluded himself for life from gambling
at the casino. In an action by the casino against him on a cheque which had had
given to the casino in payment for chips,[172b] he counterclaimed for damages for
breach of the contract alleged to have been contained in the VSE. The claim was
rejected by Simler J. on the ground that the VSE did not amount to a contract
since the requirement of consideration was not satisfied. Her reason for this
conclusion was that "nothing moved from the Defendant to the Claimant"[172c]
and that it was "difficult to see what consideration flows from the defendant
when he enters a self exclusion agreement providing nothing in return".[172d] This
reasoning, with respect, gives rise to some difficulty since it makes no reference
to the generally accepted principle that, though consideration must move from
the promise, it need not move to the promisor.[172e] Evidently the gambler was
regarded as the promisee and the casino as the promisor, though it is not
altogether clear what promise was made to the gambler by the promisor; presumably it was one to deny him the gambling facilities from which he had asked
to be excluded. The loss of those facilities, even if only for a limited time,[172f] can
plausibly be regarded as a detriment to the gambler (just as is the case where a
promisee has, in response to the promise, given up smoking or drinking). The
doctrine of consideration does not impose any further requirement that anything
should "move to the Claimant"[172g] (i.e. to the casino). It could perhaps be argued
that the gambler's self-exclusion did not amount to consideration because the

gambler's signature of the VES form had not been requested by the casino; but that is not the ground given in the judgment in its short discussion of the consideration point.[172h]

[172a] [2015] EWHC 2294 (QB), [2015] L.L.R. 860.

[172b] See above, para.41–018 n.102.

[172c] [2015] EWHC 2294(QB) at [137].

[172d] *ibid.*

[172e] See Main Work, Vol.I, para.4–040.

[172f] The self-exclusion form signed by the gambler was expressed to be "for life" but the VSE agreement was in fact revoked by mutual consent (see at [125]) of the parties to it less than a year after it had been made: see at [2(iii)], [3(ii)], [137].

[172g] See above at n.172c.

[172h] In the passage quoted at n.172c above, Simler J. relies on statements by Briggs J. in *Calvert v William Hill Credit Ltd* [2008] EWHC 454 (Ch), [2008] L.L.R. 583 at [175], [178], [180] to the effect that a voluntary self-exclusion agreement was "without consideration"; the decision was affirmed [2008] EWCA Civ 1427 where the same view is stated at [26]. No reason is given for this view either by Briggs J. or by the Court of Appeal but it should be pointed out that the judgments in the *Calvert* case dealt with a transaction concluded before the Gaming Act 2005 had come into force: (see [2008] EWCA Civ 1427 at [2], [13] and when the earlier gambling (or gaming and wagering) legislation referred to in Main Work, Vol.II, para.41–001 was still in force. The gambler would therefore be excluding himself from making bets that were void in law, while in the *Al Geabury* case he had excluded himself from transactions which, in general, were legally enforceable. This difference makes the argument that the gambler had provided consideration in the *Al Geabury* case more plausible (for the reason given in the *Calvert* case). This would not be the only situation in which the change in the law, making gambling contracts enforceable in law, could affect issues of consideration arising from gambling contracts or related transactions: see, for example, the discussions of *Lipkin Gorman v Karpnale Ltd* [1991] 2 A.C. 548 in Main Work, Vol.II, paras 41–047 and 41–048 and also in Main Work, Vol.I, para.4–190.

"Unlawfulness"

[*Add to note 176, line 4, after* "904, 928 (synallagmatic)"*: page* [1744]]   **41–027**
; *Arnold v Britton* [2015] UKSC 36, [2015] A.C. 1619 at [21] ("Given that a contract is a bilateral, or synallagmatic, arrangement . . . ")

CHAPTER 42

INSURANCE

1. The Nature of Insurance

[*In note 1, update reference to MacGillivray on Insurance Law to: page* [1763]] 13th edn (2015)

Indemnity insurance

42–003   [*Add to paragraph, at the end: page* [1766]]
However, this third consequence will change upon the entry into force of ss.13A and 16A of the Insurance Act 2015 on May 4, 2017.[18a] This new legislation will

introduce into every insurance contract an implied term that the insurer must pay insurance claims within a reasonable time (allowing for investigation and assessment of the claim). If there is a breach of this implied term, the assured will have remedies (e.g. damages) available at common law (and otherwise) in addition to the payment of the claim under the policy and statutory interest.[18b]

[18a] These provisions of the Insurance Act 2015 were introduced by the Enterprise Act 2016 ss.28–30.
[18b] s.13A. See Parliament's Explanatory Notes, para.264. See below para.42–111A.

2. Insurable Interest

Types of insurable interest

[In note 51, update reference to MacGillivray on Insurance Law to: page [1769]] **42–008**
13th edn (2015), para.1–161

Impact of Gambling Act 2005

[In note 123, update reference to MacGillivray on Insurance Law to: page [1776]] **42–016**
13th edn (2015), paras 1–027, 1–039

3. The Event Insured Against

Event insured against

[Add to note 137, at the end: page [1778]] **42–018**
See also AIG Europe Ltd v OC320301 LLP [2016] EWCA Civ 367, [2016] Lloyd's Rep. I.R. 289.

(a) The Nature of the Event

Public policy

[In note 166, update reference to MacGillivray on Insurance Law to: page [1781]] **42–023**
13th edn (2015), para.30–010

[Add to note 167, at the end: page [1782]]
In Les Laboratoires Servier v Apotex Inc [2014] UKSC 55, [2015] A.C. 430 at [23]–[29], the Supreme Court said that generally the conduct should be criminal or quasi-criminal before public policy might be engaged.

[Add to paragraph, at the end: page [1783]]
The principles of public policy as they apply to insurance contracts have been cast into some doubt by the recent decision of the majority of the Supreme Court

in *Patel v Mirza*,[175a] where it was held that a claim will not be enforced if it is contrary to the public interest, meaning that it would be harmful to the integrity of the legal system (or, possibly, certain aspects of public morality). The Supreme Court decided not to follow the reliance test adopted by the House of Lords in *Tinsley v Milligan*.[175b]

[175a] [2016] UKSC 42, [2016] 3 W.L.R. 399 at [101], [120], [174], [186].
[175b] [1994] 1 A.C. 340. See above, paras 16–014A et seq.

4. UTMOST GOOD FAITH AND FAIR PRESENTATION OF THE RISK

(a) *Existing law applicable to non-consumer insurance contracts*

Utmost good faith

42–033   [*In note 222, update reference to MacGillivray on Insurance Law to: page* [1788]] 13th edn (2015), Chs 16–17

Exceptions to the duty of disclosure

42–036   [*In note 264, update reference to MacGillivray on Insurance Law to: page* [1794]] 13th edn (2015), paras 17–063—17–067

Affirmation and waiver by estoppel

42–043   [*Add to note 320, at the end: page* [1800]]
As to the requirement of knowledge of the legal right to avoid in circumstances where the insurer is being advised by solicitors, see *Moore Large & Co Ltd v Hermes Credit and Guarantee Plc* [2003] EWHC 26 (Comm), [2003] Lloyd's Rep. I.R. 315 at [92]–[100]; *Involnert Management Inc v Aprilgrange Ltd* [2015] EWHC 2225 (Comm), [2015] 2 Lloyd's Rep. 289 at [157]–[161].

Modification of the duty by contract

42–044   [*Add to paragraph, after note 327: page* [1801]]
or that the policy is voidable only if the assured is guilty of a fraudulent non-disclosure or misrepresentation,[327a]

[327a] *Mutual Energy Ltd v Starr Underwriting Agents Ltd* [2016] EWHC 590 (TCC), [2016] B.L.R. 312.

(b) *Existing law applicable to consumer insurance contracts*

The insurer's remedies

42–049   [*Add to paragraph, line 8, after* "relevant to the insurer) or careless"*: page* [1804]]
The finding that an assured's breach of duty was deliberate or reckless may be supported by the presumptions allowed under s.5(5), in particular that the

consumer knew that a matter about which the insurer asked a clear and specific question was relevant to the insurer.[346a]

[346a] *Tesco Underwriting Ltd v Achunche*, Unreported, July 7, 2016.

(c) *Insurance Act 2015*

The insurer's remedies for unfair presentation of the risk

[*Add to note 387, at the end: page* [1809]]   **42–057**
As to what constitutes a deliberate non-disclosure, see *Mutual Energy Ltd v Starr Underwriting Agents Ltd* [2016] EWHC 590 (TCC), [2016] B.L.R. 312.

5. THE PARTIES

Agents of the insurer

[*Add new note 419a, after* "agents to solicit business." *in line 2: page* [1813]]   **42–065**
[419a] As to the regulatory requirements for the authorisation of agents and representatives, see s.39 of the Financial Services and Markets Act 2000 and art.25 of the Financial Services and Markets Act 2000 (Regulated Activities) Order 2001 (SI 2001/544). See *Personal Touch Financial Services Ltd v Simplysure Ltd* [2016] EWCA Civ 461 (private medical insurance).

[*Add to paragraph, at the end: page* [1813]]
The insurer's agent is not, by reason of the agency alone, a party to the insurance contract.[427a]

[427a] *Temple Legal Protection Ltd v QBE Insurance (Europe) Ltd* [2009] EWCA Civ 453, [2009] Lloyd's Rep. I.R. 544; *PM Law Ltd v Motorplus Ltd* [2016] EWHC 193 (QB), [2016] 1 Costs L.R. 143 at [58]

Broker

[*Add to note 433, line 19, after* "[1996] 2 Lloyd's Rep. 619"*: page* [1814]]   **42–066**
; *Involnert Management Inc v Aprilgrange Ltd* [2015] EWHC 2225 (Comm), [2015] 2 Lloyd's Rep. 289 at [288]–[292]

Lloyd's

[*In note 440, update reference to MacGillivray on Insurance Law to: page* [1816]]   **42–067**
13th edn (2015), Ch.37

6. THE CONTRACT OF INSURANCE

Renewal

[*In note 475, update reference to MacGillivray on Insurance Law to: page* [1820]]   **42–073**
13th edn (2015), paras 7–038—7–039

Payment of premium

42–075   [*In note 481, update reference to MacGillivray on Insurance Law to: page* [1821]]
13th edn (2015), paras 7–019—7–021

Return of premium

42–076   [*In note 505, update reference to MacGillivray on Insurance Law to: page* [1823]]
13th edn (2015), para.8–030

Construction of insurance contracts

42–077   [*Add to paragraph, after note 516: page* [1824]]
If the insurance contract is based on a standard form of contract to which the
parties have added special clauses, greater weight will be given to the special
provisions, and, in the event of conflict or inconsistency between the general and
special provisions, the latter will prevail.[516a]

[516a] *Milton Furniture Ltd v Brit Insurance Ltd* [2015] EWCA Civ 671, [2016] Lloyd's Rep. I.R.
192 at [24].

7. THE TERMS OF THE INSURANCE CONTRACT

Conditions precedent

42–079   [*In note 524, update reference to MacGillivray on Insurance Law to: page* [1825]]
13th edn (2015), paras 10–010—10–011

Promissory warranties and their effect: existing law

42–080   [*In note 531, update reference to MacGillivray on Insurance Law to: page* [1827]]
13th edn (2015), paras 10–026—10–027

Waiver

42–086   [*In note 573, update reference to MacGillivray on Insurance Law to: page* [1831]]
13th edn (2015), paras 10–103—10–126

Consumer Rights Act 2015

42–088   [*Add new note 599a, after* "the services provided," *in line 13: page* [1834]]
[599a] See *Van Hove v CNP Assurances SA*, Case C-96/14, [2015] 3 C.M.L.R. 31, at [34]–[35].

8. ASSIGNMENT

Assignment of the policy

42–089   [*In note 603, update reference to MacGillivray on Insurance Law to: page* [1834]]
13th edn (2015), paras 26–070—26–113

9. CLAIMS

Notice of loss

[*Update note 632, line 6: page* [1837]]   **42–093**
Maccaferri Ltd v Zurich Insurance Plc [2015] EWHC 1708 (Comm) is now
reported at [2015] Lloyd's Rep. I.R. 594.

[*Add to note 635, line 2, after* "[2009] 1 Lloyd's Rep. 8": *page* [1838]]
; *Involnert Management Inc v Aprilgrange Ltd* [2015] EWHC 2225 (Comm),
[2015] 2 Lloyd's Rep. 289 at [225]–[243].

Fraudulent claims

[*Delete text of paragraph and substitute: page* [1842]]   **42–098**
There appear to be three species of "fraudulent claim",[669] namely: (a) a fraudulent claim for a loss, which is non-existent; (b) a fraudulent claim for a loss,
which is itself genuine, but which is excluded or not covered by the insurance
policy; (c) a fraudulent claim for a loss which is otherwise genuine and covered
by the policy but which is exaggerated.[670] Each of these will attract the same
remedy. The precise definition of a fraudulent claim has not been authoritatively
stated, although it is likely to require proof of the elements of deceit (other than
inducement).[671] In order to be fraudulent, the claim must be substantially fraudulent, that is if the fraudulent element of the claim was de minimis, the assured
would not bear the legal consequences of a fraudulent claim.[672] Mere exaggera-
tion is not conclusive evidence of fraud,[673] though it affords strong evidence of
fraud if the claim is out of all proportion to the true loss,[674] as does gross
negligence.[675] The availability of the remedy for a fraudulent claim does not
depend on actual inducement of the insurer, so that the fraud does not have to be
successful; the mere making of the fraudulent claim is sufficient to engage the
appropriate remedy.[676] In order for the fraudulent claim rule to apply, the fraud
must be material to the recoverability of the claim under the insurance policy or,
in other words, to the insurer's liability under the policy. That is, if the insurer
would be liable to indemnify the assured in respect of the claim, absent any lie,
the making of such a lie is necessarily collateral and will not constitute a
fraudulent claim in itself. This was the finding of the Supreme Court in *Versloot
Dredging BV v HDI Gerling Industrie Versicherung AG*,[677] overriding earlier
authorities.[678] The fraud of the assured will preclude his trustee in bankruptcy,[679]
and any joint assured, from recovering, and the same appears to be true for an
assignee of the policy.[680] Where, however, the contract is a composite one
insuring several parties for their different interests, an innocent assured is not
prejudiced by another's fraud.[681] The assured, although himself innocent, may be
affected by a claim presented fraudulently by his agent insofar as the latter was
acting within the scope of his authority.[682] The duty of utmost good faith does not
impose any duty to disclose or not to misrepresent material facts in connection
with a claim wider than the duty not to present a fraudulent claim.[682a]

[669] In *Agapitos v Agnew (The Aegeon)* [2002] EWCA Civ 247, [2002] 2 Lloyd's Rep. 42 at
[15]–[18] the Court of Appeal considered that an originally honest claim which was subsequently

appreciated as unfounded or exaggerated would be a fraudulent claim and that the deliberate suppression of a valid defence would render a claim fraudulent. See also *Versloot Dredging BV v HDI Gerling Industrie Versicherung AG* [2016] UKSC 45, [2016] 3 W.L.R. 543 at [96]. A fraud committed in performance of a contract of compromise of an insurance claim will not be a fraudulent claim attracting the remedies discussed in this paragraph: *Direct Line Insurance Plc v Fox* [2009] EWHC 386 (QB), [2009] 1 All E.R. (Comm) 1017.

670 As to exaggerated claims, see *Versloot Dredging BV v HDI Gerling Industrie Versicherung AG* [2016] UKSC 45, [2016] 3 W.L.R. 543 at [25]–[26], [36], [51], [92]–[93].

671 *Lek v Mathews* (1927) 29 Ll.L. Rep. 141; *Aviva Insurance Ltd v Brown* [2011] EWHC 362 (QB), [2012] Lloyd's Rep. I.R. 211 at [61]–[73], although in this case it was submitted that there was an additional requirement of dishonesty within the meaning discussed in *Twinsectra Ltd v Yardley* [2002] UKHL 12, [2002] 2 A.C. 164; such an additional requirement would appear to go beyond the bounds of the authorities. There is also a question whether the fraudulent claim can be constituted by a non-disclosure, as well as by a misrepresentation: *Marc Rich Agriculture Trading SA v Fortis Corporate Insurance NV* [2004] EWHC 2632 (Comm), [2005] Lloyd's Rep. I.R. 396; *Aviva Insurance Ltd v Brown* [2011] EWHC 362 (QB), [2012] Lloyd's Rep. I.R. 211 at [64].

672 *Galloway v Guardian Royal Exchange (UK) Ltd* [1999] Lloyd's Rep. I.R. 209; *Tonkin v UK Insurance Ltd* [2006] EWHC 1120 (TCC), [2007] Lloyd's Rep. I.R. 283 at [176]–[178]; *Aviva Insurance Ltd v Brown* [2011] EWHC 362 (QB), [2012] Lloyd's Rep. I.R. 211 at [76]–[77].

673 *London Assurance v Clare* (1937) 57 Ll.L. Rep. 254, 268; *Orakpo v Barclays Insurance Services Co Ltd* [1995] L.R.L.R. 443 at 451.

674 *Chapman v Pole* (1870) 22 L.T. 306; *Herman v Phoenix Assurance Co Ltd* (1924) 18 Ll.L. Rep. 371; *Dome Mining Corp Ltd v Drysdale* (1931) 41 Ll.L. Rep. 109; *Central Bank of India Ltd v Guardian Assurance Co Ltd* (1936) 54 Ll.L. Rep. 247; *Shoot v Hill* (1936) 55 Ll.L. Rep. 29.

675 *Goodman v Harvey* (1836) 4 Ad. & El. 870.

676 *Versloot Dredging BV v HDI Gerling Industrie Versicherung AG* [2016] UKSC 45, [2016] 3 W.L.R. 543 at [28]–[36], although Lord Sumption in that case appeared to curtail the principle underlying the fraudulent claim rule to the fact that inducement was not required.

677 [2016] UKSC 45, [2016] 3 W.L.R. 543, at [36], [39], [92]–[93], [100]–[103], [109]. See also *K/S Merc-Scandia XXXXII v Lloyd's Underwriters* [2001] EWCA Civ 1275, [2001] 2 Lloyd's Rep. 563 at [35].

678 *Agapitos v Agnew (The Aegeon)* [2002] EWCA Civ 247, [2002] 2 Lloyd's Rep. 42 at [38].

679 *Re Carr and Sun Insurance* (1897) T.L.R. 186.

680 *Black King Shipping Corp v Massie (The Litsion Pride)* [1985] 1 Lloyd's Rep. 437, 517–519.

681 *General Accident, Fire and Life Assurance Corp Ltd v Midland Bank Ltd* [1940] 2 K.B. 388; *Lombard Australia v NRMA Insurance* [1969] 1 Lloyd's Rep. 575. See also *Woolcott v Sun Alliance and London Insurance Ltd* [1978] 1 Lloyd's Rep. 629. *New Hampshire Insurance Co v MGN Ltd* [1997] L.R.L.R. 24; *Arab Bank Plc v Zurich Insurance Co* [1999] 1 Lloyd's Rep. 262.

682 *Savash v CIS General Insurance Ltd* [2014] EWHC 375 (TCC), [2014] Lloyd's Rep. I.R. 471 at [55]–[59].

682a *Royal Boskalis Westminster NV v Mountain* [1997] L.R.L.R. 523; reversed on other grounds [1997] 2 All E.R. 929; *Manifest Shipping & Co Ltd v Uni-Polaris Insurance Co Ltd (The Star Sea)* [2001] UKHL 1, [2001] 2 W.L.R. 170. See also *Alfred McAlpine Plc v BAI (Run-off) Ltd* [2000] 1 Lloyd's Rep. 437, where it was held that mere negligence in supplying details of claim pursuant to a notice provision in the policy did not constitute a breach of the obligation of utmost good faith.

Remedy for fraudulent claims: existing law

42-099   [*Add to paragraph, line 9, after* "applicable to a fraudulent claim": *page* [1844]]
In *Versloot Dredging BV v HDI Gerling Industrie Versicherung AG*, Lords Sumption and Hughes were similarly sceptical.685a

685a [2016] UKSC 45, [2016] 3 W.L.R. 543, at [8], [67].

[*Update note 689, line 3: page* [1844]]
Aviva Insurance Ltd v Brown [2011] EWHC 362 (QB) is reported at [2012] Lloyd's Rep. I.R. 211.

[*In note 690, delete from* "In *Versloot Dredging BV v HDI . . .* " *in line 3 to the end*: *page* [1844]]

[*Add to paragraph, after note 690: page* [1844]]
In *Versloot Dredging BV v HDI Gerling Industrie Versicherung AG*,[690a] the Supreme Court appeared to assume that forfeiture of the insurance claim (including the genuine parts of the claim)—as opposed to the forfeiture of any other benefit under the policy—was the consequence of a fraudulent claim.

[690a] [2016] UKSC 45, [2016] 3 W.L.R. 543.

Causation

[*Add to note 716, at the end: page* [1847]]   **42–103**
; *ARC Capital Partners Ltd v Brit Syndicates Ltd* [2016] EWHC 141 (Comm), [2016] 4 W.L.R. 18.

The amount recoverable

[*Add to note 730, at the end: page* [1849]]   **42–105**
Upon the entry into force of ss.13A and 16A of the Insurance Act 2015 on May 4, 2017, the assured will be entitled to recover damages for the late payment of a claim under an insurance contract in breach of a term implied by s.13A requiring the insurer to pay insurance claims within a reasonable time. In non-consumer insurance contracts, it is open to the parties to agree to a modification of this implied term to the insurer's benefit subject to the restrictions imposed by s.16A of the 2015 Act and the transparency requirements of the Insurance Act 2015. See below, para.42–111A.

[*Add new paragraph 42–111A: page* [1853]]
   Late payment of insurance claims. At common law, if the insurer unreason- **42–111A**
ably failed to pay an insurance claim within a reasonable time, the assured had no remedy over and above the entitlement to an insurance indemnity and statutory interest.[777a] This was the result of a peculiarity of insurance law in that the claim for an indemnity is, as a legal fiction, a claim for unliquidated damages for breach of contract by the insurer (the breach being constituted by the assured's suffering an insured loss),[777b] and in that a contracting party is not entitled to recover damages for the late payment of damages.[777c] In addition, the Court held that there was no implied term in the insurance contract obliging the insurer to assess and pay an insurance claim with reasonable diligence and due expedition.[777d] In order to address the perceived unfairness with this state of the law, the Enterprise Act 2016 ss.28–30 were passed so as to amend the Insurance Act 2015 (by the addition of ss.13A and 16A). This legislation enters into force on May 4, 2017 and introduces into every insurance contract an implied term that the insurer must pay insurance claims within a reasonable time (allowing for investigation and assessment of the claim).[777e] If there is a breach of this implied term, the assured will have remedies (e.g. damages) available at common law (and otherwise) in addition to the payment of the claim under the policy and statutory interest.[777f] By s.13A(4), if the insurer shows there are reasonable

grounds for disputing the claim, there is no breach of the implied term while the dispute is continuing. Insofar as any term of the insurance contract puts the assured in a worse position as regards the implied term provided for in s.13A, such term is invalid insofar as consumer insurances are concerned and insofar as any breach of the implied term by the insurer is deliberate or reckless. Otherwise, such a term is valid if it satisfies the transparency requirements of the Insurance Act 2015.[777g]

[777a] *The Italia Express* [1992] 2 Lloyd's Rep. 281; *Sprung v Royal Insurance (UK) Ltd* [1999] Lloyd's Rep. I.R. 111; *Callaghan v Dominion Insurance Co Ltd* [1997] 2 Lloyd's Rep. 541; *Tonkin v UK Insurance Ltd* [2006] EWHC 1120 (TCC), [2007] Lloyd's Rep. I.R. 283 at [34]–[38]; *Turville Heath Inc v Chartis Insurance UK Ltd* [2012] EWHC 3019 (TCC), (2012) 145 Con L.R. 163 at [36].

[777b] *Grant v Royal Exchange Assurance Co* (1816) 5 M. & S. 439, 442; *Swan and Cleland's Graving Dock and Slipway Co v Maritime Insurance Co* [1907] 1 K.B. 116, 123–124; *William Pickersgill & Sons Ltd v London and Provincial Marine & General Insurance Co Ltd* [1912] 3 K.B. 614, 622; *Seele Austria GmbH & Co KG v Tokio Marine Europe Insurance Ltd* [2009] EWHC 2066 (TCC) at [50]–[52].

[777c] *President of India v Lips Maritime Corp* [1988] 1 A.C. 395, 424–425.

[777d] *Insurance Corp of the Channel Islands Ltd v McHugh* [1997] L.R.L.R. 94, 136–138.

[777e] What constitutes a reasonable time depends on all of the circumstances of the case, including the type, size and complexity of the claim, compliance with statutory or regulatory rules or guidance and factors beyond the control of the insurer (s.13A(3)).

[777f] Parliament's Explanatory Notes, para.264. See also s.13A(5) of the 2015 Act. By amendment to the Limitation Act 1980 s.5, introduced by the Enterprise Act 2016 s.30, a claim for breach of the implied term may not be brought after the expiration of one year from the date on which the insurer has paid all the sums due under the insurance contract.

[777g] Insurance Act 2015 s.16A. As to the transparency requirements, see Main Work, Vol.II, para.42–060.

10. THE RIGHTS OF THE INSURER UPON PAYMENT

Salvage

42–113   [*In note 781, update reference to MacGillivray on Insurance Law to: page* [1854]] 13th edn (2015), paras 24–006—24–010

Subrogation

42–114   [*In note 789, update reference to MacGillivray on Insurance Law to: page* [1855]] 13th edn (2015), para.24–032

Subrogation: rights of action

42–115   [*Add to note 805, line 6, after* "(1999) 20 W.A.R. 380 Full Ct, WA": *page* [1856]] ; *Cape Distribution Ltd v Cape Intermediate Holdings Plc* [2016] EWHC 1786 (QB).

[*Add to note 807, line 1, after* "[1986] Q.B. 211": *page* [1857]] ; *Fresca-Judd v Golovina* [2016] EWHC 497 (QB), [2016] 4 W.L.R. 107.

11. Specific Types of Insurance Contract

(a) *Liability Insurance*

[In note 834, update reference to MacGillivray on Insurance Law to: page [1860]]
13th edn (2015), Ch.30

General characteristics

[Add to note 839, at the end: page [1861]]   **42–119**
In *Cape Distribution Ltd v Cape Intermediate Holdings Plc* [2016] EWHC 1786
(QB) at [161]–[163] the Court held that the contractual liability exclusion applied
only to claims which could be made only in contract.

The Third Parties (Rights against Insurers) Act 2010

[In paragraph, lines 3–4, delete "Although the 2010 Act has . . . " *to* "of this new   **42–122**
Act." *and substitute: page* [1864]]
The 2010 Act entered into force on August 1, 2016.[856a]

[856a] Third Parties (Rights against Insurers) Act 2010 (Commencement) Order 2016 (SI 2016/550).
See also Third Parties (Rights against Insurers) Regulations 2016 (SI 2016/570).

(b) *Motor insurance*

[In note 864, update reference to MacGillivray on Insurance Law to: page [1865]]
13th edn (2015), Ch.31

Road Traffic Act 1988

[Add to note 867, line 4, after "[1986] R.T.R. 1.".: *page* [1865]]   **42–123**
In *UK Insurance Ltd v Holden* [2016] EWHC 264 (QB), [2016] 4 W.L.R. 38 the
Court held that repairs undertaken to a motor vehicle did not amount to "*use*" so
that damage caused during repairs was not covered by a motor insurance policy.

[Add to note 867, at the end: page [1865]]
See *Vnuk v Zavarovalnica Triglav dd* (C-162/13) [2015] Lloyd's Rep. I.R.
142.

[Add to note 868, at the end: page [1865]]
In *UK Insurance Ltd v Holden* [2016] EWHC 264 (QB), [2016] 4 W.L.R. 38 the
Court held that a motor insurance policy might extend beyond roads, if there was
no express limitation in the policy to use on roads. The Court also discussed
whether "*roads*" under the Road Traffic Act 1988 s.145(3) meant "*public
roads*".

Third parties and uninsured drivers

42–125 [*Add to note 895, at the end: page* [1868]]
; *Wigley-Foster v Wilson* [2016] EWCA Civ 454.

(c) *Reinsurance*

[*In note 901, update reference to MacGillivray on Insurance Law to: page* [1869]]
13th edn (2015), Ch.35

(d) *Insurance against Financial Loss*

[*In note 922, update reference to MacGillivray on Insurance Law to: page* [1873]]
13th edn (2015), Ch.33

(e) *Fire Insurance*

[*In note 932, update reference to MacGillivray on Insurance Law to: page* [1874]]
13th edn (2015), Ch.28

Special features

42–130 [*In note 933, update reference to MacGillivray on Insurance Law to: page* [1874]]
13th edn (2015), Ch.28

(f) *Life Insurance*

[*In note 936, update reference to MacGillivray on Insurance Law to: page* [1874]]
13th edn (2015), Ch.26

CHAPTER 43

RESTRICTIVE AGREEMENTS AND COMPETITION

1. INTRODUCTION

Relationship between the EU competition rules and the provisions of domestic law

[Add to paragraph, at the end: page [1879]]   **43–003**
Clearly the substance of this paragraph may require fundamental change following withdrawal by the United Kingdom from the European Union pursuant to the
referendum of June 23, 2016.[9a]

[9a] For a general note on "Brexit", see above, paras 1–013A et seq.

2. COMPETITION RULES UNDER THE TFEU

(a) *In General*

Principal sources of law

43–008   [*In note 22 update reference to Butterworths Competition Law Handbook to: page* [1880]]
22nd edn (2016)

3. UNITED KINGDOM COMPETITION LAW

(a) *Introduction*

Reform of the law

43–077   [*Add to paragraph, at the end: page* [1909]]
The withdrawal by the United Kingdom from the European Union pursuant to the referendum of June 23, 2016 is likely to lead to significant changes to the domestic competition law of the UK in due course.[225a]

[225a] For a general note on "Brexit", see above, paras 1–013A et seq.

(g) *The Competition Appeal Tribunal*

The Competition Appeal Tribunal

43–139   [*Add to paragraph, at the end: page* [1926]]
It is also now possible for the Competition Appeal Tribunal to hear so-called "standalone" actions for an injunction and/or damages as a result of changes introduced with effect from October 1, 2015; that is to say it can now hear cases where there has been no prior decision by a competition authority in the UK or the EU.

CHAPTER 44

SALE OF GOODS

1. In General

(b) *Definitions*

Definitions

44–015   [*Add to note 85, line 19, after* "[2010] NSWSC 267.": *page* [1938]]
In *Software Incubator Ltd v Computer Associates UK Ltd* [2016] EWHC 1587 (QB) HH Judge Waxman (sitting as a Judge of the High Court) held that the sale of computer software was a sale of goods for the purposes of the Commercial Agents (Council Directive) Regulations 1993. Although he stressed that context was all and that it was possible that there could be a different answer under the Sale of Goods Act, he reviewed the authorities on the Act (at [47] et seq.) and concluded that the case law was scarce and limited in effect.

2. Formation of the Contract

(a) *Contract of Sale*

Sale and agreement to sell

44–020   [*Add to note 103, at the end: page* [1940]]
; and the transfer of property must be the essence of the contract: see *PST Energy 7 Shipping LLC v OW Bunker Malta Ltd (The Res Cogitans)* [2016] UKSC 23. The Supreme Court, upholding the decision of the Court of Appeal ([2015] EWCA Civ 1058; see Shmilovits [2016] L.M.C.L.Q. 20 and Tettenborn [2016]

L.M.C.L.Q. 24), held that a contract for the supply of fuel bunkers, which contained a retention of title clause and permitted the purchasing vessel owners to consume the bunkers during the credit period, was not a contract for the sale of goods within the meaning of s.2(1). See below, para.44–174A.

[*Add to note 104, line 3, after* "connection with future goods": *page* [1940]]
. In *Hughes v Pendragon Sabre Ltd (t/a Porsche Centre Bolton)* [2016] EWCA Civ 18 there was a contract to sell if the seller was allocated one of a new model of car by the manufacturer. The contract was construed as an agreement to sell future goods to be acquired by the seller which depended on a contingency:

Conditional sale agreements

[*In note 145, delete* "[2015] EWHC 2022 (Comm)" *and substitute: page* [1944]]   **44–028**
[2016] UKSC 23

(b) *Capacity of Parties*

Capacity of parties

[*In note 170, update the reference to Treitel, The Law of Contract to: page* [1947]]   **44–033**
14th edn (2015), para.12–008

(d) *Subject Matter*

Future goods

[*Add to note 175, at the end*: *page* [1948]]   **44–037**
, applied in *Hughes v Pendragon Sabre Ltd (t/a Porsche Centre Bolton)* [2016] EWCA Civ 18 (at [42]).

Contracts for the sale of future goods

[*Add to note 178, at the end*: *page* [1948]]   **44–038**
See *Hughes v Pendragon Sabre Ltd (t/a Porsche Centre Bolton)* [2016] EWCA Civ 18.

3. Terms of the Contract

(a) *Conditions, Warranties, Misrepresentations and Puffs*

Measure of damages

[*Add in note 266, line 3, after* "This is, however, arguable.": *page* [1958]]   **44–061**
The Singapore Court of Appeal doubted the correctness of *Royscot* in *RBC Properties v Defu Furniture Pte Ltd* [2014] SGCA 62, [2015] 1 S.L.R. 997; see Liau [2015] L.M.C.L.Q. 464.

(b) *Implied Terms*

(i) *Implied Terms about Title*

Breaches of s.12

44–077   [*Add to note 330, at the end: page* [1965]]
; in the context of retention of title clauses, see *PST Energy 7 Shipping LLC v OW Bunker Malta Ltd* [2015] EWCA Civ 1058 (noted Tettenborn [2016] L.M.C.L.Q. 24), affirmed [2016] UKSC 23.

4. Effects of the Contract

(a) *Transfer of Property as between Seller and Buyer*

"Romalpa" clauses: retention of title

44–174   [*Add to note 741, at the end: page* [2015]]
However, where the buyer is at liberty to consume the goods before the price becomes due, such that the transfer of the property in the goods may never happen, the contract may not be a contract of sale at all: see *PST Energy 7 Shipping LLC v OW Bunker Malta Ltd* [2016] UKSC 23 where the Supreme Court characterised a bunker contract with these characteristics as a sui generis supply contract. See below, para.44–174A.

[*Add new paragraphs 44–174A and 44–174B: page* [2015]]

44–174A   **Right to consume before property has passed.** If the contract provides for possession of goods to be given, coupled with a legal entitlement to consume them before the property in them is transferred upon payment, then, according to the Supreme Court in *PST Energy 7 Shipping LLC v OW Bunker Malta Ltd*[747a] the contract is not one of sale but is sui generis as a bailment coupled with a licence to consume the goods. Since almost all retention of title clauses allow the buyer to use or resell the goods before property in them has passed, this means that a very large number of contracts with reservation of title clauses will no longer be contracts of sale within the meaning of the Sale of Goods Act.

[747a] [2016] UKSC 23, [2016] 2 W.L.R. 1193, [2016] 1 Lloyd's Rep. 589.

44–174B   **Sui generis supply contracts analogous to contracts for the sale of goods.** A consequence of the conclusion in *PST Energy 7 Shipping LLC* is that a body of common law parallel to the Sale of Goods Act will have to be elaborated to deal with sui generis supply contracts. Although the Court of Appeal was clear that the incidents of the sui generis contract should track those of a sale of goods contract,[747b] it cannot be assumed that the entire Sale of Goods Act can be applied by analogy to sui generis contracts. The Supreme Court gave consideration to an obligation comparable to the right to sell goods that is the equivalent of s.12 of the Act. However, the judge at first instance saw no need for a warranty of quiet possession akin to the one that exists for sale of goods contracts in s.12(2)(b).[747c] The first reason given was that the recipient of the goods obtained sufficient protection from the implied term of lawful permission to use or consume. The second reason was that the warranty of quiet possession in sale of goods contracts was concerned with events after the passing of property. However, neither reason seems compelling and there may be a practical need for such a warranty. It is likely that equivalent common law rules should apply to such sui generis contracts in relation to matters such as delivery (including time and quantity of delivery and delivery by instalments) payment and quality (although, on a strict view, the statutory provisions which modify the common law rules on merchantable quality, etc. would not apply). The potential applicability of the statutory exceptions to the *nemo dat* rule is complex. The supplier of goods under a sui generis contract is not a "seller" for the purposes of s.24, nor is the recipient a "buyer" of goods for the purpose of s.25. However, it is likely that the receipt of goods with a licence to use or consume them should be regarded as a disposition for the purposes of these sections. The definition of a mercantile agent in s.1(1) of the Factors Act 1889 may be broad enough to capture a person who buys and resells under a sui generis supply contract, given that such contracts are "in commercial terms" regarded as contracts for the sale of goods[747d] and that the Factors Act is not confined to sale of goods contracts as these are defined in the Sale of Goods Act. Thus the provisions of s.2(1) of the Factors Act may apply. By contrast, certain provisions of the Sale of Goods Act are statutory inventions and did not codify existing common law. Such sections cannot apply by analogy at common law. For example, it is possible, though perhaps unlikely, that a bulk may consist of goods supplied to two or more recipients under sui generis supply contracts and that the bulk has not been exhausted by the time that one or more recipients has paid in full. Section 20A, which is not declaratory of the common law, cannot apply to such contracts by analogy. Similarly, ss.15A and 30(2A) cannot apply.

[747b] "There is no reason why the incidents of a contract of sale of goods for which the Act provides should not apply equally to such a contract at common law": Moore-Bick L.J., [2015] EWCA Civ 1058 at [33].

[747c] [2015] EWHC 2022 (Comm) at [63].

[747d] [2015] EWCA Civ 1058 at [33].

Disadvantages of "Romalpa" clauses

[*In paragraph, lines 4–5, delete* ", the seller will ordinarily not . . . action for the price and" *including n.813: page* [2021]]   **44–183**

[*Add to paragraph, after note 814: page* [2021]]
It had been held[814a] that an action for the price would not be available unless either s.49(1) or s.49(2) were satisfied and that accordingly the presence of a "Romalpa" clause, which prevented property from passing to the buyer, would ordinarily mean that the seller could not maintain an action for the price. In *PST Energy 7 Shipping LLC v OW Bunker Malta Ltd*[814b] the Supreme Court held that the bunker supply contract fell outside the Sale of Goods Act and accordingly it

was not necessary to decide whether an action for the price under the Act would have been maintainable in the circumstances. However, the Supreme Court indicated, obiter, that the price would have been recoverable on the date stated by virtue of the contract's express terms providing the goods had been delivered, indicating that they would have overruled the decision of the Court of Appeal in *Caterpillar* on this point.[814c]

[814a] *Caterpillar (NI) Ltd (formerly FG Wilson (Engineering) Ltd) v John Holt & Co (Liverpool) Ltd* [2013] EWCA Civ 1232, [2014] 1 All E.R. (Comm) 393 at [60], [61] and [75]–[76].
[814b] [2016] UKSC 23.
[814c] See further below, para.44–365.

(c) *Transfer of Title*

(i) *Sale by Person not the Owner*

(gg) *Disposition by Buyer in Possession*

Possession of buyer

44–221   [*Add to note 952, at the beginning: page* [2035]]
See for example *Carlos Soto SAV v AP Moller-Maersk AS* [2015] EWHC 458 (Comm), where the buyer had obtained a bill of lading in good faith and without notice.

6. Remedies of the Seller

(a) *Rights of Unpaid Seller against the Goods*

(ii) *Stoppage in Transit*

Other provisions as to transit

44–334   [*In note 1452, update the reference to Scrutton on Charterparties and Bills of Lading to: page* [2085]]
23rd edn (2015), paras 1.013 et seq.

[*In note 1452, delete "Scrutton, above": page* [2085]]

(b) *Action for the Price*

Claim for price due on "a day certain"

44–364   [*Add to note 1643, penultimate line, after* "within a fixed period after delivery.": *page* [2103]]
This point was not considered in detail by the Court of Appeal [2015] EWCA Civ 1058 or Supreme Court [2016] UKSC 23. In *Caterpillar (NI) Ltd (formerly FG*

Wilson (Engineering) Ltd) v John Holt & Co (Liverpool) Ltd [2013] EWCA Civ
1232, [2014] 1 All E.R. (Comm) 393 Longmore L.J. (at [44]) indicated that a
term for payment 30 days after invoice would have fallen within s.49(2), but as
the sending of an invoice itself depended on delivery, it seems questionable
whether this is a term for payment on a day certain "irrespective of delivery".

Action for the price outside s.49

[*Add to paragraph, after note 1654: page* [2104]]   **44–365**
In *PST Energy 7 Shipping LLC v OW Bunker Malta Ltd*[1654a] the Supreme Court
held that the bunker supply contract fell outside the Sale of Goods Act and
accordingly it was not necessary to decide whether an action for the price under
the Act would have been maintainable in the circumstances. However, Lord
Mance, delivering the unanimous judgment of the Court, said that he would have
overruled the decision of the Court of Appeal in *Caterpillar* on this point. Section
49 was not a complete code of situations in which the price may be recoverable
under a contract of sale. There was room for claims for the price in other
circumstances, including the present case, where the bunkers remained the
seller's property but were at the buyer's risk and where under the contract the
buyer was permitted to use the goods before payment.

[1654a] [2016] UKSC 23 at [40]–[58].

[*Add to note 1655, at the end: page* [2104]]
While noting the artificiality, Lord Mance, delivering the unanimous judgment of
the Supreme Court in *PST Energy 7 Shipping LLC v OW Bunker Malta Ltd*
[2016] UKSC 23, saw no reason why a claim for damages for non-payment
should not in principle be available (at [48]–[49]).

(c) *Action for Damages*

An available market

[*Add to note 1682, at the end: page* [2107]]   **44–368**
In *Hughes v Pendragon Sabre Ltd (t/a Porsche Centre Bolton)* [2016] EWCA
Civ 18 a rare new limited edition Porsche was sufficiently specialised for there
to be insufficient activity to evidence a market.

[*In note 1683, update the reference to McGregor on Damages to: page* [2107]]
19th edn (2015), paras 23–118 et seq.

7. REMEDIES OF THE BUYER

(a) *Damages for Non-Delivery*

Damages where there is an available market

[*Add in note 1816, penultimate line, after* "9th edn (2014), para.17–009": *page*   **44–388**
[2120]]
; Peel [2016] L.Q.R. 177 and Yip and Goh [2016] J.B.L. 335.

Damages for non-delivery in the absence of an available market

44–397   [*Add new note 1880a, after* "the cost of the nearest equivalent," *in line 8: page* [2127]]
^{1880a} *Hughes v Pendragon Sabre Ltd (t/a Porsche Centre Bolton)* [2016] EWCA Civ 18.

(c) *Damages for Defective Quality*

(i) *Diminution in Value*

Damages for diminution in market value

44–412   [*Add to note 1977, at the end: page* [2138]]
See, applying the market price rule, *Amira G Foods Ltd v RS Foods Ltd* [2016] EWHC 76 (QB).

(ii) *Losses other than Diminution in Value*

Compensation paid by the buyer to a sub-buyer

44–433   [*Add to note 2089, line 1, after* "[1951] 2 K.B. 314, 320": *page* [2150]]
(applied in *Meadowbank Vac Alloys Ltd v Eurokey Recycling Ltd*, Unreported, May 16, 2016 (QBD Manchester District Registry))

CHAPTER 45

SURETYSHIP

1. IN GENERAL

Performance guarantees

[*Add to note 44, line 4, after* "[2002] 1 Lloyd's Rep. 617 at [16]": *page* [2173]]   **45–009**
; *Caterpillar Motoren GmbH & Co KG v Mutual Benefits Assurance Co* [2015]
EWHC 2304 (Comm), [2016] 2 All E.R. (Comm) 322 at [13]–[15], [19]–[22]
and [25]–[27]. But where a contract contains a clause as is mentioned in (iv) of
"*Paget's* presumption" (quoted in the Main Work) this may be explicable as
inserted so as to put beyond doubt that the rule applicable to true guarantees does
not apply: [2015] EWHC 2304 (Comm) at [21], referring to *Caja de Ahorros v
Gold Coast Ltd del Mediterraneo* [2001] EWCA Civ 1806, [2002] 1 Lloyd's
Rep. 617 at [25].

[*Add to note 45, at the end: page* [2173]]
cf. *Caterpillar Motoren GmbH & Co KG v Mutual Benefits Assurance Co* [2015] EWHC 2304 (Comm), [2016] 2 All E.R. (Comm) 322 at [20] (no material distinction between bank and other financial institution, such as an insurance company engaged in the business of providing bonds to its customers).

2. FORMATION OF THE CONTRACT

(b) *Consideration*

Guarantee of past and future transactions

45–024   [*Add to note 121, at the end: page* [2183]]
cf. *Tailby v HSBC Bank Plc* [2015] B.P.I.R. 143 Ch D (earlier provision of a continuing facility to principal debtor was a "real commercial benefit" to the guarantor and this constituted consideration).

4. CONSTRUCTION OF THE CONTRACT

The role of "business common sense"

45–068   [*Add to note 340, at the end: page* [2210]]
See also (though not in the context of suretyship) *Arnold v Britton* [2015] UKSC 36, [2015] A.C. 1619 at [15]–[23], [66] and [76]–[77].

Guarantee and penalty clause in main contract

45–074   [*Add to note 376, at the end: page* [2214]]
On the general common law governing penalty clauses see below, paras 26–178 et seq.

Conditional guarantees

45–075   [*Add to note 381, at the end: page* [2214]]
And if A (a bank) requires B (the director of C Co) to provide both real security and his own personal guarantee for a loan to C Co, but executes only the guarantee, A may enforce the guarantee against B as A may waive the condition designed to protect its position: *Barclays Bank Plc v Sutton* [2015] EWHC 3192 (QB) at [21] and [26].

6. DISCHARGE OF SURETY

(b) *Discharge of Surety through Discharge of Principal Debtor*

Discharge of debtor by bankruptcy

[*In paragraph, line 27, delete* "s.260(1)(b) of the Insolvency Act 1986" *and**45–098**
substitute: page* [2228]]
s.260(2)(b) of the Insolvency Act 1986

[*Add new note 488a, after* "these arrangements on sureties." *in line 31: page*
[2228]]
488a [1999] Ch.117 at 129–130. (The wording of s.260(2) of the 1986 Act has been amended, but
without relevant substantive change.)

(d) *Discharge of Surety on Other Grounds*

Neglect of creditor in relation to securities

[*Add to note 597, at the end: page* [2241]]**45–120**
; *Alpstream AG v PK Airfinance Sarl* [2015] EWCA Civ 1318, [2016] 2 P. & C.R.
2 at [115]–[118].

Creditor free to decide whether to realise security

[*Add to note 603, at the end: page* [2241]]**45–121**
; *Alpstream AG v PK Airfinance Sarl* [2015] EWCA Civ 1318, [2016] 2 P. & C.R.
2 at [121]–[124].

Implied term

[*In paragraph, lines 9–11, delete* "(although it may ... *Belize Telecom Ltd).": page***45–122**
[2243]]

[*Delete text of note 617 and substitute: page* [2243]]
On the general approach to the implication of terms, see Main Work, Vol.I,
Ch.14.

Statutory demands under Insolvency Act against guarantor

[*Add to note 624, at the end: page* [2244]]**45–123**
; applied in *Inbakumar v United Trust Bank Ltd* [2012] EWHC 845 (Ch), [2012]
B.P.I.R. 758.

[*Add new paragraph 45–124A: page* [2245]]
Creditor estopped from enforcing guarantee. In principle, a creditor may be**45–124A**
estopped from enforcing a guarantee under the doctrine of promissory estoppel
(sometimes known as forbearance in equity).636a However, where, for example,

a creditor promises not to enforce a guarantee "indefinitely" while the guarantor works (unpaid) for the principal debtor, such a promise to postpone enforcement is likely to be interpreted as applying only where the creditor agrees to the continuation of the work rather than so as to allow the guarantor unilaterally to prevent the enforcement of the guarantee by continuing to undertake the work.[636b]

[636a] *Dunbar Assets Plc v Butler* [2015] EWHC 2546 (Ch), [2015] B.P.I.R. 1358. On this doctrine generally see Main Work, Vol.I, paras 3–085 et seq.
[636b] *Dunbar Assets Plc v Butler* [2015] EWHC 2546 (Ch) at [49]–[50].

8. LEGISLATIVE PROTECTION OF SURETIES

Introduction

45–146   [*Add to note 736, line 1, after* "above, para.38–335": *page* [2256]] (as amended by this Supplement).

(c) *Unfair Contract Terms Act 1977*

Unfair Contract Terms Act 1977 and Consumer Rights Act 2015

45–150   [*Add to note 768, line 2, after* "contracts made on or": *page* [2259]] after

Exclusion of surety's rights to be discharged

45–153   [*In note 785, update reference to Treitel on The Law of Contract to: page* [2261]] 14th edn (2015), paras 7–074—7–075

(d) *Unfair Terms in Consumer Contracts*

Application of these controls to contracts of suretyship; and English decisions

45–156 to
45–158   [*Delete the text of paragraphs 45–156 to 45–158 and substitute: pages* [2263]–[2266]]
45–156–   **Application of these controls to contracts of suretyship.** The question
158   whether the 1999 Regulations and, for contracts made on or after October 1, 2015, the Consumer Rights Act 2015 Pt 2, apply to contracts of suretyship received no definitive answer until the recent decision of the Court of Justice of the EU in *Tarcău v Banca Comercială Intesa Sanpaolo România SA*.[800] The 1999 Regulations (following the 1993 Directive itself) did not specify the types of contract to which they applied beyond defining their parties; and these parties were referred to as the "seller and supplier" (the person contracting in the course

of business) and "consumer" (the individual not contracting in the course of business), this reflecting closely the terminology used by the English language version of the 1993 Directive.[801] This terminology suggested that the business sells goods (or other property) or supplies services (including financial services) *to* the consumer,[802] and this in turn suggested that the 1993 Directive (and therefore also the 1999 Regulations) applied to contracts of suretyship only in the rare situation where the *creditor* is a consumer, and the surety the person acting in the course of business.[803] However, other language versions of the 1993 Directive instead refer more openly to a "professional" or "tradesman" defined in a similar manner,[804] and, noting this, the Court of Justice of the EU has clarified that the 1993 Directive applies to *all types* of consumer contract, defined merely by reference to their parties: persons contracting in the course of business on the one hand, and consumers, viz, natural persons contracting other than in the course of business, on the other.[805] According to the Court of Justice, this interpretation gives effect to the purpose of the Directive in the protection of consumers as "weaker parties" as regards both their bargaining power and their level of knowledge.[806] This general view was then applied to the context of contracts of suretyship by the Court of Justice in *Tarcău*.[807] There, the parents of the director and sole shareholder of a commercial company had guaranteed and provided real security for the payment of sums owed by that company to a bank. The national court making the preliminary reference considered that the 1993 Directive (and therefore its national implementing legislation) applied only to contracts for the supply of goods or services *to* consumers,[808] but the Court of Justice confirmed that the Directive applies to "all contracts" between consumers and sellers or suppliers and that "[t]he purpose of the contract is thus, subject to the exceptions listed in the recital 10 of the Directive[809] . . . irrelevant in determining the scope of the directive".[810] As a result, the 1993 Directive could apply to a contract of guarantee undertaken by a "consumer" or to another contract under which a "consumer" provides security for the performance of an obligation by another person, even if that other person is a commercial company rather than another consumer.[811] Indeed, in the view of the Court of Justice, the protection provided by the 1993 Directive for consumers as "weaker parties"

> "is particularly important in the case of a contract providing security or a contract of guarantee concluded between a banking institution and a consumer. Such a contract is based on a personal commitment of the surety or guarantor to pay a contractual debt owed by a third party. That commitment involves onerous obligations for the person entering into it, the effect of which is to subject that person's own property to a financial risk which is often difficult to quantify."[812]

For this purpose, "consumer" is an "objective" concept (and therefore does not depend on the knowledge or bargaining power of the individual) and is to be assessed by reference to the "functional criterion" of whether the contract arose in the course of activities outside his trade, business or profession.[813] The question whether a particular person is to be categorised as a "consumer" in this way remains for the national court to determine taking into account of all the circumstances,[814] but in the case of security being provided for performance of the obligations of a commercial company, this would turn on whether he "acted for purposes relating to his trade, business or profession or because of functional links he has with that company, such as a directorship or non-negligible share-holding" or whether instead "he acted for purposes of a private nature".[815] Earlier English decisions on the application of the 1999 Regulations to contracts of suretyship must now be read subject to this very clear ruling by the Court of Justice on the application of the 1993 Directive.[816] Similarly, the provisions of the Consumer Rights Act 2015 which implement the 1993 Directive by subject-ing the terms of a consumer contract to a test of unfairness must also be interpreted as applying to contracts by which a "consumer" guarantees the debt or other obligation of a third party.[817] This interpretation fits more naturally the terminology used by the 2015 Act, as it calls the business party the "trader" rather than the seller or supplier.[818] It should also be noted that the 2015 Act extends (or appears to extend) the definition of "consumer" to an individual contracting "wholly or *mainly*" for purposes outside that individual's trade, etc.[819]

[800] C-74/15 (Order of CJEU) November 19, 2015 ("*Tarcău* (C-74/15)"). Main Work, Vol.II, para.45–156 and corresponding paragraphs in earlier editions have argued that the 1993 Directive (and, therefore, its UK implementing legislation, the 1999 Regulations) apply to contracts of suretyship where the surety is a "consumer" by reference to the same textual and teleological grounds as formed the basis of the reasoning of the CJEU in *Brusse v Jahani BV* (C-488/11) May 30, 2013 and *Siba v Devènas* (C-537/13) January 15, 2015, on which its decision in *Tarcău* (C-74/15) was based.

[801] See Main Work, Vol.II, para.38–207.

[802] See Main Work, Vol.II, para.38–207.

[803] An example of a contract covered in this way would be a loan by a private individual to another person, whether for that person's business or not, which is guaranteed by a bank or other financial institution. Here, the guarantor (the bank) would be acting in the course of a business and the creditor (the lender of the money) could fall within the definition of a "consumer".

[804] The non-consumer party to the contract is termed *professionnel* in the French and *Gewerbe-treibender* in the German versions of Directive 93/13/EEC art.2(c).

[805] *Brusse v Jahani BV* (C-488/11) May 30, 2013; *Siba v Devènas* (C-537/13) January 15, 2015, on which see Main Work, Vol.II, para.38–203.

[806] *Brusse v Jahani BV* (C-488/11) at para.31.

[807] C-74/15 (Order of CJEU) November 19, 2015.

[808] *Tarcău* (C-74/15) at para.14.

[809] On these "exceptions" see Main Work, Vol.II, para.38–203 n.1280.

[810] *Tarcău* (C-74/15) at para.22. On the status of these "exceptions" see Main Work, para.1280 n.1280. The CJEU contrasted the position under the former Council Directive 87/102/EEC of 22 December 1986 concerning consumer credit (itself repealed by Directive 2008/48/EC of the Euro-pean Parliament and of the Council of 23 April 2008 on credit agreements for consumers) which applied only to "contracts whereby a creditor grants or promises to grant a consumer a credit" which has led the Court to exclude contracts of guarantee from its scope: *Tarcău* (C-74/15) at para.22, citing *Berliner Kindl Brauerie AG v Siepert* (C-208/98) [2000] E.C.R. I-1741 at paras 17–23.

[811] *Tarcău* (C-74/15) paras 24–25. The CJEU therefore confirmed the view taken by the Main Work, para.45–156 that the 1993 Directive clearly applies to contracts of suretyship. It is submitted that no distinction is to be made for this purpose between contracts of guarantee and contracts of indemnity as this distinction is understood by English law and as explained in the Main Work, Vol.II, paras 45–006—45–008. Indeed, in *Bucura v SC Bancpost SA* (C-348/14) July 9, 2015 (available only in French) at paras 35–38 the CJEU held that the 1993 Directive could apply to a contract under which the alleged "consumer" contracted as "co-debtor" to a person concluding a contract of consumer credit.

[812] *Tarcău* (C-74/15) at para.25.

[813] *Tarcău* (C-74/15) at para.27 citing *Costea v SC Volksbank România SA* (C-110/14) April 23, 2015 para.21, on which see above, para.38–032.

[814] *Tarcău* (C-74/15) at para.28.

[815] *Tarcău* (C-74/15) at para.29.

[816] *Governor and Co of the Bank of Scotland v Singh*, Unreported June 17, 2005 (QB, Mercantile Ct, Manchester); *Manches LLP v Freer* [2006] EWHC 991 (QB) at [25]; *Williamson v Governor of the Bank of Scotland* [2006] EWHC 1289 (Ch) (1999 Regulations cannot apply to contracts of guarantee undertaken by a natural person acting other than in the course of business). cf. *Barclays Bank Plc v Kufner*; *Royal Bank of Scotland v Chandra* [2010] EWHC 105 (Ch), [2010] 1 Lloyd's Rep. 677 at [102] (affirmed [2011] EWCA Civ 192, [2011] Bus. L.R. D149 on other grounds); *United Trust Bank Ltd v Dohil* [2011] EWHC 3302 (QB) at [73] (1999 Regulations can apply to contracts of guarantee undertaken by a natural person acting other than in the course of business).

[817] The 2015 Act sets out the general scheme of controls of unfair contract terms in Pt 2: see Main Work, Vol.II, paras 38–334 et seq.

[818] Consumer Rights Act 2015 s.2(2), above, para.38–352.

[819] 2015 Act s.2(3); s.76(2).

Vulnerable types of clause

[*In paragraph, lines 1–4, delete* "If the Directive (and, . . . " *to* "fairness may be significant." *and substitute: page* [2266]] **45–159**

There are a number of areas where the terms of a contract of suretyship by a consumer surety and a creditor acting in the course of business (and therefore a "trader") may be open to the charge of unfairness within the meaning of the 1999 Regulations or Pt 2 of the Consumer Rights Act 2015.

[*Add to paragraph, line 21, after* "creditor (the "supplier"": *page* [2267]] **45–160**

or "trader"

[*Delete text of note 837 and substitute: page* [2267]]

See above, para.45–156.